Psychology

3rd Edition

by Adam Cash, PsyD

A Wiley Brand

Psychology For Dummies®, 3rd Edition

Published by: **John Wiley & Sons, Inc.**, 111 River Street, Hoboken, NJ 07030-5774, www.wiley.com

Copyright © 2020 by John Wiley & Sons, Inc., Hoboken, New Jersey

Published simultaneously in Canada

For general information on our other products and services, please contact our Customer Care Department within the U.S. at 877-762-2974, outside the U.S. at 317-572-3993, or fax 317-572-4002. For technical support, please visit https://hub.wiley.com/community/support/dummies.

Wiley publishes in a variety of print and electronic formats and by print-on-demand. Some material included with standard print versions of this book may not be included in e-books or in print-on-demand. If this book refers to media such as a CD or DVD that is not included in the version you purchased, you may download this material at http://booksupport.wiley.com. For more information about Wiley products, visit www.wiley.com.

Library of Congress Control Number: 2020942317

ISBN 978-1-119-70029-6 (pbk); ISBN 978-1-119-70030-2 (ebk); ISBN 978-1-119-70032-6 (ebk)

Manufactured in the United States of America

SKY10023887_010821

Contents at a Glance

Table of Contents

Introduction

So you've bought *Psychology For Dummies*. How does that make you feel? I hope you're feeling pretty good. And why shouldn't you be? You're going to discover all kinds of interesting information about the basics of human mental processes and behavior.

I think that everybody is interested in people, their thoughts, emotions, and behavior. People are fascinating, and that includes you! Humans often defy explanation and evade prediction. Figuring people out can be pretty hard. Just when you think that you've figured someone out, bang, he surprises you. Now I know that some of you may be thinking, "Actually, I'm a pretty good judge of people. I've got a handle on things." If that's the case, that's great! Some folks do seem to have a more intuitive understanding of people than others. For the rest of us though, there's psychology.

About This Book

Psychology For Dummies is an introduction to the field of psychology. I tried to write this book using plain English and everyday examples with the hope that it will be real and applicable to everyday life. I've always felt that tackling a new subject is more enjoyable when it has real-world importance. Psychology is full of jargon, so much jargon that it even has its own dictionary, aptly named *The Dictionary of Psychology* (Penguin Reference Books). This book is for those of you who are interested in what people do, think, say, and feel, but want the information presented in a clear and easily understandable manner.

WARNING

The information in this reference is not intended to substitute for expert psychological, healthcare, or medical advice or treatment; it is designed to help you make informed choices. Because each individual is unique, a psychologist, healthcare practitioner, or physician must diagnose conditions and supervise treatments for each individual health problem. If an individual is under a psychologist's or physician's care and receives advice contrary to information provided in this reference, the psychologist's or physician's advice should be followed, as it is based on the unique characteristics of that individual.

Conventional language for psychologists can sound like gibberish to someone who has never had a psychology class. As I state earlier in this chapter, I try to stay away from jargon and technical language in this book. You may come across an attempt at a joke or two. I tend to take a lighter approach to life, but sometimes people don't get my sense of humor. If I try to crack a joke in the text and it bombs, please don't be too harsh. I'm a psychologist after all, and I don't think we're known for our sense of humor. I hope I don't come across as insensitive or cavalier either — that is certainly not my intention.

Sometimes, talking about psychology can be pretty dry, so I try to liven things up with examples and personal stories. I make no references to any patients I've ever had in treatment or seen in my practice. If there appears to be a resemblance, it's purely coincidental. In fact, I took great care in preserving the privacy and confidentiality of the people I have worked with.

Foolish Assumptions

You can find a lot of psychology books out there. Many of them are either too technical and specialized or cover too narrow an area of psychology. Here are some of the reasons why I think *Psychology For Dummies* is the book for you:

» You've got a lot of questions about people.

» You've got a lot of questions about yourself.

» You're thinking about going into the field of psychology.

» You're currently studying psychology or a related discipline, such as social work or counseling.

» You're interested in psychology but don't have the time or the money to take a psychology course.

» You've got people all figured out, and you want to see if I'm on track.

Icons Used in This Book

Throughout this book, you find icons in the margins. They're there to help you easily find certain types of information. Here's a list of the icons you see:

When you see this icon, I'm trying to emphasize a bit of information that may come in handy someday.

With this icon, I'm trying to alert you to information that is a "must know" if you're going to learn psychology.

Don't forget it. When you see this icon I am reminding you of the highlights from that section. It flags the "if you learn just one thing from this chapter" type of stuff, so pay attention.

This icon flags discussions that may rise above the level you need to basically understand the topic at hand. These sections can safely be skipped without harming your comprehension of the main point.

Beyond the Book

Check out the online Cheat Sheet for quick access to information about the differences between psychologists and other mental health professionals and coping with psychological crises. To get this Cheat Sheet, simply go to www.dummies.com and type "Psychology For Dummies Cheat Sheet" in the Search box.

Where to Go from Here

Psychology is a broad field. I think you'll find that the organization of this book lets you check out what you're interested in and leave the rest of the stuff behind, if you want.

Use the table of contents and index to see what grabs your interest. If you're new to the subject, by all means start with Chapter 1 and go. But you don't have to read it cover to cover. Kind of like a cafeteria — take what you like and leave the rest.

But hey, if I can write an entire book on psychology, I think you can read an entire book on this stuff. Besides, I think you'll like it. Psychology is a great subject. Enjoy!

1
Getting Started with Psychology

Chapter **1**

The Purpose of Psychology

What is the purpose of psychology?

» To gain knowledge of human minds and behavior through scientific study and research

» To apply that knowledge for the benefit of society, and to improve lives of people by using scientific methods

» To communicate and teach that knowledge and application to others

And what's the purpose of this book?

Well, to fulfill those three goals above, of course! I wrote it to educate, teach, and to be helpful. Honestly, I am a serious psychology nerd. I see psychology as an extremely interesting subject, a set of useful methods, and a great opportunity to learn more about people. I geek out on this stuff. I used to wander the psychology stacks of my university library just looking for something interesting, something that caught my eye, to discover something, to learn more. In essence, this book is a cumulation of my effortful curiosity. I hope to stimulate and fuel yours.

REMEMBER

We're all psychologists really. Some of us just happen to be "professional" psychologists. The difference between a professional psychologist and a non-professional psychologist is really a matter of degree (get it?), separated by focus, time spent, materials consumed, and methods used. Over the years, I have been asked (sometimes respectfully and nicely, sometimes not) these questions: "What makes you better at this than me? What do you know that I don't?" Well, I believe it's really a matter of degree, perspective, and the psychologist tools I use to see and do the "psychologist thing." Professionals in any field seem to immerse themselves in it. Again, it's a matter of degree. We all occupy the space of a "psychologist" to one degree or another. Psychologists just spend more time engaged in conscious and deliberate effort to stay in that space and look at the world from that viewpoint. We spend our time and careers occupying that space and doing the "psychologist thing," occasionally coming out of the trance to share what we have seen, think, and found to be objectively true, at least as far as science allows us. But ultimately, psychology is only one way of looking at people and the world they interact with.

Is psychology "right" about people? It may or may not be, but in an attempt to live up to that challenge, psychology uses the standards of science to do so, and if conducting and practicing psychological science lends itself to some use, exposes someone to one new idea or way of thinking, and helps just one person live a better life, then it has served a valuable role in the world. It is not privileged per se. It cannot explain everything about being human. Come on, that would just pompous and downright impossible.

Humbly, psychologists go about their business and hope to offer something to the world. One psychologist "figuring it all out" isn't the goal. I have countless more bad ideas than good ones, so I need to be part of a community of thinkers, other psychologists, and other scientists. I can put my ideas to the empirical test, share what I find, allow corrective feedback, and revise as I move forward conducting psychological science. Doing psychology is a thinking, doing, and communicating endeavor. I hope to do that with this book.

Before I give you a definition, I'm going to engage in a therapy cliché: Tell me what you think? Tell me how you feel? (There's an old joke about psychologists: How many psychologists does it take to screw in a light bulb? Two! One to do it and the other one to ask, "How does that make you feel?") What are some of the ideas that come to mind when people think about the topic of psychology? It depends on whom you ask. Sometimes, I imagine myself as a guest on a television talk show. I'm bombarded by questions from the audience that I can't answer. My heart starts to pound. I begin to sweat. I start to stand up so that I can run off the set, but then something comes to me that keeps me in my seat. I imagine asking the people in the audience what they think psychology is and why they think a psychologist can answer questions about people.

Whys, Whats, and Hows of People

Before I provide a definition of psychology, I want you to take a few minutes to jot down some of your ideas on what psychology is.

Why did this book catch your eye?

Are you looking for answers? Looking for advice?

How are you going to get those answers?

These are the three main questions that psychology is concerned with as well:

>> Why do people do what they do?"

>> What are the component parts of why and how?

>> How do people do what they do?

Here are some "Why?" questions:

>> Why am I happy?

>> Why can't I stop feeling sad?

>> Why did she break up with me?

>> Why didn't I say that? (as I walk away from an argument)

>> Why did I just say that? (as I get into an argument)

Here are some "What?" questions:

>> What are emotions?

>> What is mental illness?

>> What is intelligence?

>> What are thoughts?

Here are some "How?" questions:

>> How can I remember more?

>> How can I get my 2-year-old to stop throwing tantrums?

>> How does the mind work?

>> How does language develop?

These why, what, how questions comprise the intellectual and philosophical core of psychology.

REMEMBER

So it's finally time to define it: *Psychology is the scientific study of human behavior and mental processes.* Psychology attempts to uncover what people do along with why, what, and how they do it.

A useful metaphor: Building a person

Metaphors abound in psychology. They are used to provide extremely oversimplified and overarching "explanatory" models of people. Psychologists Dedre Gentner and Jonathan Grudin conducted a review of the metaphors used in psychology and identified 256! Over the years, people have been likened to "hairless apes," computers, machines, nervous systems, and a host of others. However, remember that people are not "models," but the models can be helpful in understanding people!

Now I'm going to enter into the fray with my own metaphor for better or worse. I don't think this metaphor is particularly unique, however, and there's likely chance that I borrowed it from someone else. But I think it's a good one, so here it is:

When I try to imagine all the reasons people do what they do, what they use to do it, and how they do it, I often run with a "mad-scientist" approach. I've always thought that one of the best ways to answer the why, what, and how questions would be to think about building a person and then set that person out performing the tasks of personhood, doing what persons do. Well, I'm not talking about actually building one like Dr. Frankenstein did — out of parts and brains and electricity — but creating a blueprint of a person's mind and behavior, performing functions, embedded in context, like a "performance space" of sorts, in the way that basketball players play basketball, singers give performances, and people do people stuff.

In therapy, when people try to explain a particular behavior or situation to me, I often say, "Can you make it happen now? Can you show me?" For example, a parent may be telling me how his child hits him when he tells the child to do something. And I'll say, "Show me. Make it happen." (I can assure you that everyone is kept safe and this is done ethically!) The most common response is a puzzled or disturbed look on the parent's face.

The point is, if they can cause it to happen, then they can un-cause it to happen, too. And that means they understand why and how it's happening. This is a type of reverse psychological engineering for figuring out the why, what, and how questions of human behavior. (It's also a good example of an empirical approach in as much as the process is observable and testable.)

There may be a day when psychology reaches a pinnacle of knowing and understanding all the determinants of behavior, all the ingredients of the human mind, and all the processes. Maybe the field can figure it all out through that reverse engineering process mentioned earlier. Or, at the very least, maybe psychology will figure out people, and all the information that experts gather can be stored or formulated into an *algorithm* or "recipe" for "making" people that, one day, a super-intelligent robotic life form can utilize to re-create the human species thousands of years after it becomes extinct. I did say that I sometimes think like a mad scientist, right?

Yes, this is the kind of blueprint or overlay I like to use to understand what psychology is: Why do the parts and processes do it? What are the parts or ingredients of a person? How do we go about performing functions using those parts and ingredients to achieve the why?

So I guess my metaphor is Frankenstein's Monster. Maybe think about it as "Frankenstein's Machine" or "Dr. Cash's Machine" or maybe even a "Monster Machine."

Why?

A first principle of my mad-scientist vision of psychology is that building a human requires you to know what the person's function is. After all, engineers don't build things without knowing what they're supposed to do. Only with a purpose in mind can you know what to materials are necessary and how they work together.

The foundations of this function approach are built on a philosophy know as *functionalism*, which is the notion that the mind, mental processes, and behavior are "tools" for adaptive functioning that lead to a human functioning most effectively in his or her environment (survival and perpetuation of the species).

Like all other carbon-based living organisms on planet Earth, human beings are "staying alive" machines. I'm not saying there is no meaning to life. Quite the contrary; I'm saying that the function of life is to be alive, to stay alive, and to perpetuate life. But there's got to be more than that, right? Wrong book. Try *Philosophy For Dummies* or *Religion For Dummies*.

What?

From a psychological standpoint, what does the human "staying alive machine" need in order to fulfill its function of existing, staying alive, and perpetuating?

Well, if you've ever put together a do-it-yourself piece of furniture, you know that the instructions usually start out with a parts list.

Psychological science has already put together quite an impressive psychological parts list:

>> **Bodies** (and all the subparts — see Chapter 3 for more)

- Brains

- Hearts

- Hormones

- Genes

- Motor skills

>> **Minds** (and all the subparts — see Chapters 4 to 9)

- Consciousness

- Sensations and perceptions, including vision, hearing, taste, smell, touch, balance, and pain

- Thinking, which manages attending, remembering, forming concepts, problem solving, deciding, and intelligence

- Communicating, including verbal and nonverbal expressions such as body language, gestures, speech, and language

- Motivations

- Emotions

- Selves

>> **Other people**

- Their minds

- Their feelings

- Their motivations

- Their brains

How?

I've talked about the why and the what, so what about the how? This is where psychology can get extremely interesting. This is where the rubber meets the road, how whys and whats interact through the operations and processes of the mind and behavior. Here is a list of some of those operations and processes:

>> Sensing and perceiving

>> Moving

>> Fueling

>> Learning, as in the ability to learn from the environment

>> Thinking, paying attention, remembering

>> Being motivated

>> Feeling

>> Socializing

>> Growing

Troubleshooting

All these parts, developed and assembled, go about their tasks within the world, right? But the world acts upon them, influences them, impacts them. Whether that context is dealing with other people, interacting with technology, or being chased by something dangerous, the mad scientist's job would be incomplete without looking at the world around the assembled parts.

So I've assembled my human being, switched it on, and let it loose to go about its primary function of surviving. I think I've equipped it with all it needs in order to survive.

But then it happens: change. That's right, something unexpected happens, and my human begins floundering, struggling, and verging on failing to achieve its primary function. How could I have forgotten that the world is not a static place?

My creation is dealing with the environment in ways that I should have anticipated. So I go back to the drawing board to add the following functions and abilities to keep the why going, with its parts and processes:

>> Coping and adapting

>> Repairing

>> Thriving

Putting It All Back Together Again

In case you were wondering (and worried), I am not engaged in an actual "build a human" project, except for having a "model" to work from. But if I did want my own Frankenstein's monster, I'd have a very solid foundation and a good blueprint. Each of a person's parts, processes, and sources of help represents a section or chapter of *Psychology For Dummies*, 3rd Edition.

REMEMBER

However, before we dive in to later chapters, I feel compelled to mention one last thing. It is obvious that psychology can be very reductionist. That is, it tries to take an extremely complex phenomenon, *people,* and break it down into parts and simple explanations. We've broken apart Humpty Dumpty, but can we put him back together again? People are not made up of X, Y, and Z. People are not just whys, whats, and hows. We're not theories, models, experiments, or Dr. Cash's "monsters."

The longer I am psychologist, the longer I appreciate the complex, messy, and mysterious nature of people, despite doing this for over 25 years. There is never a day that goes by that I don't learn something new about people, realize I was wrong about something or someone, and am humbled. I just want readers to know that despite my efforts to "break down" psychology, and in turn, people, this is only my reductionist attempt to understand people, and I hope I do it with respect, compassion, and humility.

Chapter **2**

Thinking and Behaving as a Psychologist

Why psychologists do "psychology" is to figure people out and help them. But *how* do they do that exactly? Well, let's use the definition of psychology to ask it another way: "What mental processes and behaviors do psychologists do and engage in when they are doing psychology? Psychology is a thinking, doing, and communicating endeavor.

Each of us is an amateur psychologist of sorts. Professional psychologists aren't the only ones who try to figure people out, we all do! We all think, do, and communicate about people (Stop gossiping!). When I started taking psychology courses, I had my own ideas about people. Sometimes I agreed with what I was exposed to and learning about, and sometimes I disagreed wholeheartedly. I'm not alone. Most people seem to have specific ideas about what makes others tick. Sometimes they match up with reality and sometimes they don't.

This "matching up" process is at the core of scientific inquiry. We want our ideas to match up with reality, don't we? In order to get it right or find the truth, we develop theories, conduct research (for example, collect data by observation and with interviews, tests, surveys, on so on), and conduct experiments. We do this over and over again until we are satisfied that we've got it figured out, have a solid idea of what is real, and have a solid set of facts. But there's a catch. Just when we think we've got it right, something comes along that throws it all into disarray.

New data requires a reconfiguration of what we thought we knew. As such, science is a constantly updating endeavor. The more we know, the more we question, and the more we need to update our understanding of reality.

One of my favorite professors, Dr. Jay Brand, sums it up very eloquently:

> Science represents a protracted attempt to contribute to a public edifice of knowledge founded on probabilistic evidence that the piecemeal construction achieves some important similarities with reality. No one sincerely believes that his or her single experiment will answer any useful question once and for all. . . .
>
> . . . theory development (knowledge) integrated across many single investigators (and experiments and data analyses) represents the true value of science to society.

Working with other scientists is critical. Think about billions of neurons with trillions of connections and then multiply all of that by 7 billion people. Wow, that's nearly infinite. How could anyone know it all? We are better when we work together, although we may not be so bad when we work alone. I thank every professor I've ever had, every supervisor, every patient, every family, and every book and article I've ever read. When there's more than one person looking for truth, we are more likely to find it.

REMEMBER

One of the cardinal rules of science is that whatever is being investigated must yield to the *empirical test* and be replicated. That is, the existence of something, be it a theory for example, must be verifiable or disprovable by repeated observation, measurement, and experimentation.

I'll never forget the time two of my professors got into a heated debate as one presented a theory as "fact" even though it had not been empirically tested and replicated. The other argued, "That is an empirical question. Run some experiments and then get back to me!" One professor was claiming "fact" from theory; the other argued to slow down and do some research before going off claiming facts here and facts there. There are rules of verification and falsification. Scientists don't just say, "Take my word for it!" They say, "I'll test it and if I'm right, okay. If I'm not, then we'll make adjustments."

In this chapter, we are interested in "how" psychologists look for the truth. You'll find out about how psychologists go about their business, the major branches of psychology, how overarching theories frame the questions they ask, and the variables they look at. Finally, you'll see how the discipline of psychology works to be as scientific as possible by basing its knowledge on solid theory, research, and statistical methods, which shore up its credibility among the other scholarly disciplines, and how all of that is done ethically.

The Core Activities of a Psychologist

Psychologists are professionals and experts. But what are they expert at? What do they do? Fundamentally, psychologists are scientists armed with theories, models, research, and data as they go about their business.

There are four main "types" of psychologists that are defined by what they spend the bulk of their time doing. I cover them in the sections that follow.

Experimental and research psychologists

These psychologists spend the majority of their time conducting research, and they often work in academic settings. Experimental psychology covers a wide range of topics, but individual researchers typically have a specialty such as social psychology or developmental psychology.

Here's a list of some of the areas of experimental- and research-based psychological science:

>> Cognitive science

>> Behavioral neuroscience

>> Personality

>> Social psychology

>> Developmental psychology

>> Psychopharmacology

>> Health psychology

>> Sexual orientation and gender studies

>> Media psychology

>> Trauma psychology

>> Abnormal psychology

>> Research methods and statistics

Applied psychologists

These psychologists directly apply research findings and psychological theory to everyday settings and problems. Applied psychologists work in a wide variety of settings, such as business, government, education, and even sports.

Here's a list of some of the areas of applied psychological science:

>> Industrial/organizational psychology

>> Forensic psychology

>> Military psychology

>> Clinical psychology

>> Educational and school psychology

>> Engineering and human factors

>> Rehabilitation

>> Couples and family psychology

>> Sports, exercise, and performance psychology

>> Clinical neuropsychology

Teachers/educators/professors

These psychologists work in high schools, community colleges, universities, and a variety of settings. They also can engage in writing books for the general public and articles for popular magazines and websites.

Theoretical and philosophical psychologists

These psychologists engage in discussions, debates, and analyses of theories, looking at philosophical issues such as epistemology, method, scientific progress, and other "big picture" concepts.

Of course, a lot of psychologists wear more than one hat. Some psychologists fit into more than one of these categories, for example, clinical psychologists conduct research. Researchers teach. Teachers do research. Consultants do research. Research is conducted on consulting. I think you get the point.

How Do I Become a Psychologist?

The American Psychological Association states that in order for an individual to be considered a psychologist, he or she must possess a doctoral degree (a PhD, PsyD, or EdD, for example), and although requirements may vary from country to country, this is a generally accepted standard in much of the world as well. And nearly all U.S. states require the individual to obtain a license to practice psychology, which typically involves taking an intensive licensing exam. In the United Kingdom, the British Psychological Society requires doctoral-level training in order to practice as a clinical psychologist, and practitioners are regulated by the Health and Care Professions Council.

REMEMBER

So does that mean I can't be a psychologist without a doctorate? Yes and no. Maybe you can't call yourself a psychologist per se, but with a master's degree or a bachelor's degree, people can still use their psychology education and training to engage in a wide range of activities including research, consultation, and teaching. A psychology degree is an excellent degree that can apply to a lot of other fields, including government, nonprofits, politics, surveying, business, media, and education.

Getting Started with Metatheory and Frameworks

At a very basic level, psychology is a branch of knowledge. Psychology exists among and interacts with other scientific and scholarly disciplines in a community-like environment of knowledge, and contributes a vast collection of theories and research to help answer questions related to human behavior and mental processes. A number of other fields of study — physics, biology, chemistry, history, economics, political science, sociology, medicine, and anthropology — attempt to use their own perspectives to answer the same basic questions about people that psychology addresses.

One comment I get from students from time to time is, "What makes you think that psychology has all the answers?" My answer is, "Psychologists are just trying to provide a piece of the puzzle, not all the answers."

To enable psychology to contribute to the community of knowledge about people, over the years, psychologists as a group have come up with a basic set of *broad theoretical perspectives*, or frameworks, to guide the work of psychology. These broad theoretical frameworks are sometimes referred to as *metatheories.* The lion's share of psychological research is based on one or more of these broad frameworks or metatheories.

Each metatheory provides an overarching framework for conducting psychological research and comes with a different point of emphasis to figure out what people do, and why and how they do it. Other perspectives represent hybridized approaches, such as motivational science and affective neuroscience. But for now, I'm just sticking with the basics.

In this section, I describe the most common metatheories psychologists use when they find a behavior or mental process they're interested in researching. Work typically begins from within one of these theories.

Biological

The biological approach centers on the biological underpinnings of behavior, including the effects of evolution and genetics. The premise is that behavior and mental processes can be explained by understanding genetics, human physiology, and anatomy. Biological psychologists focus mostly on the brain and the nervous system. (For more on biological psychology, see Chapter 3.) Neuropsychology and the study of the brain, genetics, and evolutionary psychology are included within the biological metatheory.

For an example of biology's impact on behavior, just think about how differently people act when they're under the influence of alcohol. Holiday office parties are good laboratories for applying the biological perspective. You walk into the party and see Bob, the relatively quiet guy from accounting, burning up the cubicles. Bob's transformed into a lady's man. He's funny. He's drunk. Do you think Bob will remember?

Behaviorism

Behaviorism emphasizes the role and influence of a person's environment and previous learning experiences to understanding behavior. Behaviorists don't traditionally focus on mental processes per se because they believe that mental processes are too difficult to observe and measure objectively. In the framework of behaviorism, the "why" of behavior can be explained by looking at the circumstances in which it occurs and the consequences surrounding someone's actions. Classical conditioning and operant conditioning are ways of understanding behavior and they lead to behavior modification, a specific approach to modifying behavior, and helping people change that comes from the metatheory of behaviorism. (See Chapter 8 for details on some behavior-modification techniques that are based on classical and operant conditioning.)

Cognitive

The cognitive framework centers on the mental processing of information, including the specific functions of attention, concentration, reasoning, problem solving, and memory. Cognitive psychologists are interested in the mental plans and thoughts that guide and cause behavior and affect how people feel. Intelligence testing and information-processing theories are examples that fall within the cognitive metatheory.

Whenever someone tells you to look at the bright side, they're coming from a cognitive perspective. When something bad happens, most people feel better if the problem gets solved or the issue is resolved. But how should you feel if nothing changes? If circumstances don't change, do you have to feel bad forever? Of course not; in most cases, people can change the way they think about a situation. You can choose to look on the bright side — or at least not look solely at the downside. That's the gist of cognitive therapy.

Sociocultural

The sociocultural approach focuses on the social and cultural factors that affect behavior. Therefore, as you might expect, social and cross-cultural psychology fall within the sociocultural metatheory, which is all about the enormous power of groups and culture on the why, how, and what of behavior and mental processes.

Tattoos and body piercings are good examples of this power. At one point in mainstream culture, people who got ink and piercings were perceived to be acting outside of the status quo, so "status quo" people weren't lined up outside the tattoo or piercing parlor. Nowadays, both are widely accepted, and even Mr. Status Quo may have a tat or piercing (or two or three).

Developmental

The Greek philosopher Heraclitus is credited with saying, "The only constant in life is change." Developmental psychology is a metatheory that is built on the idea that mental processes and behavior change over time, from one mental process and behavior to another in a progressive manner. Mental processes are built from and upon previous ones. Behaviors are built from and upon previous ones.

Early approaches focused mostly on children, and this is typically what people think when it comes to developmental psychology. But the contemporary approach covers the span of a human life and is known as *lifespan development*. A critical contribution from developmental researchers is the concept of *age-related norms*. These are guidelines for what mental processes and behaviors "should be" present at certain ages. For example, children "should be" speaking in two-word combinations by 18 to 24 months old. If they are not, then they are considered outside this norm and can be considered delayed. So if you ever feel pressured to move out of your parents' house by the age of 25, thank a developmental psychologist.

Evolutionary

Evolutionary psychology searches for the causes and explanations for mental processes and behavior through the lens of adaptive fitness and natural selection. The basic idea is that mental processes and behaviors are the product of the "selection through mating" for processes and behaviors that helped solve recurring problems facing humans across large swathes of time. Whereas developmental approaches emphasize change over the lifespan of an individual, evolutionary psychology emphasizes change over generations. Traits that were particularly helpful for survival, such as problem-solving and cooperating with others were "kept" and passed on to subsequent generations. Mental process or behavior that led to a person living long enough to pass on his or her genes stayed in the gene pool. Those that did not were dropped from the gene pool. Additionally, there is a branch of psychology known as *comparative psychology* that studies animal behavior as an analog for human behavior. Studying animals can help us understand humans, and evolutionary psychology is the foundation of and justification for this approach.

Humanistic and existential

The humanistic and existential metatheory emphasizes that each person is unique and that humans have the ability and responsibility to make choices in their lives. I'm not a victim of circumstance! I have choices in my life. Humanists believe that a person's free choice, free will, and understanding of the meaning of events in his or her life are the most important things to study in order to understand behavior. The works of Victor Frankl, Rollo May, and Fritz Perls along with the study of spirituality and religion are examples that fall within this framework.

In your own life, have you ever felt like just another nameless face in the crowd? Has your life ever seemed as if it's controlled by the winds of chance? How did it feel? Probably not very good. Feeling like you have choices — and making good choices — gives you a sense of true being and affirms your existence. That's the case with most people anyway, and psychologists who work within the humanistic and existential metatheory believe that behavior is simply a result of choice.

Psychoanalytic/psychodynamic

The psychoanalytic/psychodynamic metatheory emphasizes the importance of unconscious mental processes, early child development, personality, the self, attachment patterns, and relationships. This approach explores how these mental and developmental processes interact with the challenges of life and everyday demands to affect the person you are and how you behave.

Sigmund Freud founded psychoanalysis in the early 1900s; since then, hundreds of theorists have added to his work. The later theories are typically labeled *psychodynamic* because they emphasize the dynamic interplay between various components of mind, the self, personality, others, and reality. Object Relations Theory and Self Psychology are two specific theoretical perspectives that fall within the psychoanalytic/psychodynamic metatheory.

Feminism

Feminist psychology focuses on the political, economic, and social rights of women and how these forces influence the behavior of both men and women. Although feminism had some earlier influence, the feminist perspective in psychology gained momentum during the women's movement of the 1960s.

One issue in particular that has caught the attention of feminist researchers and clinicians is eating disorders. From the perspective of feminists, eating disorders are largely the consequence of excessive pressures to be thin that mass media and culture place upon females of all ages. Feminists draw attention to the fashion magazines and female role models in popular culture.

Postmodernism

The Postmodern metatheory questions the very core of psychological science, challenging its approach to truth and its focus on the individual. Postmodernists propose, for example, that in order to understand human thinking and reason, we need to look at the social and communal processes involved in thinking and reason. Reality is not something that is out there independently; it is something that humans, as a community, create.

Postmodernists make the argument that people in powerful positions have too much to say about what is "real" and "true" in psychology, and they advocate a *social constructionist* view of reality, which states that the concepts of "reality" and "truth" are defined, or constructed, by society. These concepts, according to this framework, have no meaning apart from the meanings that society and its experts assign to them. Narrative and constructionist theories are examples that fall within the metatheory of Postmodernism.

A Unifying Model? Working with the Biopsychosocial Model

Over the years, each of the major metatheories I just covered has enjoyed its day in the sun, only to be put on the shelf when the next big thing came along. This revolving door of explanatory frameworks makes it tough to sort through the different metatheories and choose the best one for finding the answers you're seeking. Where do you begin?

One alternative to picking a metatheory is to combine several views together, thus adopting an integrationist or *unifying* approach. The *biopsychosocial model* of psychology represents a popular attempt at integration.

REMEMBER

The basic idea behind this model is that human behavior and mental processes are the products of biological, psychological, and social influences. Biopsychosocialists try to find out how these influences interact to produce behavior. They believe that any explanation of behavior and mental processes that doesn't consider all three primary factors (body, mind, and environment) is incomplete.

Feeling out the role of the body

As material beings, humans are made of flesh and bones. Any discussion of thoughts, feelings, and other psychological concepts that doesn't factor in biological makeup and function, especially the brain and nervous system, ignores the fundamental facts of human existence.

Take the mind for example. Most people agree that they have a mind and that others (well, most others) have one too. But where does this mind exist? Psychologists accept that the mind exists in, or is synonymous with, the brain. The biological metatheory is integrated into the biopsychosocial model because of this component. You may say that, just as digestion is what the stomach does, "mind" is what the brain does.

Thinking about the role of the mind

When most people think about psychology, they have this aspect of the biopsychosocial model in mind (no pun intended). Thoughts, feelings, desires, beliefs, and numerous other mental concepts are addressed by the biopsychosocial model through analysis of the role of the mind.

What if this book was about botany? Would the biopsychosocial model apply? Only if you believe that plants have minds. In other words, it'd be a stretch! This highlights the uniqueness of the biopsychosocial model of psychology: The mind is central to understanding behavior and mental processes.

Behaviorists neglect the mind. Biological psychologists study the mind as the brain. By considering a person's mental state in the context of the biological systems and social environment, biopsychosocial psychologists get a broader view of a person's behavior and mental state than those who focus exclusively on one aspect of the three-part model.

Observing the role of the outside world

Brains don't work and minds don't think in a vacuum. Behavior and mental processes are embedded within a context that includes other people and things in the environment in which people live. Therefore, the social aspect of the biopsychosocial model also includes parent-child relationships, families, communities, and culture.

Other people have enormous power in shaping and influencing an individual's behavior and mental processes. If you're unsure, consider the detrimental effects that negative social events or experiences, such as physical or sexual abuse, can have on a person. Overlooking the impact of a person's interaction with family and friends is to neglect reality.

Do behaviors and mental processes vary across cultures? Let me put the question to you this way: If I only conducted research with white, middle-class, college students, can I state that my results apply to all people? Definitely not. This subject has been a hot topic in psychology over the last 30 years or so. Technological advances help make our world a smaller place and different cultures come into contact with each other more often than ever before, making a person's social life increasingly complex. Thus, just as the influence of family and friend relations is critical, it is also vital that psychologists consider cultural differences.

So it's safe to say that the culture in which an individual is raised as well as the cultures he experiences or adopts throughout life impact his behavior and mental processes.

Cultural influence needs to be addressed in psychology for at least two reasons:

>> **Science seeks objectivity and truth.** Everyone is vulnerable to cultural bias, and psychologists are no exception. Therefore, psychology should try to identify the influence of culture on their own thinking, theories, and research in order to provide the most objective and complete picture of reality possible.

>> **Accuracy depends on the relativity of truth in a specific culture.** So just because research with Americans shows that using baby talk to communicate with infants stunts the growth of mature speech, this doesn't mean that these findings hold true in other countries.

RESOLVING THE NATURE VERSUS NURTURE DEBATE

Consider professional athletes, those elite performers who are lucky enough to get paid to play games for a living. How much luck do you think is involved? A common misconception about professional, elite athletes is that their natural raw talent accounts for their success. Yet anyone who has worked with or known one of these individuals will tell you that hard work has a lot to do with his success.

So which is it? Talent or hard work? This question lies at the heart of a long-running debate within psychology; it's known as the nature versus nurture debate. Talent versus hard work. Inborn ability versus learning and effort.

Nature refers to the concept that behavior and mental processes are innate, inborn, and hard-wired and will unfold over time as a person develops and her genetic blueprint is revealed. *Nurture* refers to the idea that behavior and mental processes are not inborn and instead are learned from the environment in which people live.

Both perspectives have their proponents. John Locke, a 17th-century British philosopher, espoused the concept of *tabula rasa,* the "blank slate" and believed that, given the right learning experiences, a person can become anything in life. On the other side is Charles Darwin, the father of evolution and nature advocate, who believed that a person's destiny is found in his or her biology and genes.

A quote by John Watson, considered by some historians as the founder of behaviorism, epitomizes this perspective:

> Give me a dozen healthy infants, well-formed, and my own specified world to bring them up in and I'll guarantee to take any one at random and train him to become any type of specialist I might select — doctor, lawyer, artist, merchant-chief, and, yes, even beggarman and thief, regardless of his talents, penchants, tendencies, abilities, vocations, and race of his ancestors. I am going beyond my facts and I admit it, but so have the advocates of the contrary and they have been doing it for many thousands of years. — John B. Watson, *Behaviorism,* 1930

Most modern psychologists consider this debate over. The simple answer is that *both* nature and nurture impact a person's behavior and level of success. This means that making sense of what people do and why they do it is ultimately accomplished only by investigating and understanding the relative contributions of innate biological influences and learned environmental influences.

Developing a good theory

A *theory* is a set of related statements about a set of objects or events (the ones being studied) that explains how these objects or events are related. Knowing this is important because a significant amount of psychological knowledge is based on theory. Theories perform two main functions: They combine what is already known into a simpler package of knowledge and they help psychologists plan future investigations: Theories *summarize* and *guide*.

Theories and hypotheses are similar but not exactly the same thing. Psychologists test theories by studying their logical implications. Hypotheses are specific predictions based on these implications. You can add new information to theories, and you can use existing theories to generate new ones.

REMEMBER

Not every theory is a good theory. In order for a theory to be good, it must meet three criteria:

>> **Parsimony:** It must be the simplest explanation possible that still explains the available observation.

>> **Precision:** It must make precise, not overly large or vague, statements about reality.

>> **Testability:** It must lend itself to scientific investigation. There must be some way to show that the theory can be wrong. It is easy to collect more information consistent with one's theory. It is braver to be a scientist: to examine situations that may prove one's theory wrong.

Seeking Truth

It seems that I've always been looking for *the* truth. When I was in college, I frequented a little bookstore near campus that specialized in spiritual, philosophical, and popular-psychology books. At least once a week, I would peruse the shelves looking for something interesting. The books were arranged by topic: metaphysics, Eastern wisdom, Western wisdom, Buddhism, Taoism, Judaism, Islam, Christianity, new age, channeling, and so on. I read books from every section. I was searching for some kind of ultimate truth, some kind of answer.

One day, I realized that I had sampled works from every section in this bookstore, but I still wasn't satisfied. Then, I had a strange thought: This bookstore is full of opinions! How was I supposed to find the answers or the truth when I was only getting opinions? Many of the books contained testimonials, logical arguments, and stories, but very little, if any, evidence or proof. If I questioned something, I simply had to take an author's word for it and trust it was true. But they couldn't all be right because some authors contradicted or criticized others. So who *was* right?

I guess I'm just one of those people who needs proof. It would be an exaggeration to say that I'm finding all the answers in psychology, but, as a field, psychology makes a serious effort to establish the truth of its claims with proof, or *empirical evidence,* which comes from applying the *empirical method,* an approach to truth that uses observation and experiment.

Psychology, as the scientific study of human behavior and mental processes, uses the empirical method. It relies on data and information obtained from research, experimentation, observation, and measurement. The empiricist motto is "Show me the data." This is not to deny the importance of theory. But theory is insufficient as a working position for reliable psychologists.

Psychologists act responsibly when they are working with empirical evidence and less responsibly when not. These scientists are expected to base their work on solid data and information, not opinion.

REMEMBER

From an empirical perspective, just because a psychologist says something doesn't make it true. A psychologist is compelled to base her claims on empirical evidence gathered from research and statistical analysis. Is it really worth paying for a psychologist's services to treat depression or a phobia, for example, if what she is saying and doing is just based on her opinion? What makes her the expert? You expect professionals to possess a credible amount of specific knowledge about their area of expertise, and this knowledge and expertise should be based on empirical evidence.

The authority of these experts is maintained through the ways in which they know and investigate their subject matter.

Words like *knowledge* and *truth* can be tricky sometimes. Knowing where psychologists' knowledge comes from is an important first step in learning about psychology. In this section, I explore the different ways that psychologists gather evidence and try to substantiate the truth of their claims and knowledge. Specifically, I describe scientific research and theory development, the two primary tools psychologists use to establish expertise in human behavior and mental processes.

Applying the scientific method

Most everyone has an opinion about the behavior and mental processes of others and ourselves. "She left you because you're emotionally unavailable." "If you don't express yourself, it just stays bottled up inside." We're full of answers to the why, how, and what questions regarding people. But how do we really know that not talking about feelings leads to bottling them up? I may think that not express-ing feelings allows them to drift away like clouds on a windy day. Who's right? You may be thinking that it doesn't matter, but we've got this whole group of psy-chologists who claim to be experts on these matters. On what grounds can they make this claim to expertise?

Psychologists strive to maintain their expertise and knowledge through the use of three forms of knowledge acquisition or ways of knowing:

>> **Authority:** Utilized to transmit information, usually in a therapy setting or the education and training process. Patients and students don't have time to go out and research everything that they're told. They have to take someone's word for it at some point.

>> **Rationalism/logic:** Used to create theories and hypotheses. If things don't make logical sense, they probably won't make sense when researchers use the scientific method to investigate them.

>> **Scientific method:** Used as the preferred method of obtaining information and investigating behavior and mental processes. Psychologists implement the scientific method through a variety of different techniques.

REMEMBER

Let me be perfectly clear: Not everything that psychologists do, talk about, and believe is based on scientific research. A lot of stuff is based on the authority of well-known personalities in the field. Other knowledge is based on clinical expe-rience without any systematic investigation. A good-sized chunk of information that's out there is also purely theoretical, but it makes sense on rational or logical grounds.

The vast majority of psychologists prefer to use the scientific method when seek-ing truth because it's seen as a fair and impartial process. When I do a research study, I'm expected to outline exactly what I'm doing and what it is I claim to be looking for. That way, if people want to try to prove me wrong, they can repeat my work, step by step, and see if they get the same results. If knowledge is based on authority alone, I can never be sure that the information I receive is unbiased and trustworthy. When the scientific method is in place, a theory that doesn't match the empirical results experienced in a research study is labeled inaccurate. Time for a new theory!

WARNING

Scientists should never change their experimental data to match their original theory; that's cheating!

Researching Matters

Psychologists use two broad categories of research when they want to scientifically evaluate a theory: descriptive research and experimental research. In this section, I describe these approaches and dig into matters related to statistics, understanding cause and effect in correlational studies, and the fascinating placebo effect.

Understanding descriptive research

Descriptive research consists of observation and the collection of data without trying to manipulate any of the conditions or circumstances being observed. It's a passive observation of the topics being investigated. Descriptive studies are good for developing new theories and hypotheses and are often the first step for a researcher investigating things that haven't been studied much. However, they don't help much if you're interested in cause and effect relationships.

If I'm only interested in the content of bus-stop conversations, I may videotape people talking to each other at a bus stop and analyze the video. But, if I want to know what causes people to talk about certain subjects at bus stops, I should conduct an experiment.

Doing experimental research

Experimental research involves the control and manipulation of the objects and events being investigated in order to get a better idea of the cause and effect relationships between the objects or events.

Say I have a theory about bus-stop conversations called the "five-minute or more rule" that states, "Strangers will engage in conversation with each other only after having been in each other's presence for five or more minutes." My hypothesis is, "After five minutes, apparent strangers will engage in a conversation beyond the simple pleasantries and greetings afforded to strangers." That is, I am hypothesizing that after strangers at a bus stop have been there for five minutes, they will start having a conversation. How can I test my hypothesis?

I can just hang out at a bus stop and watch to see if it happens. But how do I know that my five-minute-or-more rule is behind my observations? I don't. It maybe any number of things. This is a problematic issue in research I like to call the z-factor. A *z-factor* is something affecting the hypothesis that I am unaware of or not accounting for. It is an extraneous variable that I need to control in order to have confidence in my theory. Some possible z-factors in the bus-stop study may be culture, age, and time of day. Good research studies try to eliminate z-factors or extraneous variables by controlling for their influence and factoring them out of the explanation.

A descriptive or observational study won't account for z-factors, so instead, I set up an experiment in which *I* approach people at bus stops and try a variety of things to test my hypothesis. I may go up and try to talk to someone after two minutes. I may wait for ten minutes. I may conduct studies during a thunderstorm or while dressed in particular ways, and I would try to prove my hypothesis wrong! I seek to find that people have conversations at bus stops before five minutes. If this is the case, then the five-minute rule is inaccurate. The more often I fail to prove my five-minute-or-more rule wrong, the more it deserves my confidence.

This is confusing. Why would I try to disprove my hypothesis instead of just proving it right? In any scientific investigation, I can never really prove a hypothesis true. Instead, I set out to disprove the opposite of my hypothesis. For example, people once thought the earth was flat. Everything observed at that time was consistent with this idea. However, someone came along and provided evidence that disputed this idea, which showed the flaw in the thinking. If I have a hypothesis and I keep finding evidence for it, I can be more and more confident in my hypothesis but never really know for sure. But if I can find just one example that contradicts my hypothesis, then this casts doubt on my hypothesis. If I say all swans are white, what happens when I find one black swan? The notion that all swans are white is false!

Measuring one, measuring all with statistics

Good psychology is based on solid theory and good data, whether the data is obtained through observation or experimentation. And psychology claims to make statements about all people. That is, psychologists claim that their research applies to people in general most of the time. They seek the truth as it applies to all people. But without conducting research on everyone on Earth, how can psychologists possibly make this claim?

A branch of mathematics called *statistics* comes riding in on a white horse to enable a psychologist to make claims about humanity based on studies and research conducted on only a few dozen or a couple hundred people. After a theory is developed, the scientific method dictates that that theory then be put to the test, either through observation or experimentation. Again, we run into the problem of not being able to observe or experiment with everyone and this is where statistics helps out.

Statistics is concerned with the rules of data collection and analysis. Generally, two types of statistical analyses are used in psychology, descriptive and inferential:

>> **Descriptive statistics** refer to the direct numerical measurement of characteristics of a *population* such as how many of something there are, what the average number of some phenomenon is, or what the range of a particular value of something is. I am describing what is there, but not going beyond the data. If I conduct descriptive statistics on all swans to test my hypothesis that all swans are white, I would have to describe every swan. Formally, a *population* is defined as a well-defined, complete collection of things, objects, and so on. A descriptive analysis requires a description of the entire swan population.

>> **Inferential statistics** comes to the rescue when I can't measure all swans, because this approach allows me to measure a *sample* of swans, a subset of the swan population, and then make inferences or estimates about the population as a whole from the sample that was drawn.

Inferential statistics solves the measurement dilemma as long, of course, as you follow some basic rules such as *randomization* and appropriate *sample size*.

Randomization allows researchers to make inferences about a population based on the way a sample is chosen. Every member of the population must have the same chance of being in the sample.

Collecting a random sample ensures that the population is well represented. If you don't randomly choose the people to measure, then you can fall prey to *sampling bias*, choosing in a way so that some members of the population are less likely to be included than others. Sampling bias prevents you from being able to make statements about an entire population.

This issue often comes up in the use of polls during election season. A pollster claims that a result from measuring a sample extends to the population of likely voters, and critics are quick to point out that the sample consisted of 20- to 25-year-old graduate students at a liberal arts college in the Northwest. Is this a representative sample of likely voters?

Another key ingredient to ensuring that your sample is representative of the population is *sample size*, the number or *n* of individuals in your sample. Certainly the larger the sample the better because you get closer to measuring the population more directly and less inference is required. Of course, the size of your sample, your *n*, is determined by logistics and practicality so you typically have to settle for something much smaller than anything approaching the total population.

This brings up a pet peeve for psychologists, and scientists in general, known as the "N of One" problem. Everyone gets advice and information from friends about dieting and nutrition. My buddy tried the "caveman diet" and swears he lost 40 pounds. My officemate was on the "cupcake" diet and lost 20 pounds. My cousin was on the "carbs only" diet and gained 100 pounds. These people are offering data from their own experience. However, they have only sampled one individual from the population, themselves. They have a sample size of one. So, from a statistical perspective, how likely is it that their sample represents the population as a whole? Not likely at all. Correspondingly, this is why most people are more likely to trust advice if the same data comes from multiple people.

Relating variables: Correlation versus causation

A *variable* is the thing, characteristic, behavior, or mental process that is being measured or observed. Psychologists are interested in how variables relate, that is how do the things that are measured affect, impact, or alter each other? How does child abuse affect school performance? How does work stress affect depression? How does obsessive thinking affect relationships? In research, there are two types of variables, *independent* and *dependent*. A *dependent variable* is the thing that is impacted or altered as a function of the independent variable. The *independent variable* impacts the dependent variable as it changes.

My pulse and heart rate go way up when I am involved in a near-miss car accident situation. The dependent variable is my heart rate. The independent variable is the near miss. So the near miss *causes* my heart rate to go up. This is a *causal relationship*. The value of the dependent variable is directly caused or influenced by the independent variable.

Does that mean that if two variables are related that there is a causal relationship? No, sometimes variables can be involved in a non-causal manner known as a *correlation* or a correlational relationship. A *correlation* exists between two variables when the value of one is related to the value of the other but not necessarily in a causal manner. For example, a semifamous correlation is that the crime rate tends to be higher in the summer months. So there *is* a relationship between heat and crime rate; when one is high, the other is too. But does that mean that hot weather *causes* crime to go up? Not necessarily; it can be rather that youth and adolescents have more free time on their hands and therefore get into more trouble and commit more crime. This is conjecture, of course, and is just to prove the point that simply because hot weather and crime are related does not mean that one causes the other to happen. Correlation, not causation.

DOING NOTHING IS SOMETHING: THE PLACEBO EFFECT

Psychologists want to test the impact of independent variables on dependent variables. They may want to test the impact of a new medication (independent variable) on levels of anxiety (dependent variable). This can be done by comparing people with anxiety who get the medication with those who do not. If anxiety goes down (or up), then maybe the medication is helping (or making things worse). This is considered a simple experimental and control group approach. An experimental group is the group that is getting the independent variable, and the control group is not; it is getting nothing in essence.

This is a solid experimental approach but there is another variation of this approach that is often used to help make the impact of the independent variable stand out more. This is done by using a placebo group in addition to the control group. A *placebo* is a decoy variable of sorts, a fake independent variable that is not expected to have an impact on the dependent variable, but the person in the study thinks it is an actual treatment or independent variable. Of course, some psychologists fit in more than one of these categories, for example, clinical psychologists conducting research.

From the preceding anxiety example, there would then be three groups, the medication group (independent variable group), the no-medication group (control group), and the placebo medication group (another control group). So, if at the end of the experiment, the findings are that the medication group's anxiety went down substantially, we can conclude the medication worked, right? This can be said only in contrast to the no-medication group. But with the placebo group, another level of confidence exists because sometimes in studies like this both the independent variable and the placebo group show change. That would shed doubt on the trustworthiness of the finding from the independent variable group. But if the independent variable group shows change and neither the control group nor the placebo group showed change, we can be that much more confident in that finding.

What is interesting about this, however, is that the placebo group quite often shows change or improvement. This is known as the placebo *effect*, when an experimental effect is related to the presence of the placebo. For example, it is amazing how often a sugar pill (placebo) produces reductions in anxiety in experimental subjects. This truly fascinating phenomenon is one that scientists from all fields are trying to learn more about but have not quite figured out yet.

Being "Good": Ethics in Psychology

Human conduct is guided by codes of behavior known as *ethics*. Simply put, ethics refers to the prescribing of *right* behavior and the proscribing of *wrong* behavior. In addition to psychologists being guided by the principles of science, they are also guided by their own code of ethics, their own understanding of right and wrong behavior.

The American Psychological Association (www.apa.org) is the largest organization in the world representing psychology as a profession. Other countries, including the UK, have their own professional bodies, with similar regulatory frameworks. The mission of the APA is to advance the field of psychology and to benefit society. The APA's *Ethical Principles of Psychologists and Code of Conduct* is the ethical rule book for psychologists. The main components of this rulebook are the "General Principles" and specific "Ethical Standards." The Ethical Standards are numerous and cover topics ranging from resolution of ethical dilemmas to competence, education and training, and therapy.

The General Principles consist of several overarching declarations that compel psychologists to act in the best interest of the people they are working with or for (for example, clients, patients, students, or research subjects) and to avoid any harm. They are expected to act responsibly, with best practices in mind, and with honesty and integrity. Basic human rights and dignity should be respected, and justice should be preserved and pursued. Here is the list of the *General Principles:*

>> **Principle A — Beneficence and Nonmaleficence:** Benefit those whom psychologists work with and take care to do no harm. Safeguard the welfare and rights of those the interacted with professionally.

>> **Principle B — Fidelity and Responsibility:** Engage in relationships based on trust, uphold scientific responsibilities, uphold standards of conduct, clarify roles and obligations, and accept responsibility for professional behavior.

>> **Principle C — Integrity:** Promote accuracy, honesty, and truthfulness in science, teaching, and practice.

>> **Principle D — Justice:** Recognize that fairness and justice entitles all persons access to and benefit from psychology and with equal quality.

>> **Principle E — Respect for People's Rights and Dignity:** Respect the worth of all people and uphold their rights to privacy, confidentiality, and self-determination.

REMEMBER

Although all the ethical standards are important, the one that is often considered tantamount is the ethical principle of *confidentiality* — that information of a research participant or therapy client information is kept private and there are limits on how and when it can be disclosed to a third party. The APA's code is enforceable for members of the association, and a breach of the code can result in expulsion from the association. Most state licensing boards in the United States have adopted the APA's code as their guide and standard as well and can enforce compliance through various forms of disciplinary action including revoking licenses.

The rest of this book introduces you to various theories and research. There's a lot of stuff in here! Because psychology is about people, some people may argue that everything about people is psychology. I couldn't write a book about everything. This is not *Everything about People For Dummies*. In establishing a way to decide what to put in the book and what not to, I used scientific research and theory as my measuring rod. The information you find in this book is considered part of legitimate psychological science and theory.

2

Picking Your Brain (and Body)

IN THIS CHAPTER

» Biologizing psychology

» Getting up the nerve

» Slicing and dicing the brain

» Discovering DNA

» Finding out how medications change behavior

Chapter **3**

Brains, Genes, and Behavior

Psychology can seem pretty abstract, seemingly having more in common with philosophy than biology. In this book, I introduce you to all kinds of psychological concepts — thoughts, feelings, beliefs, and personalities among them. But have you ever wondered *where* all of these phenomena "exist"? If I need to find or locate a thought or feeling, where do I look?

Obviously these things happen in the mind. But where is a person's mind? The quick response for many people: It's inside my skull, in my brain! So, I wonder, if you opened someone's skull and gazed upon the brain, would you see various kinds of thoughts, feelings, and other psychological stuff tucked away in there? Definitely not. You'd see a wrinkled and convoluted mass of grayish-pinkish-whitish tissue. There are no visible thoughts, feelings, or beliefs. Yet you know they exist because you experience them every day. Some ancient people's knew that whatever "caused" behavior was inside the skull. We know this because when someone acted in a bizarre or disruptive manner, they would bore holes into their skulls to let out whatever was in there causing the problem. The causes could have been bad spirits or demons. Either way, when they went looking for the source of someone's problematic behavior, they looked to the skull, or what was inside of it.

The question of where the mind, the home of psychological concepts, exists is an age-old philosophical question. Is the mind in the brain? Is the mind somewhere other than the brain? Are the brain and the mind the same thing? Most scientists today hold the position that the mind and the brain are one and the same. Scientists taking this position, known as *monism*, believe that in order to achieve the most full understanding of mental processes and behavior, we have to include the brain and the body in that formulation, acknowledging the very reality that we have brains and bodies in which mental processes and behavior "live."

Psychologist Neil Carlson states, "What we call the 'mind' is a consequence of the functioning of the human body and its interactions with the environment." This is a powerful idea — the key to unlocking the mysteries of such psychological concepts as thinking and feeling lies in a thorough understanding of human biology.

REMEMBER

The idea that all of human psychology can be reduced to biology is known as *biological reductionism*. This idea seems to insult our closely guarded and esteemed sense of free will, self-awareness, and consciousness. I mean, how can all this complex stuff going on inside my mind be reduced to a hunk of flesh resting between my ears? If you feel this way, maybe you're not a biological reductionist. But for the sake of this chapter, I'm going to be one, and I'm asking you to be one too.

In this chapter, you're introduced to the major components of biological psychology, the brain, and the role of genetics in understanding behavior and mental processes is covered as well. The chapter closes with a discussion of medications and newer forms of brain-based treatments for mental disorders.

Believing in Biology

People haven't always believed that human behavior and mental processes are the consequences of biology. In the times of ancient Greeks and Romans, human behavior was seen as the consequence of supernatural forces, namely the whims and passions of the gods. But somewhere along the line, suspicion grew that maybe the human body had something to do with it. Where would such a radical idea come from?

REMEMBER

The history of research in this area is long, but at the core of all the research is a very simple observation: Changes in a person's biology result in changes in her mental processes and behavior.

Take alcohol consumption, for example. No question that people act differently when under the influence of alcohol. They may flirt, dance like an idiot, get emotional and sentimental, or even become angry and violent. Alcohol has a chemical effect on the brain; it alters the biology of the drinker's brain. It goes something like this:

Alcohol consumption → chemical effect on brain → thinks he's super cool

What about more serious changes in biology like brain injury? People who suffer from brain injury can exhibit drastic changes in their mental processes and behavior. They may go from being very organized to very messy. Or a once very laid-back, easygoing person may fly into a rage at the slightest frustration. They may have difficulty with memory or understanding.

I think you probably have an intuitive understanding that what goes on within your brain has an effect on your mental processes and behavior. *Biological psychologists* are a group of psychologists who have extended this intuitive belief and these casual observations, using techniques and methods of modern science to investigate the idea that changes in biology lead to changes in psychology. We can't escape our brains and genes, so biology and psychology are stuck with each other. But this relationship doesn't have to be contentious as long as we adopt the monist stance.

Although a lot of this seems logical, you may be thinking that there must be more to you than biology. And I say, that's just the dualist in you acting up. Try not to struggle with it too much, at least while you read this chapter. Even if you think you're more than just cells and molecules, you can still benefit from the research of biological psychology.

Did you read about the *biopsychosocial model* in Chapter 2? (If not, you may want to check it out. Trust me, it's a good chapter.) That model proposes that human psychology is a function of the three important levels of understanding:

>> The biological level

>> The psychological level

>> The social level

This chapter focuses on the biological level, and the remainder of the book focuses on the other two. But you need to find out how the three levels interact — that is, how biology influences psychology, how psychology influences biology, and so on — to really get a handle on behavior and mental processes.

TIP

A useful metaphor for describing how the different levels interact is the modern computer. You may know that a computer has at least two functional components: hardware and software. The hardware consists of the actual physical components of the computer: the processor, hard drive, wires, USB ports, and various other components. The software includes the operating system, a word-processing program, and several other tools you use to actually work on a computer. There's even a "cloud" now that functions as software but isn't actually on your hard drive. That's cool!

In this metaphor, the hardware of a computer represents the biological level of understanding. This is the physical body, the brain, the nervous system, the sense organs, and other physical systems that are more or less involved in mental processing and behavior. So does that mean your toe plays a role in mental processes and behavior? It kind of does but in a limited way compared to your brain and other systems. Your toe may not tell you what to do, but pain in your toe can definitely influence your mental processes and behavior. However, this influence is mediated by the peripheral nervous system and the central nervous system (the brain). That's why this chapter is not called "Shoulders, Knees, Toes, and Behavior." But it could be called "Head and Behavior."

The Biological "Control Room"

The human nervous system consists of two large divisions: the *central nervous system (CNS)* and the *peripheral nervous system (PNS)*. The CNS includes the brain and spinal cord. The PNS includes the nerves outside the CNS; they are in the rest (the periphery) of the body.

The basic building blocks of the nervous system are nerves, neurons, and neurotransmitters and glial cells. The nerves are, essentially, bundles of neurons, like a box of spaghetti is a bundle of individual strips of pasta. The neurons are individual nerve cells. Usually, they receive signals from other neurons, evaluate those signals, and then transmit new signals to other parts of the nervous system.

Neurochemical electrical changes throughout the nervous system serve as a basic mechanism for psychological functions. I say "a basic mechanism" because some researchers go deeper or smaller by looking at molecular actions in the brain, and still others go even deeper or smaller to look at the role of genetics in mental processes and behavior. (More on that later in the chapter.) Because these electrical changes involve the movement of chemical ions, the transmission system is called an *electrochemical system*. Neurotransmitters are chemicals that play a critical role in transmitting signals between neurons. The glial cells are cells within the nervous system that play a variety of support roles for the neurons; they protect neurons from damage, repair them when they are damaged, and remove damaged or dead tissue when it can't be repaired ("taking out the trash").

So neurons, networks of neurons, and all the biological stuff (I know, not very scientific but I'm not a neurobiologist) underlying their function make up the neurobiology of mental processes and behavior. Some scientists propose that the biological study of the brain is really the study of neurons in networks. This approach is known as the *neurocomputational* approach to brain functioning. It's "computational" because these researchers base their models of brain functioning on the calculation processes of neurons in networks as they interact with each other by turning each other on and off with electrochemical signaling. For more about this check out the excellent book by Steven Pinker, *How the Mind Works* (W.W. Norton & Company, 2009).

The nervous system is a living part of the body and, therefore, has the same basic needs as any other body part: It needs fuel and immune protection. The components of the nervous system stay alive and healthy thanks to the circulatory system and other regulatory body functions. If you've studied any physics, chemistry, or biology, you may remember that some of the basic building blocks of life are atoms (operating under the laws of physics). Atoms are grouped in particular ways to make up molecules that then form compounds. In the brain, molecules create cells, and cells interact with each at the cell-to-cell level. Cells interacting with each other form neuronal networks, and the neurobiology of behavior are cells and their interactions with each other. There are billions of neurons and trillions of connections. That's a lot going on.

REMEMBER

So how do scientists sort all of that out? They look at the nervous system in two basic ways: *anatomical organization* and *functional organization*. Looking at the nervous system from an anatomical (or anatomy) viewpoint essentially focuses on the parts, and the functional organization view is concerned with what those parts do with respect to mental processes and behavior.

The anatomy of the CNS consists of both the brain and the spinal cord. Although the spinal cord is critical, the focus of this section is on the brain, which is considered to be the underlying physical foundation for psychological functioning. It is, literally, the command center for behavior. The brain, with billions of cells and sophisticated networks, is among the most complex biological structures known to scientists.

Cells and Chemicals

At the cellular level of brain anatomy is what many brain scientists consider to be the fundamental unit of the brain and the nervous system: the *neuron*, a specialized cell that provides the foundation for brain functioning, which is communication among nerve cells. Actually, there is another important type of cell in the brain: the *glial cells*. Glial cells provide the basic structure to the nervous system and nourish the neurons. But neurons are the star of the brain show according to most scientists.

A neuron is considered the information cell; it's involved in the processing and storage of information. Neurons contain the following parts:

>> **Soma:** The cell body of the neuron containing the nucleus and supportive structures of the cell, including the mitochondria

>> **Dendrite:** Projections from the cell body that receive information from other neurons

>> **Axon:** The nerve fiber that conducts the electrical impulse

>> **Terminal button:** The end of the axon involved in neurotransmitter release and signaling to other neurons

The action in the brain happens when a neuron is activated and sends electrochemical signals to other neurons. Neurons become activated by input from other neurons, which in turn impacts the other neurons in a given network. Simply put, when information from the environment (or inside the brain itself from other neurons) comes into the brain through the sensory organs and activates a particular neuron (or, more often, a set of neurons), an *action potential* is created.

Action potentials are the movement of electrochemical energy through a neuron toward its terminal button, toward other neurons. Something called the *all-or-none law* states that neurons are either "on" or "off"; they are either firing an action potential or not. After a neuron is activated, it fires. If it's not activated: no action, no fire!

Some people consider the firing of a neuron (the action potential) to be an electrical process; others say it's a chemical process. In essence, however, it's both. The action potential consists of electrical energy that's created and activated by the exchange of positive and negative chemical ions between the inside and the outside of the neuron. It's electrochemical.

When a neuron is not firing, it is considered to be in the state of a *resting potential* and its electrical charge is more negative on the inside relative to the outside.

There are more negatively charged ions inside than outsid...
receives a signal from another neuron, gates in the cell m...
open and positive ions rush into the negatively charged ir...
istry and physics point out that positive charges move t...
they attract! So as the inside of the cell spikes to the posi...
is created and the neuron fires! In many ways, the actior...
disturbance in the axon that travels along the axon, like ...
fuse of a firecracker.

When the action potential occurs, the cell cannot fire again for a short period of time. During this refractory period, small pumps in the cell membrane work to reset the neuron by moving positive ions back out of the cell, returning the chemical balance of the neuron to its original state to prepare for another round of action.

In the subsections that follow, I cover how neurons communicate with each other by sending signals from one neuron to another in a process called *synaptic transmission*.

Networking and crossing the divide

As an action potential speeds through a neuron toward its terminal button, how does it propagate that signal to other neurons in the network? Before I can answer, you need to know that neurons don't actually connect to each other in a physical sense. There are gaps between them known as *synapse*, spaces between axon terminals of one neuron (the neuron sending the signal) and the dendrites of the next neuron (the neuron receiving the signal); this is where inter-neuronal communication happens through chemical messengers called *neurotransmitters*. Figure 3-1 shows a neuron and a synapse. Although they are only millionths of an inch apart, the sending neuron throws its "message in a bottle" into the sea-napse, where it drifts to the other shore (the receiving dendrite). The message says, "Please hear me; please fire!" Dramatic stuff!

Neurotransmitters are stored in the axon of the sending cell. An action potential stimulates their release into the synapse. They travel (actually drift) to a receiving neuron in which specialized docks known as *receptor sites* are present. Different shaped neurotransmitters have different docks.

Basically, neurotransmitters have one of two effects; they either *excite* the receiving neuron (make it more likely to fire) or *inhibit* the receiving neuron (make it less likely to fire). Some neurotransmitters are excitatory and some are inhibitory. Whether a particular neuron fires (transmits a signal) depends on the balance between excitatory and inhibitory neurotransmitters.

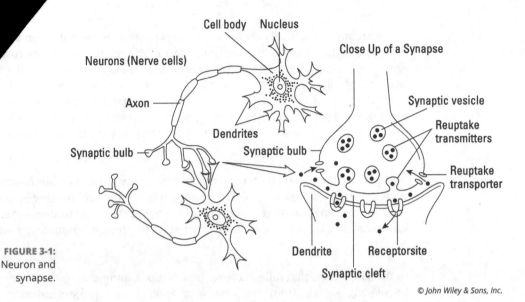

FIGURE 3-1:
Neuron and
synapse.

Labels: Cell body, Nucleus, Close Up of a Synapse, Neurons (Nerve cells), Synaptic vesicle, Reuptake transmitters, Axon, Dendrites, Synaptic bulb, Reuptake transporter, Synaptic bulb, Dendrite, Receptorsite, Synaptic cleft

© John Wiley & Sons, Inc.

Following the docking process, neurotransmitters are either broken down by enzymes or reabsorbed by the sending neurons in a process called *reuptake*. These two processes clear neurotransmitters from the synapse after they have done their job (enough, already!). This is critical to prepare the cells for the next signal. Neurotransmitter manipulation is a primary mechanism of action for most psychiatric medications (find information on the actions of medications in the "Understanding Psychopharmacology" section later in this chapter).

Scientists have discovered more than 100 neurotransmitters in the human brain. Many, including the following, play a major role:

>> **Glutamate:** The most common excitatory neurotransmitter

>> **GABA:** The most common inhibitory transmitter; involved in eating, aggression, and sleep

>> **Acetylcholine:** A common neurotransmitter with multiple excitatory and inhibitory functions; involved in movement and memory

Another group of four chemically similar neurotransmitters modify behavior in many ways. These neurotransmitters are particularly important regarding psychological disorders:

>> **Serotonin:** An inhibitory transmitter that is involved in balancing excitatory transmitters as well as mood, sleep, eating, and pain

>> **Dopamine:** Can be either inhibitory or excitatory and is implicated in attention, pleasure and reward, and movement

> » **Epinephrine:** An excitatory transmitter related to stress responses, heart rate, and blood pressure

> » **Norepinephrine:** An excitatory transmitter involved in energy regulation, anxiety, and fear

Branching out

An estimated 86 billion neurons live in the human brain and form trillions of connections among themselves. So you can think of the brain as a massive collection of nodes in a well-connected network. Just exactly how information is kept and processed in the brain remains the focus of incredible amounts of neuroscience research, but here's what scientists do know.

REMEMBER

The brain is a "massively parallel" information-processing system. (Flip to Chapter 6 for more about information processing.) If each neuron was connected to only one other neuron, the neuron system would be considered "massively serial." Compared to electronic signals, neural signals travel very slowly (like 5–100 mph), so it is efficient to do many things at once — called *parallel processing*. Think of it like finding a person who is lost in a large national park. The search party probably doesn't stay together and follow each other on the same path (serial processing); instead, they "branch out" (parallel processing) to cover more ground in the same amount of time. Likewise, the brain, with its billions of neurons and trillions of connections, uses the branching-out method to process, store, and find information among its cells and cell clusters.

Not every neuron is connected to every other neuron, but neurons are connected to multiple others that form clusters or networks involved in particular psychological processes and behaviors. For example, if seeing a red ball activates neurons #3, 4, 192, X, A, and 56, then the network for "seeing a red ball" would be called 3-4-192-X-A-56. Neuroscience researchers are working hard to map the brain and its networks in order to connect cell clusters to respective mental functions and behavior. The International Consortium for Brain Mapping (ICBM) is one such group of scientists that is dedicated to this endeavor.

Activating brain change

Have you ever scratched your nose and noticed that your foot stopped itching? Okay, well, that's a slight stretch, but there is something called *phantom limb syndrome* in which people who have lost a limb (an arm or leg for example) continue to report feeling sensations from that limb such as pain, cold, touch, and so on. How can this be? The limb is gone so where are the sensations coming from?

In his book, *Half a Brain Is Enough: The Story of Nico,* Dr. Antonio Battro tells the story of a boy named Nico who has a very significant portion of his brain surgically removed to control seizure activity (a drastic but sometimes necessary surgery for individuals with intractable seizures). However, after having that large portion of his brain removed, Nico remains relatively normal and maintains a fair amount of brain functioning — as if the brain tissue had not been removed. Why does Nico remain relatively unimpaired while working with half a brain?

Both phantom limb and Nico's brain demonstrate what brain scientists refer to as *neuroplasticity,* which is the notion that the brain's neural networks and connections continually reorganize. At one point in time, scientists believed that the brain's organization was "fixed," but this is simply not the case. The brain can change its size and connections throughout a person's lifetime.

The ability for the brain to update itself in response to new stimulation and input represents the neurobiological foundation of learning. In phantom limb syndrome it was found that the neural networks devoted to the lost limb (arm, leg, and so on) had been co-opted by neurons and networks proximal to it such as neurons associated with sensation in the in nearby body parts. So when the face had a sensation, the neurons that were previously associated with the lost limb were being stimulated, and other parts of the brain interpreted the sensations as coming from the limb.

In Nico's case, the functions performed by the lost brain cells from surgical removal were taken over by neighboring or other cells and networks. Other parts of the brain essentially learned how to do the functions once performed by the lost cells. In both cases, phantom limb and Nico, the brain essentially rewired itself in response to new inputs and learning experiences.

Neuroplasticity is good news for people who lose brain tissue through trauma or disease. But what about growing new brain cells? After all, new skin cells grow after a cut. Does this happen in the brain?

For many years scientists believed that it was not possible to grow new neurons or brain cells. However, research has shown that *neurogenesis* (regeneration of nerve cells) is possible in specific regions of the brain, particularly the lateral ventricles and the hippocampus. More research is being conducted to see if this process is happening in other parts of the brain as well. If neurogenesis is found to be more widespread or possible in other brain areas or if scientists can find a way to stimulate the process, manipulate it, or otherwise impact it, then there may be a great ray of sunshine for people who now suffer from diseases or trauma such as Alzheimer's, stroke, traumatic brain injury, or spinal cord injury. However, the science and research is very preliminary in this area and much more work needs to be done before such a thing is possible.

Because everything people do involves the brain, one might wonder what happens when some part of the brain gets damaged? The behavior and mental processes associated with the damaged portion of the brain are adversely affected or altered. Clinical neuropsychologists are particularly interested in the behavioral and mental consequences of brain injuries.

The brain can be damaged in numerous ways:

>> **Closed-head injuries:** These injuries occur when someone sustains a blow to the head but the skull is not penetrated. A common form of closed-head injury is a *contrecoup* injury, where the injury occurs to the part of the brain opposite from where the individual was struck. For example, if you're hit in the back of the head, this could cause the front of your brain to hit the inside of your forehead, and you may sustain damage to your frontal lobe, thus affecting your organizational and planning abilities. Even though the skull is not broken, serious damage can occur if the brain bleeds or swells resulting in pressure and additional damage beyond the site of injury.

>> **Open-head injuries:** These injuries occur when the skull is either penetrated or fractured; both closed-head and open-head injuries can lead to serious brain damage.

>> **Other brain disorders:** Degenerative diseases such as Alzheimer's can produce brain damage in the form of atrophied (for example, a reduction in size or loss of cells) brain tissue and cellular death. Strokes (a blood clot or bleed in the brain) and other vascular accidents also can result in brain damage by denying parts of the brain blood and oxygen, causing cellular death.

The Organization of the Brain

If you to open up the skull and look at the brain, one of the first things you'll like notice is that anatomically, the "one" brain is really two halves called *hemispheres*. These two halves are connected by a large bundle of nerve fibers called the *corpus collosum*.

Structurally, there are three main divisions of the brain: *forebrain, midbrain,* and *hindbrain.* Each of these divisions consists of many substructures that are involved in various behaviors and activity.

REMEMBER

The brain is a complex, integrated system. All of its components work together to produce the complexity of human behavior. The concept of *localization* refers to the idea that there are specific parts of the brain for specific components of behaviors. Various parts work together to produce vision, hearing, speech, and so forth.

Neurological techniques such as post-mortem brain examination, CT (co-axial tomography) scans, MRI (magnetic resonance imaging) scans, and PET (positron-emission tomography) scans have been used to identify and explore these systems.

Forebrain

The human forebrain is involved in a wide range of mental processes, including the sensing, perceiving, and processing of information. It is also involved in thinking, problem solving, organizing, and language functions.

The human forebrain consists of four sections:

>> **Cerebral cortex:** If you think of the brain as a mushroom, with a top and a stalk, then the cerebral cortex is the top of the mushroom. It's divided into two halves, called *cerebral hemispheres* (the left and the right — pretty creative, I know). These halves are connected by a bundle of nerve fibers known as the *corpus collosum.* Without the corpus collosum, the halves wouldn't be able to communicate with each other.

Figure 3-2 shows the four major divisions of the cerebral cortex and their corresponding functions:

- **Frontal lobe:** Planning, organizing, coordinating, and controlling movements (in an area known as the primary motor cortex), reasoning, and overall monitoring of the thinking process

- **Parietal lobe:** Sensation, spatial and somatosensory (bodily) awareness

- **Temporal lobe:** Hearing, language, and other verbal activity

- **Occipital lobe:** Vision

>> **Limbic system:** Located on the underside of the mushroom top (the cerebral cortex), the limbic system is involved in learning, memory, emotional behavior, and mating or reproduction.

>> **Basal ganglia:** This part of the brain is involved in controlling movement.

>> **Thalamus:** This "neural switchboard" is a relay station for the different parts of the brain. However, it is more than simply a connection. It analyzes inputs to construct organized outputs.

>> **Hypothalamus:** The hypothalamus takes part in the control of the endocrine system and works with the limbic system to control behaviors such as aggression, eating, protection, and mating.

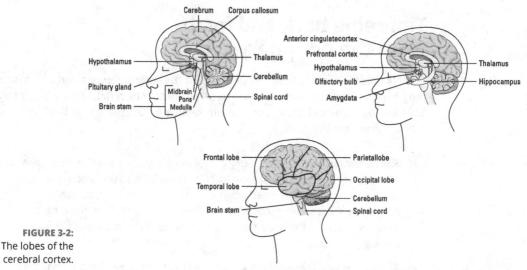

FIGURE 3-2:
The lobes of the
cerebral cortex.

Midbrain

The midbrain is involved in the auditory and visual processes and in motor control. The midbrain consists of the following divisions and their respective areas of responsibility:

>> **Tectum:** Auditory and visual systems

>> **Tegmentum:** Movement, sleep, arousal, attention, muscle tone, and reflexes

Hindbrain

The hindbrain is involved in the autonomic functions of the body such as heart rate and breathing as well as the coordination of movement. The hindbrain includes two divisions with assigned duties:

>> **Cerebellum:** Motor movement and its coordination

>> **Pons:** The bridge connecting the cerebellum to the rest of the brain

>> **Medulla:** Vital functions of the body such as the cardiovascular system, breathing, and the movement of skeletal muscles

Tiptoeing back and forth from the periphery

There's that toe again! Of the two divisions of the body's nervous system, think of the peripheral nervous system (PNS) as a system of connections that make it possible for the brain and spinal cord to communicate with the rest of the body. Two sets of nerves are involved:

>> **Spinal nerves:** These nerves carry neural signals both to and from the spinal cord. Sensory nerves carry information from the body to the central nervous system: For example, they carry signals from sensors in your foot when somebody steps on your foot. Motor nerves carry signals from the central nervous system to the body; they cause the muscles in your limbs to move (raising your hand).

>> **Cranial nerves:** These nerves are involved in the muscular (motor) and sensory processes, except that they are connected directly to the brain itself, not to the spinal cord. Cranial nerves support functions occurring in your face and head, including seeing and hearing, blinking and speaking.

Finding Destiny with DNA

I look a lot like my father's father. But do I act like him, too? Does your personality come from your parents? Do people inherit intellect and good looks? The field of psychology known as *behavioral genetics*, the study of the role of genetics and heredity in determining mental processes and behavior, investigates these questions.

The brain influences behavior. The endocrine system influences behavior. But what about your genetic makeup? Scientists have answered this question with a resounding "yes"; genetics do matter! Research implicates genetic contributions to cognition and intelligence, personality, and even psychopathology.

Genetic contributions to psychology have been traditionally performed using *twin and adoption studies*, in which identical twins (who share a common genetic code) who've been adopted separately at birth and raised in different environments are compared for some psychological construct or disorder (such as the presence of ADHD). This testing setup allows for the control of the influence of different environments, so if the identical twins show similar findings on the construct in question, then it is deduced that it must be due primarily to their genetic similarities — DNA. Research continues to evolve, and other techniques, such as large-scale DNA sampling and gene manipulation, push the field of behavioral genetics.

REMEMBER

Researchers are looking for *genetic markers* for particular behaviors, including disorders. A genetic marker is a gene with a known location on the human genome. Genetic markers for such disorders as autism, schizophrenia, and reading disabilities have been found. Just keep in mind that the presence of a genetic marker in a person's genome does not guarantee that he will have a particular trait or disorder; it simply increases the odds of such.

Although the complexity of behavioral genetics leaves much to be discovered, one thing is clear: Genes matter. But where do these inherited traits, behaviors, and mental processes come from? How do gene–behavior relationships come about? Evolution.

Evolutionary psychology is a branch of psychology that says human psychology (behavior and mental processes) is the result of the evolutionary process of natural selection. *Natural selection* is the process by which specific genes become more or less common in a population of a species through reproduction and mating. In other words, genes that contribute to survival are more likely to be passed on than those that don't. After all, if your genes help you live long enough to pass them on to your offspring, then those genes perpetuate. If they don't, and you don't perpetuate, then your genes don't survive either.

Evolutionary biologists look at biological phenomena (such as opposable thumbs and walking upright) as adaptations that thrived. Evolutionary psychologists take the same approach with psychological phenomena such as language, memory, attention, visual perception, happiness, and so forth. Finding out how these psychological phenomena helped our ancestors adapt as a way to explain why they exist in us today is a matter of extreme interest. An evolutionary psychologist, for example, may look at attachment theory (covered in Chapter 10) and propose that the behaviors and mental processes underlying the mother–infant bonding process evolved over time to the state they can be observed today because these behaviors and processes enable the human species to survive.

Understanding Psychopharmacology

The use of medications in the treatment of mental disorders and their symptoms (such as schizophrenia and major depressive disorder) gained significant prominence over the last half of the 20th century. Prior to that, medications were used to a lesser extent, along with psychotherapy, psychosocial, and behavioral treatments. But advances in research and drug development have led to the creation of more effective drugs, which in turn spurred an increase in their use. Hundreds of drugs have been developed that are used to target the specific symptoms of a particular mental disorder. The primary goals of pharmacotherapy are to produce improvements in behavior and thinking, alleviation of suffering, and enhancement of functioning.

Although pharmacotherapy has a history of being "disorder specific," a more up-to-date view of psychiatric treatment with medications is the use of medications for more symptoms than disorders as a whole. This change has led to the breaking down of medication categories from simply seeing medications as treatment for "schizophrenia" or for "depression." So depression might be treated with an antipsychotic medication if the neurochemical mechanisms of the medication are deemed helpful for a particular patient. This approach may seem confusing, but it is not uncommon to see someone with major depressive disorder taking an antipsychotic medication or someone with bipolar disorder doing the same. The point of this practice is to use medications to improve patients' symptoms as opposed to treating their "disorder" per se. Nonetheless, the basic categories of medications are unchanged despite more flexible use in practice.

Before I go on, I think it is important to address an ongoing controversy in the use of medication in mental health treatment. Some people see the expanded use of medications for disorders other than what the drugs were initially developed for as an advance, while others see it as an example of the inexact nature of psychiatric medical practice. Some people have very little trust and a healthy dose of skepticism when it comes to the pharmaceutical industry and its influence on psychiatrists. Still others have found profound relief from years of suffering. This perhaps is a value judgment for each individual to make for him- or herself. And the picture gets complicated when it comes to children or minors. In either case, I am a psychologist and really have no skin in the game. I don't prescribe medications but I am willing to refer patients and clients for a medication evaluation so they can get informed and make a decision for themselves, with the assistance from and collaboration with a medical doctor. Medications can help. Medications can make things worse. Some people don't like to take them; some people wouldn't think of living without them. It's your call either way.

Now back to the meds! Many brain systems involved in the symptoms of mental illness involve one particular neurotransmitter, and drugs used for the treatment of a particular illness are designed to affect the functioning of that specific neurotransmitter. The sleep difficulties and appetite disturbance often seen in major depressive disorder, for example, are thought to be related to the limbic system. For these symptoms, most drugs for depression target the neurotransmitter serotonin.

In this section, I describe common pharmacological treatments for the symptoms of depression (such as sad mood), schizophrenia (such as hallucinations), and anxiety (such as hyperarousal). For these three of the better known mental disorders, I discuss various medications and their biological mechanism of action.

Easing depression

Medications that are used to treat depression are called *antidepressants*. Most antidepressants affect one or both of two neurotransmitters: *norepinephrine* and *serotonin*. Basically, there are three major classes of antidepressant medications (although there are some that don't fit in either class, such as Wellbutrin, Remeron, or Effexor) differentiated by their mechanism of action:

>> **Tricyclic antidepressants:** Block the presynaptic neuron's re-absorption of mostly norepinephrine (NE). This allows for a functional "increase" in the level of NE in the synapse and prolongs the activation of the postsynaptic neuron when stimulated by NE.

>> **Selective serotonin reuptake inhibitors (SSRIs):** Block the re-absorption of serotonin rather than NE and have the similar effect of prolonging activation. Some of the more popular brands of SSRIs are Prozac, Paxil, and Zoloft.

>> **Serotonin norepinephrine reuptake inhibitors (SNRIs):** Block the re-absorption of both serotonin and NE. These drugs are essentially a combination of the tricyclic and SSRIs.

Shushing the voices

The experience of auditory hallucinations or feeling like someone is out to get you can be extremely troubling. These are common symptoms of psychosis and the mental disorder schizophrenia. However, psychotic symptoms can occur in mood disorders as well such as a Major Depressive Disorder with Psychotic Features or Bipolar I Disorder. One of the most powerful treatments for psychotic symptoms are *antipsychotic medications.*

Antipsychotic medications have a specific effect on the neurotransmitter dopamine. The *dopamine dysregulation hypothesis* of psychosis proposes that the symptoms of psychosis result from disruptions in the action of dopamine in the brain. Antipsychotic medications block the postsynaptic receptor sites of dopamine. This blockage keeps dopamine from being able to activate the postsynaptic neuron and has been found to reduce the presence of psychotic symptoms substantially.

WARNING

Unfortunately, antipsychotic medications, as do all medications, don't just affect the neurotransmitters in the brain areas theorized to be implicated in the disorder. Most medications also affect other brain areas and can often lead to very unpleasant side effects. Side effects associated with antipsychotic medication can include weight gain; repetitive, involuntary motor movements (known as tardive dyskinesia); or sexual dysfunction, to name just a few. The experience of these side effects often leads people to stop taking their medication, which can have serious negative consequences. This situation keeps drug researchers searching for even more selective drugs.

Relaxing

Anxiety disorders are the most common mental disorder in the United States. Millions of people suffer from intolerable worry, panic attacks, and disabling phobias. The good news is that medications can help with these symptoms.

Anxiolytic medications are drugs designed to relieve the symptoms of anxiety disorders. Psychiatrists and family physicians prescribe one class of Anxiolytics, *benzodiazepines,* quite often. Benzodiazepines affect the neurotransmitter GABA, which has a suppressing effect on the central nervous system. In other words, it slows things down in the brain.

Benzodiazepines are very effective in reducing anxiety. Unfortunately, they are also highly addictive. Benzodiazepines have a near-immediate effect and often produce sedation and an overall feeling of calmness. These feelings are highly pleasurable, and patients sometimes don't want to stop taking these medications even after their anxiety disorder has been successfully medicated. Table 3-1 gives an overview of some frequently prescribed medications.

TABLE 3-1   ## Major Medication Groups

Problem	Class of Medication	Common Example
Depression	SSRI	Prozac
	SNRI	Effexor
Obsessive-Compulsive Disorder	SSRI	Paxil
Insomnia	Benzodiazepines	Xanax
	Antipsychotics	Seroquel
	SSRI	Citalopram
Generalized Anxiety Disorder	SSRI	Zoloft
Panic Disorder	SSRI	Citalopram
	Benzodiazepines	Ativan
Psychosis	Antipsychotic	Haldol
		Abilify
		Risperdal

Problem	Class of Medication	Common Example
Mania	Mood Stabilizer	Lithium
	Antipsychotic	Zyprexa
Bipolar Depression	Mood Stabilizer	Lamictal
	Antipsychotic	Seroquel
Bipolar Disorder, Mania, and Depression	Mood Stabilizer	Depakote
	Antipsychotic	Zyprexa
ADHD	Psychostimulant	Ritalin

Remember what I said about medications being used "across" diagnoses? When it comes to anxiety, this is very much the case. It is not unusual for someone who is experiencing panic symptoms, obsessive compulsive symptoms, or generalized worry and anxiety to be given an antidepressant. In fact, this is a more common course of treatment for anxiety symptoms because of the abuse and addictive potential of other anxiolytics. So it's official: Psychiatry has confused all of us. Antidepressants as anxiolytic agents? Yep.

NO-KNIFE BRAIN SURGERY

Changes in biological functioning can and do result in psychological changes. Medications have a direct biological effect on the brain. Neurosurgeons lesion, excise, and cut brain tissue. But imagine a day when doctors can change your brain directly without a pill or surgery.

Dr. "Bones" McCoy of *Star Trek* used a device that he placed on the head of patients with neurological conditions. Using some form of energy field, the device alleviated all sorts of conditions, including brain injury and bleeding. Well, Dr. McCoy, that day has arrived!

Transcranial Magnetic Stimulation (or TMS) is a technology right out of *Star Trek*. TMS devices are placed on the head and use electromagnetic pulses to activate specific parts of the brain. This technique is being used to treat migraines, stroke symptoms, hallucinations, and even depression.

For depression, TMS stimulates the brain's frontal lobe and limbic system, parts impacted by the disorder. The medical world is excited and hopeful about the prospects of TMS as a treatment for a broad range of other disorders.

Chapter **4**

From Sensation to Perception

S eeing is believing! I have no idea where that phrase came from, but it says something important about people. That is, people have an easier time understanding or comprehending things if they can see them, touch them, hear them, and so on. Why doesn't everyone believe in ghosts, UFOs, or any number of things that most people have not experienced firsthand? Precisely the point. Most people haven't experienced these phenomena with their own senses, so they don't believe in them. How do you know if something is part of the world you live in or not — and whether it's real?

In this chapter, I focus on the why and how of sensing and perceiving the world. They're as obvious as the nose on your face, but it's easy to overlook the impact of senses to everyday thoughts, moods, and actions. Psychology as the study of behavior and mental processes includes taking a look at how our senses — the ability to see, hear, taste, touch, feel, and so on — actually work.

Humans aren't just little brains floating around inside a body with no contact with the outside world. Quite the contrary; most people are typically in full contact with the world around them, taking in information, processing it, and using what they perceive to navigate a wide range of possibilities. So why is understanding materialism important? Because the way people actually maintain contact with the information that's processed is through the physical materials that create it.

Building Blocks: Our Senses

Physicists and chemists have, for a long time, been pointing out that the world is made up of material stuff: particles, atoms, molecules, and various forms of energy. Basically, the universe is one big ball of energy. Everything consists of a particular configuration of energy. A working definition of *sensation* is the process by which we receive raw energy/information from the environment. If you want a definition in a suit and tie, then *sensation* is the process of mentally acquiring information about the world through the reception of its various forms of energy.

Here are the forms of energy that humans most commonly experience:

>> Light (electromagnetic energy)

>> Sound (acoustic energy, or sound waves)

>> Heat (thermal energy)

>> Pressure (mechanical or physical energy)

>> Chemical energy

Some organisms experience the same kinds of energy as humans do, but other forms of life are sensitive to different ranges of the energy forms. Sharks can smell chemical particles (of blood, for example) in far smaller quantities than people can, and dogs can hear much higher frequencies of sounds.

REMEMBER

For each form of energy that humans sense, a specific organ system or "device" is used to receive it. Aristotle, an ancient Greek philosopher (around 350 BCE, who some say was the last man to know everything there was to know) claimed that humans have five basic senses. Each of the five basic human senses are receptive to a specific form of energy. Psychologists now know that humans have at least ten different senses, but Aristotle recognized the major ones:

>> **Sight** receives light energy.

>> **Hearing** receives sound energy or sound waves.

>> **Touch** receives mechanical energy.

>> **Smell** receives airborne chemical energy.

>> **Taste** receives chemical energy.

The sensing process

When light travels from a light bulb or sound waves travel from a radio speaker, sensing devices, or *accessory structures*, intercept them. The eyes, ears, skin, nose, and mouth are called *accessory structures* because they provide access to the environment. After the energy reaches a sensory structure, it has to get inside the brain somehow. Light, sound waves, and heat waves don't bounce around inside a person's head — not in mine, at least. So how do they get inside?

First, keep in mind that the brain uses its own form of energy. In Chapter 3, I describe a specific type of energy in the brain; it's called *electrochemical energy*. Electrochemical energy involves the creation of an electrical signal from chemical reactions. Electrochemical processes occur in many areas of nature. For example, some sea creatures such as eels can generate electric charges by using the electrochemical process. In the brain, this energy is how neurons communicate with each other and operate.

So in order for the brain to process the various forms of energy that a person's sense organs receive, each form of energy has to undergo a transformation process, called *transduction*, that turns the raw energy into electrochemical, or *neural*, energy. Transduction is a fairly common process encountered often in today's digital world as sounds and images are transduced or transformed into digital "bits" or code and transmitted via the Internet and cellular phone networks across the world.

The presence of specific types of cells, *receptors*, in each of the sensory systems makes transduction possible. Each sensory system has its own type of receptor cell. After the receptor cells *transduce*, or convert, the environmental energy, a neural signal travels along a *sensory nerve*, taking the information to the parts of the brain that are involved in processing and analyzing the information.

Does the music you listen to or human voices have only one tone? Does the light you see come in only one color? Of course not! Each of these sensory experiences, or *stimuli*, is made up of a complex array of wavelengths of light, frequencies of sound, intensities of smells and tastes, and so on. And your sensory systems are on the job to sort it out for you. Through the process of *coding and representation*, your brain captures the complexity of the environmental stimuli you encounter.

Humans experience the complexity of a stimulus after the brain translates its different features into a specific pattern of neural activity. The theory of *specific nerve energies* states that each sensory system provides information for only one sense, no matter how nerves are stimulated. In other words, specific parts of the brain always label the stimulation they receive as light or sound.

Psychologists have worked with neurosurgeons to conduct experiments with patients who, for various medical reasons, need a portion of their skulls removed, which exposes their brains. The neurosurgeons took an electrode and zapped specific parts of the exposed brains with a little jolt of electricity. When they applied this shock, a weird thing happened. The people in the experiment said, "I can hear chickens squawking." If they zapped the part of the brain that processes taste, a person may have said, "I can taste tomato soup. Mmm, that's good."

How is this possible? When a particular part of the brain is stimulated, the brain thinks that it's receiving a specific kind of information from the sense organ it processes, even if it's not. So specific sensory systems are wired into specific brain regions, permitting the brain to know the difference between hearing a sound and seeing a light.

Different aspects of a stimulus are coded in the brain depending on which neurons are activated and the pattern of neuron activation. If neurons in the visual system are activated, for example, the brain senses light. If the pattern of neural activation differs, the brain senses different wavelengths or intensities of light so it can distinguish between sunlight and candlelight. The end of the sensory trail leads to a neural *representation* of the sensation in a specific region of the brain where you finally hear the music or see the colors.

Seeing

Sight is arguably one of the most important human senses. Although the other senses are also important, being able to see is critical for getting along in the modern world. In this section, I chronicle a little journey — the journey light takes through the eye and into the brain, completing our sensation of light.

SYNESTHESIA

Some people claim to hear light and see sounds. Other people report that certain sounds have a color. *Synesthesia* is the name of an ability that certain people have to sense one (or more) forms of energy with a sensory system other than the one typically used for the stimulus. This phenomenon is estimated to affect about one in every 2,000 people. Scientists suspect that this experience is a result of some "wires" or neural connections in the brain being crossed.

Simon Baron-Cohen, a world-famous autism researcher and psychologist, hypothesized that synesthesia is possible when extra connections in the brain allow for otherwise separate sensory systems there to interact. Whatever the cause, I think it sounds kind of cool. I'd love to be able to see the music when I dance because I sure can't feel it!

The journey begins with *electromagnetic radiation,* more commonly known as light. Visible light occupies wavelengths between 400 and 750 nanometers. I remember from physics class that light travels in waves. The intensity of light is calculated by measuring the size of the waves, and its frequency is measured by how many peaks of a wave pass a particular point within a specific period of time. Wavelength is important to the topic of how people sense light because different wavelengths make it possible to experience colors.

Here's the process:

1. Light enters the eye through the *cornea.*

2. Light passes through the *pupil.*

3. The *lens* of the eye focuses the light onto the *retina.*

4. Light energy is converted into neural energy — an action known as light *transduction.*

Grasping the process of light transduction requires a closer look at the retina, a part of the eye that's located on the back lining of the eyeball. The retina contains some special cells called *photoreceptors* that are responsible for transduction. These cells contain chemicals called *photopigments* that are broken apart when the photons of light traveling in the light wave make contact with them. This event starts a chemical reaction that tells the cell to fire a signal to the *optic nerve.* The signal then travels to the *visual cortex* of the brain, the part of the brain responsible for analyzing visual stimuli. So light is transformed into neural energy by literally breaking up chemicals in the retina, which triggers a neural signal. These chemicals are stored in two different cells (called photoreceptors) in the retina, *rods and cones.*

Rods contain a chemical called *rhodopsin,* which is very light-sensitive. This chemical reacts to very low-intensity light and helps with peripheral vision. That is why we see mostly in black and white when it is dark; it's also why we can sees stars at night better if we don't look right at them.

Cones contain chemicals known as the *iodopsins,* which are closely related to rhodopsin. Each of three types of cone contains a different form of iodopsin. The three types of cone respond to different wavelengths of light and are involved in seeing color.

Seeing colors

Some people are colorblind to particular shades of blues, greens, and reds. This condition means that these people have a hard time sensing the specific wavelengths of light associated with those specific colors. They lack a photo pigment that is sensitive to the wavelengths. Typically, they only have two types of cones, not three. Fortunately, most people get to see the world in all its rainbow-hued glory.

There are two basic theories of color vision: the *trichromatic theory* and the *opponent-process theory.*

>> **The trichromatic theory** is really basic. The idea is that the retina contains three different types of cones (photoreceptors) that each responds to different wavelengths of light, and these provide our experience of different colors.

- *Short-wavelength* cones respond to light around 440 nanometers, or blue light.

- *Medium-wavelength* cones respond to light around 530 nanometers, or green light.

- *Long-wavelength* cones respond to light around 560 nanometers, or greenish-yellow light.

  When each cone system is partially activated, combinations of these three basic colors are visible as colors like aquamarine and orange. But the point here is that the human experience of all colors originates from these three basic cone inputs.

>> **The opponent-process theory** of color vision states that the brain contains different types of neurons that respond differently to different colors. The idea is that these cells fire more — when compared to their baseline, or background, level of firing — when stimulated by one type of light, and they fire less when stimulated by another. So if you're looking at red, your specialized red cells increase their firing rate. When you're looking at green, your red cells chill out with the firing rate and your green cells increase their firing rate. "Cell sets" exist for yellow and blue as well.

  This theory explains something called the *negative-afterimage effect* images in your mind's eye that are different colors than the actual image you're seeing. The most popular example uses a U.S. flag that has black instead of white stars, green stripes replacing the red ones, and yellow instead of a blue background. After looking at the image for a while, a person can close her eyes and see the flag in its real colors because the cells being stimulated by black, green, and yellow light are recovering from the stimulation and begin "seeing" white, red, and blue light instead. Try it. Stare at a 1-inch yellow square for about 30 seconds and then look at a white sheet of paper. You should see a blue square instead of the white paper.

So which theory is correct? As is the case frequently in psychology, and in science more generally, an either/or question ends up being answered "both!" Psychologists now know that the trichromatic theory describes what happens in the retina of the eye, whereas the opponent-process theory describes what happens in the brain.

Figuring distances and depth

How can you tell how far away something is from you just by looking at it? Well, maybe you can't, but some people are really good at eyeballing distances. Personally, I need a tape measure, ruler, land-surveyor, and a global positioning satellite to figure distances, but depth and distance are calculated by the body's visual systems, using two inputs: *monocular cues* and *binocular cues*.

>> **Monocular cues** are simple; you know that some things are bigger than other things. Dogs are bigger than mice. Cars are bigger than dogs. Houses are bigger than cars. Because you know these things from experience, whenever you see a mouse's image on your retina that's bigger than an image of a dog in the same scene, you know that the mouse is closer to you than the dog. Similarly, if you see a dog that's bigger than a car, you figure the dog is closer.

  The rule is that things that cast bigger images on our retinas are assumed to be closer. Artists use this rule all the time when they want to depict a three-dimensional scene on a two-dimensional canvas.

>> **Binocular cues** are interesting and a little weird. Remember the Cyclopes from the *Sinbad* movies? He only had one eye. According to binocular vision rules, he would have had a hard time figuring out distances because binocular distance cues depend on two eyes providing information to the brain.

  * *Convergence* is a binocular cue and refers to information provided by the muscles of the eyes to the brain in order to calculate distances. When your eyes are pointing inward, toward the nose, the brain knows that you're looking at something close to you. When your eyes are pointing outward, the brain knows that you're looking at an object farther away.

  * *Stereoscopic* vision is the other, and more important, type of binocular cue. Try this real quickly. Make a square, a viewing frame, with your hands by connecting your thumbs and index fingers at the tips while keeping the rest of your fingers folded. Then close one eye and focus on an object around you. Frame the object in the middle of the box. Now, close that eye and open the other. What happened? The object should have moved. This happens because of stereoscopic vision. Each of your eyes gives you a slightly different angle on the same image because they are set apart. Your brain judges distance by using these different angles by calculating the difference between the two images.

Hearing

Sound travels in waves and is measured by its *amplitude* or *wave size* and *frequency* or *number of waves per unit time*. Each of these translates into a psychological experience: Amplitude determines loudness (my neighbor's rock band), and frequency provides pitch or tone (the screeching lead singer of said neighbor's rock band). The structures of the ear are specifically designed to *transduce,* or convert, sound-wave energy into neural energy.

A sound first enters the ear as it is funneled in by the *pinna.* A human's crumpled-up outer ear is designed as a "sound scoop." As the wave passes through the ear canal, it eventually reaches the eardrum, or the *tympanic membrane.* The vibrating eardrum shakes three little bones *(malleus, incus,* and *stapes,* Latin words for *hammer, anvil,* and *stirrup),* which amplifies the vibration.

After the sound wave reaches the inner ear, the *cochlea,* auditory transduction occurs. The cochlea contains the hardware for the transduction process. The cochlea is filled with fluid, and its floor is lined with the *basilar membrane. Hair cells* (they actually look like hairs) are attached to the basilar membrane. The sound waves coming into the inner ear change the pressure of the fluid inside the cochlea and create fluid waves that move the basilar membrane. Movement of the basilar membrane causes the hair cells to bend, which starts the transduction ball rolling. When the hair cells bend, their chemical properties are altered, thus changing their electrical polarity and positioning them to fire and send a neural signal. The sound waves, now turned into neural electrochemical energy, travel to the *auditory cortex* (the part of the brain responsible for hearing) for perceptual processing.

Touching and feeling pain

The sense of touch includes sensing pressure, temperature, and pain. Specialized cells in the skin sense touch by sending a signal to the spinal cord and then on to the brain. Transduction in touch is a physical or mechanical process; it's much more straightforward than the chemical transduction in the eye for vision. When heat, cold, or weight stimulates touch receptors in the skin, a neural signal travels to the brain, much the same way that the hair cells of the inner ear operate.

Pain is a special case for the sense of touch because it would be difficult to avoid harm and survive in this world without a sense of pain. Because it hurts when you touch fire, you're motivated to avoid getting too close to it, which helps you avoid damaging your flesh and possibly dying. Pain is an important signal that something is harming, damaging, or destroying the body.

Two specific nerve fibers located throughout the skin signal pain to the brain: the *A-delta fibers* and the *C fibers.* A-delta fibers carry sharp sensations and work rapidly. C fibers communicate chronic and dull pain and burning sensations.

TIP

Some people seem to have a really high threshold for pain. The *gate-control theory of pain* states that pain signals must pass through a gate in the spinal cord that "decides" which signals get through to the brain and which ones don't. If another sense is using the pain pathways at a given time, the pain signal may not reach the brain. For example, rubbing your thigh when your ankle aches seems to help dull the pain in the ankle. That's because the rubbing signal (pressure) from the thigh is competing with the pain signal from the ankle for access through the gate. Amazing, right? I'm always blown away by the complexity of the human body.

Smelling and tasting

The sense of smell is called *olfaction*. Sometimes I can smell my neighbor's barbecue on the weekend. I have that experience because little particles from the cooking food, *volatile chemical particles,* become airborne and travel over to the smell receptors in my nose. Inside my nose are thousands of olfactory receptors that can sense tens of thousands of different odors.

The molecules from the volatile chemicals cause a chemical change in the receptors in my nose, which sets the transduction process in motion. The chemical energy is then converted into neural energy by the receptor cells, and a signal hits the *olfactory bulb* in my brain where the signal is processed. The olfactory bulb also connects with the part of my brain that involves emotion. Some researchers think that this physical connection in the brain is why smells can activate emotional memories from time to time.

Perhaps you've heard talk about the impact of *pheromones,* which are scents that animals send out as signals to other animals during mating season. Some companies market pheromone products for humans, especially for men out there who are desperate to find a date. Do humans really produce pheromones? The research jury is still out, but a few recent findings seem to suggest that the answer is yes. The pheromone system depends on a second organ of smell, the vomeronasal organ, or Jacobsen's organ. This system is prominent in animals as small as moths and as big as elephants.

Gustation refers to the sense of taste. Taste is a chemical sense made possible by chemical receptors on the tongue known as *taste buds.* All tastes are variations on five themes: sweet, sour, bitter, salty, and umami. Umami has generally been accepted as a fifth taste dimension. The receptors are activated by monosodium glutamate (MSG), often added to processed food. Approximately 10,000 taste buds are on every tongue, reacting to the molecules of food and converting chemical energy into neural energy that sends information to the area of the brain involved in analyzing taste information.

Balancing and moving

Smart as he was, Aristotle missed some important sensory systems. Ballerinas and ice skaters can appear to float through space, their movements balanced and defying gravity. These marvelous abilities are possible in part due to the *body senses*, the sensory processes of the body's orientation (in space) and movement — oftentimes referred to as the *kinesthetic sense*. Without the senses of balance and movement, it would not be possible to walk in a straight line or even stand up.

Structures known as the *vestibular organ*, located in the inner ear, and receptors located throughout the body are involved in balance and the kinesthetic sense. The vestibular organ consists of a set of "canals" that are filled with fluid that contain hair-like receptor cells. As the head moves around, the fluid inside the canals moves or flows, bending the receptor cells and causing these cells to fire, telling the brain that the head is in motion. Movement of the fluid triggers the sensation of movement.

The kinesthetic sense results from the firing of receptors located throughout the body in the skin, muscles, and joints. The firing of these receptors provides sensory information to the brain about the particular body part in motion, pressure, and the orientation of the body parts to each other. When the sense of movement, balance, orientation, body part in motion, and the body parts in relation to each other are all working together in a well-coordinated manner, graceful and fluid movement is possible.

Finishing the Product: Perception

The world is much more complex than a bunch of singular sounds, smells, tastes, and other sensations may indicate. You hear symphonies, not just notes. You see fireworks, not just single photons of light. You indulge your taste buds with flavorful foods, not individual salty, sour, bitter, umami, and sweet tastes. So take a moment to thank your ability of perception for these pleasures. I'll wait.

Perception is the process of organizing, analyzing, and providing meaning to the various sensations that you're bombarded with on a daily basis. If sensation provides the raw material, perception is the final product.

REMEMBER

Here are two popular views of the complex process related to perception:

>> **Ecological:** This idea states that the environment provides all the information you need to sense the world; very little interpretation or construction is

required. For example, when I perceive a tree, it's not because I've constructed a perception of it in my mind. I perceive the tree because the tree has provided me with all the necessary information to perceive it as it is.

>> **Constructionist:** In this view, the process of perception relies on previous knowledge and information to construct reality from fragments of sensation. You are not just a passive recipient of sensory information. Instead, you are actively constructing what you see, hear, taste, and feel.

Regardless of whether you're an ecologist or a constructionist, the process of perceiving has some basic tenets. If sensation is the process of detecting specific types of energy in the environment, how do you know what information is worth detecting and what's just background noise? After all, you can't possibly respond to every bit of sensory energy you encounter. All the roaring traffic, howling wind, bustling pedestrians, and other stuff would easily overwhelm a person. That's why the perceptual systems have a built-in mechanism for determining what information should be detectable.

Threshold theory

The concept of an *absolute threshold* refers to the minimum amount of energy in the environment that a sensory system can detect. Each sensory system has an absolute threshold below which energy does not warrant or garner perceptual attention. A stimulus must be higher than your absolute threshold for you to notice it's there.

Another type of threshold, the *difference threshold*, is described by *Weber's law*, which introduces the *just-noticeable difference (JND)*. The JND is the smallest difference between two stimuli that lets you know they are different. Each sensory system determines a constant fraction of intensity for each form of energy that represents the smallest detectable difference between energy intensities. The idea is that the difference between two stimuli has to exceed the JND in order for it to be detectable; otherwise, an observer will think the two stimuli are the same. For example, the just-noticeable difference for brightness is about 1/60th: I can barely tell the difference in brightness between a 60-watt and a 61-watt bulb, if they made 61-watt bulbs.

Signal-detection theory

Another theory known as *signal-detection theory* takes a slightly more complicated look at the problem. An overwhelming amount of environmental energy is considered background noise (think traffic sounds when you are in your automobile). When you encounter a stimulus, called the *signal* (think your car radio), you need to distinguish between the signal (car radio and traffic noise) and the background noise (just the traffic sounds). That's why you have to turn up the car radio when there is heavy traffic at rush-hour; there's more noise, so you need to increase the strength of the signal. Signal-detection theory says that your ability to perceive stimuli is based on your individual *sensitivity* and *response criterion.* Sensitivity refers to a basic characteristic of each perceptual system: what it is able to distinguish. The response criterion is determined by situational factors, like emotions and motivations. Based on your sensitivity and response criterion, you can either correctly detect a stimulus *(hit),* fail to detect a signal when one is available *(miss),* detect a signal when there isn't one *(false alarm),* or report no signal when there isn't one *(correct rejection).*

To understand response criterion, imagine that your task is to tell whether I turned a light on. Compare two situations: In one, you earn $100 every time you see the light when it occurs (a *hit*), but you lose $1 every time you say the light was on when it actually wasn't (a *false alarm*). In the other situation, you earn $1 for each *hit* and lose $100 for each *false alarm.* Would you behave the same way in each situation? I wouldn't — in the first case I would say "light" every time I even suspected it had come on; in the second case I would not say "light" unless I was really sure.

REMEMBER

Individual biases and motivations determine response criterion and affect whether a person makes an accurate detection or not. This means when people think I'm not listening to them, it's not my fault. I'm not detecting their signal because my response criterion is set too high. See? I'm an innocent victim of my perceptual processes.

Organizing by Principles

The perceptual system is not made up of a bunch of arbitrary rules and random processes. Psychologists and other researchers over the years have discovered principles that guide the way human perceptual systems organize all the information they receive from the sensory systems:

>> **Figure-Ground:** Information is automatically divided into two categories: either figure or ground, or foreground and background. Figural information is obvious and immediate; ground information is not very meaningful.

>> **Grouping:** This large category contains principles that people use to determine whether information belongs in a specific group with similar stimuli. These characteristics of the information or stimuli help with the grouping process:

- **Proximity:** Stimuli that are close together in space are perceived to belong together.

- **Common fate:** Stimuli that move in the same direction and at the same rate are grouped together.

- **Continuity:** Stimuli that create a continuous form are grouped together.

- **Similarity:** Similar things are grouped together.

>> **Closure:** This principle is the tendency to fill in missing information to complete a stimulus. There is a smartphone game app that demonstrates this nicely in which only a portion of a popular company's or corporation's logo is presented and you have to guess the correct the company by completing or "closing" the rest of the logo.

REMEMBER

Most psychologists today are in the *constructionist* camp. (See the "Finishing the Product: Perception" section earlier in this chapter.) They view perception as a process of building your sense of reality out of fragments of information. People are born with some of the rules for organizing information, but a few other factors can influence the way you perceive things.

Personal experiences have a powerful impact on how you analyze sensory information. The concept of a *perceptual set,* defined as an expectation of what you will perceive, attempts to capture this. You use cues from context and experience to help you understand what you're seeing, tasting, feeling, and so forth. For example, if I'm driving down the street and see someone in a police uniform standing next to someone's car window, I assume that an officer is making a traffic stop. I could actually be seeing a person in a police uniform asking for directions, but my past experience suggests otherwise.

A person's culture is another powerful influence on how stimuli is perceived. A good example of the impact of cultural influences on perceptions involves figuring out a story line based on a series of pictures. If I have four pictures, each containing a different piece of a puzzle that, when viewed in sequence, can tell a story, I'm likely to imagine a story that's different from the one my Spanish colleague imagines. For example, say I'm looking at a series of pictures that show these images:

>> A woman is carrying a bag.

>> A woman is crying.

>> A man is approaching a woman.

>> A woman is standing with no bag.

What's going on here? I may see a woman who is upset because she dropped her bag and a man who is coming to help her. Or I may see a woman crying out of fear because a man is coming to steal her bag. Depending upon my culture or subculture, not to mention my personal experience, I may see two very different stories.

TRICKING THE EYE

The organizing principles of the perceptual systems make perceptual illusions possible. You may see things that aren't really in front of you or see things moving when they're motionless. Illusionists, including magicians, use your perceptual organizing rules against you. They have a keen understanding of how the perceptual systems work, and they take advantage of this knowledge to perform their tricks.

Chapter **5**

Exploring Consciousness

C onsciousness is an elusive concept. You know it's there, but it's hard to put your finger on it. Is my consciousness that inner voice and my awareness of myself, my surroundings, and my experience? I'm not typically aware of numerous mental processes, bodily sensations, and things going on in my mind. For example, I don't usually hear my heart beating as I'm walking down the street, but I can hear it when I try to hear it. Nonetheless, I know what it "feels like" to have a heartbeat if I focus on it. When I become conscious of something that I was unconscious of before, I become *aware* of it. Let's start trying and pin down the elusive topic of consciousness with a two-part working definition:

Consciousness is . . .

» Our current, in-the-moment awareness of external (outside the brain) and internal (inside the brain) stimuli. The philosopher John Locke described this as an "outer sense" and an "inner sense." Psychologist Joseph LeDoux refers to this as an inner awareness of one's mental functioning.

» The experience of what it is "like" to "be" a being.

The first part of the definition is relatively easy to understand. We are aware of sounds, smells, movement, people, things, and so on. The second part is a little more challenging. Think of consciousness like a flashlight. There is the actual flashlight (the source of the light), the light that shines (the action), and the "objects" that are illuminated (the content).

So when we think about consciousness, where does it come from? How does it work? What is it pointed at and showing us? Still confused? Okay, most of us know what a 3D movie is. But what about a 5D movie? These are immersive experiences that include seeing, hearing, sensing, moving, and acting, and there is a "me" who is immersed. I heard the Buddhist psychologist Jack Kornfield put it this way: There is the content we are aware of and awareness of awareness (part 1 of the definition above), and there is the "me" or "self" that is experiencing all of this (part 2 of the definition above).

In this chapter, I introduce you to consciousness, both normal and altered states. I will talk about scientific models of consciousness and its proposed function. I cover different states of consciousness including sleep, its stages, and that ever so interesting phenomenon, dreaming. Finally, I discuss how consciousness can be manipulated or altered with meditation and hypnosis.

Carving Awareness and Being at Its Joints

The philosopher Plato said in his work *Phaedrus* that we should "cut up each kind according to its species along its natural joints, and to try not to splinter any part, as a bad butcher might." So let's get cutting without splintering. The joints we are going to look at are consciousness as a skill and as a state or level.

Consciousness as an ability, skill, or process of the mind (and the brain)

Think of consciousness as mental ability or skill, like doing math, having a conversation, or just plain old thinking that occurs on or within the brain. David Chalmers, a professor of philosophy in Australia, outlines the following criteria for the mental ability/skill/process of consciousness:

>> The ability to discriminate, categorize, and react to environmental stimuli

>> The integration of information by a cognitive system

>> The "reportability" of mental states — both the ability to report on, and those states being available to be reported on

>> Ability of the system to access its own mental states

>> Focus of attention

>> Deliberate control of behavior

>> Being able to tell the difference between wakefulness and sleep

If consciousness is an ability, a skill, or even a tool, then what is it for? What does this tool help us do? Dr. Antonio Damasio, neurologist and neuroscientist, considered by many to be one of the foremost authorities on consciousness, gives us and idea. According to Damasio, consciousness helps us do the following:

>> **Being mentally flexible:** We are able perform novel responses to new situations. We can carry out new mental and behavioral processes in environments and under demands we have never encountered.

>> **Thinking ahead:** We have the ability to anticipate our needs before they are critical. Like planning to eat before we get hungry (growing food, going to grocery store, storing food in the fridge and pantry).

>> **Having motivation:** We possess the ability to be aware of our feelings and emotions, which allows us to make decisions about the positives we should move toward and the negatives we should avoid. (For more on emotions and motivation, see Chapter 7.)

Consciousness as a state or type of awareness

People can be unconscious, passed out, sleeping, sleepy, out of it, or in another world. These are all descriptions of states, levels, and types of consciousness. The following is a list of consciousness states:

>> **Normal consciousness:** Awake, responsive to environment in speech and behavior with some fluctuations relative to concentration and attentiveness.

>> **Confusion:** Atypical thinking with altered speed, clarity, and coherence, including inattentiveness and disorientation, lowered awareness of immediate environment, and distractibility, which is sometimes referred to as delirium.

>> **Drowsiness and stupor:** Mental and physical activity substantially reduced, with difficulty sustaining wakefulness and/or ability to be aroused only by intense and continuous effort.

>> **Sedation:** A drug induced state of consciousness that exists on a continuum from minimal sedation or *anxiolysis* (cognitive and physical impairment, reflexes are intact, but can respond to verbal commands) to *general anesthesia* (complete loss of consciousness and cannot be aroused even by painful stimulation).

>> **Coma:** Appearance of being asleep and incapable of responding to external stimuli.

- >> **Subjective experience of your own awareness:** Have you ever had a dream in which you knew you were dreaming? Really, you were aware that you were asleep. Being aware of your own awareness involves realizing or being aware that you are either awake or asleep.

- >> **Others' observations of deliberate actions:** One of the most important features of consciousness is that it mediates our behavior. Sometimes I act impulsively and reflexively. I don't think about what I'm doing; I just do it. Other times, there's a step of conscious deliberation, an act of will, before acting. In that case, I am consciously analyzing what I am going to do. Willful or voluntary acts are a signal of conscious awareness. Consciousness is attributed to acts of deliberation and intention. When someone does something willfully, it is assumed he is conscious.

- >> **Measurement of the brain's electrical activity:** Consciousness can be observed physiologically, in addition to behaviorally, through the measurement of brain activity. Different EEG (electroencephalogram — a test that records the "brain waves" or electrophysiological activity of the brain) measurements of electrical activity in the brain correspond to different levels of observable consciousness.

Once again, Dr. Antonio Damasio says that emotions, feelings, and a sense of self are central to consciousness. He famously refers to consciousness as the "movie within the movie" of our life. Damasio's classifies consciousness this way:

- >> **Consciousness of the proto-self:** Awareness of bodily states and "here and now" moment-by-moment awareness

- >> **Consciousness of the core-self:** A sense of "me" or "selfness," of being in the present

- >> **Consciousness of autobiographical-self:** Awareness of a linear timeline of the core self over time in both past and future

Catching some zzzzs

Sleep represents a change in consciousness. When I'm asleep, I am unconscious. Sleep is characterized by a change in brain wave activity, also called *electrophysiological activity*. Sleep, as a level of consciousness, can be distinguished from other levels of consciousness by measuring the electrophysiological energy of the brain with an EEG. When someone is awake and alert, his brain emits a wave with a frequency of 13 to 30 hertz (Hz), called *beta activity*. When awake but relaxed, the brain shows *alpha activity* — a frequency of 8 to 12 Hz.

A WAKING NIGHTMARE?

Imagine waking up in the middle of surgery? We can see, hear, feel pressure, and sometimes even feel pain. But we can't speak, move, or signal in any way to the doctors and nurses that we are awake! This phenomenon is called *anesthesia awareness*. According to the American Society of Anesthesiologists, it happens in about 1 to 2 out of every 1,000 administrations of general anesthesia every year. What a nightmare, right? But this state isn't just dreaming or remembering things just before or just after you are fully sedated. This can sometimes be a very traumatic experience for some people, and they may even develop posttraumatic stress disorder as a result. (For more about PTSD, see Chapter 14).

Scientists and physicians are working to fix this problem by working on technological devices to monitor a surgical patient's level of consciousness. There have been some missteps along they way, and they have yet to come up with a solid tool, but with advances in EEG, MRI, and other approaches of looking at and monitoring brain activity, they remain optimistic. (For more on these technologies, see Chapter 13.)

Generally, sleep is divided into four stages with one *substage*. Each stage is characterized by specific brain activities.

>> **Stage 1:** When you close your eyes and begin to relax, getting into sleep mode, your brain waves are at an alpha frequency. As you drift deeper into Stage 1, your brain waves become less regular, and they have a higher amplitude. This is *theta activity*, 3.5 to 7.5 Hz. This stage is a transition period between being awake and asleep, and it lasts approximately 10 minutes.

>> **Stage 2:** During Stage 2 sleep, brain wave activity is irregular and contains spikes of very high-amplitude EEG waves called *K-complexes*. There are also short bursts of 12 to 14 Hz waves called *spindles*. You are sound asleep at this stage, but you may think you're not actually sleeping. My wife wakes me up while I'm sleeping in front of the television set all the time to tell me that I'm snoring, but I always tell her I wasn't sleeping. I must have been snoring while awake. I don't know which is worse — snoring while asleep or awake!

>> **Stage 3:** Stage 3 is characterized by the presence of high-amplitude, low-frequency waves (3.5 Hz), which are an EEG signal of *delta activity*. Stage 3 lasts about an hour and a half.

>> **Stage 4:** This stage is signaled by the presence of more theta waves interrupting the smooth waves of delta. During Stage 4, your eyes begin to move back and forth very rapidly, which is called *rapid eye movement (REM)*. REM sleep is characterized by the presence of beta activity. Here, part of the brain is active but disconnected from skeletal muscle systems; however, you *are* asleep.

You dream during REM sleep. After you reach this stage, usually about an hour and a half into the whole sleep process, the rest of the night is characterized by alternating periods of REM sleep and non-REM sleep (activity of Stages 1, 2, and 3).

Understanding tired brains, slipping minds

I don't necessarily know why other people sleep, but I usually sleep because I'm tired. For the most part, researchers still don't know exactly why people sleep, but some believe that sleep has a *restorative* function. Research that looks at the effects of a lack of sleep, or sleep deprivation, suggests that people engage in sleep so that the body can restore what was lost or damaged during waking hours. Still others have proposed that during sleep, neural connections formed during the day are solidified during sleep.

When people have difficulties sleeping, they may be suffering from a formal *sleep disorder* in which there are abnormalities in the amount, timing, or the mental activity or behavior of the sleeping person. There are two broad categories of sleep disorders: *dyssomnias* and *parasomnias:*

» **Dyssomnias** consist of difficulties in the amount, quality, or timing of sleep. *Insomnia* is a common type of dyssomnia in which people have difficulty either falling to sleep or staying asleep. *Hypersomnia* is a condition of excessive sleepiness. Anybody with infants or young children at home? Can you say "hypersomnia"? *Narcolepsy* involves repeatedly falling fully asleep just out of nowhere. It can be in the middle of driving, during a conversation, or in the middle of lecture. Quite inconvenient!

» **Parasomnias** consist of the activation of bodily actions at the wrong time. For example, *nightmares* are a type of parasomnia that involve the inappropriate activation of cognitive process or thinking during sleep characterized by extremely frightening dreams in which a person feels threatened or in danger. *Sleepwalking disorder* is another parasomnia that involves getting out of bed during sleep, walking around, having a blank stare on one's face, looking awake but being unresponsive, and being extremely difficult to awaken. I used to get out of bed, unlock the door, and walk down the street. Still other people have been known to engage in some pretty sophisticated behavior while sleepwalking — ranging from making a sandwich to driving to the next town. There are even famous court cases where defendants have claimed that they committed murder while sleepwalking. In 1994, for example, Michael Ricksgers claimed that he accidently killed his wife while sleepwalking. The jury didn't buy it. *Sleep apnea,* a parasomnia characterized by abnormal pauses in breathing or abnormally low breathing rates, has been shown to have important health consequences such as high blood pressure and heart attacks.

WARNING

Sleep deprivation is a big problem in today's do-more, fast-paced, and stimulation-packed 24-hour lifestyle. And the consequences of sleep disorders can be significant, ranging from slowed thinking, low alertness, poor work performance, and irritability. This does not mean that people who are sleep deprived are akin to zombies or the "walking dead." It's not quite that dramatic, but sleep deprivation has been related to an experience of feeling brain dead or having impaired thinking and cognition, feeling mentally more slow, and of being in a mental fog.

So get to sleep! After you finish reading, of course! Ultimately, the long-term health effects of sleep disorders are only now being appreciated. A good source of information on sleep disorders is the National Center on Sleep Disorder Research website at www.nhlbi.nih.gov/sleep.

Arriving at Work Naked: Dreams

I once had a dream that I told a group of attractive women that my name was "Lion's Den." Maybe there's meaning behind it, or maybe it was just mental gibberish. I think if you ask most people, they would tell you they believe that dreams have some symbolic meaning or importance. Dreams represent another altered state of consciousness, and some psychologists have postulated that dreams have meanings that can be interpreted. I'm not sure what my Lion's Den dream meant or what my dream persona was trying to convey, but perhaps I thought it was impressive to be a "House of Lions," or that I am dangerous, hostile, or sinister. That's dark!

Dreams can occur during REM sleep and non-REM sleep. The dreams most people think about when they talk about their dreams occurs during REM. They can be strange, hallucinogenic experiences that make little sense. The content of dreams and how they are experienced by a person in REM sleep may be the result of different regions of the brain being active at that particular time, such as the visual cortex (what we "see" when we dream) or the auditory cortex (what we "hear" when we dream), or the motor areas of the brain (what we do and how we move in a dream). So when I am having a dream where I walk into work naked, hear everyone laughing, and see the reactions on their faces, these brain areas may be to blame! (Not my deep seated unconscious exhibitionistic wishes!)

Psychoanalysis has provided a comprehensive look at the psychological importance of dreams and dreaming. Freud and other psychoanalytic theorists make a simple point: Dreams have deeper meanings than their surface content suggests. In *The Interpretation of Dreams,* Freud states that dreams often represent our attempts to fulfill wishes that we're not consciously aware of. Through the technique of dream interpretation, a psychoanalyst helps a patient get to the bottom of the meaning of his or her dreams. If I have a dream about getting a new car, it means more than I want a new car. It can mean any number of things, but the meaning is something unique to my psychological makeup, something idiosyncratic. The car may represent a repressed desire to be free; the car is a symbol of movement.

REMEMBER

Understanding the meaning of many dreams is oftentimes not that complex. They can simply be reflections of events, worries, or experiences that are at the forefront of our minds. Yet other times the "true" meaning of a dream is extremely difficult, if not impossible, to discover. Dreams and their meanings are very personal and subjective phenomena. But just because dreams and their symbolic meanings are difficult to analyze scientifically, it shouldn't take away from anyone's belief that his dreams have some deeper meaning. The process of discovering the meaning of dreams in therapy, whether factually correct or not, can be an exciting and often helpful experience.

Psychologist Alan Hobson in 1977 proposed a theory of dreaming that postulates that dreams have no inherent meaning at all, and they are simply hallucinations created by random neurons firing and the rest of brain tries to make sense of it after the fact. However, this model is not widely accepted anymore. Many psychologists have come to view dreaming as a memory process that combines recent past and remote past memory fragments into novel, imaginary scenarios.

Dreams represent the memory consolidation process while we sleep. (For more on memory, see Chapter 6.) Dreaming is a type of information processing, like many others in the brain, and as such is, according to psychologist Erin J. Wamsley, an extension of and akin to waking consciousness. Research has been done to test this memory incorporation notion and has shown that, for example, when test subjects play a video game before falling asleep, the game was incorporated into their dreams. So beware, those who play *Grand Theft Auto!* However, dreams are not simply "replays" but "movies" of sorts that combine memory fragments into new experiences the dreamer has never encountered.

Altering Your Consciousness

People have been deliberately trying to alter their consciousness since the beginning of human history. Human beings have used meditation, medication, religious rituals, sleep deprivation, and numerous other means to alter their levels of everyday awareness.

Psychologist and author Stanley Krippner identified more than 20 states of altered consciousness. Among the more intriguing altered states of consciousness identified by Krippner are these four states:

>> **Rapture:** An intense feeling of overpowering emotion, experienced as pleasurable and positive. People have reported experiencing rapture after sex, ritualistic dancing, religious rituals, and the use of psychoactive substances.

>> **Trance states:** An alert but very suggestible state. An individual in a trance is focused on a single stimulus and oblivious to much of everything else going on around her. People in trances sometimes report that they feel "at one" with the world. Religious rituals, chanting, hypnosis, brainwashing, yoga, and even music can induce trance states.

>> **Daydreaming:** Rapid thinking unrelated to an individual's current environment. Daydreaming can often result from boredom, sensory deprivation, and sleep deprivation.

>> **Expanded consciousness:** Increased awareness not typical of everyday experience and awareness. People try all kinds of ways to "expand" their consciousness from using drugs to sensory deprivation. There are four levels of expanded consciousness:

- **Sensory:** An altered experience of space, time, and other sensory phenomena.

- **Recollective-analytic:** An experience in which individuals develop novel ideas and revelations about themselves, the world, and their role within the world.

- **Symbolic:** Identification with a historical figure or famous person accompanied by mystical symbols such as having a vision of a crucifix or an angel.

- **Integral:** A religious and/or mystical experience usually involving God or some other supernatural being or force. The person usually feels merged with or at one with the universe. This state has sometimes been called *cosmic consciousness.* Krippner and other experts believe that very few people are actually capable of attaining this level of consciousness.

Getting high on conscious life

Perhaps one of the most common methods for altering consciousness is the use of drugs. Drug use to alter one's consciousness is an ancient phenomenon as well as a contemporary practice. Archaeologists have found traces of cocaine in mummified bodies from ancient Egypt.

Some people claim that one of the purposes of taking drugs is to gain added insight into the concept of consciousness itself. Most people who have used drugs report that they do so in order to get *high* or intoxicated.

REMEMBER

The state of being high actually represents a change in consciousness, perhaps going from a level of awareness that involves negative feelings to a different level of awareness where an individual no longer feels "bad." The idea that drugs are an escape rings true, if you consider that many mind- and mood-altering drugs trigger a transition from one state of consciousness to another.

Not all drugs necessarily have an impact on consciousness. I don't recall feeling altered the last time I took an aspirin or antibiotic. Drugs whose main effect is the alteration of consciousness are called *psychoactive drugs.* Common psychoactive drugs and substances include LSD, psilocybin, PCP, marijuana, cocaine, amphetamines, barbiturates, ecstasy, and alcohol.

WARNING

Although some people consider drug use for the claimed purpose of expanding their consciousness to be a good thing, as a health professional, I feel compelled to warn you of many of the negative effects of psychoactive substance use and abuse. Addiction, brain injury, mental health issues, psychological distress, and social and legal problems are common consequences of psychoactive drug use. With these in mind, I strongly caution anyone considering the use of drugs to avoid them, and I argue that seeking higher states of consciousness without the use of substances might be far more enlightening and less risky.

Being conscious of my mind (meditative states)

Meditative states of consciousness are considered a special form of consciousness but not necessarily abnormal or maladaptive. As with other states of consciousness, the focus of or object of attention differs with meditation. There is an intense concentration and focusing of attention upon a particular facet of experience, mental activity, or physical experience.

The meditative state has often been referred to as watching yourself think. The purpose or goal is to engage in the practice as a form of mental training to increase a person's ability to concentrate, stay calm, and be aware. It's also used as a positive coping strategy in the face of distress or adversity.

Meditation is considered to be a mental enhancement technique. There are many different forms of meditation that differ in subtle ways; the focus of meditation may be one's own thoughts or on a statement or phrase repeated over and over (as in religious chanting or with some prayer). *Transcendental Meditation (TM)* is a practice that moves practitioners toward a state of "pure consciousness" in which there is no effortful concentration but an experience of being free and untethered. *Mindfulness Meditation* on the other hand involves the attentive monitoring and detection of sensations, feelings, and thoughts against a background of "non-grasping" awareness. (I am aware . . . there is a thought of a dog, an image of a cat, now pleasantness, now a breath . . . and so forth.)

Practicing meditation has been associated with positive health benefits such as reduced stress and muscle tension. It has been used in conjunction with psycho-therapy for depression and posttraumatic stress disorder (PTSD). Although historically associated with Buddhism, many consider meditation to be a nondenominational and non-religious practice and applicable to medical-, edu-cational-, athletic-, and even business-related goals. Besides, why should the Buddhists have all the fun?

BEING NATURALLY HIGH

Stanley Krippner defines an altered state of consciousness as a mental state that is sub-jectively experienced as representing a difference in psychological functioning from an individual's normal, alert, waking state. The importance of the subjectively experienced difference can be illustrated by a story told by Baba Ram Das in his book *Be Here Now* (Crown Publishing Group).

Baba Ram Das's original name was Richard Alpert. Alpert was a psychology professor at Harvard in the 1960s, where he and Timothy Leary conducted experiments with LSD. Perhaps one Timothy Leary's most famous sayings was "Turn on, tune in, drop out." Eventually, both Alpert and Leary were fired.

Ram Das traveled to India to seek the path of Hindu wisdom and to find out if anyone could explain why LSD seemed to have such a profound effect on consciousness. One day, Ram Das encountered a very wise and respected guru. Ram Das asked the guru if he could explain the effects of LSD. The guru asked for some LSD, and Ram Das com-plied. The guru took more LSD than Ram Das had ever seen a human being take, but the guru seemed completely unaffected! He didn't have an "acid trip" at all. There was no change in his current state of consciousness; he didn't experience an altered state of consciousness when he took the LSD. Does that mean that the guru was already on some sort of "reality trip" or "spiritual LSD"? The guru simply replied that his conscious-ness was "beyond" what LSD could provide, and therefore it had no effect on him.

Falling into hypnosis

Close your eyes and relax. You are *soooooo* relaxed. Your breathing is slow. You're beginning to feel sleepy. You are *soooooo* relaxed.

Well, did it work? Hello? Are you under my hypnotic spell? Probably not. I'm not even trained in hypnosis. It's a special skill, and not all therapists or psychologists are trained in it. *Hypnosis* is a procedure in which a person called a *hypnotist* suggests changes in sensations, feelings, thoughts, or behaviors to a subject. Some psychologists think hypnosis is simply an increase in suggestibility that allows the hypnotist to "control" a subject's behavior. Other psychologists propose that hypnosis is actually an altered state of consciousness in which a person *dissociates* (separates) from her normal or regular state of consciousness.

REMEMBER

The key to understanding the mechanism of hypnosis is *suggestion*. A *suggestion* is a directive given to the subject to act, feel, or think in a particular way. A hypnotist begins the process with some pleasant suggestions and progresses to more sophisticated requests. This process is called *hypnotic induction,* and it's considered a light hypnotic trance.

Hypnosis has been used for many different purposes ranging from entertainment to helping people stop smoking. The more controversial applications of hypnosis involve past-life regression and the recovery of repressed memories. There is little scientific evidence supporting the legitimacy of past-life regression through hypnosis. It's virtually impossible to prove. Why? Anything that someone reports can only be verified through historical records, and if I can look it up for verification, the individual in question could have looked it up to fake a regression.

3

Thinking and Feeling and Acting

Get exposed to the thinking on human thought, which psychologists call cognition, including both the contents of thoughts and the thought process.

Realize what being smart is all about via a discussion about communication, language, intelligence, and the different theories of "being smart."

Get in touch with your feelings in a chapter on motivation and emotion.

Check out the psychological understanding of learning with a refresher on Ivan Pavlov and his famous dogs and the theory of operant conditioning that followed.

IN THIS CHAPTER

» **Thinking about thinking**

» **Booting up the mind**

» **Understanding memory and other brain processes**

» **Discovering facts about intelligence**

» **Comprehending language**

Chapter **6**

Thinking and Speaking

Before I get into the complex psychological concept of thinking, here's a little mental experiment: Imagine yourself lying in your bed having just awakened from a good night's sleep. You reach over to shut off your annoying alarm, toss the blankets to the side, and head for the bathroom. Now, here's the experimental part. When you get to the bathroom, you forget why you're in there. The answer may seem obvious because you just got out of bed and walked straight to the bathroom, but you've forgotten. You look around and can't figure out where you are. Nothing seems familiar, and you're surrounded by a strange world of shapes, figures, objects, sounds, and lights. You look into an object that reflects an image of some other thing back at you, but you don't know what it is. You're confused, disoriented, and basically lost. Your mind is completely blank. You can't even think of anything to say in order to cry out for help. You're stuck there. What are you going to do?

If the example seems a little strange, or at least a bit abstract, it's because the situation *would* be strange. Without the ability to think, life would be similar to the bathroom situation I just described. Thinking enables you to recognize objects, solve problems, and communicate. You'd really be in trouble if you couldn't think. You wouldn't even be able to figure out how to get out of the bathroom.

In this chapter, I describe the concepts of thinking (cognition) and language and their component processes such as attention, memory, decision making, intelligence, language (including speech and nonverbal language such as American Sign Language), and comprehension.

What's on Your Mind?

What exactly is thinking? A bit later in this chapter, I ask you to analyze your own thought processes, so it would help if you knew what you're analyzing. In psychology, the term, *cognition* refers to the mental processing of information including memorizing, reasoning, problem solving, conceptualizing, and imagining.

Studying thinking (or, more strictly, cognition) is pretty difficult. Why? It's hard to see! If I opened up your skull and looked inside, would I see thinking? No, I'd see a wrinkly, grayish-pink thing (your brain). In the early years of psychological research on thinking, psychologists asked people participating in studies on thinking to engage in something called introspection. *Introspection* is the observation and reporting of one's own inner experience. Psychologists gave participants a simple math problem to solve and asked them to talk out loud as they performed the calculations. These exercises were intended to capture the steps involved in the thinking process. It is important to keep in mind that a great deal of thinking or cognition occurs outside of conscious awareness. In that sense, introspection would not be very helpful, now would it?

Try it! Get a piece of blank paper and a pencil. Your instructions are to solve the following math problem and write down each step that you take, one by one:

$$47,876 + 23,989$$

The answer is 71,865. If you didn't get this right, don't worry about it; everyone has weaknesses. Actually, if you got the wrong answer, the introspection technique may be able to reveal what you did wrong. Take a second to go over each of the steps you went through to solve the problem.

You just participated in a psychological experiment, and it didn't hurt a bit, did it?

Now, imagine how hard it would be to use introspection to analyze all of your thinking. It would be pretty difficult — impossible, in fact. Part of the reason psychologists don't rely on introspection anymore is that people are blind to most of what our minds (or brains) are doing. Introspection can't capture sophisticated thought processes, and it's not a very reliable measure because it's based on subjective report. These days, psychologists use computer modeling, formal experiments, lesion studies, PET scans, fMRI, event-related potentials, and other complex means for researching thinking. Psychologists try to build models systems that think the way people do.

 Cognitive psychologists are measuring thinking "behavior" as it manifests on a test someone takes, their overt behavior, or how their brain lights up when engaged in a thinking task.

REMEMBER

Thinking like a PC

Finding out how thinking works has been a pursuit of inquiry since Aristotle, through the Renaissance with Descartes, and into the modern era. A useful tool that thinking thinkers use to explain the workings of the mind is *metaphor*. Numerous metaphors have been developed through the ages, including the mind as a steam engine, a clock, and even a computer. In this section, I introduce you to the concept of the mind and thinking as computational processes, in which representations of information are manipulated as the actual process of thought. Where did the idea of the "computing mind" come from?

Turing's challenge

Alan Turing came up with something called the *Turing Test*. Turing (1912–1954) was a British mathematician and computer scientist who was instrumental in helping crack secrete German submarine codes during World War II. He developed a "computing machine" to crack the code. There's a great depiction of this machine in the movie about Alan Turing starring Benedict Cumberbatch called the *Imitation Game* (2014).

In his time, a popular parlor game involved placing a man and a woman behind two different doors; guests had to communicate with them by typewritten notes. The point was to guess correctly if it was the man or the woman behind a particular door based only on their answers to the guests' questions. Turing proposed that the comparison be changed from a man and a woman to a computer and a human being to find out if guests could determine whether the computer or a human was answering their questions. If guests couldn't tell the difference, then the computer would have to be considered to be a suitable "stand in" for the human. That is, such a test result would mean that a computer could "represent" human thought in its own way — in a *symbolic or cognitive architecture*, or computer language.

According to the Merriam-Webster dictionary, the word "cognitive" has its origin in the Latin *cognitivus*, which essentially means to "know," "knowing," or "get to know." A machine that passes Turing's test essentially "knows" the same things and "possesses" (stores) the same "knowledge" as its human competition. It just stores that knowledge in a set of symbolic "codes" that it uses to compute and produce an answer to a question. Turing proposed that if machines can do the thinking thing through computing, then maybe the human mind does the same thing.

The Turing test is a demonstration of how computation can be performed on symbols or representations and is an analogy for how the human mind can perform computations on symbols and represent the real world in mental terms. The title of the movie mentioned before is clever because the "imitation game" is when a machine imitates and models human thinking.

Computing

Building on Turing's work and with the eventual advent of the modern computer, psychologists and related investigators began to look more seriously at the operations performed by computers, called *computing* or *computation*, as potential models for human thought processes. This was a significant breakthrough. Using the computer as a model for how thinking occurs is called the *computational-representational model of mind* (and thinking). The idea is both profound and simplistic: The mind and all of its complex processes, such as perceiving, thinking, problem solving, and so forth, make up an information-processing machine that performs computations.

What is a "computation"? A computation is a manipulation of symbols according to a preset rule that transforms one set of symbols into another. For example, assume that there is the following rule for representing the letters W, S, D, O, and R:

W = 1

S = 2

D = 3

O = 4

R = 5

So the word "words" would be represented as "14532," and the word "sword" would be represented as "21453." That transformation is a computation. So the brain, as a computational "device," transforms one type of information, such as light waves (or the letters in the "words" example), into another type of information, neural patterns (or the numbers in the "words" example).

The computational-representational model of mind is also called the *information-processing approach* to cognition. Cognitive researchers began designing and "building" programs of computational/information processing models that could run on computers to see if the computer programs could do the same things human thinking could. These models were essentially computer simulations of human thinking and are often referred to as *cognitive architectures*. Buildings have architectural plans, and just like a building's plans, these models have them too. Richard Samuels, Professor of Philosophy at Ohio State University, states that cognitive scientists generally agree on the notion that the mind is a "mechanism" consisting of "parts" and says, "On this assumption, a central project of cognitive science is to characterize the nature of this mechanism — to provide an account of our cognitive architecture — which specifies the basic operations, component parts (for example, processes), and organization of the mind."

Representing

Computations are performed on mental representations. A *mental representation* is a symbol of a particular stimulus (like a tree) in the mind. The term "symbol" is used here in a very loose sense to refer to something standing in for something else. So the stimulus "tree," for example, may come to be symbolized by the activation of a specific set of neurons in the brain.

Sit back for a second, get comfortable, and conjure up an image of a pink rose in your mind. Concentrate so that the image is clear; see the green stem and leaves, the pink petals, the thorns. Try to imagine the rose in detail. If someone comes into the room as you're doing this and asks if there is a rose in the room, what would you say? If there isn't actually a rose in the room, then you'd say "no." But consider the idea that there is actually a rose in the room, or at least it's in the room because there's one inside your mind, the rose that you're imagining. So if I cut open your skull and looked into your head, I'd see a pink rose, right? Of course not! The rose only exists in symbolic or representational form inside of your mind.

Remember, thinking consists of symbols that represent information about the world, the objects within it, and the manipulation of those symbols. The mental manipulation of symbols is based on combining, breaking down, and recombining symbols into more complex strings or systems of symbols that have meaning. Take the word "rose" again. It consists of simpler parts called letters, and the specific combination of those letters gives rise to the specific word and image of the object called "rose." The letters can be rearranged to spell the word "sore," which is an entirely different thing and thus an entirely different thought. This reveals that even a simple system like the alphabet can give rise to an almost infinite set of larger and more meaningful symbols or representations.

REMEMBER

Where do all these symbols come from? Symbols are generated by sensing things in the world. When I see a rose, there's a corresponding symbolic representation of that rose in my mind as I think about it. From this point on, the *Psychology For Dummies* definition of thinking is the mental processing of information as computations performed on representations and the various operations involved in that process.

Processing

Your mind goes through four basic steps when processing information:

1. Stimulus information from your senses reaches the brain. (You see Lebron James slam dunk for the first time.)

2. The information is analyzed. (Your brain thinks, "Wow. Those are impressive moves.")

3. Different possible responses are generated. (Your brain tries to figure out how he's doing it.)

4. A response is executed and monitored for feedback. (You throw on your basketball shoes and head for the court.)

These basic mechanisms of information processing are sometimes called the *architecture* of thought. These are the *rules of thought* and require all the following basic components:

>> **Input:** Sensory information that comes in from your world or from within your own mind and is considered.

>> **Memory:** System necessary for storing knowledge. Information about people and other elements in the world is stored in the mind and memory.

>> **Operations:** Rules that determine how information in the memory system is utilized (reasoning, problem solving, and logical analysis). Take math as an example: If I have 100 numbers stored in my memory and am confronted with a mathematical problem, operations determine how I solve that problem.

>> **Output:** Action "programs" that involve telling the rest of the mind and body what to do after the thinking operations have been carried out.

Modules, Parts, and Processes

Jerry Fodor (born 1935) is an American philosopher who proposed that the mind's complicated information-processing system can be divided into specific operations, or modules, that perform specific thinking tasks: an attention module, a problem-solving module, and so forth. In the sections that follow, I introduce some of the more significant mental operations or procedures, including attention, memory, concept formation, and problem solving.

Over 60 years later, well known Harvard psychologist Steven Pinker agrees with Fodor stating strongly that the "mind is a system of organs of computation . . . organized into modules . . . each with a specialized design." It is important to remember that these "organs" are not "brain parts" in the material sense. It is a strange use of the word "organ," but what cognitive scientists are talking about are the cognitive processes that occur within the brain's neural network structure.

The attention process

There's a great scene from one of my favorite movies, *Dumb and Dumber* (1994), starring Jim Carey (Lloyd) and Jeff Daniels (Harry) in which Harry tells Lloyd a story about how a girlfriend broke up with him in high school.

Harry tells Lloyd that he didn't know why she ended the relationship — something about him not listening to her — but he wasn't paying attention when she told him the reason.

Harry didn't pay *attention,* one of the most critical and primary thinking processes. The world and your own mind are full of information and stimulation. It's extremely noisy, buzzy, fuzzy, colorful, blurry, and chock-full of stuff. How can you select and focus on what is important and ignore all the rest?

REMEMBER

As part of information processing, attention is defined as the cognitive process of selecting stimuli and information from the environment for further processing while excluding or inhibiting other stimuli and information. There's simply too much information buzzing around in people's minds and in the environment to attend to it all. Efficient and effective information processing requires selection.

Psychologists Daniel Simons and Christopher Chabris conducted an experiment that illustrates this selective feature of attention. In short, experimental subjects were asked to watch a video of people innocently passing a basketball to each other. Partway through the video, a person in a gorilla suit enters the frame, pounds on his chest, and then leaves the frame. Subjects were asked if they remember seeing the gorilla; about half of them reported never noticing a gorilla. This is known as *inattentional blindness;* when a person is focusing on something, he misses unrelated information. This is an active principle in magic shows and sleight-of-hand tricks. Sorry, I don't think David Copperfield is a wizard, but he sure knows how to harness inattentional blindness!

Different types of attention processes exist:

>> **Focused attention:** Concentration on one source of input to the exclusion of everything else

>> **Divided attention:** Focus on two or more inputs simultaneously

Psychologist Donald Broadbent developed a cognitive model of attention in which attention is characterized as a channel with limited capacity for input to pass through. Sensory information is processed first, and then semantic (or meaning) information is processed. The key to Broadbent's model is that inputs need to be attended to in order to be further processed.

Broadbent's model does not explain all the data being collected through research so other models have been developed. One research finding known as the *cocktail party effect* presented a challenge to Broadbent's model. Ever been at a noisy party and suddenly you hear your name mentioned from across the room? Well, you weren't particularly attending to or waiting to hear your name, but you did anyway because it's important. Your mind attends to *important* information.

Experiments have lead cognitive psychologists to characterize attention as a dynamic process in which both selection for attention and selection for "non-attention" are made at the same time. Guided search theory is a dynamic model of attention that proposes that attention is guided by salient information from previous searches or episodes of attending. It is considered a top-down model of attention in that people are considered to be actively searching rather than passively receiving inputs as is more the case in Broadbent's model.

Going back to concept of a "module," "part," or even "organ," the notion is that if this module was missing from the architecture in a person's mind, then they wouldn't be able to attend. No part, no process.

The memory process

Thinking involves the manipulation of mental symbols that you store as concepts — representations of the objects you encounter in the world. How are these mental symbols stored? Memory!

To conceptualize memory, envision a bank. Think about your checking account and your savings account. Each of these accounts does something a little different with your money because they have different purposes. Checking accounts typically function for everyday and short-term use. Savings are intended to be for longer-term storage. Your memories store information in different ways as well.

Three separate storage systems are involved with memory: *sensory memory, short-term memory,* and *long-term memory.*

Sensory memory

Sensory memory is a split-second memory system that stores information coming in through your senses. Have you ever looked at the sun and then closed your eyes and looked away? What happens? You can still see a type of sun in your mind. This afterimage is a visual sensory memory known as an *iconic* memory. For auditory stimuli, it is called *echoic* memory. This process happens so fast that it is sometimes considered a part of the perceptual process (for more on perception, see Chapter 5), but is, in fact, part of the overall memory system.

Short-term memory

Short-term memory (STM), also known as *working memory*, consists of the information that is active in your consciousness right now, the things you're aware of. The light on the book page, these words being read, the grumbling in your stomach, and the sound of traffic outside your window are all parts of your conscious awareness, and they're all being stored in your STM. Things you are not aware of can simply be forgotten in many cases.

How much information can your STM store? The general consensus is that it can store seven items of information, plus or minus two items. This is sometimes called the "magical number seven" of STM capacity.

Does that mean that I can only store seven words, seven numbers, or seven other simple items in my STM? No. Thanks to a process called *chunking*, I can store a lot more information than that. A classic example of chunking is the use of *mnemonics*, which enables you to take a big chunk of information and break it down into a little phrase, so it's easier to remember.

TIP

Here's an easy way to form a mnemonic. If you have a list of things you want to memorize, take the first letter of each word on the list and make a catchy phrase out of it. I learned this one in eighth grade and never forgot it: "Kings play chess on fine green silk." Do you know what that stands for? It stands for the way biologists classify different organisms on the earth: Kingdom, Phylum, Class, Order, Family, Genus, and Species.

The duration of memory for the STM system is approximately 18 seconds. You can extend the length of time that you store information in STM only by engaging in something called rehearsal. *Rehearsal* is the process of actively thinking about something. Rote rehearsal is repeating something over and over again in your mind or out loud so that you don't forget it. Rote rehearsal will work, but not as effectively as a more effortful type of rehearsal, such as building a mnemonic like "Kings play chess on fine green silk."

Long-term memory

If the information in STM is rehearsed long enough, it eventually ends up in your memory's savings account, the *long-term memory* (LTM). You basically have two ways to deposit information into your long-term memory bank:

» **Maintenance rehearsal:** You transfer the information from your STM through repetition until it's committed to long-term storage.

» **Elaborative rehearsal:** Your mind elaborates on the information, integrating it with your existing memories. When information is meaningful and references something that you already know, remembering is easier and forgetting becomes harder.

TIP

The more you process the information, linking it to what you already know, the better you will remember it!

You can break down the LTM into three basic divisions:

>> **Episodic memory:** Events and situations unique to your experiences (marriages, birthdays, graduations, car accidents, what happened yesterday, and so on)

>> **Semantic memory:** Factual information such as important holidays, the name of the first president of the United States, and your Social Security number

>> **Procedural memory:** Information on how to do things like riding a bike, solving a math problem, or tying your shoes

Theoretically, the size and time capacity of LTM is infinite because researchers haven't found a way to test its capacity. It has enough capacity to get the job done. This may sound kind of strange when you consider how much information you seem to forget. If the information is in there somewhere, why do you forget it?

Forgetting information stored in LTM is more of an issue of not being able to access it rather than the information not being there. Two forms of access failure occur, and both involve other information getting in the way:

>> **Retroactive interference:** Having a hard time remembering older information because newer information is getting in the way

>> **Proactive interference:** Having a hard time remembering newer information because older information is getting in the way

The next time you watch a sitcom on television, try to remember the details of the first 10 to 12 minutes, the middle 10 to 12 minutes, and the last 10 to 12 minutes of the program. Or listen to a lecture and try to remember what was said during the beginning, middle, and end of the presentation. You may notice something psychologists call the *serial position effect.* Information from the beginning and end of the show or lecture is easier to remember than the middle. Why is that?

REMEMBER

The serial position effect occurs because the information at the beginning of the show or lecture is usually committed to long-term memory due to the amount of time that elapses. The information at the end of the show is being kept in your short-term memory because it's fresh in your mind. The middle stuff? It's just gone.

FAHGETABOUDIT!

Have you ever been told to forget about something? Try this: Forget about cheese. Did it work? Did you forget about cheese or did you actually think more about cheese? The irony of someone telling you to forget something is that it's impossible to forget about something you're actively thinking about, making "forget about it" bogus advice. If someone really wants you to forget about something, then she shouldn't mention it to you at all.

The knowing process

When was the last time you went out with a friend just to talk? Did you go to a coffeehouse? Did you talk about recent romances and frustrating relationships in your life? Did you talk about politics or the weather? It doesn't matter; you were talking about a concept.

A *concept* is a thought or idea that represents a set of related ideas. *Romance* is a concept. *Relationship* is a concept. *Politics* is a concept. *Weather* is a concept. All these concepts are represented as symbols in your information-processing system of thought, and they get into this system through learning. In other words, concepts are derived and generated; they are formed. When objects share characteristics, they represent the same concept. Some concepts are well-defined, others are not.

Consider the following words:

Tail, Fur, Teeth, Four Legs

What do these words describe? It could be a cat, a dog, a lion, or a bear. The fact is, you really can't tell just from those words. Some crucial detail is missing, some piece of information that clearly defines the concept and separates it from others.

Now, consider this list of words:

Tail, Fur, Teeth, Four Legs, Bark

What is being described now? This has to be a dog. Why? Cats, lions, and bears don't bark. The feature "bark" uniquely defines the concept of "dog." "Bark" is the concept's *defining feature*. It is an attribute that must be present in order for the object to be classified as an example of a particular concept. Consider the following words:

Feathers, Beak, Eggs, Fly

These words describe a bird. Hold on a minute. Aren't there at least two birds that don't fly? Penguins and ostriches don't fly, but they're still birds. So flying is not a defining feature of a bird because animals don't have to have that attribute in order to be considered a bird. However, most birds do fly, so "flying" is what is called a *characteristic feature* or attribute. It is an attribute that most, but not all, members of a concept group possess.

Think about a chair. Try to imagine and picture a chair. Now, describe it. (Describe it to someone else or you'll look funny describing an imaginary chair to yourself.) Your imagined chair probably consists of wood, four legs, a rectangular or square seat, and a back constructed of two vertical supports on each side of the seat connected by a couple of horizontal slats. This is a typical chair. It's common. In fact, it may be considered as a prototypical chair. A *prototype* is the most typical example of an object or event within a particular category. It is the quintessential example of the concept being represented.

REMEMBER

Thinking is much more complex than simple one-word descriptions. When developing a thought, single word concepts are combined into sentence-long concepts, sentence-long concepts into paragraph-long concepts, and so on. In other words, attributes are combined into concepts. Concepts are combined into propositions. Multiple propositions are combined into mental models. Finally, mental models are combined into schemas, which are used to represent the world in a language of thought.

For example, check out this process, which continuously builds upon itself:

>> **Proposition:** "War is hell" is a combination of two related concepts, war and hell being related.

>> **Mental model:** Clustering thoughts help you understand how things relate to each other:

- War is hell.
- World War II was a war.
- World War II was hell.

>> **Schemas:** Organizing mental models into larger groups form basic units of understanding that represent the world. An example here is "Some of the soldiers who fought in WWII experienced psychological trauma. Some people believe that this was due to the extreme nature of war. Some people have even said that war is hell."

Another example may be to consider the concept "book." Combine the concept of book with another concept, like reading. Then connect those concepts to another concept, like library. Now you have three related concepts: book, reading, and library. This set of concepts may form the proposition of studying (as opposed to reading for pleasure). You can then embed studying into larger divisions, or schema, of school or a certification process.

Concepts are formed from co-occurring features encountered in experience. They represent ideas in relation to each other. That is, in order to understand, comprehend, or grasp the meaning of a concept, the representational mind relates concepts to other concepts.

For example, anyone who regularly interacts with kids will tell you how difficult it is to explain certain concepts to a curious toddler because it's tough to find words she already knows and can use as a reference.

> Child: "What's a computer?"
>
> Parent: "A computer is like a . . . a . . . um . . . TV . . . um . . . but . . . um . . . you can type on it."
>
> Child: What's type mean?

See where this is going?

Some cognitive scientists and psychologists have found their way out of this concept trap by suggesting that all concepts are innate and inborn. One of the more interesting and fruitful approaches to this problem comes from the theories of *embodied cognition (EC)* and *embodied simulation (ES)*.

The core idea behind EC and ES is that the mind comprehends or grasps concepts through a process of simulation that uses the motor and perceptual parts of the thinker's brain to represent the experience. This simulation allows for comprehension because people understand concepts through reference to the bodily experiences they associated with them.

> "In over your head"
>
> "Slap in the face"
>
> "Eye-opening experience"

All capture the essence of EC and ES. You understand the meaning of these phrases in terms of bodily experience. Bodily, sensory, and motor experiences are the meaning; they are the experience, the concept. If I want to understand a new concept, I use my body, sensory, and motor experiences to come to an understanding. I understand "eye-opening experience" because I have opened my eyes and know (because I've experienced it) what that means.

Interestingly, EC/ES proponents say that the parts of the brain that you use to actually open your eyes, or move your arm, or see the sunrise are the same parts of that you use when you conceptualize the meaning of "eye-opening" and other such phrases. Ultimately EC/ES are relative newcomers to the cognitive psychology arena, but they hold a lot of promise and are being hotly researched.

The reasoning process

Reasoning is a thinking process that involves two basic components:

>> **Premises:** These are statements about some object or event that support a conclusion. Premises declare some state of affairs such as, "All fire trucks are red." Another premise may be, "My dad drives a fire truck at work."

>> **Conclusions:** The points derived from the premises. They are only valid if they can be logically or reasonably drawn from the premises. A logical conclusion for the premises stated here may be, "My dad drives a red truck at work."

Reasoning is the act of drawing conclusions based on the truth of the premises that precede the conclusion. Reasoning can help people figure out if their conclusions are valid or if they make logical sense. When arguments make logical sense, reasoning is good. It makes logical sense that my dad drives a red fire truck at work because this follows from the premises.

But what if it went like this: All fire trucks are red. My dad's truck is red. Therefore, my dad's truck is a fire truck. This is not logical because the first premise doesn't state that all trucks are red, only that fire trucks are red. So other trucks can be red, including fire trucks. My dad may drive a red Toyota. Logic is like a measuring stick for verifying our reasoning.

There are two basic types of reasoning: inductive and deductive.

Inductive

In inductive reasoning, you begin with making observations (the premises) in order to collect facts to support or disconfirm (validate) some hypothetically stated outcome or situation (the conclusion). Consider the following:

Monday it rained.

Tuesday it rained.

Therefore, I conclude that Wednesday it is going to rain.

This is an example of inductive reasoning. Two observations or premises are used to predict a third outcome. I think my local weather person uses inductive logic to make his forecasts, not the million-dollar computer technology that the TV station advertises.

Deductive

Deductive reasoning uses premises that claim to provide conclusive proof of truth for the conclusion. A conclusion based on deductive logic is by necessity true provided that it begins with true premises. Deduction often begins with generalizations and reasons to particulars. Consider the following example of deductive reasoning:

> All men should be free.
>
> I am a man.
>
> Therefore, I should be free.

The conclusion follows logically from the two premises. It has to be that way based on what is stated in the premises. Here's an example of a false conclusion:

> All chickens lay eggs.
>
> My bird laid an egg.
>
> Therefore, my bird must be a chicken.

This is false because the first premise refers to a subset of the larger category, birds. The second premise includes this larger category, and therefore refers to some events not covered by the first premise. If you turn the two premises around, you can create a logically valid argument:

> All birds lay eggs.
>
> My chicken laid an egg.
>
> Therefore, my chicken must be a bird.

The decision-making/choosing process

Go left and get there five minutes late. Go right and *maybe* get there on time; it's a risk because sometimes there's major traffic that way. It may mean you'll be 20 minutes late. For many people, the morning commute is a daily problem. How can you get to work on time with the least amount of travel time, encountering the least amount of traffic, and experiencing the least amount of stress? You have to solve this problem, and part of solving this problem requires you to make some decisions. Perhaps you'll use reasoning to choose your course; maybe you won't.

People solve problems all day long and make hundreds, if not thousands, of decisions every day. In fact, a condition related to mental exhaustion is called "decision fatigue" — simply having too many problems and making too many decisions in a given day. Some choices are life or death, some less so; but it all adds up.

Decision making is the act of choosing an option or action from a set of options based on criteria and a strategy. The study of decision making is really a complex cross-discipline science in and of itself, spanning economics, political science, computer science, management and business, and marketing. And I don't know about you, but sometimes I just flip a coin.

I once worked at a job in which the most important decision made all day long (at least as perceived by my co-workers) was where to go for lunch. We had a "Wheel-O-Lunch" we'd spin; where it stopped was where we'd go — theoretically. Usually we ended up discussing and ultimately overriding the wheel's "choice" due to recollections of bloating, large bills, or "I had that for dinner last night" qualifiers and caveats. This illustrates a point well discussed in decision-making research: There is more than one way to make a decision, and most people use a variety of approaches.

Flipping a coin is one way to make a decision, but that's not really a cognitive process, is it? It's simply a way of letting chance choose for you — it's not really choosing at all. But people do make choices by using processes such as *intuitive decision making* which refers to choices based on what is most easy, familiar, or preferred. I'm sure you can see how this may work some of the time, but sometimes a decision to do what is preferred is the wrong choice. Just think about the last time you ended up eating that fourth piece of cake only to regret it later.

Decisions can also come from a more scientific approach based on *empirical* evidence through trial and error, experiment, estimation, experience, or consultation with an expert. *Consumer Reports* provides experimental evidence to tell you which blender to buy or which brand of deodorant to use.

If you are pressed for time or need to make a lot of decisions with limited resources, then your choice for choosing may be to use a *heuristic*, which is a mental short cut based on principles, rules, maxims, and so forth. Ethical decision making can be considered heuristic, choosing based on a code of ethics. My religious beliefs may be factored in to my decision making.

Amos Tversky and Daniel Kahneman studied heuristic decision making and identified different types of this model. Here are two commonly used heuristics:

>> **Representative heuristic:** Making a choice based on the situation in question being similar to another situation. If you were lost in the forest while on a horse-riding outing you may try to retrace your tracks to find your way out. You start looking for your tracks and by using the representative

heuristic, decide that the tracks you find are, in fact, horse tracks because you are familiar with and know what horse tracks look like. Too bad you don't know what bear tracks look like!

>> **Availability heuristic:** Making a decision based on how easily or readily available information is. This is the "first thing that comes to mind" approach to choosing. News agencies are guilty of spreading the use of this heuristic. Oftentimes they all report on the same story or similar stories so the most recent story of the latest fad diet is fresh on your mind. The next time you choose a diet, let the heuristic choose for you, fad all the way!

People make decisions in some pretty haphazard ways. What happened to deliberation, to thinking things through, to being rational? *Rational* decision-making models are all based on the assumption that people make decisions after weighing the costs and benefits of options and ultimately choosing the option in which the benefits outweigh the costs. These costs may include factors such as utility, risks, functionality, and quality.

The famous psychologist Herbert Simon proposed that although humans can be rational decision makers, this rationality has *bounds*, or limits. In his theory of *bounded rationality*, Simon proposes that because the environment is so complex, a prospective decision maker cannot possibly rationally weigh out *all* the options in order to come to the optimal decision. So rational decisions are bound; therefore, decisions must be based on limited information, short cuts, and reasonable estimation. Simon does not lament this situation; he states that bounded rationality is a fact of cognition and the human mind, and it usually results in relatively solid and good decisions.

Dan Ariely in his well known book *Predictably Irrational: The Hidden Forces that Shape Our Decisions* (2008), further addressed the concept of limited rationality. He experimentally identified many situations in which decisions are not only based on incomplete information but also are sometimes downright irrational and based on nonoptimal information. Bottom line: People make irrational decisions. What's interesting is that Ariely shows that people make irrational decisions in predictable ways:

>> **Relativity:** Sometimes a choice between two options is based on the relation between them, not on the absolute quality of each choice. For example, in U.S. presidential elections, many people say they dislike both candidates, but end up picking the one they determine is "less bad."

>> **It's free:** Free things are good right? Well, not always, but sometimes a less good choice is made (irrational) because of its free status. Waiting in line for three hours to get a free gift with purchase isn't always worth the three hours of waiting.

>> **Hot and cold:** Decisions made when you're emotionally aroused are different from the choices you make when you're calm. This is an oldie but goodie when it comes to common sense and decision making, yet people violate it all the time. Decisions made when emotions run strong can be predictably irrational.

The problem-solving process

Problem solving sounds pretty straightforward. You have a problem, and you solve it. Did you ever watch that television show *MacGyver* from the 1980s? Mac-Gyver could solve just about any problem that came his way. He could turn a toothpick into a Jet Ski or a rocket launcher. I'd sit back and watch in amazement, and then I'd get out my trusty toolbox and dismantle the toaster, trying to turn it into a satellite receiver — four hours later, I'd just have a pile of parts and no way to make toast. MacGyver clearly had better problem-solving skills than me.

Newell and Simon (1972) are pretty much the godfathers of problem-solving psychology. Nearly every research study on the topic cites their study. They defined these basic steps of the problem-solving process:

1. Recognizing that a problem exists.

2. Constructing a representation of the situation that includes the initial state of the problem and the eventual goal (a solution).

3. Generating and evaluating possible solutions.

4. Selecting a solution to attempt.

5. Executing the solution and determining if it actually works.

TIP

These steps are sometimes identified by the acronym IDEAL, which Bransford and Stein formulated in 1993:

I — Identify the problem.

D — Define and represent the problem.

E — Explore possible strategies.

A — Action.

L — Look back and evaluate the effects.

The world has as many problem-solving strategies as there are problems, but most people tend to use the same ones over and over again. For instance, *trial and error* is a popular way to solve a problem. I've seen young children use trial and error when trying to put shapes into their respective holes in a bucket. A child will pick up the circle block and try putting it in every cut-out until it fits, and then move on to the next block.

The trial-and-error strategy is pretty inefficient, but sometimes it's the only strategy available, particularly for situations that have no clear definition for the problem, when part of the process is figuring out what the problem is.

Here are a couple more common problem-solving techniques:

>> **Means-ends analysis:** This strategy involves breaking the problem down into smaller sub-problems to solve to get to the end result.

>> **Working backwards:** This way to solve a problem is like taking something apart and putting it back together again in order to figure out how the object (or problem) is built.

>> **Brainstorming:** A technique that involves coming up with as many possible solutions to the problem without editing them in any way. It doesn't matter how implausible, unfeasible, idiotic, or ridiculous the solutions are; you just put them all out there and eliminate them after you can't think of any more possible solutions. Even my idea to have Superman use his super-cool breath to stop global warming is included in this technique.

>> **Analogies and metaphors:** These strategies involve using a parallel or similar problem that has already been solved to solve a previously unrelated problem. The Cuban Missile Crisis was like a nuclear-powered game of chicken, and whoever flinched, blinked, or chickened out first was the loser. I guess President Kennedy was pretty good at playing chicken.

REMEMBER

In wrapping up the process list, let's go back to the concept of a "module," "part" of even "organ" for a minute. Think about this: If a module was missing from the architecture in a person's mind, then he wouldn't be able to pay attention, remember, know, reason, decide, choose, or solve problems. No module, no process. If someone was missing all of it, then you might say he was "thoughtless" — like a bad gift from your secret Santa at the office.

It's All about Connections

One of my favorite professors, Dr. Jay Brand, said in our cognitive science class that any model of cognition that doesn't map onto the actual biological constraints in the brain is useless at best and dead wrong at worst. In other words, if it doesn't match the meat in our heads, then it's not an accurate model. Computational models are excellent and indispensable, but they don't tell us much about how the brain does all this computing.

Along come the connectionists to save the day. In 1996, James McClelland and David Rumelhart proposed a model to account for the cognition in terms of neural functioning known as the *neural network* or the *parallel distributed processing approach (PDP)*. The PDP proposes that cognition is characterized by networks in the brain, very much like the neurons and synapses, operating in massively parallel fashion. "Massively parallel" means that all kinds of thinking processes can happen simultaneously, not simply in linear fashion. Information cannot be "stored" in the brain in one location but instead is distributed across neurons in a network. So instead of a "location" per se, you have networks as "locations." Think of it like this: If you are building a piece of furniture from Ikea (poor thing), all the parts are "scattered" around, and only when they come together do you have the "table." But the table is just a collection of parts put together in a particular way, held together by the network of interacting parts. You can take the table apart and you still have parts but no table. Connectionists believe that the "table" exists in your mind as parts spread across neurons, but when the network of neurons all work together and coalesce, you get the table — in your mind anyway. Experiments based on the connectionist model have been able to simulate some of what the brain does, but much more research is being done as we speak.

REMEMBER

Ultimately, both the computational model and the connectionist model are correct and useful. The computational model does explains how thinking is done generally and connectionist models show how these processes might manifest and operate in the actual brain.

Bodies and Minds

So far we've had some good, clean, machine-like models of thinking. So why mess with a such a clean model? Let's talk about robots for a minute. There are a lot of depictions of robots in film and literature. Take the robots in the film *iRobot*. They are thinking machines, but they have a metal (or some kind of futuristic composite) body. There are the robots (cyborgs actually) from the movie *Bladerunner* with bodies made of flesh. There are the various forms of robots in the *Terminator* films, like the one with skin (Arnold), the ones without skin, the ones without skin made of some crazy liquid metal, and in the most recent film, there's even a human with robot parts. Which one thinks most like a human? Would Turing's machine think differently if it was made of flesh, bones, and blood? Does the fact that some of them have flesh and some of them don't matter when it comes to figuring out cognition? Well, the fleshy Arnold robot was the nicest, after all!

A CYBORG IN YOUR POCKET?

Here's something to think about: What kind of "mind" does an iPhone have? Is it fleshy or not? It "walks" around (with you as you walk). It can monitor aspects of you biological, psychological, and social functioning (through apps). It knows where it is in space with GPS. It knows if it's upside down or not. It anticipates your wants and needs with ads, reminders, and prompts. It has a memory and remembers everything you do on it, especially with the help of the massive storage capacity of iCloud. It's plugged in and connected to a larger network of other versions of itself through social media.

As Dr. Frankenstein might say, "Its alive!" Well, as long as we take it with us everywhere and continue to feed it (via charging), then maybe it is a hybrid version of Turing's machine with flesh (our flesh). But it needs us as much as we need it. We could live without it; we've managed to live without smartphones for the vast majority of human history. But it can't live without us. Or can it? Not until it has legs, wheels, or appendages, I think.

There's a famous thought experiment in philosophy that gets to the heart of whether flesh matters in understanding thinking. It's called the "Brain in a Vat" experiment. Picture a brain in a jar with wires connected to it. The wires run to a computer where the activity of the brain is running on its hardware and through its software version of the brain. Is the activity of that brain different from a brain inside an actual body? Some philosophers and cognitive scientists say yes. This is where the model of cognition known as *embodied cognition* comes in. Evan Thompson and Diego Cosmelli state the baseline premise of embodied cognition is that the minimal requirement for human-like cognition is a living body.

Remember back in Chapter 3 where I talk about dualism and monism? We're monists, right? Embodied cognition is a logical extension of the monist perspective. The mind and the body, including the brain, are not separate because the brain can't live without the body and vice versa. By logical extension, human cognition can't exist without the body either. Sorry, Turing.

REMEMBER

The main tenet of embodied cognition is that cognition is the product of the interplay between the brain, the body, and the brain's connection to the outside world of sensations as the body interacts with that world. The mind processes information about the world via the body. Our eyes, ears, mouths, hands, and all the other body parts are the mind/brain's connection to the world. No flesh, no human cognition. That's not to say that computers don't think, but they just don't think like humans.

Support for the embodied mind model comes from some interesting observations, such as the fact that we use gestures (with our hands and faces) when we speak to convey information back and forth between each other. Visual perception happens because we have eyes, retinas, and optic nerves. We often do better on learning tasks when we can touch, feel, and interact physically with what we are trying to learn (hands on). According to George Lakoff and Mark Johnson in their book *Metaphors We Live By* (University of Chicago Press, 2008), we even use physical metaphors when we speak such as "handing off a project" or "circling back" to an idea. Both are metaphors based on physical movement.

Thinking You're Pretty Smart

Acting intelligently is perhaps the pinnacle and most grand cognitive process of the human mind. After all, the cognitive processes of managing information and the various components of attention, remembering things, and so forth ought to produce something useful, right? Indeed, you can view intelligence as the collective output of human cognition that results in an ability to achieve goals, adapt, and function in the world. This is *intelligent behavior.*

Psychologists have been trying to figure out what intelligence is for a long time. Plenty of examples exist to support the theory that humans lack intelligence. Just take a look at those goofy home-video shows. A guy forgets to turn off the electricity before rewiring a room, or a hiker tries to feed a bear and almost becomes dinner. Maybe I'm entertained by these misfortunes of others caught on videotape because these people couldn't have been any less intelligent. Or perhaps I feel giddy because I did not suffer their fate.

REMEMBER

People differ in their abilities to solve problems, learn, think logically, use language well, understand and acquire concepts, deal with abstractions, integrate ideas, attain goals, and so on. This impressive list of human abilities represents some of the ideas of what intelligence actually is; these abilities *are* the stuff of intelligence. For a more concrete definition, *intelligence* can be understood as a collection of cognitive abilities that allows a person to learn from experience, adapt successfully to the world, and go beyond the information presented in the environment.

Considering the factors of intelligence

Sure, intelligence is a collection of cognitive abilities, but a unifying construct called "intelligence" that can be measured and quantified must exist, right? Psychologists think so, and they've been working tirelessly to test and measure intelligence for a long time. As part of this work, psychologists have developed intelligence tests and worked with militaries, schools, and corporations, trying to sort individual differences in intelligence in the service of job selection, academic honors, and promotions. From all this testing has emerged the concept of "g" as a general and measurable intelligence factor.

The g-factor is comprised of subcomponents known as *s-factors*. Together, the g- and s-factors comprise what is called the *two-factor theory of intelligence*:

>> **g-factor:** Some psychologist comes up with a test of mental abilities and gives it to a lot of people. When a score is calculated and averaged across abilities, a general intelligence factor is established. This is factor one of the two-factor theory, commonly referred to as the *g-factor,* or the general intelligence factor. It is meant to represent how generally intelligent you are based on your performance on this type of intelligence test.

>> **s-factor:** The individual scores on each of the specific ability tests represent the s-factors. An s-factor score represents a person's ability within one particular area. Put all the s-factors together, and you get the g-factor. Commonly measured s-factors of intelligence include memory, attention and concentration, verbal comprehension, vocabulary, spatial skills, and abstract reasoning.

So intelligence according to the psychometric theory is a score on an intelligence test. How can this be? Each test is made up of subtests, and typically, people who score high on one test do well on the other tests, too. This reveals a relationship among the individual abilities as measured by the subtests; the general intelligence concept underlies that relationship.

TECHNICAL STUFF

In a related theory, psychologist and intelligence research pioneer Louis Thurston (1887–1955) came up with a theory of intelligence called *primary mental abilities*. It's basically the same concept as the s-factor part of the two-factor theory, with a little more detail. For Thurston, intelligence is represented by an individual's different levels of performance in seven areas: verbal comprehension, word fluency, number, memory, space, perceptual speed, and reasoning. Thurston's work, however, has received very little research support.

Getting a closer look

Psychologists continue to divide general intelligence into specific factors. The *Cattell-Horn-Carroll Theory of Cognitive Abilities* (CHC Theory) proposes that "g" is comprised of multiple cognitive abilities that when taken as a whole produce "g." Early work by the individual contributors to CHC theory, Raymond Cattell, John Horn, and John Carroll, converged to produce a model of general intelligence consisting of ten strata with numerous individual abilities within those strata. They are as follows:

>> **Crystallized intelligence (Gc):** Comprehensive and acquired knowledge

>> **Fluid intelligence:** Reason and problem-solving abilities

>> **Quantitative reasoning:** Quantitative and numerical ability

>> **Reading and writing ability:** Reading and writing

>> **Short-term memory:** Immediate memory

>> **Long-term storage and retrieval:** Long-term memory

>> **Visual processing:** Analysis and use of visual information

>> **Auditory processing:** Analysis and use of auditory information

>> **Processing speed:** Thinking fast and automatically

>> **Decision and reaction speed:** Coming to a decision and reacting swiftly

Researchers continue to work with the CHC model and have developed research programs looking into adding to the ten strata. Many professionals believe that sensory and motor abilities need to be more fully included in this theory, and researchers are looking at "tentative" factors such as tactile abilities (touch), kin-esthetic ability (movement), olfactory ability (sense of smell), and psychomotor ability and speed. Wait a minute, you mean I can be a smart smeller?

Many intelligence researchers and practitioners have accepted CHC as a triumph of psychological science and the consensus model of psychometric conceptions of intelligence. It is, however, a working model, and many intelligence investigators and theorists consider CHC theory as a strong beginning or second act but not the final word on intelligence.

Adding in street smarts

Robert Sternberg developed the *Theory of Successful Intelligence* in part to address the street smarts controversy, which holds that many intelligent people may be smart when it comes to academics or in the classroom but lack common sense in real life or practical matters. A cultural myth claims that Albert Einstein, unques-tionably gifted in mathematics and physics, couldn't tie his own shoes. I don't know if this is true or not, but Sternberg seems to agree that an important aspect of being intelligent is possessing a good level of common sense or practical intel-ligence. The three intelligence components of his theory are as follows:

>> **Analytical intelligence:** The ability to analyze, evaluate, judge, decide, choose, compare, and contrast.

>> **Creative intelligence:** The ability to generate novel or creative ways to deal with novel problems.

>> **Practical intelligence:** The type of intelligence used to solve problems and think about actions of everyday life. Like Einstein tying his shoes, opening up a jar of pickles, or figuring out how to log into a streaming service or how to send a group text.

Excelling with multiple intelligences

Have you ever wondered what makes Michael Jordan such a good basketball player? What about Mozart? He wrote entire operas in one sitting without editing. That's pretty impressive! According to Howard Gardener (1983), each of these men display a specific type of intelligence.

REMEMBER

Gardener generated a theory known as *multiple intelligences* from observing extremely talented and gifted people. He came up with seven types of intelligence that are typically left out of conventional theories about intelligence:

>> **Bodily kinesthetic ability:** Michael Jordan seems to possess a lot of this ability. People high in bodily kinesthetic ability have superior hand-eye coordination, a great sense of balance, and a keen understanding of and control over their bodies while engaged in physical activities.

>> **Musical ability:** If you can tap your foot and clap your hands in unison, then you've got a little musical intelligence — a little. People high in musical intelligence possess the natural ability to read, write, and play music exceptionally well.

>> **Spatial ability:** Have you ever gotten lost in your own backyard? If so, you probably don't have a very high level of spatial intelligence. This intelligence involves the ability to navigate and move around in space and the ability to picture three-dimensional scenes in your mind.

>> **Linguistic ability:** This is the traditional ability to read, write, and speak well. Poets, writers, and articulate speakers are high in this ability.

>> **Logical-mathematical ability:** This intelligence includes basic and complex mathematical problem-solving ability.

>> **Interpersonal ability:** The gift of gab and the used-car salesman act are good examples of interpersonal intelligence. A "people person" who has good conversational skills and knows how to interact and relate well with others is high in interpersonal ability.

>> **Intrapersonal ability:** How well do you know yourself? Intrapersonal intelligence involves the ability to understand your motives, emotions, and other aspects of your personality.

Any one of us can have varying degrees of Gardener's intelligences. I may be one heck of a baseball player and a singing math whiz, but I may be unable to carry a conversation, get lost walking home from the grocery, and have no idea how I feel about all that.

Making the grade — on a curve

Psychologists like to measure stuff, especially stuff related to human behavior and thought processes, like cognitive abilities. Measuring and documenting individual differences is at the core of applied psychological science.

REMEMBER

Whether you ascribe to CHC, Sternberg's model, or the concept of multiple intelligences, don't forget the concept of average. Intelligence is considered to exist in the human population along what is called a *normal distribution*. A normal distribution is essentially a statistical concept that relates to the ultimate range of any particular trait or psychological phenomenon across a population.

Individuals vary in how intelligent they are. A normal distribution (see Figure 6-1) is established by assuming that if the full population took an intelligence test, most people would center around average scores with some variation — from slightly less than average to slightly higher than average. A normal distribution is also referred to as a *bell curve* because it looks like a bell with a bulky center and flattening right and left ends. Most people are somewhere in the range of average intelligence. Increasingly fewer people are at intelligence levels that are closer to the highest and lowest ends of the spectrum.

At the high end of the intelligence curve are people considered *intellectually gifted*; at the low end are those considered *intellectually disabled.* (See Chapter 15 for more on intellectual disability.)

Shining bright

Einstein was a genius, right? So what exactly is a genius?

Psychologists typically refer to super-smart people as intellectually gifted rather than use the term genius. But there is no uniform cutoff score on an intelligence test to determine giftedness. An average standard intelligence score is 100 and, generally speaking, any score above 120 is considered superior. Giftedness is granted to people in the top 1 to 3 percent of the population. That is, out of 100 people, only one, two, or three are considered gifted.

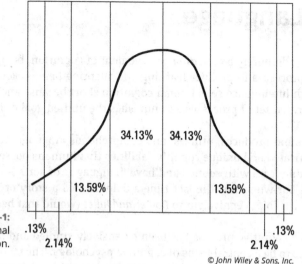

FIGURE 6-1:
Normal
distribution.

34.13% 34.13%

13.59% 13.59%

.13% .13%

2.14% 2.14%

© John Wiley & Sons, Inc.

WARNING

Many psychologists are wary of defining giftedness in such numerical and statistical terms and warn that cultural and societal context must be factored in. One culture's genius is another culture's madman? I'm not sure it's that dramatic, but it is important to consider that giftedness is multifaceted and not so easily tied to a cutoff score.

Numerous attempts have been made to pin down a definition of intellectual giftedness. Eminent American psychologist Robert Sternberg proposed that giftedness is more than superior skills related to information processing and analysis; it also includes superior ability to capitalize on and learn from one's experiences to quickly solve future problems and automatize problem solving. He proposed that gifted people are especially skilled at adapting to and selecting optimal environments in a way that goes beyond basic information processing and what is considered general intelligence or "g."

Researchers continue to examine the concept of intellectual giftedness, and one consistent finding is that gifted individuals have stronger *metacognitive skills,* or knowledge of their own mental processes and how to regulate them. These three specific metacognitive strategies are often used by gifted individuals:

» **Selective encoding:** Distinguishing between relevant and irrelevant information

» **Selective combination:** Pulling together seemingly disparate elements of a problem for a novel solution

» **Selective comparison:** Discovering new and nonobvious connections between new and old information

Figuring Out Language

Intelligence is definitely a crowning achievement of cognition, bringing together component processes to produce learning and adapting beings, you and me! But stopping with intelligence sells human cognition short because another amazing and sophisticated set of processes accomplishes the unified goal of language.

The human mind produces, utilizes, and comprehends language. It is one of the most sophisticated and unique cognitive abilities that humans possess. Yes, other species communicate with sounds and have "language" of sorts — think whales and birds — but when was the last time a dolphin told a story or wrote the *sus scrofa domesticus* (pigs) equivalent to *Romeo and Juliet* (would that be *Hamlet?*)

Language as a cognitive process has been extensively studied and hotly debated, and continues to be a central focus of cognitive psychology. The study of language in general is called *linguistics,* and the psychological study of language is called *psycholinguistics.*

Babel-On

Perhaps one of the most amazing things about language is that you and I ever learn how to do it. Babies don't come out talking. They take their time, absorbing and learning. Eventually sounds, words, sentences, paragraphs, stories, and treatises all come out.

In Chapter 12, I introduce language developmental milestones to give you a sense of what kinds of language should be happening when. This section describes the underlying cognitive models of how language develops in the first place.

Numerous models of language development exist in the fields of linguistics and psycholinguistics, but the three most prominent are *nativist, behaviorist,* and *interactionist.*

Nativist

Noam Chomsky, a philosopher, linguist, and political thinker, is the foremost proponent of nativist theory. The core of the nativist argument is that language is innate, essentially inborn, and wired into your DNA and brain development. In many ways it simply unfolds as does the development of the brain, liver, pancreas, and that weird-shaped birthmark on your back.

The rules of language are inborn in what Chomsky calls *Universal Grammar.* All speakers in the world, regardless of individual language differences possess this universal grammar as part of their human genetic endowment. Children can even create their own languages or various forms of slang with its own grammatical rules and structure because of something Chomksy calls the *language acquisition device* — an inborn cognitive module or mechanism that is triggered by language in the environment. Note that, according to his view, the module is only triggered; there is no learning from the environment going on.

Behaviorist

The behaviorist model says language is learned. People learn it by observing speakers in the world and through classical and operant conditioning processes. (See Chapter 8 for more on classical and operant conditioning.) Evidence in support of the behaviorist perspective includes the fact that it can take months and sometimes years for a person to develop proper language skills. Behaviorists believe this illustrates the learning process.

Interactionist

Nature or nurture? Both! Language is innate *and* learned according to this model. A prominent version of interactionist theory is the *social interactionist* approach, which holds that parents and mature language speakers model and provide a learning scaffold for language learners, guiding them toward mature and correct language use through social interaction.

Rules, syntax, and meaning

To understand how the mind does language, researchers have broken the it into different parts. Language, it seems, can be understood in terms of the rules of its use, known as *grammar.* Grammar is divided into three parts:

>> **Phonology:** The smallest units of speech (phonemes) that determine how sounds are used to make words

>> **Syntax:** Ways in which words and phrases are combined to make sentences

>> **Semantics:** Meaning

An estimated 800 or so different phonemes exist in the human language family. English speakers use 52; some languages use well over 100. Think about how various languages sound. Some seem faster. Some use guttural sounds; other seem smooth and airy. Different languages have different sounds and phoneme (the smallest distinct unit of sound in a language) use.

Consider this sentence: Store the to Jon went. Does that sound right to you? Probably not, because the rules of syntax determine how words are put together in a way that makes sense in a given language. Also, subtle changes in positions of words within a sentence can change the meaning of a particular phrase and convey a very different thought. Take the following words, for example, and see how rearranging them changes the meaning of each phrase drastically: robbed, Louis, bank, the.

Louis robbed the bank.

The bank robbed Louis.

These mean two very different things. Same words, different meanings depending on syntax. Either way, poor Louis.

I've noticed an interesting phenomenon when conducting cognitive testing and administering vocabulary tests. Certain wrong definitions occur over and over again. I ask a person the meaning of the word "yesterday," and she answers, "The things I did yesterday." Now, I'm not sure what that means per se, but the fact that this definition, albeit not really the right one, occurs again and again is fascinating. To these people, "yesterday" refers to the set of actions he or she engaged in on the previous day. The word means something different to them than it does to me.

Because I don't really know what they are talking about, we are not really communicating or understanding each other. The other person is not responding to the semantic rule of grammar that determines the shared and agreed upon definition of the word "yesterday."

Semantic rules determine that the meanings of words are universal or widely understood and agreed upon, which makes it possible to communicate. When you say "elephant," I know you're talking about a large animal with a long nose because of semantics. This all applies to signed languages, too, which have their own grammar and which will develop in the same way as spoken languages provided there is a rich signing environment around a deaf child.

Chapter 7

Needing, Wanting, Feeling

Why do people get up and go to work every day? Why did my teenage cousin get her bellybutton pierced? Why do people go to the gym? Honestly, I think the best part of psychology is getting to ask all these interesting questions!

But there isn't always a lot of mystery behind why people do what they do. Most of us work to pay the bills and earn money for vacations, comfort, and entertainment. You eat to stay alive. You tolerate irritating neighbors to avoid going to jail. These things make sense and don't usually require much thought. But when someone does something extraordinary, extremely difficult, or horrific, the "Why?" question comes up.

Why would Mother Teresa dedicate the greater part of her life to working with the sick and the poor in India? She lived in abject poverty, sacrificing all comfort in order to help the poor and seemingly forgotten. Why would she do such a thing? Mother Teresa's dedication to her religious calling and duty was remarkable. She endured harsh conditions and stayed the course; her motivation was strong and unyielding. Were her actions a result of love for the people she helped?

In this chapter, I introduce the psychological approach to motivation. Simply knowing the nuts and bolts of an action leaves a gaping hole in what you know about behavior if you don't know why someone chooses a certain course of action — or at least why he thinks he does something.

In addition to exploring the various theories of motivation, I also take a look at emotions, which some psychologists tag as the primary motivating factors for all of us. Psychologists make a big deal about emotions because of the central role emotions play in human behavior and mental processes. "Why we do what we do" has a lot to do with the way we feel.

What's My Motivation?

You're auditioning for a part in a movie. You're given a few lines to read in front of a panel. Now, get into character and start acting! Action! You go for it, and the panel interrupts you saying, "I'm not feeling it." You start up again. They stop you again. They just aren't convinced! Finally, in frustration you say, "What's my motivation? Why am acting this way and saying these things" It's a cliché by now but it is said that actors will often need to understand where characters are coming from or what they are motivated by in order to "get into character." In other words, why is that character acting that way? Isn't the character "driven" to do something, get something, achieve something, avoid something, go for something?

Just like understanding a character's motivation, psychologists want to know what people's motivations are, where they come from, and what we do because of them. Many of the chapters in this book talk about "how" mental processes and behavior are "done." There is some motivation-related material here and there, but this chapter focuses on the "why" question so central to so much of psychology. I've never conducted a scientific survey, but anecdotal data shows that the question of why people do what they do is at least in the top two of questions I am asked. (The other is "Why do I feel this way?" We'll get more into emotions later in the chapter.)

Professor Lambert Deckers at Ball State University states that to be "motivated" is to be moved into action by either a *motive* or an *incentive*. He defines a motive as an internal state that pushes us toward a desired result. An incentive is something valuable in the environment that we are driven to pursue or acquire. Motives can be biological, such as hunger, or psychological, such as the need to create or be creative. Incentives can be biological, like food, and psychological, such as a good grade.

In the following sections, I describe the various theories related to the sources and structures of motivation — ranging from basic genetics to striving for independence and relief from psychological pain.

Would you like some adrenaline with that bear?

Over the course of human evolution, certain behaviors were naturally selected (put in the "to keep" pile) because they contribute to the survival of particular individuals in a species. Imagine a group of people that lives in a forest with wolves, bears, and various other dangerous beasts. Now, imagine that a group of three men and three women from this community encounters a bear. One man and one woman take off running the instant they see the bear, and they get away. Another man and woman stand there, frozen in their tracks. They become the bear's lunch. The final couple tries to fight the bear with sticks and rocks. They lose.

If the man and woman who ran away decide to have a child, there's a good chance that their child will be a runner when it comes to encounters with bears. The other couples (the freezers and the fighters) died, so they can't have children. This is a crude illustration of how evolution selects for traits that help us survive. Those who survive reproduce. It is safe to assume that the couple that ran away had better instincts than the other two couples. Their instincts were better in the sense that they were able to stay alive. Instincts that help keep us alive stay in the gene pool.

From an evolutionary perspective, motivation is behavior directed at passing on our genes. In 1976, evolutionary biologist Richard Dawkins wrote a seminal book called *The Selfish Gene* (Oxford University Press). Dawkins proposed that that we are driven or motivated to pass on our genes. For Dawkins, the basic "unit" of motivation is the gene. So the next time you do something and are questioned, you can claim, "My selfish genes made me do it!"

How do genes get passed on? We survive by adapting, and when we survive, we mate and pass on our genes. Adaptation is key. If we don't adapt, then we die, and if we die before we mate, we don't pass on our genes.

Before you jump to conclusions that this whole thing sounds like a justification for selfishness and self-centeredness, think about that mating component. In order to mate effectively, we have to cooperate. Cooperative mating works best. We need to pass on our genes; we have to mate before we die; we have to cooperate to mate.

Dawkins was really an advocate for cooperation in the form of *altruism.* Zoologists A. Gardner and J.J. Welch tell us that altruistic genes are the best guarantors of survival of a species. Altruism can be defined as a behavior that benefits another's chance of adapting and surviving at the expense of oneself. This might sound contradictory because how can sacrificing myself help my selfish genes go on? To answer that question, we have to look at whom we are most likely motivated to be altruistic towards. We are most motivated to be altruistic to family or kin. Altruism makes sense when it comes to family or kin because we share genes with them. So if I have to sacrifice my individual genes for the sake of my family's genes, then I've increased the probability that my genes will go on. Sacrificing oneself in this case is a better genetic bet and a better play. So help out. It's good for your genes.

Feeling needy

Many people can relate to being worried about money and finances. I'm sure that even the billionaires of the world have spent one or two sleepless nights of their lives mentally counting their Benjamins. Some of us have learned to live on a budget, setting aside money for the mortgage, car payments, medical insurance, and household costs — even keeping a little money for entertainment if there's any left over. When I started living on a budget, something weird began to happen. When I went to a store and saw something I liked, such as a pair of shoes or fancy power tool, I asked myself if I really needed it. Part of developing a budget involves figuring out what you truly need and what your financial priorities are.

I first spend my money on what I need. My needs are a powerful determinant in what I do with my money. I may even say that I'm *driven* (or pushed) by my prioritized needs. Satisfying my needs is one of my top, if not the top, drives in my life. Needs drive my behavior; they motivate me.

Clark Hull came up with a theory of motivation that emphasized need satisfaction. Needs are generated from two things: *homeostasis* and *equilibrium restoration*. I experience homeostasis when my needs are met and I feel balanced — not in need of anything. When my needs aren't being met, I find myself out of balance, and I'm then motivated to restore the equilibrium through the satisfaction of my needs.

Hull's theory is called *drive reduction theory* because people are driven to satisfy their needs. *Drives* are motivations toward satisfaction and homeostasis. There are two kinds of drives:

>> Biological needs that are necessary for survival are called *primary drives*. Hunger, fatigue, and thirst are all examples of primary drives. If you think about it, primary drives play a pretty big role in everyday life. A large part of the day revolves around satisfying hunger and obtaining shelter.

>> Any need other than a primary drive is called a *secondary drive*. A lot of these are learned from families, social groups, and the larger culture. The importance of secondary drives is determined by how they become associated with primary drives. People are driven to go to school and get good grades in order to have a better life and provide for themselves and their families. Secondary drives have no inherent worth; they only matter as they relate to primary drives.

REMEMBER

One of the limitations of drive reduction theory is that it leaves no room for needs that seem only peripherally related to our biological survival. Does a day of surfing restore my homeostatic balance? What basic need does surfing satisfy? I may be able to stretch it a little and say that I make it a point to go surfing because if I don't, I'll get depressed and then I won't be able to go to work and then I won't be able to eat. That would make surfing a secondary drive at the bottom of a long chain of other secondary drives. But most people probably don't reduce, consciously anyway, their every activity to the lowest common denominator of biological survival.

Although it's not technically an instinct theory, Abraham Maslow's motivational theory states that motivations stem from a basic set of needs that you naturally strive to satisfy. Maslow believed that some needs are more basic than others. Eating is more basic than getting an A on your English final. They're both needs (for some people anyway), but one is more fundamental than the other.

REMEMBER

Maslow created a priority list of needs that he arranged into a triangle called the *hierarchy of needs:*

>> At the lowest and most foundational level are *basic physical needs* for food, water, and sleep. These needs direct behavior until they are satisfied.

>> The next level of the triangle contains needs for *safety and security* such as proper shelter and protection.

>> *Love and belonging* is the next level of need.

>> The fourth level of need is *self-esteem*, striving toward situations that enhance self-worth.

>> *Self-actualization* — the need to fulfill our top potential and to live at a high level of awareness of ourselves and our desires — is the top level. When someone has reached the highest part of the triangle/hierarchy, he has a *peak experience,* or a feeling that signals arrival at the highest level of motivation. It is important to point out though that even for one who self-actualizes, these peak experiences are brief and infrequent. A person does not settle in at the level of peak experiences.

Knowing who's the boss

Freedom may be the best motivator of all. Throughout history, societies and large groups have sacrificed their lives for the right to determine their own fates, make their own decisions, and be masters of their own lives. The U.S. Declaration of Independence, authored by Thomas Jefferson, is perhaps the quintessential document of such self-determination, the right to determine one's actions without compulsion from others or outside influence.

Edward Deci and Richard Ryan proposed a psychological theory of motivation known as *self-determination theory (SDT)*. It states that the human motives for competence, autonomy, and relatedness are at the center of what drives behavior. These fellows may even be considered the "Thomas Jeffersons" of motivational psychology. They propose and cite research to support the concept that the needs to feel competent, autonomous, and related are universal human needs and found in all cultures. These needs are considered necessary for people to feel a sense of well-being and to perform or achieve at an optimal level at life's tasks such as work, school, and relationships. SDT acknowledges two different kinds of motivation:

>> **Autonomous motivation** is *intrinsic,* or internal, to a person; it comes from within and reflects a sense of non-coercion and freedom of choice.

>> **Controlled motivation** is a function of external contingencies and rewards or punishments such as shame, pay, or public recognition.

Controlled motivation is associated with feelings of being pressured to think, feel, or act according to some external standard as opposed to an individual's internal standard. A wonderful historical example of autonomous motivation is the great American Rosa Parks, an African American woman who challenged racial segregation in the United States by sitting in the "white only" seats on a public bus. She was brave enough to sit on a bus seat of her own choosing. Despite the pressure to conform and concede and have her motivation "controlled," *she chose* where to sit, was autonomously motivated, and changed history. According to SDT, it is best to be in control of one's self, to be one's own boss, to have the freedom to make choices; this satisfies a basic human need and drives motivation.

Deci and Ryan consider autonomy to be synonymous with being in control of oneself, to regulate oneself, to engage in *self-regulation*. Whereas SDT refers to the human need and motive to be autonomous and in control of oneself, *self-regulation* is a set of psychological controls over emotions, behavior, and thoughts in a manner that is consistent with meeting personal goals. SDT can be considered the "why" of human behavior but self-regulation is the "how."

Psychologist Andrea Burger defines self-regulation as an individual's ability to monitor and modulate cognition, emotion, and behavior to accomplish goals, and/or to adapt to the demands of specific situations. Self-regulated behavior involves controlled, focused, and attentive thought and action as opposed to impulsive and reactive action. Self-determination, it would seem, is not possible without adequate self-regulation.

Being autonomous and in control of yourselves is all well and good, but many people have had the experience of letting themselves down after a resolution to diet, exercise, quit smoking, or change some other undesirable aspect of their behavior. They "want" to diet but they overeat. They want to exercise, but they end up watching that movie they rented instead.

This is where the concept of willpower comes in. There is a struggle for self-control going on, a struggle of the will. Roy Baumeister defines *willpower* as the ability to resist short-term temptations in order to meet long-term goals. Some psychologists consider willpower a logical component of self-regulation, to be in control of oneself in the face of competing or contradictory motives or impulses. You can diet and lose weight or enjoy eating that entire plate of kung pao chicken and bloat.

Psychologist Walter Mischel in the 1960s conducted a very simple but powerful set of experiments popularly known as the "marshmallow studies." Basically, the experimental subject, a child, is offered a small reward such as a marshmallow but is told by the researcher that he or she could get a bigger reward if they don't eat the marshmallow while the researcher steps out of the room for a short time. If they delay their gratification for a short time, they will get a bigger reward. Well, some children could do it and some could not. Those who could were considered to have stronger abilities to delay gratification. Follow-up research on those same children many years later showed that children who could delay had better academic outcomes and were less likely to be overweight.

Research suggests that willpower is a psychological ability that exists in all people to a greater or lesser extent. Willpower has been likened to a "mental muscle" that can grow, get stronger, weaken, fatigue, and even atrophy. Strong willpower has been associated with success at behavioral change such as quitting smoking or sticking to an exercise regime.

REMEMBER

Stress and needing to resist too much temptation have been found to weaken will-power. This is why it's probably a good idea to avoid going to a donut shop when all you want is a cup of coffee. Unless of course you've already "chosen" to eat an apple fritter or a chocolate twist.

Arousing interest in prime rib

Optimal level of arousal theory is considered a more refined version of drive reduction theory. Instead of just being driven to satisfy basic biological needs at a minimum level, this theory states that people are motivated to reach the highest level of satisfaction possible.

What do I mean by "highest level of satisfaction"? Think of this as the "prime rib theory" of arousal. When my body needs energy, I get hungry, and I develop a primary drive or motivation to eat something. Now, if this theory was the "hamburger theory" of arousal or the "minimal level of arousal theory," then I'd just get a greasy drive-through cheeseburger and be done with it. But why would I eat hamburger if I can eat steak? I can satisfy the primary need and also enjoy great flavor at the same time.

REMEMBER

Another component of the optimal level of arousal theory involves being driven to seek the best (optimal) level of arousal in order to maximize performance. In an example of how optimal level of arousal theory may work, in 1908 psychologists Yerkes and Dodson found that people perform activities best when moderately aroused — not too relaxed, not too uptight. This is called the Yerkes-Dodson law.

Have you ever had to make a presentation in front of a large group or class? Were you nervous? If so, how nervous? Throwing-up, passing-out nervous? Being that nervous constitutes an extreme level of arousal; and if you've been there, you know it doesn't contribute to a top-notch performance. Similarly, if someone is too relaxed, he may not put out enough effort to properly prepare for the presentation, and he may end up giving a terrible performance. The best place to be is right in the middle.

Getting cheaper long distance is rewarding

When I come home and find the red light on my answering machine flashing, I wonder who called. Was it a friend I haven't talked to in a while? A long-lost relative? No, it was one of those annoying long-distance phone companies trying to get me to change my provider.

A lot of marketing efforts are based on a motivational theory called *expectancy theory*. Expectancy theory holds that motivations are the product of an individual's analysis of the potential rewards associated with a particular behavior and the likelihood of achieving those rewards. Long-distance carriers count on me associating a switch with an expectation of a reward. This is a straightforward but powerful means of motivating people, especially if you can get them thinking that the rewards are likely to come rolling in!

Incentive theory, which is closely related to expectancy theory, simply states that we are motivated to seek rewards and avoid negative experiences such as pain. My experience with spam email ads has led me to expect pain in my inbox from unsolicited purveyors of stuff I don't need every day, which overpowers the expected reward of saving a few bucks from their "great deals." What I expect, whether it's really the case or not, ultimately has a powerful effect on my behavior. When I see these emails I don't even open them, I just delete them.

Facing your opponent-process theory

Sometimes I am motivated to do things that aren't much fun, like going to the gym — at least I don't think that's much fun. Some people may like it. But the point is that people can engage in behaviors that seem more painful than pleasurable on the surface. This doesn't mean that they have some masochistic need or instinct. Motivations that may appear outwardly painful and not so pleasurable can sometimes be explained with the *opponent-process theory*, which states that people are motivated not by the initial response or incentive, like the pain of a tough workout, but by the reaction that occurs after the initial response, like the reflection of a toned, fit, and healthy body in the mirror looking back at me.

For every response that occurs, there's an opposite reaction called the *opponent process*. After being exposed to a particular stimulus for a while, the initial response diminishes, and the opposite response grows stronger.

A lot of people like to eat hot and spicy foods. Personally, I like to taste my food, not feel it for 20 minutes after I take a bite, but to each his own. What's the opposite response, the opponent process, of hot foods? It's the endorphins — those natural painkillers released by the body to combat pain. Spicy foods actually chemically burn the tongue, and the body combats those burns with these natural painkillers. It feels good when the endorphin painkillers kick in to soothe the burning. People who enjoy hot foods think that they eat spicy foods for the spice, but according to opponent-process theory, they're just a bunch of endorphin junkies. Yep, they're burning their tongues in order to benefit from the opposite or *opponent* reaction of endorphin release!

The opponent-process theory has been used to explain the sometimes baffling affliction of drug addiction. Of course, when a substance or drug is used there is a high, euphoria, and an experience of pleasant feelings. Once the effects of the drug wear off, however, there is an unpleasant experience from the aftereffects of the drug. According to the opponent-process theory, the addicted person then uses the drugs again to get relief from those unpleasant experiences. They don't use for the initial high necessarily — they use to alleviate the negative aftereffects.

Believing in yourself

Everyone knows Lebron James, right? He's perhaps the best professional basketball player of all time. Looking at Lebron James provides a good primer to discuss the *social-cognitive theory of motivation*. To many (at least those who root for the team Lebron is not on), James looks like an ego-maniac who's cocky and too self-assured. Regardless of whether you have a negative view of him or not, Lebron shows us how believing in oneself can fuel us and motivate us toward a goal. Lebron wanted to be the best and has worked his tail off to get there. The point is not that Lebron has succeeded but that his belief in himself drives him obsessively and relentlessly. Lebron works out all year long; he watches his diet; he practices and practices and practices. Because Lebron believes these efforts will get him there, he keeps working hard.

The social-cognitive theory of motivation proposes that people are motivated to act towards meeting their goals and that the evaluation of their ongoing behavior provides feedback as to whether they are moving in the right direction. This process can be broken down into five critical components laid out by Dale Schunk and Ellen Usher as follows:

>> **Goals and self-evaluation:** These are the targets of our behavior, what we are trying to achieve or maintain. Without goals, we have no targets, and without targets, we have unfocused motivation, which really amounts to little motivation. (Unless one's goal is to not have goals, but that's another discussion for you nihilists.) The self-evaluation component refers to the process in which we evaluate our current progress relative to the goal. Are we moving in the right direction? If we are, we keep going, and if there's a gap, we can double or triple our efforts. Either way, we are motivated to close the gap; we don't just give up! Lebron hasn't.

>> **Outcome expectations:** We are motivated to act in ways that we *believe* are going to move us closer to our goals. We also seek to interact with people who we believe are going to help us get there. Expectations can motivate us over long periods of time, as we believe we will get there eventually if we just keep going.

>> **Values:** We are motivated to act in ways that are in accordance with what we value. For example, I am motivated to work hard during the week so that I can take my kids surfing on the weekend. I value my time with them, teaching them something fun and healthy, watching them gain confidence, and just watching them feel good and have a good time.

>> **Social comparison:** We are motivated to engage in behavior that shows improvement relative to other people who are working toward the same goals we have. Lebron is motivated to be the best basketball player, so he compares himself to the his peers and the best that came before him, like Michael Jordan. He strives to have more points than Karl Malone or Kareem Abdul-Jabbar.

>> **Self-efficacy:** The more we believe in our ability to achieve our goal(s), the more we will be motivated towards it. This isn't saying that self-efficacy is a guarantee of success, but it can be fuel for the road. We base this belief on four sources of information:

- **Mastery experiences:** We look at what we've actually accomplished or achieved so far to tell us if we are efficacious.

- **Vicarious experiences:** Watching others achieve our goals gives us confidence that it "can be done!"

- **Forms of social persuasion:** We are motivated by the encouragement from others who are seen as qualified and credible.

- **Physiological indexes:** Anxiety, stress, and other strong emotions can provide feedback about actual progress or anticipated progress towards a goal. Anxiety might let me know that I'm off target or that something is blocking me, for example.

Pleasure and pain

It is as close to truism as there is in life that we are motivated to seek out pleasure and to avoid or escape pain. These motives cut across the animal kingdom. Nobel Laureate and musician Bob Dylan says as much in his song "Silvio":

Since every pleasure's got an edge of pain, Pay for your ticket and don't complain

Bob Dylan would have made one heck of a psychologist.

Over the years, psychoanalysis has had much to say about motivation with regards to pleasure and pain. In his 1920 essay "Beyond the Pleasure Principle," Sigmund Freud proposes that our primary motivation is the *pleasure principle*, a life instinct relentlessly driven by a force Freud called the *libido* (essentially "desire"). Freud's psychoanalytic theory of motivation is used more in psychoanalytic/psychodynamic therapy than as a scientific model of motivation. It nonetheless places pursuit of survival stimuli front and center in the study of motivation.

Whether one is a follower of Freud and psychoanalysis or not, the importance of the study of desire for understanding of motivation is critical. Wilhelm Hofmann and Loran F. Nordgren state, "Desire propels us to action" and "Desires are key motivators in our lives."

In the 1950s, James Olds and Peter Milner discovered what they considered a "pleasure center" in the brains of rats. Rats would obsessively and repeatedly press a lever to receive electrical stimulation to that center in the brain. They would do it thousands of times per hour. The rats would even choose this stimulation over food. But before you start thinking that rats are just greedy and lustful little buggers, these results were repeated in primates and human subjects as well.

Later research showed that this "pleasure" center was an area of the brain with a high concentration of the neurotransmitter dopamine. However, still later research showed that viewing dopamine as the "pleasure chemical" was not quite right. Research has continued to develop an understanding of the brain systems involved in pleasure seeking. Research by Pecina and Berridge showed that pleasure in the brain is tied to a network of sites in the brain known as *hedonic hotspots* that serve to amplify the "pleasure-ness" of a stimulus or stimuli. But researchers still weren't content (their hotspots were not fired up) and eventually returned to dopamine as a primary motivator in driving us toward pleasurable experiences. This research makes a distinction between "liking" and "wanting." Dopamine is involved in the "wanting" process, driving motivation.

Of course we go for the pleasure! But don't we also avoid pain? The psychologist E. Tory Higgins reminds us that "people are motivated to approach pleasure and avoid pain." This is called the *hedonic principle,* which is the "basic motivational assumption of theories across all areas of psychology." In 1959, psychologist Theodore Christian Schneirla, in his study of aplysia (sea slug), showed that at a very basic level, organisms approach stimuli that represent "survival" and avoid stimuli that represent "not surviving" or threats. Although they are essentially synonymous, a survey of the literature will lead you to two "versions" of this "going towards and going away" conceptualization of motivation: *appetitive/defensive* and *approach/avoidance.*

However, E. Tory Higgins proposes that a simple approach/avoidance concept is limited and introduces the concept of *regulatory focus* to improve upon it. The key point is that people are motivated to reduce the gap between current states and desired end states. We approach stimuli that get us closer to our desired end state and avoid stimuli that move us away or block the achievement of that end state. These focus us on promotion of end state behaviors and prevention of "not end state" behaviors.

Escaping psychological pain

So far, I've discussed motivation from the perspective of moving toward pleasure and avoiding threat. But what if the treat is already on you and you haven't successfully avoid it? What then? There's more to staying alive than avoiding. Of course, tell that to someone who suffers from agoraphobia. This is where the concept of *escape* or *escape motivation* comes in. Escaping a threat or dangerous situation is a "no brainer," studied in animals and humans alike. For animals, research has posited this escape response as something they do to avoid predation or getting eaten, which doesn't really apply to humans except in zombie movies and when swimming with sharks. The difference between escape and avoidance is that escape motivations kick in once avoidance is not possible.

Pain is a hell of a motivator. Psychological pain is no different. According to psychologist Alan Fogel, the same brain areas that are activated during physical pain are also activated during emotional pain. Fogel asks the question, "Where does emotional pain hurt?" After all, it's not like we skinned our knee. So where is the corresponding skinned emotional knee? Fogel proposes that emotional pain must have a location. Fogel cites research done on social rejection and cites that both behavioral medicine and health psychology show that when we are in the presence of loved ones, we have a vagal-parasympathetic response that makes us feel calm, slows our heart rate down, and slows are breathing. The opposite happens when we are withdrawn from our loved ones. The sympathetic nervous system kicks in and we get stressed out. All of this happens in the chest area by the way, so heartache really is a physiological reality.

Psychological pain is our achy sympathetic nervous system. Is that it? That's what is going on when we are wrought with emotional pain when our child suffers from cancer, a loved one is hurt in an accident, or our marriage of 20 years comes to a crashing end? People who suffer from depression or schizophrenia have described it as a painful experience. What are they talking about then? Biologists, neurobiologists, and the like might argue that the concept of psychological pain is too elusive, too subjective, to be adequately studied. Psychologists have never shied away from subjectivity. Moreover, the International Association for the Study of Pain (IASP) states, "If people regard their experience as pain and if they report it in the same ways as pain caused by tissue damage, it should be accepted as pain."

Finding relief

Relief from mental pain can come from many sources. Seeking proximity and connection from a nurturing person, self-care in the form of engaging in healthy behaviors such as exercise or eating right, psychotherapy, and prayer are all ways people use to find relief from psychological pain. Unfortunately these aren't the only ways. Some people seek to relieve mental pain in less than healthy or helpful ways, such as abusing alcohol or drugs, self-harm, and even suicide. These motives seem paradoxical and self-contradictory. Unfortunately, there are people who are driven in these directions. We may know someone or have family members that have displayed one or all of these behaviors.

Self-destructive behaviors

Research on self-destructive or self-damaging behavior (drug abuse, risk-taking behavior, self-harm) demonstrates that these behaviors are used as an attempt at controlling chaotic, dangerous, fear-inducing, and emotionally painful experiences. We often ask why someone continues to drink when the consequences are so dire. Why would someone cut themselves? Why would someone kill themselves? Although discussion of this goes way beyond this section, one consistent finding is that avoiding and escaping psychological pain is a common denominator. Painful emotion can be a trigger for relapse in recovering alcoholics. A breakup can be a trigger for someone cutting their arm with a safety pin. Being trapped in an abusive relationship can be a trigger for a suicide attempt. Again, all of these behaviors are examples of avoiding or escaping pain, even if they seem to be paradoxical and self-defeating. These seemingly self-destructive behaviors are essentially "rational" in this regard. They are attempts to alleviate suffering and therefore not so paradoxical after all.

Psychological pain and suicide

There is perhaps no other psychologist more associated with the concept of psychological pain than Edwin Shneidman. Dr. Shneidman started looking into the relationship between psychological pain and suicide in the 1950s when he engaged in a research study looking at the suicide notes of people who completed suicide. From these notes, he began to formulate the concept of *psychache*. In his book *Suicide as Psychache: A Clinical Approach to Self-Destructive Behavior* (Rowan & Littlefield Publishers, Inc, 1993) he states,

> Nearing the end of my career in suicidology, I think I can now say what has been on my mind in as few as five words: Suicide is caused by psychache. Psychache refers to the hurt, anguish, soreness, aching, psychological pain in the psyche, the mind. It is intrinsically psychological — the pain of excessively felt shame, or guilt, or humiliation, or loneliness, or fear, or angst, or dread of growing old, or of dying badly, or whatever.

There is of course the subjective experience component to this concept, and Dr. Shneidman proposes that it depends upon an individual's threshold for enduring psychological pain. He states that any attempt to understand suicide in terms of sex, age, race, or socioeconomics will fall short. It is the simple motivation to escape and find relief from suffering.

Launching Countless Bad Poems: Emotions

Emotion and motivation are intimately related. When I need something, I am motivated to satisfy that need. When my stomach growls, I know I'm hungry. But how do I know when other, more psychological needs aren't being met, like the need for self-esteem? When certain personal needs aren't being met, emotions send out a signal. Emotions can indicate that you are not reaching your motivational goals (in the form of disappointment, for example) or that you are meeting your motivational goals (perhaps in the form of happiness). They can tell us when something feels good and we should do more of it and when something feels bad and we should do less of it. In a word, emotions are adaptive. Psychologists have been interested in emotions since the inception of the formal field. Nowadays, emotion theory and research is sometimes referred to as *affective science*, the scientific study of emotion or affect.

Before we go on I think it's important to address a few definitional issues. Many terms are out there that refer to emotions such as *affect*, *mood*, and *feelings*. Here is what the APA Dictionary of Psychology offers:

>> **Affect:** A person's *experience* of a feeling or emotion.

>> **Emotion:** A complex *reaction pattern* involving experiential, behavioral, and physiological elements by which an individual attempts to deal with a personally significant matter or event. The specific quality of the emotion (for example, fear or shame) is determined by the specific significance of the event.

>> **Mood:** Any short-lived *emotional state*, usually of low intensity (like a cheerful mood or an irritable mood). Moods differ from emotions in lacking an object. For example, the emotion of anger can be aroused by an insult, but an angry mood may arise when one does not know what one is angry about or what elicited the anger.

>> **Feeling:** A self-contained *phenomenal experience*. Feelings are subjective, evaluative, and independent of the sensations, thoughts, or images evoking them.

From these definitions it looks, like affect and feelings are most similar. Mood is more long term and lasting, like a sustained emotion over a period of time. Emotion has a lot more going on than the rest and is probably our best bet in terms of it being observable and measurable. For our purposes, I am going to use emotion for the remainder of the chapter. In the following sections, I define emotion, explore its functions, and discuss how emotions can be "used" to improve functioning.

REMEMBER

An *emotion* is a complex reaction pattern with three interrelated components:

>> **Experiential/subjective experience:** When I have a particular emotion, I call this a *feeling*. My experience of sadness may consist of wanting to cry and lacking energy or motivation. This is my experience of sadness; it's subjective.

>> **Behavioral/expressive component:** Each emotion is expressed and communicated in a unique way. Facial expressions, body language, posture, words, phrases, gestures, and numerous other means of expression accompany and communicate the experience of an emotion.

>> **Physiological response:** All emotions are comprised of responses that involve brain and nervous system activity. When I'm angry, my heart beats quickly and my breathing rates increases. When I'm sad I may feel tired.

Watch out for that sabertooth!

Research on emotions over the years spans the whole range of psychological science, with *evolutionary psychology* being no exception. Psychologists subscribing to this perspective view specific behaviors and mental processes as adaptive responses developed through natural selection. Emotions are assumed to be part of this adaptation process.

Cosmides and Tooby propose an extensive set of behavioral and mental programs (think computer programs) that help people address the challenges of survival. Each program functions independently, which creates a logistical nightmare. If you think getting ready for a camping trip is logistically difficult, try coordinating all the behaviors and mental processes that humans possess! This is where emotions come into play.

Cosmides and Tooby view emotions as "master programs" of sorts, working to organize and integrate all those behaviors and thoughts. From this perspective, emotions serve a regulatory function. They help people figure out what they need to do in a particular situation and whether or not they've accomplished a desired goal. Cosmides and Tooby list the following "programs" regulated by emotion:

>> Perceptual mechanisms

>> Attention

>> Memory

>> Categorization

>> Motivational priorities

>> Current goals

>> Information gathering adaptations

>> Specialized inference mechanisms

>> Communication and expression

>> Learning processes

>> Reflexes

>> Energy level, mood, and effort allocation

>> Physiology

>> Behavior

So this list essentially places emotion at the center of coordinating nearly all mental processes and behavior for the sake of survival.

More thoughts on the evolutionary "usefulness" of emotions comes from a field called *evolutionary psychiatry*. Randolph M. Nesse, MD, proposes a similar role for emotions in adaptation but comes at it from the angle of mental illness in his book, *Good Reasons for Bad Feelings: Insights from the Frontier of Evolutionary Psychiatry* (Dutton–Penguin Randomhouse LLC, 2019). Nesse proposes that evolution not only "selected" emotions for an adaptive purpose but also kept mental disorders related to emotions around for a good reason as well. He states the following:

> Why do mental disorders exist at all? Natural selection could have eliminated the anxiety, depression, addiction, anorexia, and the genes that cause autism, schizophrenia, and manic-depressive illness. But it didn't. Why not?

He proposes that in studying emotional disorders, we learn more about why emotions exist in the first place. He states that there are obstacles in understanding the evolutionary role of emotions such as viewing negative emotions as "not useful." He proposes that the symptoms often presented to mental health professionals provide useful clues to something that is "wrong" and needs to be addressed, emotional symptoms included. Think of it like this: If I have strong sadness around an issue or event, then my attention (and my therapist's) should be drawn to that issue or event, not just the strong sadness. Negative emotions are indicator lights on the dashboard of functioning. Hesse calls this the *Smoke Detector Principle*. Emotions in general and negative emotions in particular are useful. He states,

> In the face or threats or losses, anxiety and sadness are useful, but happy relaxation is worse than useless. . ..The advantage [however] goes not to individuals who are constantly anxious, sad, or joyful but to those who experience anxiety when loss is threatened, sadness after a loss, and enthusiasm and joy in the face of opportunity and success.

I once told a professor of mine that PTSD (posttraumatic stress disorder) exists to show us that trauma is bad and that if we only pay attention to the symptoms, we wouldn't work to reduce or eliminate the causes of it, like war, violence, abuse, or neglect. So I was proposing that PTSD is useful! He looked at me like I was crazy. Maybe.

Your brain on emotion

Ever met someone who gets really lovey, nostalgic, and overly emotional when under the influence of alcohol? You know, the sentimental drunk? This common phenomenon is a pretty good indicator that our brains definitely have something to do with emotions. Researchers looking for emotions "in the brain" have made pretty good progress over the years.

FEELINGS SAVE LIVES

TIP

In addition to signaling whether someone has achieved his or her goals or not, emotions have a couple of other functions. Emotions prepare people for and alert them to potentially dangerous situations. Gavin De Becker sings high praises for this function of emotions in his book, *The Gift of Fear* (Dell Publishing). In a sentence, fear saves our lives. Have you ever been in a situation where you got that feeling that something just wasn't right? That "feeling" was your emotions alerting you to the possible presence of danger that you may have not consciously observed or been aware of. De Becker advocates listening to that voice more often and being more attuned to it as a powerful survival tool.

Positive emotions can provide relief from the trials and tribulations of life. Happiness feels good. What would life be like if you never felt happy? Pretty miserable, obviously! It's easier to have a good relationship with someone who is happy. Happiness also leads to socializing, which may lead to romance, which may lead to children, which may lead to passing on whatever genes worked to produce that happy procreator in the first place. Positive emotions have the potential to make people more attractive and allow for social connection.

Antonio Damasio tells us that emotions are at the center for evaluating what is ultimately of value for us as we go about interacting with the environment. He even proposes that emotions play a significant role in our construction of and experience of the self. He states, "Emotions proper are merely an integrated jewel of life regulation." (*Self Comes to Mind: Constructing the Conscious Brain*, Pantheon Books, 2010). Images of objects or events in the current environment or from recall and memory trigger a chain of emotional responses across multiple regions of the brain and body that are mobilized to address the stimulus with coordinated actions of mental processes, behavior, and physiological responses. The brain receives a signal; emotions are activated and set in motion other parts of the brain to mobilize action; other parts of the brain look for feedback through perception or external or internal events (called *interoception*) and so on until the situation, problem, or event is dealt with successfully or resolved. The whole process is complicated and beautiful.

Psychologist Josepeh Ledoux is a rock star in psychology (along with Albert Bandura, Martin Seligman, Mary Ainsworth, Carol Gilligan, and many others). He has extensively studied emotion in general and fear specifically. Ledoux defines emotions as "non-conscious brain states that connect significant stimuli with response mechanisms." Ledoux's study of fear led him to propose that there is difference between our conscious experience of an emotion, the *feeling*, and the brain activation underlying it, emotion. The emotion of fear is the activation of an underlying brain circuit that is designed to detect and help us respond to threat and danger. He calls this brain circuit the *defense motive state*.

When I see that car barreling up on me in the rearview mirror while I'm standing dead still in traffic with no option for escape, I'm not having the emotion of fear; I'm have the emotion of "brain responding to threat or danger state activation" (formally known as the artist "fear"). It is interesting to note that psychoanalysts have long thought that unconscious processes (like the activity of the defense motive state) influence our behavior outside our conscious awareness, and by bringing that experience to conscious awareness (into the feeling experience), a client could modify that process for the better. Freud seemed to be on the right track, but he didn't have an MRI or electrodes to help him out.

Yes, all of this "processing" is fine and dandy, but you might be asking, "Where *in* the brain are emotions?" Anita Deak of the University of Pecs in Hungary provides an excellent overview of research that answers that very question. She summarizes the literature that identifies the following brain areas as critical to emotion:

>> **Amygdala:** This brain area can be found in the inside layer of the temporal lobe and is involved in emotional learning, emotional memory, the processing of emotional signals from other parts of the brain, and emotion detection.

>> **Insula:** This area is located at the outside layer of the temporal lobe and is involved in the perception of emotional triggering events that are recalled from memory or imagined and the coordination of sensory and motor (movement) responses to unpredictable, threatening stimuli.

>> **Anterior cingulate cortex:** This is part of the limbic system and is located on the "top" of the brain toward the front. It is involved in the monitoring and evaluation of emotion by integrating autonomic nervous system functions (like heartrate and respiration), emotional signals from other parts of the brain, and attention systems in the brain.

>> **Orbitofrontal cortex:** Located just above the eyes, in the forehead, the OFC is involved in integrating sensory information in order to modulate sensory and cognitive processes through feedback and subsequently influence autonomic and motor responses.

Which comes first, the body or the mind?

If emotions consist of three components — subjective experience, physiological reactions, and the expressive component — which comes first? Do I think and feel angry before my muscles tense up? Do I say I'm angry before I know I'm angry? Figuring out this process can get confusing; it's like the chicken or the egg argument for emotions. But don't worry; Farmer Cash — that's me! — is here for you to put all the eggs in the right basket. Three main theories address the birth order of emotion components.

James-Lange theory

The *James-Lange theory* attempts to make sense of this mess. When a person encounters a situation or stimulus that leads to an emotional reaction, his body reacts first. There is a set of automatic physical reactions to emotional stimuli. The sensory systems respond by sending signals to the emotional centers of the brain, creating a state of arousal. After this physiological reaction, the brain analyzes what is occurring. Finally, after arousal and appraisal, the subjective experience of the emotion occurs. The brain then recognizes fear, for example, after interpreting this long chain of physiological reactions. Emotional expression comes after recognition of an experience of emotion.

First you see the bear. Then your heart starts pounding, and other fear-related physiological reactions occur. You think to yourself that your heart is pounding, and you are running away from the bear and must be scared. Only after the analysis are you able to communicate that you are "scared."

Cannon-Bard theory

The *Cannon-Bard theory* of emotion is a variation on the James-Lange theory. This theory also proposes that the physiological reaction to stimuli occurs before the subjective experience of an emotion, but there's a little twist. Cannon-Bard doesn't agree that the complex activities of muscle activation and the subsequent actions (like running from a bear) are the first physiological processes to get involved.

Specific parts of the brain that are considered less sophisticated are activated first, according to Cannon-Bard. These "lower" parts of the brain then simultaneously send signals to three "higher-level" brain areas: the appraisal area, the arousal area, and the experience area. When compared to James-Lange, the main difference here is that arousal, analysis, experience, and expression all occur at the same time, but only after more basic areas of the brain are cued or activated.

So I encounter the bear, my lower brain areas activate, and then I run, analyze my running, realize I'm scared, and yell out, "Help, I'm going to die" all at the same time. If this fascinates you, check out Chapter 3 to read more about the brain.

Two-factor theory

Stanley Schacter of Columbia University and Jerome Singer of Penn State University are psychologists who came up with a third variation on the emotional process. Their *two-factor theory* takes elements from James-Lange and Cannon-Bard but changes things around just a tiny bit. Instead of having an initial reaction from the body or lower brain areas followed by the evaluation process, the two-factor theory states that physiological reactions and cognitive appraisal occur together, creating a feedback loop and co-producing the subjective experience of an emotion. Information from the situation and the environment are used in the appraisal process. Emotional arousal is seen as *generic* (not specific to a particular emotion) until an evaluation is conducted.

According to this theory, I see the bear and experience physiological arousal and cognitive appraisal at the same time. "I'm aroused and there's a dangerous animal in front of me. I must be scared."

Constructivist theory

Lisa Feldman Barrett has proposed a significant upgrade to the James-Lange, Cannon-Bar, and Two-Factory theories of emotion. She proposes that emotion as we know it is a *construction* of your mind. I tell my kids all the time that I'm not being strict with them; their minds are just telling them that. (Talk about gaslighting. I'm ashamed of myself.) Dr. Feldman Barrett has developed the *theory of constructed emotion*. She states,

> Emotions are not reactions to the world. You are not a passive receiver of sensory input but an active constructor of your emotions.

We receive sensory input, and with the input of past experiences stored in memory, we construct meaning and engage in action. She states that without past experience, these sensory inputs would be just "noise" and you wouldn't know what to do in response to them. You wouldn't even experience them as an emotion. This view of emotion is an extension of the work of Jean Piaget into the field of emotion. Piaget did not see people as passive recipients of information but rather active participants in the construction of knowledge through actively constructing knowledge by creating and testing their own theories of the world around them. Okay, so I don't feel totally ashamed about what I tell my kids; it's kind of true.

Expressing yourself

When someone is smiling, is she happy? What about someone who glares at you, puffs out his chest, and turns red in the face? Can you guess what emotion he's experiencing? Of course you can. All emotions have an expressive and communicative component that consists of verbal signals, facial expressions, eye contact, and other body movements and nonverbal expressions.

Some people believe that the expressive components of emotions are innate or inborn. The same goes for the ability to discern what someone is feeling by observing these expressions. Some emotional expressions seem to be universal, such as smiling when happy and frowning when sad.

Certain situations place constraints on these aspects of emotions as well. Although not always the case, people don't typically cheer and laugh at funerals and they don't usually scream angrily at people when given a compliment or a gift. In some cultures, funerals are somber, quiet affairs in which there is very little public display of emotion, although in other cultures there may be a great outpouring of emotion with people screaming, hitting themselves in the head, and grabbing at the casket of the deceased.

REMEMBER

Culture has a lot to do with how and when emotions are expressed, including what emotions are appropriate to feel and express.

Speech gives expression to feelings in several ways:

>> **Rate of speech:** Rate of speech can increase or slow down depending on how a person is feeling.

>> **Tone of voice:** A person's voice can be friendly or sharp, and this tone variation says a lot about the emotions being experienced.

>> **Volume:** Volume of voice conveys information as well. When someone is angry or excited he may talk more loudly, for example.

TIP

If you want to appear calm when you're angry, make an effort to speak slowly, use soft tones, and keep the volume down. If you're looking to intimidate someone, speak fast, in harsh tones, and very loudly. This sends the signal that you're angry.

Human beings experience many different emotions: fear, sadness, elation, and disgust to name just a few. Take a second and think about your life: What emotions do you experience most often? As a therapist, I've seen the whole range. Covering all of them would go way beyond the scope of this chapter, but I am going to go over two very important ones (actually, they are all important): anger and happiness.

Acknowledging anger

Speaking of issues, anger is an issue that deserves a lot of attention. On the one hand, anger can be suppressed and not expressed enough. But on the other hand, anger is expressed in inappropriate and extreme ways every day. Either way, anger is a natural emotion and is as important to human relationships as love.

Have you ever seen that T-shirt that has "I'm not prejudiced, I hate everybody" printed on it? Wonderful message, right? That ranks right up there with the bumper stickers with the cartoon character Calvin, from the American cartoon *Calvin and Hobbes,* peeing on everything from the symbols of different car manufacturers to the Internal Revenue Service. Sometimes it seems like there's a heck of a lot of anger out there.

Where does anger come from? Lots of theories exist. One is that anger is a consequence of experiencing negative or painful feelings. All kinds of things can lead to negative feelings: unpleasant physical conditions, physical pain, limits on our movement, and even loud noises. I like to refer to this theory as the "grouch factor." Psychologists theorize that the following things trigger anger:

>> **Feeling depressed:** People who are depressed are more at risk for feeling angry. Even sadness and grief can generate angry feelings. It is not uncommon for people to become extremely angry when someone they are close to dies.

>> **Being separated from desires:** When people are unable to engage in a desired activity or carry out a desired action, they tend to become angry. Sroufe proposed the existence of an *anger* system, which works like a pressure cooker. A person gets increasingly frustrated as his desires and activities are blocked time and time again, which eventually leads to the experience of anger with the blockade. There are no guidelines in this theory about where the breaking points are.

>> **Separation from attachment figure(s):** An *attachment figure* is someone we have attached to or formed a strong emotional bond with. When someone you are attached to leaves you, you may react with anger. These types of anger reactions were determined by researchers observing young children's reactions to being separated from their mothers. This seems to happen as adults as well. Have you ever seen someone fly into a rage when their romantic partner wants to break things off? This has been the story in many horrific romantic related crimes, unfortunately.

Although it can be quite destructive, anger is a valid and important emotion, and there are some positives to it. Anger can be pretty adaptive. It can aid in self-defense, fuel ambition, and sometimes prevent someone from acting aggressively toward another person. If someone is going to hurt you, sometimes a display of anger can make her think twice.

WARNING

Keep in mind that some people react to anger with even more anger, so be careful with this tactic. Anger can mobilize a lot of physical energy in a short period of time. If two angry people meet up, who is going to be the one to back down first? Maybe neither. When I worked in the prison system, I witnessed this often. Tough guys with a lot to prove would meet anger with anger and the result was not pretty; usually both people got hurt and put other inmates and correctional staff at risk as well.

Anger need not be destructive, as long as it is expressed appropriately and constructively. Research shows that children who appropriately express their anger have fewer emotional and social problems growing up. Infants and toddlers sometimes use anger as a signal that they're frustrated and may need help with something, like eating.

Being happy

The other day, in the middle of my workday, I caught myself feeling good and particularly positive and I stopped to think about what I was doing, what was going on around me, and what may be producing this positive experience. Was I happy?

Philosophers, poets, and many a middle-ager in midlife crisis would agree: Happiness is an elusive concept. Psychologists do not disagree. The exact definition of happiness and how to study and research it has been controversial, in part because research consistently shows that happiness is more than having the experience of positive emotions. Happiness can be understood as a multifaceted experience consisting of many things, including a person's self-view of life satisfaction, positive beliefs about life, and having more positive emotions than negative ones on average. Happiness is considered synonymous with well-being in psychological research.

Was my positive experience the other day the product of my exceptional cup of coffee, the unexpectedly delicious breakfast burrito, the warm welcome I got from the clinic staff, or my sense of being helpful to my first few clients? What were the ingredients of my happiness that day? What are the ingredients of my well-being?

Subjective well-being

Take two people: One has a good job, friends, a loving spouse, and well-behaved children; the other has unpredictable work, few friends, and no spouse. Which person is happier? This question gets to the heart of the approach to happiness known as *subjective well-being (SWB)*.

University of Illinois psychologist Ed Diener has done some important work on subjective well-being and the self-evaluation process involved. The SWB approach to happiness posits that well-being is essentially the strong positive emotions a person may experience as she reflects on and evaluates her life. SWB is the "whatever floats your boat" approach to happiness. The answer to the initial question is whoever evaluates her life more positively — the friendly person with a good job or the single guy with unstable work. Maybe neither; maybe both; the answer does not come from some objective list of "happiness ingredients." The happiest person of the two is the one who individually and subjectively judges himself or herself to be happy. That's it!

Perhaps this approach seems rather simplistic; to some people it is wholly profound. Whichever position a person may take, the subjective well-being theory of happiness leaves one's judgment of happiness up to individuals to judge for themselves.

Some think the SWB approach to happiness is too limited because it does not address why or how someone has high SWB or what she bases her SWB evaluations on. It doesn't address what "leads" to SWB and therefore is not prescriptive, not helpful, cannot be learned from, and cannot be taught.

Psychological well-being

Psychologist C. D. Ryff presents a more "list like" approach to happiness known as the *psychological well-being approach*. Ryff's model proposes

>> **Self-acceptance:** Feeling positive about yourself

>> **Positive relations with others:** Good relationships

>> **Autonomy:** Being independent with self-control and self-determination

>> **Environmental mastery:** Being able to choose and create environments that fit your needs and wants

>> **Purpose in life:** Having beliefs that give meaning to your life

>> **Personal growth:** Developing your potential and growing as a person

PERMA

Martin Seligman is another psychologist who approaches happiness from a broader perspective than the "whatever floats your boat" approach of SWB. Seligman's ingredients to happiness and the good life are captured in the acronym *PERMA*:

>> **Positive emotions:** Feeling good more often than feeling bad

>> **Engagement:** Feeling absorbed and highly focused on what you are doing — akin to being "in the zone" during a sports performance or composing a piece of music

>> **(Positive) relationships:** Having good relationships with good people in your life

>> **Meaning:** A sense that your efforts and talents are serving a purpose greater than oneself

>> **Accomplishment:** Mastery and success at the highest level or a particular pursuit, be it work, sports, or school

TIP

Taking the SWB approach, psychological well-being approach, and PERMA models all together, it would seem that some degree of positive subjective evaluation, good relationships, mastery, and meaning are core components to the good life, to happiness. So the next time I'm feeling happy, it just may be a result of that good cup of coffee and breakfast burrito (SWB), warm staff (good relationships), and knowing I'm helping somebody (mastery and meaning)!

Discovering your smart heart: Emotional intelligence and styles

In 1996, psychologist Daniel Goleman introduced the public at large to the concept of *Emotional Intelligence* in his book, *Emotional Intelligence: Why It Can Matter More than IQ*. In the years since, there has been a great deal of research on Emotional Intelligence (EQ) — a person's ability to perceive, control, and utilize his emotions in a productive manner. EQ has been likened to a form of intelligence because it is seen as a particular mental skill or ability and has been found to be associated with some positive outcomes in a person's life, just as being traditionally (cognitively) intelligent has, as in success at work.

Psychologists Mayer, Salovey, and Caruso define EQ as the ability to accurately reason about emotions and use that knowledge to enhance thinking. Dr. Reuvan Bar-On considers EQ to be a set of emotional skills that help a person cope and succeed in the world and environment. Perhaps an example of "emotionally unintelligent" behavior or skill can illustrate the point best. During a staff meeting I once saw a well-respected colleague scream and berate a graduate student for making a menial clerical error on some documentation. This caused quite an uproar, but it was later revealed that the colleague had received very distressing news about his personal health just a few minutes before the meeting. The poor student was the target of a lot of emotion he did not deserve. The colleague was clearly not aware of how his emotions were playing out in this interaction. Not so smart, not an example of high EQ.

Richard Davidson, in his book *The Emotional Life of Your Brain: How Its Unique Patterns Affect the Way You Think, Feel, and Live and How You Can Change Them*, takes the concept of emotion perhaps a little further than the concept of a "skill" or "ability" in his model of *emotional style*. For Davidson, it's less about EQ and more about a person's predominant and consistent responses to his or her life's experiences. Davidson proposes the following six dimensions for determining a person's emotional style:

>> **Resilience:** How quickly you recover from stress and challenge

>> **Outlook:** How long you can maintain a positive perspective

>> **Social intuition:** How good you are at picking up social signals

>> **Self-awareness:** How well you perceive body sensations related to emotions

>> **Sensitivity to context:** How good you are at using your surroundings in regulating your emotions

>> **Attention:** How focused you are

REMEMBER

Both emotional intelligence and emotional style approaches look at emotion from a broader perspective that put emotional "skillfulness" and ability at the heart of coping and success. It's not enough to be "book smart"; you need to be "heart smart" — to know how you feel, what do to about it, and how to use it to your advantage.

Being in Control

With all these brain processes, parts, and constructions, someone might be feeling like all that we are just passive sailors on the ocean of emotion. Not so fast. It is clear by now that emotions are important, critically important for survival and well-being. Is there a mental process or behavioral processes that help guide the ship? This is where the concept of *emotional regulation* (ER) comes in. It is defined as the control and use of emotion that facilitates moving us toward or achieving a goal (adaptive, achievement) or away from a noxious stimulus. I've talked about how emotions themselves help us move toward or away, but the emotional regulation process itself is critically involved as well. Emotional regulation helps in relationships, everyday life, getting along, staying healthy, building bonds, being happy, and managing negative feelings.

James Gross and Ross Thompson tell us that ER can be automatic or controlled, conscious or unconscious. ER can operate across the whole process (more on the process in a minute) or at different stages along the process. With ER, emotions can be modified in terms of how fast they come up (latency), their "size" or magnitude (intensity), and how long they last (duration). Gross and Thompson spell out five processes of ER. Think of them as the control switches of emotion.

>> **Situation selection:** This ER process involves taking action in "selecting" situations that will increase or decrease the chances that a desired emotion will be experienced or an undesired emotion will not. We plan on going to a party because our chances of feeling good are higher for a positive emotion. We plan on not having a difficult conversation with a coworker about his bothersome behavior.

>> **Situation modification:** Because we can't always pre-select situations to increase our odds of feeling a certain way, we may have to modulate or adapt to a given situation. Here, we modify some aspect of the situation to move it toward or away from an emotion. If you can't avoid talking to your coworker because your boss called you both into her office to "work it out," you might ask to do it immediately in order to get it over with and keep you from ruminating about it all day in dreadful anticipation.

>> **Attention deployment:** Here, we regulate emotion without changing the situation by directing our attention toward a stimulus or some aspect (or aspects) that will increase our positive/negative odds. Some strategies include distraction, diversion, concentration, or changing one's focus.

>> **Cognitive change:** Have you ever been told, "You're thinking about it all wrong"? If we can change the way we appraise a situation, we might be able to change our emotion around it. We can "think" in a way that changes our appraisal of a situation. From the positive side, we might "look on the bright side" or see that boring party as a chance to get to know someone really well. We can see a bad date as "Well at least he's not as bad as the last guy I was out with." One tact finds the positive, and the other tact reduces the negative.

>> **Response modulation:** Let's say you got your boss to agree to do that meeting right away, but once you're in there, in the middle of it, you're starting to get really anxious, almost panicked. You can use response modulation by changing your behavior, your physiology, or your experience somehow. You can slow

your heart rate down with controlled breathing. You can sit down or create more space between you and the coworker. You can try to alter your positive/negative emotional experience with action. There's an old saying in alcohol and addiction recovery circles: "Act your way into right thinking." You can apply this advice to feelings too.

None of these five processes happen in a vacuum. They can occur when a person is alone, but they also happen within the context of a interpersonal interaction. We can be "regulated" by others such as caregivers, family, and other relationships. We can also "regulate" other people. Caregivers help children develop their ER capacity by being responsive to their signals and cues and respond in ways that reduce distress and increase positive emotion.

TIP

For a great discussion on this topic, see Daniel Siegel's book, *The Power of Showing Up: How Parental Presence Shapes Who Our Kids Become and How Their Brains Get Wired* (Ballantine Books, 2020). Families influence how their members appraise emotion, provide help with ER strategies, and help members gain confidence and self-efficacy in ER. They can also help members learn the rules of acceptable and unacceptable ER strategy use.

Benard Rime points out that one common and very powerful way that ER is done in relationships is through the process of *sharing* our emotions with others. People want to talk about how they feel (except when they don't). If someone doesn't want to talk about how they feel, then they at least want to talk about situations or occurrences that were emotionally evocative.

Trauma, stress, illness are all for grist for the sharing mill. So too are positive experiences. I got married in Israel in my wife's tiny Christian village in the north and stayed there for four months after I got my doctorate. (I was unemployed anyway!) It was an awesome experience, and when I got back, I couldn't stop talking about it. I'm still talking about it. Research shows that sharing our emotions (either by talking about them or showing our emotions to others) provides more benefit than when we just share facts or non-emotional aspects of an experience (when you say "I felt" rather than "I thought" or "I did"). Of course, psychologists would find this in research. After all, "Tell me how that makes you feel" is our banner. People feel more helped when they share their emotions. Sharing can also elicit much needed support, validation, assistance, direction, advice, and nurturing. So "Tell me how that makes you feel. It's good for you!"

Chapter **8**

Barking up the Learning Tree: Dogs, Cats, and Rats

Athletes are some of the most superstitious people around — only gamblers can outdo them in this category. When I played college baseball, I had one teammate, a pitcher, who wore the same undershirt without washing it for as long as he kept winning. Some of us kind of hoped we'd lose so he'd wash his shirt. Other athletes carry lucky charms, perform rituals, or engage in elaborate routines to keep a winning streak alive.

I had a couple of superstitions of my own during my college baseball years. For starters, I couldn't knock the dirt off just one of my cleats (shoes) with my bat. I had to do both, even if the other one was clean. And when running in from the field, I never stepped on the chalk line. The other players never questioned me about my superstitions; they had their own weird habits.

When I started studying psychology, I began to wonder where this stuff comes from. What convinced me that I'd have a bad game if I stepped on the chalk line? At some point in time, I must have stepped on the line and then had a bad game. I saw a connection between what I did (stepped on the line) and what happened to me (had a bad game). I drew a connection between my behavior and a consequence, in this case, a negative consequence. Psychologists call this *superstitious learning.*

When an actual connection exists between what you do and a particular event that follows, be it positive or negative, a specific type of learning takes place. You learn that when you do something, the action is followed by consequence. Behaviorists use the acronym A-B-C: Antecedent (what happens before) → Behavior (the action performed) → Consequence (what happens after the action). All learning is a process of *conditioning,* a type of learning in which an association between events is made.

In this chapter, I describe the learning process and point out how learned behaviors apply to *classical conditioning,* a type of learning in which in which two events become associated with each other, as well as *operant conditioning,* learning in which an important consequence follows a specific response, leading to that response being more or less likely to happen again.

Both classical and operant conditioning lead to learning. What is "learned" in classical conditioning is that two previously unassociated stimuli are now "related" or *associated.* A good example is something called *taste aversion learning.* I once ate a shrimp cocktail and got ill and vomited. From that point on, just the thought of shrimp cocktail has made me nauseated. I *learned* that shrimp cocktail and illness are related, at least for me. I *learned* that the *taste* of shrimp was *aversive* because it was associated with nausea.

In operant conditioning, the learned association is between a particular behavior and what happens after it, the consequence. If you've ever caught a fish in a particular spot on a lake or river, you know from that point on you will continue to try that spot first every time you go fishing. What you learn is that your behavior of fishing (behavior) in spot X (context) resulted in a *positive consequence,* or a reward. The receipt of that reward increases the likelihood that you will repeat the behavior that triggered the reward when you are next in the same situation.

REMEMBER

Classical conditioning is about two stimuli becoming related to each other. Operant conditioning is about the relation of two stimuli increasing the likelihood that a behavior will occur again (or not).

Learning to Behave

You've been there or at least you've seen it, and I'm not judging — too much. It's the public tantrum with all the key ingredients: parent shame, onlooker disdain, child out of control. And only the coveted toy, piece of candy, or permission has the power to end it. Desperate, you give in and appease the hostile creature.

Most people seem to agree that throwing a public tantrum to fulfill an emotional or physical goal is a *learned behavior,* a response that is taught or acquired through experience. So when a tantrum erupts, parents tend to bear blame for teaching the child that tantrums work. Because work they do! A screaming and flailing child often does get what he wants; children see it work for others (observational learning), and they experience results when they do it (operant conditioning). So why not create a spectacle?

More than a hundred years ago, a group of British philosophers asked this very same question and tried to figure out the nature of learning. They observed that when two experiences occur together in time (temporal contiguity) and space (spatial contiguity), they become associated with each other. In other words, people learn that when event or object A occurs, so does event or object B. It sounds gossipy — "A and B are always together!" The freeway and traffic stay together; hamburgers and French fries don't make individual plans; and tantrums go hand-in-hand with new toys. They go together. They're associated!

Public tantrums capitalize on associations. The child realizes, "Every time I'm in the store, my terrible behavior leads to a new toy in my hands." And unfortunately for the tired, stressed out, and impatient parent, frequency is at play as well. The parent learns that buying a toy stops the tantrum — quick relief for the weary! As this scene continues to play out over and over again, an ever-stronger association forms.

The good news is that learned behavior can be unlearned through the same learning processes, which is also known as conditioning.

Drooling like Pavlov's Dogs

Kind of a gross visual, huh?

Personally, I would rather go to the dentist than conduct research on the salivation patterns of dogs. That's just me. But one brave man, Russian physiologist Ivan Pavlov, was up for the job. Pavlov was actually studying digestion with dogs when he became interested in how the presentation of food automatically activated the salivation response in the dogs that he was studying. He found that the formation of saliva was automatic.

TIP

Try it. Think about something really tasty and see if your mouth waters automatically. Did it work? It should have because salivation is a reflexive response to food. It's the body's way of preparing to receive food. Saliva helps break down food into digestible bits.

In this section, I describe how Pavlov figured out why certain associations trigger certain natural responses and thereby discovered classical conditioning. I also point out how associations can change to alter certain learned responses.

Conditioning responses and stimuli

Pavlov constructed a device to collect the saliva directly from the dogs' salivary glands as the glands went to work. He could then measure how much saliva the dogs reflexively produced. Picture a dog strapped into a cage with a tube attached to its salivary glands and this wacky scientist counting each drop. Not even Hollywood could have imagined a more eccentric scene.

At this point, Pavlov was probably happy with his canine digestion research; but one day, he noticed something strange — the dogs salivated sometimes even when the food wasn't presented. What was going on? Was something else causing the salivation?

Pavlov came up with an *associationist* explanation. That is, the dogs had learned to associate other stimuli with the food. But what was triggering this response?

Pavlov conducted a whole series of experiments to figure out how the dogs had learned to automatically associate non-food stimuli with food in a way that produced salivation. A typical experiment went something like this:

1. Pavlov placed his dogs in their harness with the saliva tubes attached to the dogs' salivary glands.

2. He rang a bell and observed whether the dogs salivated or not. He found that they didn't.

3. Then he rang the bell, waited a few seconds, and then presented food to the dogs. The dogs salivated.

4. He repeated the bell plus food presentation several times. These pairings, by the way, are called *trials*.

5. After Pavlov was satisfied with the number of trials, he presented the bell alone, without the food.

6. He found that the bell by itself produced salivation!

REMEMBER

Conditioning refers to learning through the associative process, learning through experience. Pavlov's discovery became known as *classical conditioning*.

After conducting his experiments, he identified four necessary components of classical conditioning:

>> **Unconditioned stimuli (US):** The food that Pavlov presented to his dogs, the *unconditioned stimulus*, is the thing that triggers the unconditioned response. Food prompts salivation.

>> **Unconditioned responses (UR):** Pavlov's dogs automatically, or reflexively, salivated when presented with food. They didn't need to learn or be conditioned to salivate in the presence of food. Pavlov called this response the *unconditioned*, or not-learned, *response*. It happened without learning. It was a reflex.

>> **Conditioned stimuli (CS):** The bell that Pavlov rang in a typical experiment, called the *conditioned stimulus*, is the item that the dogs learned to associate with the food through the process of pairing trials. After enough trials, a conditioned stimulus produces a response on its own.

>> **Conditioned responses (CR):** After the CS begins producing the UR without the US, the response is called the *conditioned response*. In symbolic form, this system looks something like Table 8-1.

TABLE 8-1

Classical Conditioning

Trial Number	Result
	US → UR (food automatically produces salivation)
1	CS + US → UR (bell + food produces salivation)
2	(bell + food produces salivation)
3	(bell + food produces salivation)
4–9	(bell + food a few more times produces salivation)
10	CS → CR (bell alone produces salivation)

Becoming extinct

The power of classical conditioning is pretty impressive. Just think — if you appropriately pair two stimuli, the CS alone will eventually get the job done. But when the pairing stops, and the CS is producing the response by itself, the power of the CS eventually fades. If a CS is presented enough times without the US, the CS eventually will cease to elicit the CR.

This phenomenon is called *extinction*, and it is a way to reverse the process of classical conditioning. For example, Pavlov's dogs learned to salivate at the sound of a bell. But if the bell continued to be presented without the delivery of food, the dogs would eventually stop slobbering to the bell.

But wait, there's more!

Something even more interesting happens if the US is reintroduced sometime after extinction — *spontaneous recovery*. At this point, the CS's ability to elicit the response comes bouncing back, and once again the CS triggers the CR. This means that you can use classical conditioning techniques to teach an old dog new tricks, and you can reverse the process through extinction. With this skill, you'll never be the boring guy at the party sitting in the corner. You can dazzle your newfound friends with classical conditioning tricks and come to the rescue of parents of a toy-hungry tantrum king by teaching them to just stop giving in and let extinction take over.

TIP

Here's a fun party trick if you're thinking about testing your own classical conditioning prowess.

1. Gather a few people together — family, friends, coworkers, whomever. Get some packets of powdered, lemonade drink mix. This stuff is really sour without sugar. Give one packet to each participant.

2. Ask each person in the crowd to dip a finger in the lemonade and take a lick. (This is the US.) Ask them to observe if their mouths watered. They should have. If not, get yourself some better droolers.

3. Now choose a CS (a bell, a light, a whistle, whatever). Go through the process of pairing the CS with tasting the lemonade (CS→US→UR over and over again).

4. After 10 to 20 trials, go through a couple of trials where you present just the CS and ask the participants to observe if their mouths watered. They should have! That's classical conditioning.

5. If your crew is really into spending this kind of time with you, you can now start playing around with extinction and spontaneous recovery!

One more way to reverse the effects of classical conditioning is worth mentioning. You've conducted the lemonade test, and you've successfully taught your Pavlovian subjects to drool on command. If you want to change the effect, choose another US that produces some other response (UR) and classically condition your subjects with the new US. This process is called *counterconditioning*.

Counterconditioning works especially well if the new US produces a response that is incompatible with the old CR. If the old CR was a watering mouth, maybe you pick a new US that produces a dry mouth. I don't know what that may be — maybe eating sand.

I guarantee that if you classically condition the bell with the eating of sand, the bell will have a very hard time triggering a watering mouth ever again . . . unless, of course, you reverse the process all over again. Just be sure to give your subjects a break from time to time, and don't actually try the sand-eating thing as a parlor game; it's just an example!

Classic generalizing and discriminating

You may be thinking, "Big deal. Dogs learn to salivate to a bell; so what?"

Well, if you're going to be so tough to impress, you should know that classical conditioning is actually a very important phenomenon in terms of human survival. It helps people learn things simply by association, without effort; and this can be very beneficial. In other words, after a CS becomes associated with a US to the point where the CS produces the CR by itself, that learning can expand automatically through a process known as *generalization*.

Generalization happens when something similar to the CS — I'll call it CS-2 — elicits the CR, even if CS-2 has never before been associated with the original US. For instance, if you learn to associate certain facial gestures, like a snarl or a sneer, with eventual violence, then the snarl or sneer (CS) produces fear (CR), whereas only a flying fist or a verbal threat (US) elicited fear (UR) in the past. You may then generalize the snarl and experience fear in connection with direct and non-averted eye contact (CS-2). This generalization can save your tail. Generalization helps people adapt, because learned responses are applied to new situations.

WARNING

Generalization can backfire, though. If, for example, I am attacked by a gray-colored pit bull, I may get scared every time I see a gray dog of any type, even a Chihuahua. This "over-learning" can limit my behavior and cause unnecessary suffering because I become afraid of dogs that pose no actual danger to me, so instead of just avoiding gray pit bulls I avoid all dogs.

Another example of generalization backfiring comes from the traumatic experiences of war veterans who suffer from post-traumatic stress. If they've experienced loud explosions and heavy gunfire and developed a strong fear reaction to these events, these veterans may respond to hearing a car backfire or some other loud noise in the same way they responded to gunfire in a war zone. This can make life pretty difficult, especially for people living in an urban area with a lot of loud noises.

When people begin to overgeneralize learned behaviors, a process known as *discrimination* is absent. You know how to *discriminate*, or tell the difference, between stimuli such as the sound of a potentially fatal gunshot and the merely annoying sound of a car backfiring. Discrimination is learned when a CS-2 (or 3 or 8 or 25) is presented enough times without eliciting a response. It becomes apparent that only the CS, and not the CS-2, is necessarily going to produce the CR.

Conditioning rules!

If all it takes to trigger a natural response to an unnatural stimulus is pairing a natural stimulus with an unnatural stimulus and presenting them together for a while, it can't get much easier.

But not so fast! The process sounds as straightforward as it gets, but some specific rules must be followed in order to achieve conditioning.

In order for associations to form, they must conform to the following two very important rules:

>> **Contiguity:** Associations are only formed when events occur together. For example, I feel depressed when I wake up every Monday morning and think about going back to work. Therefore, for me, work and waking up are associated.

>> **Frequency:** The more often that two (or more) events occur together, the stronger the association becomes.

Contiguity, when one event follows another in time, is absolutely required for classical conditioning to occur. Think about it: What if Pavlov had presented the bell (CS) after he presented the food (US)? Or what if he had presented the bell 15 minutes before the food? The CS must come immediately before the US in order for the association to form.

Each of these sequence and timing scenarios represents conditioning techniques that aren't very effective. If Pavlov presented the US before the CS, which is a process known as *backward conditioning*, the dogs would have either made no association at all or an extremely weak one. If he presented the bell well in advance of the food, a process known as *trace conditioning*, the dogs may have formed a weak association, if any.

TIP

The best way to ensure that a strong or more quickly formed association is formed during the conditioning process is to follow these guidelines:

>> Present the CS just before the US and keep the CS on or around until the US appears. This way, the CS is perceived to be contiguous with the US.

>> Conduct a lot of trials with the CS and US paired frequently. The strength of the association is a direct product of the frequency of the pairing.

>> Use a strong or intense CS to condition faster. A bright light conditions faster than a dim one. A loud bell conditions faster than a faint one.

But I don't want to mislead you into thinking that all you have to do is frequently present an intense CS before a US to achieve classical conditioning. Even though the rule of contiguity states that if two stimuli are contiguous, an association will form, it's actually not that simple.

Blame it on a pesky graduate student named Robert Rescorla who questioned whether contiguity was enough. Maybe he thought it all seemed too simple.

REMEMBER

Rescorla proposed that another rule — the rule of *contingency* — be added to the list of conditioning requirements. His idea was that a CS not only has to be contiguous with a US; it also has to be an accurate predictor of the US. In other words, if the CS is presented at random times (at 1 minute, 7 minutes, 2 minutes, or 12 minutes, for example) with the US, then the CS isn't a credible predictor of the US. The learner (animal or human) gains no predictive power from experiencing the CS, so the CS fails to trigger the CR. Therefore, the CS must be presented with the US in a way that the learner can anticipate, with a fair degree of certainty, that the US is soon to come.

Adding another rule to the requirements of Pavlov's classical conditioning is quite the accomplishment for a graduate student. But Rescorla wasn't finished. Later, he and another psychologist, Allan Wagner, made another huge contribution to learning theory. Ready?

The Rescorla-Wagner model (1972) simply states that in order for a CS to be maximally effective, the US must be unexpected. The learning process is dependent on the element of surprise. If a learner expects the US every time she sees the CS, then she learns to associate it properly; but eventually, the strength of the association reaches a maximum. The strength increases dramatically at first and then levels off as the novelty of the CS wears off and it becomes more "expectable."

Therefore, the power of an association to elicit a CR is a function of surprise. The more novel the CS, the stronger the association.

Battling theories: Why does conditioning work?

Knowing how to perform classical conditioning is useful (check out the "Conditioning responses and stimuli" earlier for the how-to on this trick), and the conditioning response enables people to learn about their environment in ways that improve adaptability and a little something called survival. But why does conditioning work? Why do previously unrelated stimuli become associated with each other?

Pavlov believed that the simultaneous activation of two distinct areas in the brain form associations between a CS and a US. This activation results in the formation of a new pathway between the two areas. It's like sitting next to a stranger on the bus and, through some polite chitchat, realizing you both know the same person. These two previously unrelated people become associated through this common association and a new connection is born.

Clark Hull presented an alternative account. He believed that the association formed is actually between the CS and the UR, which then becomes the CR. Scientists are at their most creative when they figure out how to make two different theories compete with each other in predicting the outcome of an experiment. This creativity makes it possible for them to dream up a critical experimental test. Holland and Staub set out to test Hull's theory. They conditioned rats by using noise and food pellets.

According to Pavlov, the rats learned to associate the noise with the food. But Holland and Staub pitted Pavlov's idea against Hull's by trying to make the food an unattractive US. First, they taught the rats to associate noise (CS) with food (US). Then they put the rats on a turntable and spun them around to make them nauseous. Here, they taught the rats to associate food with nausea. Then, after spinning them for a while, they presented the noise again, and the rats didn't respond to it. This "devalued" the food by associating it with nausea.

Pavlov thought that the original connection was between the noise and the food. But Hull predicted that devaluing the US would not make a difference in the rats' response; he suggested that the critical association forms between the noise (CS) and eating (UR). Devaluing the US did make a difference, though. Spinning the rats on the turntable and making the food less attractive to them as a result should not have made a difference, according to Hull, but he was wrong. A connection must exist between the CS and the US; the CS can't be left out of the loop for conditioning to occur.

So Pavlov rules the day!

This isn't just rigid tradition. It actually has predictive value. Learning doesn't stop here, however. Check out Chapter 9 for new adventures in learning about learning.

Studying Thorndike's Cats

Operant conditioning takes place in all facets of everyday living — in homes, the workplace, and public spaces. Parents use rewards, or operant conditioning, to get their children to do their homework or follow through on chores. Here's how operant conditioning works.

Every month I get paid at my job. Am I paid just to sit around and take up space? No, I'm paid for performing the duties of my job, for working. I do something, and something happens. I work, and I get paid. Would I work if I didn't get paid? Probably not, for two reasons.

First, I have better things to do with my time than to work for free. (My credit card debtors wouldn't be too happy with me either.) Second, according to operant conditioning theory, I work *because* I get paid. The "something" that follows my working behavior is a reward, a positive consequence.

When I do something like work at my job, something happens; I get paid. Then what happens? I keep going to work every month, so that paycheck I get must be having an effect on me. Way back in early 1900s, Edward Thorndike created a theory, known as the *law of effect,* that addressed this idea of a consequence having an effect on behavior.

Thorndike decided to look into this phenomenon by doing research with cats. He constructed the *puzzle box* made from a wooden crate with spaced slats and a door that could be opened by a special mechanism. Thorndike placed a hungry cat inside the box and closed the door. He then placed some food on a dish outside of the box that the cat could see through the slats in the crate. Sounds kind of cruel, doesn't it? The cat would reach for the food through the slats, but the food was out of reach. The only way for the cat to get the food was for Thorndike or the cat to open the door.

Obviously, Thorndike wasn't going to open the door; he was conducting an experiment. The cat had to figure out how to open the door himself. You don't see a lot of cats going around opening doors. So what did he do? It's suspenseful, isn't it? What will the little hungry cat do there in the puzzle box? Will he open the door and feed voraciously on the prized food that was just beyond his reach only moments before? Or will he meet his demise and starve at the hands of a fiendish psychologist?

The cat had to figure out how to open the door, and Thorndike was a patient man. He waited and watched, waited and watched. The cat wandered around the box, stuck his little paw out, meowed, bounced off the walls, and acted in any number of random ways inside of the box. But then, something remarkable happened. The cat accidentally hit the latch that was holding the door shut, and the door miraculously opened! Hurray! The cat got to eat, and everyone lived happily ever after.

What did Thorndike learn from his little experiment?

Nothing. He wasn't done yet.

So he put that poor cat back inside the box to go at it again. No problem, right? The cat knew what to do; just hit the latch, little kitty! But when it got back into the box, the cat acted like he didn't know that he had to hit the latch to open the door. He started acting in the same random ways all over again.

Never fear, eventually the cat triggered the latch by accident again and was again rewarded by gaining access to the food. Thorndike kept performing this experiment over and over again, and he made a remarkable observation. The amount of time that it took for the cat to figure out that the latch was the key to freedom — well, food! — got shorter and shorter with each subsequent trial. Why was the cat getting faster? Thorndike proposed that the food helped the cat learn the association between the triggering the latch and the escape.

REMEMBER

Thorndike's law of effect states that a response that results in stronger satisfaction to an organism (for example, animal or human) will be more likely to be associated with the situation that preceded it. The greater the satisfaction, the greater the bond between the situation and response.

Basically, the consequence of getting the food served as a reward for learning how to open the box. The cat's opening-the-box behavior is like my job, and his food is like my paycheck.

So getting back to my original question of whether my paycheck has an effect on me or not — the fact is, I keep working, just like Thorndike's cat kept opening the box to get the food. Therefore, the consequence of my action does appear to lead me to perform that action again.

Reinforcing the Rat Case

When a consequence of an action or event increases the probability that the event or action will happen again, that consequence is called a *reinforcer.* It's like a reward, and rewards often motivate a repeat of actions that earned the reward. Operant conditioning is all about the effects of reinforcers on behavior.

B. F. Skinner, one of the most famous psychologists of all time, followed in Thorndike's footsteps in using animals to investigate operant conditioning. He constructed a box with a lever inside and called it a *Skinner box.* When an animal pressed the lever, a food pellet fell out of a feeder and into the box. Skinner wanted to see if rats placed in the box could learn to press the lever in order to receive the food.

This task was a lot harder than one may think. Rats aren't used to pressing levers to get food. Skinner had to facilitate the process a little bit with a procedure known as *shaping,* a technique of rewarding successful approximations to the goal. Skinner rewarded the rats with food for performing a behavior that was close to, but not exactly, the required response. Shaping was done gradually so that the rats eventually got to the point where they pressed the bar and received their reinforcers of food.

After the rats got the hang of it, they learned to press the bar for food the same way Thorndike's cats learned to open the door. The rats learned because the reward of the food taught them how to press the bar.

Finding the right reinforcer

In the cases of both Thorndike's cats and Skinner's rats, the subjects learned because they were rewarded with food. Food is a powerful reward for animals, but it's just one type of reinforcer. Anything that increases the likelihood that a behavior will occur again can be used as a reward or reinforcer. It can be food, money, recess, or vacations. It can also be something intangible like approval, praise, or attention from another person.

There are two basic types of reinforcement:

>> **Positive reinforcement** is the use of any reinforcer that increases the likelihood that a behavior will occur again.

>> **Negative reinforcement** occurs when the removal of negative stimuli leads to an increased likelihood that a behavior will occur again. A good example of this is when a student gets disruptive in class during an assignment he is trying to avoid or escape. The teacher sends him out of the room and negatively reinforces the disruptive behavior. The teacher thinks she is punishing the student but he is actually getting out of an aversive demand.

The basic idea of operant conditioning is that behaviors that are reinforced (either positively or negatively) are more likely to occur again. But is this true for all reinforcers? Are all reinforcers created equal? If Skinner had given the rats five dollars each time they pressed the lever, would they still have learned the response?

Probably not. Differences between reinforcers exist and affect the impact that the reinforcers have on responses. Not all consequences are rewarding or reinforcing as they vary from person to person (or animal to person).

REMEMBER

Two types of positive reinforcers are effective:

>> **Primary reinforcers** are rewards that don't require shaping or prior training to be effective. Examples may be food or pleasurable physical sensations.

David Premack in 1971 came up with the interesting idea that primary reinforcers can be identified by looking at what people spend most of their time doing. If they spend a lot of time watching television, riding bikes, or sleeping, then these activities may be considered primary reinforcers. His *Premack principle* states that high probability responses can be used to reinforce lower probability responses. This is like using ice cream to get your child to eat his or her vegetables. If they want the ice cream (high probability response), they'll eat their vegetables (low probability response).

>> **Secondary reinforcers** are things that become reinforcing through experience and learning. This result happens by associating the secondary reinforcer with a primary reinforcer by using classical conditioning techniques. (See the section "Conditioning responses and stimuli" earlier in this chapter.)

The best example of a secondary reinforcer is money. We aren't born knowing the value of money (and some of us never get it). But, eventually we learn the value of money as we experience its association with the things we like such as food, clothing, shelter, and expensive cars. So money "acquires" its value to us as it becomes associated with primary reinforcers. In some institutions, like schools and hospitals, caretakers reward appropriate behaviors with *tokens*, which may be cashed in for specific rewards later. This type of system is called a token economy, like local money.

After identifying what a subject considers to be reinforcing, it becomes possible to influence behavior by providing rewards for performing the appropriate responses.

For example, consider an office manager who is having a difficult time getting her employees to come back from lunch on time. What can she do? First, she needs to figure out what is reinforcing for the group or each individual. Not all rewards are the reinforcing to all people. Then, she has to start rewarding anyone who performs the desired behavior, coming back from lunch on time. She could give them little gifts, money, or smiley-face stickers.

Or the office manager could use negative reinforcement. For instance, she could send a really whiny employee out to lunch (who complains profusely and gets everyone's anxiety up at the thought of being late) with the latecomers. The latecomers hate hearing the whiny employee complain so much that they start returning on time just to avoid hearing him go on and on.

This concept of negative reinforcement confuses a lot of people. How can taking something away or removing a noxious stimulus increase the probability of a behavior? You may have some experience with this tactic if you've ever had a new puppy in your home that wouldn't stop whining while you tried to sleep. If you kept the puppy in another room or in the garage, you probably responded to the whining by getting up and checking on the cute little creature. What happened when you went to the puppy? It probably stopped crying. If you then went back to bed, I bet the crying woke you again less than ten minutes later.

The problem in this situation is that *your* behavior was under the control of negative reinforcement. The puppy's whining was a noxious (and annoying) stimulus. When you went to the garage, the whining stopped, increasing the likelihood that you kept going to the puppy every time he cried. You were negatively reinforced for going to the puppy — and that puppy got positively reinforced for whining! Oops.

Using punishment

Both positive and negative reinforcements are consequences that are likely to increase certain behaviors. But what about that other consequence, *punishment?* Punishment is any consequence that decreases the likelihood of a response and not necessarily something typically thought of as a punishment. For example, if every time you call a certain friend he seems distracted, like he's not listening to what you're saying, you may experience negative feelings of not being valued; this "punishment" is likely to lead to you calling at person less often.

One type of punishment is straightforward — the introduction of something noxious or aversive.

Another type of punishment, *negative punishment,* involves removing a reinforcer, such as taking away a child's bicycle. Again, as for reinforcement, punishment can be a very individual matter; what one person experiences as aversive or punishing may not apply to the next person.

Punishment is used to influence people's behavior all the time. Parents punish children. Courts punish convicted criminals. Credit card companies punish people for late payments. But does punishment work?

Punishment can be a very potent and effective means for decreasing the frequency of a behavior, but keep a few things in mind:

>> Punishment should be the least intense form necessary to produce the desired response. Recipients may acclimate to each subsequent increase in punishment, however, and overly intense punishment is problematic as well. In order for punishment to be effective over a long period of time, you have to adjust its intensity in a meaningful way.

>> To be effective, punishment must occur as close in time as possible to the response being punished. If a parent waits three weeks to punish a child for breaking a lamp, the kid's likely to be completely clueless about why she's being punished; therefore, the punishment has no effect on deterring future behavior.

>> Punishment should be firm, consistent, and accompanied with a clear explanation of why the punishment is being administered.

There are ethical issues associate with punishment which mean it has to be considered very carefully in all circumstances.

Of course, a lot of people are uncomfortable with the idea of inflicting pain or suffering on another person in order to alter behavior. The use of punishment can have some negative consequences:

>> **Fear:** When people are effectively punished, they may learn to anticipate future punishment and develop severe anxiety while waiting for the next shoe to drop. This can have a disruptive effect on the life of a punished person, which can lead to avoidance and apathy.

>> **Aggression:** I've worked in both jails and prisons, and I've seen men become angrier and more aggressive as a result of the harsh conditions that they face while incarcerated. When the time comes for these people to be released and face the world in a reformed manner, they are dysfunctional and institutionalized, often unable to make the transition to the outside world as a result of their punishment.

The person delivering the punishment may become an aversive CS through conditioning. For example, a child may avoid a parent who punishes the child frequently. Contiguity does its thing — that person is there every time I get scolded ("Just wait until your father gets home." Thanks, Ma).

Scheduling and timing reinforcement

Have you ever wondered why people keep going back to places like Las Vegas and Atlantic City time and time again to donate their money to the casino expansion fund? The bottom line with gambling is that the big winner is always the house, the casino. Everyone knows this, but some people can't stay away.

People keep going back because of something called a *schedule of reinforcement,* a schedule or determination for what responses to reinforce and when to reinforce them. There are four basic schedules of reinforcement, each with different effects on the response in question:

>> Fixed ratio (continuous and partial types)

>> Variable ratio

>> Fixed interval

>> Variable interval

Ongoing rewards

Perhaps the most common form of reinforcement is called *continuous reinforcement,* in which the ratio is one-to-one. One behavior, one reward. It involves reinforcing a behavior every time it occurs. Every time I pull the slot machine handle, I win! Yeah right, I wish.

Continuous reinforcement is good for the shaping phase of learning (see "Reinforcing the Rat Case" earlier for a discussion of shaping) or for what is called the *acquisition phase.* Learning a new behavior takes time. Continuous reinforcement speeds up the learning process.

The problem with continuous reinforcement, however, is that it extinguishes quickly. If I'm reinforced every time I return to work on time from lunch, then I'm likely to stop returning on time as soon as my boss stops reinforcing me for this behavior.

Patting heads sporadically

Often, reinforcement in our world is intermittent and sporadic. Of course we don't win every time we pull the lever on the slot machine. B. F. Skinner didn't design slots.

B. A. Loser, the casino behavioral psychologist, did. Reinforcement on a less frequent basis (for example, requiring more than one response) is called *partial reinforcement*. There are two types of partial reinforcement schedules, and each is further divided by how predictably or randomly the reinforcers come.

>> The first type of partial reinforcement is called a *ratio schedule that involves more than one response being required to gain a reward.* With a ratio schedule, reinforcement is only given after a specific number of responses have been given. If a parent is using this schedule with his children, he may only give a reward for some number of A's his child gets on her report card or after a certain number of times the child cleans her room. Ratio schedules can then vary based on whether a fixed number of responses or a variable number of responses are required to receive the reinforcement.

- A *fixed ratio* reinforcement schedule involves always reinforcing for the same number of given responses. If I'm going to reward my child for every two A's she earns, that never changes; reinforcement follows every two A's.

- A *variable ratio* reinforcement schedule involves giving reinforcement for a varied number of responses provided. I may reinforce my child for two A's now, but then I may reinforce her for one A, three A's, or ten A's down the line. The key to this approach is to keep the recipient guessing. Doing so has a powerful effect on the persistence of a response because people keep doing the requisite behavior because they don't know when the reinforcement will come. A variable ratio is much more resistant to extinction than continuous reinforcement.

>> The other type of partial reinforcement schedule, an *interval schedule,* is based on the amount of time that has passed between reinforcements. You still have to respond to get a reward, but you have to wait a certain time before your response "works."

- I get paid once a month. Time determines when I get paid. My pay schedule is an example of a *fixed interval* reinforcement schedule. The time frame never varies.

- The other type of interval schedule is *variable interval*. Here, responses are reinforced per a varied amount of time passed since the last reinforcement. This approach would be like getting paid at the end of one month, and then getting paid two days later, and again three weeks later, and so on. Variable interval schedules are also very resistant to extinction for the same reason as variable ratio schedules; the responder never knows when he is going to get reinforced, so he has to keep responding to find out.

Gambling is motivated by a variable interval schedule so that people keep pumping the money in, waiting for the big payoff.

I'm sure you've heard "You can't win if you don't play." The next time you think you're "due" or bound to win because you've been sitting at the same machine for three days without a shower, sleep, or anything to eat, remember that it's variable. You never know when the machine is going to hit. So try to manage your rage if you finally give up and the next person who sits down wins it all!

That's why they call it gambling.

REMEMBER

The timing of the reinforcement is also critical. Research has shown that reinforcement must occur immediately, or as quickly as possible, following the desired response. If you wait too long, the connection between the response and the reinforcing consequence is lost. Skinner's rats would have never figured out how to press that lever if they were given a food voucher redeemable only after five visits to the Rat Food Deluxe shop — instead of instant gratification for their achievement.

Stimulus Control and Operant Generalization

Have you ever noticed how people slow down on the highway when they see a traffic cop? That's probably because they've all gotten tickets from them at one time or another. What happens when a good old city (non-traffic) cop is on the road? Nobody slows down. They just ignore him. Is this an example of a blatant disrespect for the law? No. It's an example of *stimulus control*, the idea that a response can vary as a function of the stimulus present at the time of reinforcement or punishment. Although both law enforcement authorities can give tickets for speeding, most of us know that city cops don't typically give tickets on the highway. The stimuli have different effects on our behavior because they have led to different consequences. Punishment only comes from the traffic cop.

Sometimes, when we learn a response due to reinforcement, we may automatically *generalize* that response to other similar stimuli. If I generalized my traffic cop ticket experience to city cops, I would slow down for city cops, too. Or, if I'm reinforced for coming back from lunch on time, I may also generalize that behavior to coming to work in the morning on time. Generalization helps speed up the learning process because we don't have time to receive reinforcement for every single response we elicit.

Operant Discrimination

Sometimes people can over-learn a response or behavior. They then engage in the response when they shouldn't because they've generalized a little too much.

I think this happens to psychotherapists sometimes. We may be in a social situation, not working, when someone starts talking about how hard his or her day was. "Tell me how that makes you feel," may slip out. Everyone looks at the psychotherapist in question like a quack. Maybe it's time for a vacation.

TIP

I've also seen this phenomenon in movies. An ex-cop overreacts to seeing his grandson point a water pistol at him, and he takes the kid down to "remove the threat." These are problems of *discrimination*, responding to only one of two or more particular stimuli. The problem is remedied by presenting someone with both stimuli and only reinforcing the response to the correct one. Put Grandpa in the middle of a hold-up and throw his grandson with a water pistol into the mix. Only reinforce Detective Grandpa when he successfully neutralizes the threat of the robber (stimulus 1) and not for taking grandson out (stimulus 2). He's learned to discriminate between a real threat and a benign one.

4

Me, You, and Everything in Between

Discover personality theory, the most common personality types, and topics such as knowing yourself and developing identities.

Get connected to those around you and find out the influence that others have on your behavior, the different ways people behave in groups, and how we get along (or not).

Take a look at developmental psychology and trace development from conception to adolescence.

See how the digital age is affecting how we relate to each other and how we live our lives.

Chapter **9**

Myself and I

W hy psychology? It's about people right? Me, you, and everything in between. Perhaps the branch of study in all of psychology with the longest history is the study of personality, or *personality science*. Psychologist David Funder (an old professor of mine!) proposes that the study of personality is where all the different branches of psychology come together. Thinking, sensing, learning, behaving, growing, and socializing all happen where exactly? In a person of course! So who am I?

Imagine my old friend Brad contacts me out of the blue. I'm excited to hear from him, so we decide to meet up for coffee and catch up. When I walk into the café, I immediately see my old friend. He hasn't changed a bit. I walk up and say, "Brad!" He looks at me, and in that instant, I realize he doesn't recognize me. (I have an ongoing fear that when I see old friends, they won't recognize me, so I sometimes don't say anything! More on that in a minute.)

Brad looks up and says, "Can I help you?"

"It's me, Adam!"

I realize it's my old friend, but he doesn't recognize me. I'm older (obviously, and I don't think I've aged too well); put on weight; and have a different "hairstyle" (balding actually). So much has changed, but has it?

Here's a story that actually happened. I'm out eating lunch with some colleagues and I recognize an old childhood friend at a table across the way. I keep looking over at him, not sure if he recognizes me. (Remember that I think that sometimes.) Does he remember me? After looking over a few times, we make eye contact, and he says, "What's up, Adam?" I reply, "Hey, Jason! It's been a long time!"

We made some small talk. I asked about his brother and his dad. We talked about a few things and then we went our separate ways. It felt good. He still remembered me.

Both scenarios are about my personality really. The "me" is consistent over time, despite my aging looks. Sure, my personality has changed in some ways, but the "core" of who I am has obviously persisted.

These stable characteristics are what famous psychologist Philip Zimbardo describes as a complex set of unique psychological qualities that influence behavior, thinking, and emotions across situations and time — which is an excellent working definition of personality.

A *personality* is a stable system of tendencies to act, think, and feel a particular way.

Describing someone's personality is, in essence, developing a whole person picture out of the various bits of information available about them that hold true through the passing of time and changes in circumstance.

Personality theories assume that a particular set of general characteristics can serve as a summary for what a person is like. The qualities that first come to mind when you think about a person are usually the qualities that are most central to him. The more central that quality is, the more useful that aspect is in predicting the individual's behavior and distinguishing him from other people. In fact, the study of personality may very well be where psychology as a field shines. Why? Because I've always had a student in Introduction to Psychology courses who believed that psychologists are too reductionist, breaking up Humpty Dumpty and never putting him back together. Well, personality psychology is that attempt.

My "Adam-ness" is my personality. It's what makes me unique in the world. Personality is what makes me unique. Tens or hundreds of people around the world may have the same name as I do or may look like me, but nobody has my identical personality.

In this chapter, I describe the field of personality psychology and cover various theories and research personality, including biological approaches, social learning approaches, and trait-based approaches.

REMEMBER

As you read about these personality theories, keep in mind that nobody fits perfectly into these categories. An important concept in psychology is the principle of *individual differences.* No one *is* a personality theory: The theories are *tools* for understanding the complexity of human behavior, thoughts, and emotions.

Getting to the Magic Number 5

Aren't people just born with their personality? Maybe there are just fixed qualities of "personhood" present from the beginning of life — sort of "built in." This is essentially the position of *Trait theories* of personality. Trait theories represent one of the most stable and reliable lines of research in all of personality dating back to the work of psychologist Gordon Allport (1897–1967) and his book, *Personality: A Psychological Interpretation* (1937), considered to be the first textbook on personality. Allport and many personality scientists to follow proposed that personality is organized into a dynamic *whole,* and that whole is engaged in dynamic interaction with the environment, including other people.

Trait theories represent the parts that comprise the "whole." They are derived from directly describing and measuring characteristics found in the general population and are not tied to any particular theory such as psychoanalytic or cognitive theory. A *trait* is a stable feature of someone's personality that leads him or her to think, feel, and think in particularly stable ways. Traits don't vary from situation to situation, at least not that much. For more on the role of situational influences on personality, see the "It Depends on the Situation" section later in this chapter. Traits "travel with" a person *across* situations and circumstances.

REMEMBER

Trait theories propose that there are a core set of personality traits that exist to varying degrees in all people as a common and universal feature of being human. Humans walk upright and have one heart, large brains, and personality traits. Dogs, on the other hand, walk on four legs, have one heart, medium brains, and no personality traits. Wait a minute; I know some dog-lovers out there just stopped reading. Relax, I'm sure Skippy has traits, but that's another subject.

Coming back to Gordon Allport, he studied personality by looking at language as a means to determine what traits constituted the core of personality. Allport examined words used to describe people and pared them down into three essential categories of traits:

>> **Cardinal traits:** A single characteristic that guides the majority of a person's actions. Think of one personality feature that best describes someone you know: cool, kind, hotheaded, or arrogant.

>> **Central traits:** The five to ten main traits that make up a person's major personality features. For example, when describing your sweetheart, you may refer to these characteristics: funny, considerate, intellectual, passive, and genuine.

>> **Secondary traits:** Less influential characteristics that affect fewer situations than the more predominant traits.

Allport essentially started the method of trying to filter personality from a large list of descriptors to a core short list of traits. Another psychologist, Raymond Cattell, continued this method and developed a personality test that measured 16 (core) traits, called the *16pf* (16 personality factors). (For details on personality testing, see Chapter 16.)

Still another psychologist (Hans Eysenck) went even further using the same method and concluded that all personality consists of varying degrees of three traits:

>> **Extraversion:** Sociable, outgoing, active

>> **Neuroticism:** Tense, anxious, guilty

>> **Psychoticism:** Aggressive, cold, egocentric

The culmination of the trait approach over years and years of personality research resulted in an empirically acceptable and generally well-regarded trait model of personality known as the *Big Five*. This model establishes a set of five traits that are considered the most core features of personality. Think of each factor as a continuum of high and low levels of these featured traits:

>> **Openness to experience:** An "open" person is independent rather than conforming, more imaginative than practical, and prefers variety over routine.

>> **Conscientiousness:** A conscientious person is careful rather than careless, disciplined and not impulsive, and well-organized.

>> **Extraversion:** Extraverts are talkative, fun loving, and sociable.

>> **Agreeability:** Agreeable folks are more sympathetic than critical, kind and not cold, and appreciative.

>> **Neuroticism:** Neurotics are characteristically tense, anxious, and insecure.

What's your "Magic 5" formula? With a list of five factors, there is a wide range of possible combinations. That leaves a fair amount of room for individuality and considering that these are dimensions, it may just cover the billions of people on the planet.

They Made Me This Way

In 1977, Albert Bandura conducted a now-famous study that looked into the possibility of a violent personality and turned his theory into a broader theory of personality. The experiment is now called the *Bobo Doll study*. Bobo dolls are those plastic blow-up figures with a weighted bottom that bounce back when you hit or kick them. The experiment consisted of an adult punching and kicking a Bobo doll while a young child watches. Then, the child is put into the room with the Bobo doll by himself. Can you guess what happens? Little Johnny turns into Little Rocky. He punches and kicks that Bobo doll just like he saw the adult do it.

Bandura's *social-learning theory* explains this phenomenon. Basically, people can learn something just by watching or observing it. This is one of those "no duh!" theories in psychology. But hey, no one else put the theory out there the way Bandura did. Social-learning theory has become a powerful theory of personality and its development. Our personalities are a "product" of our observational learning experiences from those around us. We're all just a bunch of copycats. If you see your parents being obnoxious, you probably act obnoxious, too.

REMEMBER

Bandura continued to add to his copycat theory of personality by addressing the question of why people do what they do. In other words, what motivates people to act in certain ways?

He introduced two very important concepts to address this:

>> **Self-efficacy** is a personal belief in one's ability to successfully perform a behavior. This belief is based on what Bandura called the *self-appraisal process,* which is simply an analysis of one's actions — an evaluation of successes and failures. A sense of one's capabilities arises from this process, and a person is motivated by her beliefs about her ability to succeed and inhibited by expected failures. You do what you think you can do and vice versa.

>> **Self-reinforcement** is as simple as giving yourself rewards for doing things. Some parents give their children rewards or reinforcement for doing their homework or cleaning their room. Bandura believed that everyone does this for themselves to some extent and that most people would benefit from doing more of it. So the next time you do something, give yourself a little reward. It will help your self-efficacy.

Representing Ourselves

Some psychologists emphasize the way people represent themselves and their experiences of the world as core aspects of personality and behavior. You've probably been to an office party or holiday party at school where some genius tries to be helpful by giving everyone a nametag. I'm always tempted to put something goofy on mine or to use someone else's name.

The tag is a crude form of representation, or presentation, of yourself to other people. Sometimes I put a nickname on mine — I've had a few. Nicknames are good examples of a "tag" that tells you a little more about a person than her everyday name. When you meet someone nicknamed "Stinky" or "Psycho," you get a different impression than you would from "Lefty" or "Slim."

Nametags, nicknames, and common names are all examples of representations of who you are. They are convenient and shortened ways to organize a whole lot of information about someone. Ever have a conversation about a movie and forget the name of the main actor? "You know, that guy who was in that one movie with that one woman?" Just saying "Brad Pitt" is so much easier than explaining the person's characteristics every time you want to talk about him. This way of organizing information about people and the world is the product of the human mind's tendency to impose order and structure on our experiences.

Schemas

The structured representation of experience is based on recurrences of similar qualities of a person or experience across repeated events. This order takes the form of *schemas,* or mental constructs for "Joe," "Brad Pitt," or "me." Joe is my neighbor who plays his music too loud. Brad Pitt is a famous actor that every man envies. Me? I'm that guy who envies Brad Pitt. After these structured representations of the self and others are developed, people can use them to recognize and understand newly encountered information; the representations influence how a person interacts with the world.

Unhelpful schemas are emphasized in schema-focused therapy developed by Dr. Jeffery Young.

REMEMBER

Cognitive personality psychologists emphasize the schema-based representation of experience as the central organizing construct in human personality. Two basic types of schemas play a role in establishing regularities and patterns of personality: self-schemas and socially relevant schemas.

>> **Self-schemas** are the organized units of information about yourself; sometimes these are called *self-concepts*. What is the concept of "you" or "me"? An in-depth discussion of how a person's identity is developed is beyond the scope of this section, but, exact details aside, your identity is represented in the form of schemas.

>> **Social-schemas** are integrated conceptual networks that incorporate your own sense of identity and others' opinions of you. These schemas provide detailed information about someone, ranging from demographics (such as how old someone is) to his values, and this information can be updated automatically through experience or revised through conscious attention and effort.

Scripts

Socially relevant schemas involve the representation of categories of other people, environments, social behavior, and stereotyped expectations. These are sometimes called *scripts*, organized sequences of actions typically expected in various situations. Is an actor in a movie presenting his off-screen personality or simply acting out a script that tells him how to act, when to speak, when to cry, and so on? It's a script, of course.

Imagine, now, that everyone you see in a day is acting out a "personality" script of his or her own, written by the author of experience and development. These scripts determine the how they act out — what they say and do. This is the gist of the scripts theory of personality. Pretty simple, right?

Not so fast! A sense that personalities are actually quite complex holds water. Walter Mischel (1980) attempted to add some flavor to the rather dry basic version of personality scripts. He introduced five ways that an individual person's personality is more than just scripted by a situation: *competencies, encoding strategies, expectancies, subjective values,* and *self-regulatory mechanisms.*

>> There is so much more to personality than meets the eye, and one important aspect of personality is an individual's unique collection of skills and abilities for solving problems and analyzing the world. Mischel called these *competencies.*

How you engage and overcome the challenges in your life, in part, defines your personality. Are you a "go-getter" or an "analyzer"? Have you ever built something like an extra room, a playhouse, or maybe a doghouse? How did you go about doing it? Some people sit down and figure everything out in advance, drawing out a blueprint with precise measurements and specifications. Others just get what supplies they think they may need and figure it out as they go along. A good way to test yourself is with something I call the "Directions Test." When you buy something that needs to be assembled, do you look at the instructions, or do you toss them to the side?

>> Because cognitive personality theory puts so much emphasis on information and how it is stored and interpreted, an important aspect of personality involves the strategies and constructs used to organize information. This is the process of building those complex schemas and scripts that eventually guide your behavior. *Encoding strategies* are a person's unique way of managing and interpreting the world. It is pretty easy for two people to witness the exact same event and come up with two entirely different interpretations of it. Anyone who's ever had an argument with a wife, husband, or significant other can vouch for that!

>> You're only as special as your expectations of a situation. Are you an eternal optimist or a pessimist? *Expectancies* consist of expectations or predictions that one event will necessarily follow another. These expectations set up the rules for what to do and how to manage specific situations. If the rules match the reality of a situation, then the behavior will be effective, and a feeling of mastery will develop. If not, I guess the only option is to keep on trying.

>> Do you work for free? Not many of us do. Most of us work for the incentive of getting paid. Incentives act as motivators toward a certain behavior. People are not all tempted by the same things, though. *Subjective values* represent what things are important to individuals and determine what they are willing to do to earn them. Hey, if you like getting little golden stars on your paycheck instead of a raise for a job well done, knock yourself out. That's what makes you so unique.

>> What are your goals in life? Do you have a master plan or a blueprint? You may not realize it, but according to Mischel, all of us have what he called *self-regulatory systems and plans*. You set a goal, you go for it, you analyze whether you meet that goal or not, and you make the necessary adjustments. Each of us has a unique way of doing this that characterizes our personal style.

Ultimately, according to this representational view of personality, how a person sees themselves and views the world, and the ways that these views get planned out in the form of behavioral blueprints represent personality.

It Depends on the Situation

So by now, one might think that our "personhood" just goes with us wherever we go, showing up to events, activities, and situations, being the same, acting the same, thinking and feeling the same. But wait. What about that time your normally quiet cousin was dancing on the tables at that wedding? Or the time someone who is normally bold and brash becomes a coy little child when meeting her favorite celebrity? There's a scene in one my favorite moves, *Stepbrothers* (2008), with Will Ferrell and John C. Reilly, where the father of John C. Reilly's character (Dale), Dr. Doback, played by Richard Jenkins, meets Will Ferrell's character's (Brennan) brother Derek, played by Adam Scott. They're all eating dinner together and Dr. Doback is just smitten with Derek, his tales, his swagger, his cool. Dr. Doback is giddy, giggling, and acting very differently. Derek's mother Nancy (played by Mary Steenburgen), who is recently married to Dr. Doback, can't believe her eyes. Who is this person? Why is he laughing that way? What's going on? I highly recommend this movie by the way, despite its R rating.

Isn't personality supposed to be immutable? I can tell you that I am no stranger to this seeming inconsistency. If anyone has ever seen me at my kids' water polo games, they would tell you that there was no way I was a psychologist who specializes in working with kids. (By the way, yes, water polo is an actual sport; it doesn't involve swimming horses; and it's really quite the thing in California.) Now, I'm not inappropriate in any way, but I'm loud, really loud, and obsessed, and not the poster child for stability (not that any of those traits are bad for a psychologist).

There are personality psychologists who are attempting to address these seeming inconsistencies with a line of thinking and research known as *situational psychology*. Remember Dr. David Funder from earlier in the chapter? Well, Dr. Funder is one of the leading minds in this approach to personality, and he states that we have created a "false dichotomy" between personal and situational determinants of behavior. He cites research that demonstrates that behavior can be a product of situational changes while also maintaining stable qualities across situations. It's as if our personality is loosely pieced together but not so loose that we are not recognizable across situations. This "looseness" shows malleability and helps us be more flexible and adaptive. Imagine how annoying I would be if I acted like a "psychologist" at a water polo game or any other situation outside of my work and practice? I think most people don't want to be analyzed poolside!?

Dr. Funder proposes a solution to "variant vs. invariant" problem in terms of what he calls the *personality triad* of persons, situations, and behaviors. How's that for a unifying concept in psychology? The personality triad is as follows:

Situation = Behavior × Person

Person = Situation × Behavior

Behavior = Person × Situation

Of course, that all sounds like common sense. Situational personality researchers didn't stop there. They have proposed a "classification system of situations" to flesh out this approach. They propose that people perceive and categorize situations in the much the same way they classify other people. It's like the personification of situations. This process provides humans with an overall taxonomy of situation perception that allows for the efficient deployment of adaptive behavior without having to process every single cue, stimulus, and situation anew. These categories of situations help guide our thoughts, behavior, and feelings in optimal ways. It's a shortcut! The proposed classification system goes by the catchy acronym DIAMONDS, which represent eight dimensions of situations that are used to determine our responses:

>> **Duty:** Refers to the characteristics of a situation that require fulfilling duties, tasks, problem solving and decision making

>> **Intellect:** The characteristics of a situation that call for intellectual engagement, deep reflection, daydreaming, and display of intelligence

>> **Adversity:** The characteristics of a situation that are threatening, conflictual, competitive, and possible victimization

>> **Mating:** Situation characteristics related to sex, love, and romance

>> **Positivity:** Characteristics of a situation perceived as fun, pleasant, and easy

>> **Negativity:** Situation characteristics that elicit frustration, anxiety, anger, and other negative feelings

>> **Deception:** Situation characterized by deception, mistrust, lying

>> **Sociality:** Socializing, interacting, relating, warmth, reassurance

WHAT HAPPENED TO FREUD?

Some readers may have noticed that there is no mention of Sigmund Freud, or any other psychoanalytic/psychodynamic theorists in this personality chapter. This is deliberate and not due to any disrespect to these great thinkers. However, the scientific status of Freud's and other psychoanalytic/psychoanalytic thinkers' writings on personality has for quite some time been viewed as purely theoretical at best, and as Dr. David Funder (I know, again?) puts it, we should not be taking a "tour of the graveyard," covering "brilliant but long-deceased theorists" work. Sorry Sigmund, Heinz, Anna, Otto, Robert, Karen, Melanie, Ronald, D. W., and Margaret. You will be missed.

Feeling Self-Conscious

In case you haven't noticed, psychologists take nothing for granted. If I had John Wayne in therapy and he came in with his macho, "I know who I am, and I'm not going to change" attitude, I'd take the bait. I'd say, "Okay, who are you?" It's easy to take knowing who you are for granted. Until someone asks, most of us go around assuming we know who we are. This is the age-old question of *self*. What is a self, and how do I know if I have one? What is my identity? Who am I?

Have you ever seen a dog stand in front of a mirror? (So we're talking about dogs now? Yep!) Sometimes they bark at themselves or stand there with a puzzled look. Believe it or not, the ability to recognize oneself in the mirror is pretty advanced, and dogs have yet to demonstrate that they can do it. Some psychologists argue that it is a uniquely human ability, although some research has shown that teenage chimpanzees, magpies (a type of bird), elephants, and orangutans can recognize themselves in a mirror.

When we've developed a sense of self-awareness, we've achieved a state of self-consciousness. Why do I say "developed"? Aren't we aware of ourselves at birth? Actually, it may take up to five or six months for an infant to develop anything even remotely resembling self-consciousness.

The mirror technique is one of the tools that psychologists have used to test infants' and toddlers' levels of self-consciousness. The simplest form of this test involves just setting an infant down in front of a mirror and watching her response. Some researchers have shown that 5- to 6-month-olds will reach out and touch the mirror image, suggesting they think it's another baby, or at least someone different from them.

In 1979, Michael Lewis and Jeanne Brooks-Gunn conducted a sophisticated version of the mirror test. They applied some blush to the noses of two sets of children: 15- to 17-month-olds and 18- to 24-month-olds. The idea: If the kids look in the mirror and see the blush on their nose, they'll touch it or try to remove it in some way. But this requires the child to realize that the person in the mirror is himself. So what happened? Just a few of the 15- to 17-month-olds actually reached up and touched their noses, but the vast majority of the 18- to 24-month-old children did it. So the older children were more likely to recognize themselves in the mirror.

REMEMBER

Self-consciousness and self-awareness are the same thing. Being self-conscious just means being aware of oneself. But too much of anything can be bad. Usually when someone says that she is "self-conscious," she means that she is aware of some flaw. This is not the type of self-consciousness I am talking about in this section.

SHOWING UP IN THE BUFF

I used to have this recurring dream where I would find myself naked in some public place. In one of the dreams, I was back in elementary school, and the only thing I was wearing was a fur coat, with nothing underneath. I was pretty worried about what these dreams meant. Did I have a fur-coat fetish or was I an exhibitionist? I was glad to find out that these dreams were probably about self-consciousness. Each of us has different situations that exemplify feeling extremely self-conscious and exposed. For some people, the situation is public speaking; for others, it's dancing in a nightclub or wearing nothing but a fur coat.

Here, I'm talking about these specific types of awareness:

>> Body awareness

>> Private self-consciousness

>> Public self-consciousness

Becoming aware of your body

Body awareness begins with a simple question: Where do I physically begin, and where do I physically stop? Remember the movie *Malice* with Bill Pullman, Nicole Kidman, and Alec Baldwin? In one scene, Bill and Alec are sitting in bar, and Alec asks Bill to name the part of his body that is most expendable. In other words, Alec wants Bill to choose the part of his body that he could lose without taking a severe blow to his sense of self. If you've seen the movie, you know why he asks this creepy question; it's foreshadowing.

What part of your body is most important to your sense of self? It may sound strange, but being able to tell the difference between your body and someone else's body is crucial to self-consciousness. Think about newborns. The physical connection between a child and a breast-feeding mother is undeniable, and a child's realization of a sense of difference, or separateness, from the mother develops slowly over a period of several months.

Keeping it private

How well do you know yourself? Are you always trying to figure yourself out? The internal focus on your thoughts, feelings, motivations, and overall sense of self is called your *private self-consciousness*. When you "look within," you're privately self-conscious. But if you "look within" a little too much, you can be privately "spaced-out."

Showing it off

I was leaving for work one morning and realized, when I got outside to my car, that I'd forgotten something. I did the big finger snap and the one-eye squint, made an about-face, and went back inside. What are these things? They sound like something from a *Seinfeld* episode, but I bet you know these actions — those behaviors you do when you forget something. Why did I make these gestures? If I didn't, I'd look like an idiot for walking to my car and then walking back again for no apparent reason. Why did I need a reason? Someone was watching me!

This is the *invisible audience* phenomenon — a sense that you're on display when you're in public and that people are watching you. Teenagers always seem to be on stage. If they trip over a crack in the sidewalk, they turn bright red and run off giggling. This is an example of *public self-consciousness,* a sense of being in the presence of others or our public image — whether others are actually watching or not.

The most noticeable aspect of public self-consciousness is awareness and focus on appearances. People don't spend billions of dollars a year on nice clothes, gym memberships, and diets for nothing. Public self-consciousness is a big part of who you are and how you see yourself.

Identifying Yourself

An easy way to find out who you are is to ask other people. Your identity is often deeply tied to the way other people see you. When you look into the mirror, what do you see? Have you ever wondered how you look to other people? Do they see the same person you see in the mirror? The part of your self-concept that is based on other people's reactions to and views of you is called your *looking-glass self,* one of the most basic concepts of self. People are, after all, social creatures, and it would be hard to argue against the idea that at least part of a person's self-concept depends on the views of others.

Daniel Stern (a notable psychoanalyst specializing in infant development) proposed a theory of self-concept that gives us a good look into how people develop a unique "self." From his studies on infants, he proposed that all people are born with an innate ability to become aware of themselves through a series of experiences.

People are born with the *emergent self,* which basically consists of subjective experiences of joy, distress, anger, and surprise. Feelings! The *core self* begins to arise between the ages of 2 and 4 months, when memories start to form and people develop a sense of their physical capabilities. Next comes the *subjective self,* which emerges when an infant realizes that she can share her experiences with other people. A good example of this is when a baby tries to give you a drink off her bottle before she drinks it. And finally, the *verbal self* develops as we use language to organize a sense of self.

Arnold Buss, an American researcher and psychologist, provides a good look at the meaning of *identity.* Two aspects comprise a person's identity:

>> Personal identity

>> Social identity

Forging a personal identity

My *personal identity* consists of the things that make me stand out in a crowd — like my massive biceps and athletic prowess. Actually, I'm thinking of something a little more psychological, even though physical appearance does make up part of a person's identity. According to Buss, the personal identity is comprised of a *public self* and a *private self,* each with its own components.

Three important aspects make up the *public self:*

>> **Appearance:** As I mention earlier in the "Showing it off" section, being aware of your appearance is very much a part of your identity. This is not a uniquely western perspective. Cultures all over the world engage in elaborate and sophisticated attempts to improve appearances and enhance personal beauty, as defined by each particular culture. Some philosophers state that a sense of aesthetics is essential for the good life — central to a person's self-concept.

>> **Style:** George Clooney, Johnny Depp, and Jay Z have style. The way they talk, their body language, and their facial expressions are undeniably "them." Everyone has a peculiar way of speaking and moving. Even a person's handwriting is unique. These things make up a person's style. Don't get confused by the Clooney, Depp, or Z examples though; style isn't about being "cool." My style is unique to me, whether it's cool or not. It's the "Dr. Cash" style, and no matter what others may say, I think it's very cool.

>> **Personality:** Personality theories attempt to account for individuality based on differences among personalities. If someone put my personality inside another person's body, would my friends recognize me? Maybe not at first, but they may eventually start to notice that something is up because personalities make people unique; they make a person identifiable. Personalities are enduring, and they don't change easily. Because of their consistency and stability, personalities are good representations of who a person is, even if he acts differently from time to time. Chapter 9 is about personality.

The *private self* consists of characteristics that are difficult for others to see and observe. When a patient comes in for psychotherapy, a psychologist has a difficult time helping him if he refuses to talk about his private self — his thoughts, feelings, and daydreams and fantasies.

>> **Thoughts:** Knowing what someone is thinking is hard, unless he tells you. Some people are better than others at figuring out what people are thinking, but it's really nothing more than a sophisticated guessing process. My thoughts are unique to me.

>> **Feelings:** Mental health professionals often evaluate new patients at psychiatric hospitals with something called the *mental status examination.* The professional observes the patient, partly to figure out how the patient feels. This observable aspect of how someone feels is the *affect.* But what about what the person says? I've often not seen someone's depression even when she tells me that she is extremely sad. This is called *mood,* a person's own private experience of feeling. When patients tell me how they feel, I have to take their word for it. It's pretty hard to tell someone that he's not sad when he tells you he is.

>> **Daydreams and fantasies:** Who would you be without your daydreams and fantasies? Again, fantasies are typically private, especially the sexual ones. Yours are unique to you, and they define you.

YOU ARE WHAT YOU DO

The most interesting aspect about identity is that, as people grow older, the way they define themselves changes. Elementary school children often define who they are by the things that they do. Very young children may identify themselves by saying, "I run. I play. I ride my bike." When these children become teenagers, this shifts to psychological concepts such as beliefs, motivations, desires, and feelings. "I want to go to the dance" or "I feel very sad today." How do adults define themselves? Probably by combining both types of self-definition: activity and psychological concepts. For example, "I'm a sad psychologist who can't golf."

Carving out a social identity

What's your name? Where are you from? What's your religion? Each of these questions is a component of one aspect of your *social identity* — those things that identify you with a particular societal category.

Group affiliation refers to things such as your vocations and social clubs. Many people identify themselves by the type of work they do for a living. "I'm a fireman!" "I'm a cop!" I'm a psychologist. But another important dimension of the social identity is the kinds of social clubs and cliques a person affiliates with. One would be hard pressed to deny the strong identification that many college men have with their fraternities. Other people see themselves as "cowboys" because they strap on boots, jeans, and a cowboy hat and go line dancing at a local Western club. No matter what you're into, it often gives you a sense of uniqueness that goes beyond the other aspects of personal identity. Your social identity is comprised of certain identity factors that, when taken all together, equal the social "you." These factors include kinship, race and ethnicity, and religious beliefs.

Kinship

Most people realize that *kinship* is central to social identity. Your relatives are your "kin," and most people get their last name from their family of origin. In the United States, last names are legal names and a fairly reliable way to identify people. Although many people have the same name, many more do not.

In Arabic culture, a last name is not the primary way to identify someone's kin. Legally, last names are often used for identification, but a person is socially identified by who his father is, and a father is identified by who his oldest son is. Instead of being "Mr. Nasser Khoury," an individual in this culture would be "Father of Josef" or "Abu Josef." The son, "Josef Khoury," would be "Son of Nasser," or "Bin Nasser," or "Josef Nasser."

Ethnicity and nationality

Ethnicity is another important aspect of social identity and is defined as a classification of belonging to a particular group based on a similar cultural tradition. Often, you can find these common categories on job and school applications. The categories are rather arbitrary in name, but they do include a lot of information. Some people are more comfortable not identifying ethnic differences between people because they fear discrimination. But ethnicity is very much a part of who people are and the culture that guides their lives.

REMEMBER

Nationality is not the same as ethnicity. I can be a born-and-raised Canadian citizen with Japanese ethnicity. Both ethnicity and nationality are important pieces of information about a person because a Peruvian citizen of Japanese descent is likely very different from a Canadian citizen of Japanese descent.

Religious and group affiliations

Religious affiliation affects a person's social identity to varying degrees. In Israel, for example, most of the inhabitants of the city of Nazareth are of Arabic ethnicity, but there are two distinct religious groups: Muslims and Christians. An individual's religious identity is a core aspect in determining who she is. Some Americans strongly identify themselves by religious denomination: Roman Catholic, Presbyterian, Lutheran, Muslim, Jewish, Hindu, and so on.

Mustering up some self-esteem

Unfortunately, sometimes having a *looking-glass self* can be a bad thing. (See "Identifying Yourself" earlier in this chapter.) As long as other people see you in a good light, all is well. But this is often not the case. Children, for example, are sometimes belittled, put down, or verbally abused by their own parents. Even adults know that others don't always hold them in the highest esteem, so many people don't have very high regard for themselves.

Sorry for the depressing introduction, but many people have come to understand the concept of *self-esteem,* an individual's evaluation of her self-worth, through its absence. Most of the people I know are pretty quick to point out if someone they know has low self-esteem. These folks are a dime a dozen. I mean, have you ever seen the "Self Improvement" section of a bookstore? It's usually pretty big, and I've yet to come across the "You're Already a Great Person!" section in the bookstores and libraries I visit.

REMEMBER

Buss provides a good review of six main sources of self-esteem:

>> **Appearance:** People usually feel better about themselves when they feel attractive. A lot of social psychology research has demonstrated that people judged to be attractive are granted more favors and preferred for social interaction than those who are not. Looking good means feeling good!

>> **Ability and performance:** People feel better about themselves when they get good grades, perform well at work, and otherwise do things successfully. The more a person is able to accomplish for himself, the more likely he is going to feel good about himself.

>> **Power:** When a person feels like she's in control of her life, she's more likely to feel good about herself. There are at least three sub-sources of a sense of power: dominance, status, and money. Domination can be achieved by coercion, competition, or leadership. Status and money pretty much speak for themselves. I'm not saying that unknown, poor people feel bad about themselves, but they'd probably feel better if they had some status and a bigger bank account.

>> **Social rewards:** Three types of social rewards tend to make people feel good about who they are.

- *Affection:* People like you.

- *Praise:* Someone tells you that you're doing a good job.

- *Respect:* Others value your opinions, thoughts, and actions.

>> **Vicarious elements:** This source of self-esteem is all about feeling good about yourself because of things "outside" rather than "inside." *Reflected glory* makes you feel good because you get a boost from being around or associated with successful, powerful, or popular people. It's the I-know-famous-people form of self-esteem. Having nice material possessions can also make some people feel better about themselves.

>> **Morality:** Morality involves being a good person and living according to the standards and rules of social conduct that you admire. Being a good person never hurts self-esteem. For the most part, morality is a relative term. But, when someone feels that he's taken the moral high ground (however he defines it) in a situation, he is likely to have positive self-esteem.

In addition to these sources of self-esteem, some research also suggests that certain aspects of personality can make an impact on self-esteem. Shyness and social loneliness have been found to be associated with a sense of low self-worth. On the flip side, people who are optimistic and sociable typically report feeling better about themselves. It seems, then, that being social and having good relationships are important to feeling good about oneself. That brings me to the topic of relationships, as I leave the realm of the isolated self behind.

IN THIS CHAPTER

» **Connecting with others**

» **Enjoying family**

» **Hanging out with friends**

» **Engaging in romance and love**

» **Getting to know you**

» **Communicating with others**

Chapter **10**

Connecting

We are better together, right? Well, better or not, we all find ourselves embedded in a field of relationships with others. What happens as we leave the virtual loneliness and move towards others? How do we bridge the seeming chasm between us and the other human beings around us? That brings us to the topic of relationships and how they are formed.

Can there be a "self" without an "other"? Here's what object-relations theorist N. Gregory Hamilton says:

> Afraid of our aloneness and smallness, we need to gain courage by taking in love and nurturance from our caretakers. . . . Only after we receive the concern which we need can we grow strong and confident enough to accept our weaknesses and longings as our own and care about others.

Psychoanalysts always did have a penchant for the literary, and although his statement does not sound very scientific, Hamilton is talking about one of the pillars of psychological inquiry: *relationships*. Whether we are connected or not is really not a question. We are. So how does that happen? In this chapter, I discuss how we become connected, build relationships, love, figure each other out, and communicate.

Getting Attached

Humans are unarguably social creatures. Some are very social, and others are less so; but most people have a desire to socialize at least a little bit. In fact, if a person has an extreme disinterest in social interactions, he may have a form of mental illness called *schizoid personality disorder*. Personality disorders are tackled in depth in Chapter 15.

The most basic human relationships are between two people — husband and wife, brother and sister, friend and friend. How do you cross the divide between your isolated self and the people in the world around you? Psychologists have approached this problem by looking at what is typically a person's first relationship: mother and child. I realize that this is not the first relationship for everyone. Some people are raised by their grandparents or by foster parents. So in actuality, the earliest relationships that people have are with primary caregivers, who may or may not be their mothers.

Realizing even monkeys get the blues

Researchers often analyze the primary relationship between a caregiver and a child by using a concept called *attachment*. John Bowlby is considered the dominant figure in attachment research. (Does that mean he has high self-esteem, you think?) Bowlby's theory stated that infants are essentially dependent on their caregivers for providing the necessities of life (food, shelter, stimulation, love, and so forth). For the most part, infants are helpless, except for their ability to "attach" to and form a relationship with their primary caregiver(s). This connection or attachment ensures that the infant's needs are met.

REMEMBER

When an infant finds himself in a threatening situation, he attempts to reconnect to his primary caregiver. This is called *attachment behavior* — anything an infant does to attain or maintain closeness to someone perceived as better able to cope with the world. A primary caregiver is viewed as an *attachment figure*. If you know that your attachment figures are available when you need them, you feel more secure.

Bowlby viewed attachment as an essential aspect of leading a productive and psychologically healthy life. In fact, when attachment is lacking, infants often suffer from depression, anxiety, and a generally poor psychological well-being. In the 1950s, for example, mental health professionals began to investigate the effects of long-term hospitalization and institutionalization on infants, and they documented severe problems. The adverse effects of inadequate or absent care during infancy and early childhood were undeniable. Children need access to caregivers whom they know and are connected to.

In 1959, University of Wisconsin-Madison psychologist Harry Harlow conducted an interesting experiment with monkeys. He put baby monkeys in a cage with two different dummy versions of mother monkeys. One of the dummies was made of soft cloth and had no food; the other was made of wire but had food for the babies to eat. The babies preferred contact with the soft dummy over the wire dummy in spite of the presence of food. Harlow conducted another experiment in which he deprived baby rhesus monkeys of social contact with other monkeys for as long as six months. When these monkeys were released to be with others, their behavior resembled that of a depressed and anxious human with severe levels of withdrawal, self-harming behavior (such as biting themselves), and nervousness.

Attaching with style

It should be undeniable that attachment represents an essential relationship for all people, but I'm sure you well know that the gap between ideal and reality can be vast; the concept of human attachment is no exception. Some people are in therapy today because of the less-than-ideal relationships they had with their primary caregivers. So if Bowlby presented us with the ideal, what else is there?

Various *attachment styles* theories address the variations on Bowlby's ideal relationship. They used the *strange situation* technique to determine the nature and extent of children's attachment. In the strange situation, a child and her primary caregiver are put in a room with some toys to play with. Then, the primary caregiver gets up and leaves the room. Researchers observe and record the child's reaction. After a while, a stranger comes into the room, and the child's reaction is recorded again. Finally, the primary caregiver comes back into the room, and the child's behavior is recorded one last time.

Researchers designed the strange situation to determine if a child uses the caregiver as a secure base from which to explore the environment. A child sees a caregiver as a *secure base* — a safe place to launch explorations into the world from but someone to safely return to if there is a need. The strange situation observed the following in order to answer these questions:

>> When the caregiver leaves, does the child fuss or react with protest?

>> If there is a protest, is it because the child prefers to be with the caregiver, or is it because the child fears that the caregiver won't return?

>> When the caregiver returns, does the child welcome him or her back, or does the child react in some other, more resentful or distant manner?

The answers to these questions lead to a description of three basic attachment styles:

>> **Secure:** Securely attached children exhibit the following behavior:

- They use their primary caregiver as a secure base from which to explore their environments.

- They protest a little when their caregiver leaves but eventually calm down, seeming to trust that he will return.

- While with strangers or other adults, they're friendly but not overly so.

- Upon reunion, they go to the primary caregiver and seek connection.

>> **Anxious/ambivalent:** Anxious/ambivalently attached children act in the following ways:

- They do not use their caregivers as secure bases to explore from.

- They sometimes resist initial contact with the caregiver but staunchly resist any attempt to break it off after it has been established.

- They are avoidant or sometimes aggressive in the presence of strangers.

- They cry excessively upon separation and are difficult to console.

>> **Avoidant:** Avoidant attached children act as follows:

- They seem to need less contact from the caregiver.

- They are indifferent when left alone or cry only because they are alone and not because they seem to miss the caregiver.

- Upon the return of the caregiver, they either avoid or ignore her.

Before anybody designs his own little "strange situation" at home to see how much his children love him or not, let me tell you about *goodness-of-fit*. Goodness-of-fit refers to how well the primary caregiver and the child are matched in terms of temperament and personality. This fit can have an effect on attachment style and should be considered before anyone writes himself off as a horrible parent or "unlovable child."

TIP

Caregivers and infants sometimes can look like they're engaged in a harmonious dance, perfectly synchronized with each other. Other times, they look like they both have two left feet. If a mother is high-strung and energetic, she may not do well with a mellow baby — and vice versa. The style of interaction and how smoothly it happens is a powerful factor in establishing a secure attachment. So if you're having trouble and you think that your child is poorly attached, take a look at the style of interaction and see whether there's anything you can do differently to improve it.

Cavorting with Family and Friends

Ever wonder why so many people get depressed during the holidays? Maybe they're not looking forward to going into debt to finance all those gifts. Or maybe the holidays remind them how lonely they are. I'm not buying it. Here's my explanation: The holidays mean getting together with family, and families are pretty good at embarrassing and belittling each other by pointing out weight problems and receding hairlines or pitiful salaries. That can be pretty depressing! Fortunately, families are good for some positive things, too.

A *family* consists of at least two people related by blood, marriage, or adoption. It seems like families have changed quite a bit over the last 20 years, including increasing numbers of single-parent families, gay marriages, and blended families of divorce. A lot of marriages end in divorce, so children are learning to manage two sets of parents, half-siblings, and split holidays. Even though the modern face of the family has changed, many of the basic functions of a family have not.

The *McMaster model of family functioning* breaks down seven major components of, you guessed it, family functioning:

>> **Problem solving:** The family's ability to resolve issues and maintain family functioning.

>> **Communication:** The clarity and directness of information exchange in a family. You knew this one was coming.

>> **Roles:** The different behaviors and responsibilities of each family member in terms of meeting basic needs, performing household tasks, and providing emotional support and nurturance.

>> **Affective responsiveness:** Each family member's ability to express and experience a range, intensity, and quality of emotions.

>> **Affective involvement:** The family as a whole's interest in the values, activities, and interests of others.

>> **Behavior control:** The rules and standards of conduct. Belching at the dinner table was never a laughing matter in my family — even if we were supping on soda and cauliflower!

>> **Overall family functioning:** A family's ability to accomplish its daily tasks across the other six areas. If you had to give your family a grade, what would it be?

REMEMBER

CHILDREN OF DIVORCE

The effects of divorce on children have been a matter of controversy since the first pen scrawled across the dotted line of those famed papers. And many parents stay together "for the sake of the kids." Yet most research tends to show that children are not necessarily adversely affected by the divorce of their parents. Boys seem to do a little worse than girls in the long run, but research indicates that the most important predictor of how children will cope with a divorce is the nature of the marriage. If the parents always fight and have a tumultuous relationship while married, then the divorce is also likely to go poorly and have a negative impact on the children's adjustment. Researchers often advise couples to not argue or discuss divorce-related issues in front of children and to keep overall conflict to an absolute minimum in order to avoid undue stress and strain and coping difficulties for the children.

Parenting with panache

A good friend of mine recently had a baby. Just when I was about to offer him some psychological advice on parenting, he started talking about all the advice people had been giving him and how it bothered him. I kept my opinion to myself. "Crying opens up their lungs." "Don't give babies a pacifier." There are almost as many opinions on how to raise children as there are people on the planet. Fortunately, psychologists have been trying to simplify things.

Diana Baumrind, a clinical and developmental psychologist, took on the task of trying to boil down parenting into something a little more manageable. She came up with three main parenting styles: *authoritarian*, *authoritative*, and *permissive*:

>> **Authoritarian:** These parents are rigid and dictatorial. Some kids feel like prisoners in their own families; parents are overly strict and don't listen to what the children have to say. They're like the drill sergeants of parenting. What they say goes, and there's no discussion about it. Unfortunately, all that toughness tends to backfire. Authoritarian parents tend to have children who are either overly passive or excessively rebellious and sometimes hostile. These parents can learn a lot from the next style of parenting.

>> **Authoritative:** These folks tend to approach parenting with a more democratic style. Parents from previous generations often criticize how "today's" parents try to reason with their children too much. "What that kid needs is a good spanking!" Authoritative parents listen to their children and allow them to have input, while maintaining parental authority and control. Children seem to thrive in this environment, and they tend to act more sociable, feel more capable, and be more well-adjusted in general as they grow up.

>> **Permissive:** There are two types of permissive parents:

- **Indulgent:** Ever go to one of those backyard beer parties in high school? Me neither, but I hear they can get pretty wild. I've always wondered where those kids' parents are. Oh, I get it; they've got the "cool parents." Indulgent parents are involved with their children but shy away from control, authority, and discipline. They sometimes even enable their children to engage in questionable behavior because they don't want to alienate their kids.

- **Indifferent:** These parents are neglectful due to a range of possible factors, including career obsession, drug abuse, or self-centeredness. Whatever the reason some people adopt this style, permissive parents tend to have children who report feeling ill-equipped to deal with the demands of growing up.

Embracing your rival: Siblings

Ever wonder what siblings are good for? Those of you who are only children may have fantasized about having a brother or a sister. Those with siblings may think those creatures are pretty much only good for fighting and stealing your crush, but psychologists have found that there's actually more to it.

Siblings have a powerful effect on a person's development. They create a family environment that would be very different without them. Siblings are also good sources of friendship, companionship, and affection. Sometimes they can even be role models. Here are three other distinct functions that siblings provide for each other:

>> **Mutual regulation:** Acting as sounding boards and testing grounds for new behavior, like practicing a break-up speech before delivering it to an unsuspecting sweetheart

>> **Direct services:** Easing household burdens and sometimes providing practical support, such as rides, help with homework, or fashion advice

>> **Support:** Helping each other in times of need by forming alliances and sticking together

Many people are familiar with sibling rivalry and discord. Research shows that the most common negative qualities associated with siblings are antagonism and quarreling. Some people think that the fighting goes away as people grow older, but the truth is that the basic emotional character of sibling relationships remains pretty stable over time. Interactions can change, but the feelings remain much the same.

Getting chummy: Bridge building

So far, I've been looking at the progression from first bonding relationships and moving farther and farther out into the social world. The bridge that takes us from Mom and Dad to the "world" is often seen as relationships with peers, or *friendship*.

How does that old saying go? "Friends are forever"? Or is it "Diamonds are forever"? I never can remember. I don't have many diamonds, so it doesn't really matter much anyway. But I do have friends, and friendship is an important element in life. Good friendships hold a special place in our hearts and minds. Where would Oprah Winfrey be without her Gayle King? SpongeBob without Patrick? Butch without Sundance? Prince Harry without Megan Markle?

Psychologists Willard Hartup and Nan Stevens provide a nice review of research related to friendship. They basically define *friendship* as a relationship between mutually attracted people engaged in a reciprocal relationship of exchange. Friends are different from non-friends in that our relationships are typically mutual. There's a lot of giving and taking and giving again in most friendships.

REMEMBER

Good friends provide support and help people cope with life's problems. But making friends isn't necessarily easy; it requires a fair amount of social skill. It doesn't hurt if you're socially well-adjusted. Being equal and fair also helps. And knowing how to manage conflicts when they arise helps maintain the friendships you develop.

Who are your friends? I'm guessing they're people much like you. Friends are typically similar in age, gender, ethnicity, and ability. A lot of times friends also have a similar lifestyle. Generally speaking, as people get older, friends tend to be people you work with, which means that they're probably of the same socioeconomic class as well. This still remains relatively true despite the popularity of social media and the use of the Internet as a social tool. Shoot, guess that means no rich friends for me!

Friendship tends to have a positive effect on psychological well-being. People who have good friendships tend to be more sociable, helpful, and confident. Friends are good for your health. So go out there and make a few!

The importance of friendships in helping us become better "connectors" starts early in our lives through childhood play with peers. Playing together as children helps us learn how to regulate our emotions, thoughts, and behavior based on learning how others feel, think, and behave. Studies show that children who "play well" together are more cooperative in less "fun tasks" or nonpreferred tasks like cleaning up and doing work. When we play together, we work through scenarios with each other when there's no real pressure per se, so the stakes are low. This helps us when the stakes are actually higher. These peer to peer interactions through play are good prep work for more and more relationships as our social world grows.

Attraction, Romance, and Love

Mates, partners, love interests: There are so many ways to think about the people we are attracted to and feel romantic love towards. In today's world, these concepts are less bound by gender roles, societal pressures, and traditional norms than perhaps ever before, but the underlying principles are thought to be the same nonetheless. I love (pun intended) a comedian who said that he answered his girlfriend when she asked him if she was "the one" by telling her, "You are one of the ones," because he hasn't met all that many people, and there may be more out there. Ouch! But cynicism aside, one only has to look at the sheer amount of "find a mate" shows on television to see that love is very much alive (*The Bachelor, The Bachelorette, 90-Day Fiancé, Married at First Site*, to name just a few).

How we choose the ones we love

So how do we "pick"? Psychologists Gul Gunaydin, Emre Selcuk, and Cindy Hazan break down the process into four stages: accessibility, appeal, attainability, and the one.

Accessibility

This principle can basically be summed up by saying that one criterion is a person's proximity in location and common social connections. Think of this as the "I have someone I want you to meet" principle.

Appeal

How appealing someone is to us can be broken down into three subcriteria:

>> **Similarity:** We like people like ourselves. (Ewww!) It's not that gross actually. Research just shows that we tend to be attracted to people in our own ethnic age, education, and religious groups. We also prefer potential love interests who are similar in physical attractiveness. (For more on the concept of "opposites attract," see the section "Love's expanse" later in this chapter.)

- » **Familiarity:** The more we know about a person, the more informed our choice is. Familiarity aides in information gathering. This is like the "she comes from a good family" criterion. It's like a shortcut to all kinds of relevant data and information about a person, such as social status, personality, attitudes, and beliefs.

- » **Attractiveness:** Of course this had to be on the list! To oversimplify (because entire books are written about this topic), as a rule, what many people find attractive are people in generally good moods most of the time; people who self-disclose and share information about themselves; and socially embedded ideas about physical attractiveness of one's facial features, body, voice, and even smell.

Attainability

This factor can be thought of as the "out of my league" or not criterion. Gunaydin, Selcuk, and Hazan state that we tend to like people who like us back. We learn that they are "attainable" based on this reciprocity. Liking me when I like you makes you "attainable."

The "one"

Finally, when all the accessible, appealing, and attainable possibilities are narrowed down, we arrive at romantic infatuation. As Dorothy Tennov states in her 1979 book, *Love and Limerence: The Experience of Being in Love,* we "lock the emotional gates against further intrusion" from all possible others.

So romantic, I know! Psychologists are kind of known for breaking things down into less "sexy" ways of looking at things.

Love's expanse

"You complete me." "You make me want to be a better person." "With you, I grow a thousand miles in every direction." Like that last one? I came up with it all by myself. But I had some help from a theoretical model known as the *self-expansion model of love*. There's a great line from the movie *The Danish Girl* (2015) that captures the sentiment perfectly: "I love you because you're the only person who made sense of me, who made me possible."

The self-expansion model of love, developed by Arthur Aron and Elaine N. Aron, proposes that love is built on two motivational principles:

- » The desire to expand all that is "you" in order to better accomplish and realize your goals

- » The "inclusion of others in self" principle

REMEMBER

Research shows that when we fall in love, our self-esteem and self-efficacy go up. We feel better and more confident in ourselves when loving and loved and when our mental image and construction of our "self" overlaps with a close other's mental image and construction of us. It's the scientific version of "seeing oneself in another's eyes."

The *Self-Expansion Questionnaire* is an instrument developed by Gary Lewandowski and Arthur Aron that is designed to measure to extent that someone experiences self-expansion in a relationship by asking whether a relationship provides new experiences, new perspectives, leads to learning new things, and makes someone a better person. This model essentially holds that attraction and reciprocal like through similarity and familiarity suggest to us that a relationship is "likely" and signals the potential for self-expansion. This may explain the old adage, "Opposites attract!"

THE SCIENCE OF GOOD MARRIAGE

Marriage is interesting at the very least. Considering that the divorce rate in the United States is cited at 42 to 45 percent according to some estimates, it would seem that it's essentially a coin-flip proposition. However, there has been some light shed on some of the aspects of a marriage that seem to predict success. Psychologist John Gottman has engaged in intense scientific analysis and has gifted us with the following "ingredients" for a successful marriage, which can be found in his book with Nan Silver, *The Seven Principles of Making a Marriage Work.* The seven principles are as follows:

1. **Enhance you love maps.** Be intimately knowledgeable of your partner's world.

2. **Nurture your fondness and admiration.** Continue to stay "in-like" with each other, seeing each other as worthy of honor and respect.

3. **Turn toward each other instead of away.** Make bids for your partner's attention and respond to their bids.

4. **Let your partner influence you.** Instead of feeling "nagged" or criticized, take in the advice and consider it. And maybe even do it!

5. **Solve your solvable problems.** Engage in effective conflict resolution and prioritize.

6. **Overcome gridlock.** Help each other achieve and realize their dreams and goals. Don't "block" each other.

7. **Create shared meaning.** Have a mutually enriching engagement around what's meaningful to both of you.

Connecting to Thoughts and Action

Humans are social beings, and no small part of survival depends on a person's ability to understand and effectively engage our social environment. Social understanding — including alliances, enemies, allocations of resources, division of labor, relationships, communication, and self-awareness — is vital. Psychologists of course have investigated the role of mental processes in this social dance by looking at what is called *social cognition*. The *APA Dictionary of Psychology* defines social cognition as processes in which people perceive, think about, interpret, categorize, and judge their own social behaviors and those of others. But thinking isn't enough, of course. We have to be able to communicate with each other as well. In this section, I discuss some critical categories of social skills, including understanding other people's behavior, thoughts, and feelings with social cognition.

Explaining others with person perception

People are always watching other people. When you go to a public place like a park or a busy shopping mall, how often do you just watch people? You may notice people's clothes, the bags they're carrying, or the conversations they're having. You're noticing all kinds of things about them and using your observations to draw conclusions.

Don't believe me? How many times have you decided that the teenager with purple hair and a pierced nose is just looking for attention? When's the last time you figured that the woman driving a brand-new SUV with kids in the back is a stay-at-home soccer mom with a successful husband paying the bills? Where do people come up with these ideas? Maybe the purpled-headed kid is conducting a psychology experiment. Perhaps the woman is a CEO and single mom. How do you know? If you're like most people, you almost instinctively begin drawing conclusions about other people based on what you see, hear, and experience.

Assuming

Trying to explain other people's behavior can be difficult. You can't look inside their minds, so you can only guess what's going on in there. But this doesn't stop people from trying to explain others' actions. In fact, it's so common that there's a word for it. The complex process of drawing conclusions about other people's intentions and characteristics, based on a person's observations of them, is the social cognitive process known as *person perception*. Almost everyone uses some assumptions in the person-perception process, including these:

>> People are *causal agents;* they play an active and intentional part in producing their own behavior. Nobody or nothing else causes them to behave in a particular way.

>> People are like me, thinking and feeling in the same ways I do. Thinking like this allows people to use themselves as a baseline when trying to understand other people.

Snapping to judgment

Have you ever experienced love at first sight? I've always wondered how that works. How can you fall in love with somebody based on just looking at him or her? Maybe research in the area of *snap judgments* can help answer that question. Snap judgments of people are instantaneous, automatic, and unconscious evaluations.

Snap judgments follow two types of cues:

>> **Static cues:** Things that are relatively unchanging about a person like appearance, gender, and body type (not including clothing). People use this information to make *evaluative judgments* about other people, and these judgments can be right or wrong. I may evaluate a person with a particular hairstyle as laid-back and easygoing (long and hippie-esque), or I may see him as nerdy and uptight (high and tight around the ears). Either way, I'm using an aspect of someone's physical appearance to make a judgment about what kind of person he is.

>> **Dynamic cues:** Things that tend to change depending on the situation, such as facial expressions, clothing, and mannerisms. When I see a person smile, I may evaluate him as generally happy, or I may assume that he just heard a funny joke. Either way, I'm using relatively basic information to make snappy evaluations of a person's personality or life.

Making an impression

Snap judgments are really just the beginning of attempts to figure out other people. We all make snap judgments and usually are unaware it's happening. In the process of *impression formation*, people go beyond snap judgments and make in-depth inferences about the kind of person someone is.

Solomon Asch, at Swarthmore College, came up with a popular theory of impression formation that focuses on the existence of *central traits* that color interpretations and perceived meanings of observed traits. It's like people have an internal sense that certain traits go together. For example, an attractive person may have an easier time getting someone to help him change a flat tire than an unattractive person. This may be related to an assumption that the attribute of attractiveness is automatically connected to the attribute of gratefulness. I'm not going to help an unattractive, ungrateful person change his tire.

Implicit personality theory

Jerome Bruner and Renato Tagiuri in the 1950s considered the internal sense of traits that belong together as part of an *implicit personality theory*. People learn that certain traits go together because they've either been told that they go together or observed them going together. I was told a thousand times that polite people don't interrupt, so I guess I'm pretty rude because I interrupt all the time. Interrupting and rudeness "belong" together in my implicit personality theory.

Basically, implicit personality theories are stereotypes. Stereotypes are an inevitable consequence of attempts to make sense of the social world. Stereotypes are thinking shortcuts. No one can possibly store independent evaluations of every single person he ever meets. This would take up way too much space in the human memory. Instead, people categorize other people, and sometimes this categorization results in the formation of stereotypes. Unfortunately, in an attempt to simplify the world, people often over-generalize negative aspects of others, which too often leads to prejudice and racism.

Figuring out the causes of others' behavior

Snappy judgments based on limited information aren't the only thinking shortcut; most people also attempt to determine why a person did what she did or what caused a particular behavior. This is known as *attribution,* a process by which a person's behavior is linked to either internal or external causes.

When making an attribution, a person typically considers three important pieces of information:

>> **Consistency:** People generally behave in the same way every time a particular situation occurs.

>> **Distinctiveness:** When a person behaves differently with different people and/or in different situations, his behaviors are considered "distinct."

>> **Consensus:** There's agreement that all people act in a particular way when engaged in particular activities or within specific contexts.

Numerous possible combinations of these three pieces of information exist in varying degrees, and these variations provide clues to whether a behavior is internally or externally motivated. For example, the combination of high consistency, low distinctiveness, and low consensus leads to a *personal attribution* (internal cause or explanation for a person's behavior). When I act consistently across situations, respond to the same stimuli the same way every time, and act differently than other people in that same situation, it's probably me. High consistency, high distinctiveness, and high consensus lead to an external attribution. When I act the same across situations, but I respond differently — but the same as other people in the situation — to the same stimuli, it's probably the situation or the external environment. So what would you attribute my passion for polka music to? Doesn't everyone love polka?

All of this judging begs the question of whether or not people are accurate in their attributions. A consistent mistake is called the *fundamental attribution error.* Most of the time folks underestimate the role of external causes as determinants of other people's behavior. There's a tendency to see what people do as inherent to them, as actor-caused, because you lack significant information about a person's behavior across situations. When in doubt, attribute it to the actor. The more information you have, the better judge you become.

Conversely, people also have a tendency to see their own behavior as a result of external causes more so than other people's behavior (Jones and Nisbett). This is called the *actor-observer effect/bias.* Again, this tendency is probably due to the fact that people have access to more information about themselves.

Similarly, when it comes to success and failure, people tend to attribute their successes to internal causes and their failures to external causes. This reverses for other people's successes and failures.

Minding "you" with theory of mind

"I can't read your mind but I expect you to read mine" could be the slogan for the television show *Huh? I Don't Get You!* Okay, that show doesn't exist; I made it up. But how do we read each other's minds. We seem to do it all the time. In 1978, psychologists David Premack and Guy Woodruff in an article titled, "Does the chimpanzee have a theory of mind?" introduced the concept of *theory of mind (TOM),* starting a very well developed line of inquiry in the field of social psychology. They propose that we develop a system of inferences about the mental life and minds of other people in the form of a "theory" about what is going on inside their heads. Henry M. Wellman fleshed out the definition; our conceptual understanding of another person's mental states is derived by observing their behavior. We see someone doing something, and we infer that they have thoughts and feelings that are "behind" that behavior.

A line of research called the *false belief task* has been used with infants and toddlers to trace the developmental origins of our TOM. In this task, a puppet play is presented in which one puppet (Diego) hides a toy or some other object and leaves the scene. Another puppet (Fred) comes along and is "looking" for the hidden toy. Children with no TOM will think that Fred is going to know where Diego hid the toy because they know! They do not attribute to Fred that he didn't see where Diego hid the toy. Children with a TOM (for Fred) will know he won't know where it is. This is a cool experiment indeed!

Theory of mind consists of more than just "false beliefs" attributed to others. Our TOMs include an understanding of others' intentions, their desires, their subjective sense of self, and a sense of what they know and don't know (knowledge and ignorance). As our TOMs become more sophisticated, we understand the interactions between these various mental states.

Dancing with others: Embodied social cognition theories

Some researchers over the years have come to see person perception and TOM models of social cognition as limited and missing the point. They think there is more to understanding others than simply sitting back, observing them, and coming up with "theories" about them. They propose that from the very onset as infants, we are engaged in a perceptual, expressive, and reciprocal "dance" with others in our environment, and from this we "learn" about other people. We act, we perceive, we act, we perceive. Theories and research under this construct are generally referred to as *embodied social cognition* theories.

REMEMBER

The main notion of embodied social cognition is that as we actively engage in the perception of others' bodies, faces, and actions, we sense what is going on with them.

Psychologist Shaun Gallagher describes it this way:

> I am not taking an observational stance; I am not off to the side thinking or trying to figure out what they are doing. Rather, I am responding to them in an embodied way, and I am part of the situation. . . . What we call social cognition is first social interaction. We are engaged in a dance-like feedback loop, and the correct level of analysis is the social unit, not the individual. Through mutual mimickry, imitation, coordinated movements, and reciprocal facial expressiveness, we come to "know" others. We don't have "mental models" of people; we instead have real-time interactions that inform us of "them" and help us engage in successful social interaction by making moment by moment adjustments to stay as "in tune" as possible based on the feedback we get when we act.

Communication Skills

One of Ronald Reagan's nicknames was "The Great Communicator." Supposedly, he could really get his point across, and people responded well to his speeches. I personally haven't taken the time to analyze Reagan's communication skills. But whether you're negotiating with nations as the president of the United States or trying to order a hamburger at a drive-thru, communication skills are vital to being a socially skilled person.

Owen Hargie, Christine Saunders, and David Dickson at the University of Ulster developed a model of *interpersonal communication* that identified several important components of the communication process. All episodes of communication are goal-directed, and several goals may be pursued simultaneously. A conversation varies as a function of the intended goal. If my goal is to visit with an old friend, I may talk about different things than if I'm conducting a psychological evaluation.

There are also several *mediating processes* that shape the communication process. Any psychological process that affects the meeting of a communicative goal or the outcome of communication can be a mediating process. One important process is called *focusing* (what one pays attention to), which can have a major impact. How you connect current conversational information with previous knowledge is also important, and *inference* — going beyond the surface information being communicated — is also important.

Another core aspect of the communication process is *feedback*, which is information provided to me by the other person about how effectively I am communicating, and how I use it. If you use feedback to change the way you communicate, then you can better meet the conversation goals. But some people seem to just ramble on, oblivious to signals from other people in a conversation that they're not making any sense. These ramblers are not picking up on the feedback. Here's a hint: When someone falls asleep while you're talking to her, that's important feedback.

REMEMBER

Being a great communicator involves being good at three specific communication skills: asking questions, explaining, and listening.

Asking questions

An important feature of all effective communication is the process of questioning. Questions are a good way to open a conversation, gather information, and express to another person that you're interested in what he's saying. There are several different types of questions:

>> **Recall:** A question like "Where were you on the night of November 12 at 10 p.m.?" asks you to remember basic information. Just a little advice if the police ask you this question: Call a lawyer.

>> **Hypothetical:** Questions designed to engender some creative thought such as "If you could have any job in the world, what would it be?"

Other questions that ask the responder to analyze, evaluate, or problem solve often have different formats that solicit different types of answers:

>> **Closed-end** questions require just a yes or no or identification response.

>> **Open-end** questions require description and elaboration.

There's an art to being a good questioner. Giving the responder a context and structure often helps the responder form answers that meet your actual information needs. You may start out by saying, "I have three main questions." The point is to clue the person in to what you are trying to learn.

Explaining

In addition to being good at questioning, the gift of gab often requires a certain level of skill at explaining oneself. Explanations provide information and clarify messages, and they're often used to demonstrate a point.

When making a point in a conversation, an individual can often bolster her argument by providing a solid explanation for the position being taken. Good explanations are clear, focused, and linked to the listener's knowledge base. Being brief and avoiding a lot fillers like "um," "uh," and "ya know" also helps. These terms interrupt the fluency of communication and can lead to loss of interest.

Sometimes it helps to pause and review so the listener can organize and absorb what has already been explained. It's also very important to use language that is appropriate to the audience or listener. If you're too technical, too gross, or too basic, you may lose their interest.

Listening

A third critical aspect of effective communication is listening. One-way conversations are poor excuses for communication. If no one is listening, there's no "co" in communication.

Here are some good listener guidelines:

>> **Focus.** Turn off the TV, put away your phone, reduce extraneous noise, and don't fidget or fool with stuff around you. Doing your taxes or looking at your mobile phone while someone is talking is a dead giveaway that you're not really listening.

>> **Clear your head.** Be aware of your biases and preconceived ideas and mentally prepare yourself to pay attention and absorb the information being offered by the other person.

- » **Mentally engage.** Keep yourself focused by asking questions to clarify what the speaker is saying.

- » **Wait.** Don't interrupt if you can help it. Respond when the other person finishes making a point.

- » **Process.** Mentally identify the main point of the speaker's communication and organize what he is telling you into categories such as who, what, when, why, and how.

- » **Remain open and attentive.** Don't use *blocking techniques,* such as denying someone's feelings or changing the topic. Take in what the person is saying.

- » **Demonstrate attention.** Maintain eye contact, nod, and orient your body toward the speaker and keep an open posture. Don't cross your arms or turn away.

Asserting yourself

One of the most common problems I see in my clinical practice is that people don't know how to stand up for themselves and communicate their needs in a direct and confident manner. Complaints about pushy coworkers, jerky bosses, and grouchy spouses are commonly the result of a person's lack of assertiveness. For some people, assertiveness seems to come naturally; they're just good at telling people what they think in a way that doesn't put anybody off.

REMEMBER

I'm not talking about being aggressive; that often involves a certain level of hostility and a denial of the other person's rights in the interaction. I am talking about something a little milder than aggression, *assertiveness.*

Assertiveness can be defined as standing up for one's rights and expressing one's thoughts, feelings, and beliefs in a direct, honest, and appropriate manner that respects others. Ever have someone cut in line when you're at the grocery store? Did you tell them to go to the end of the line, or did you keep your thoughts to yourself only to get increasingly resentful about it later? What about ordering food at a restaurant and getting something you didn't order? Did you eat it anyway or did you send it back? It sounds easy, but a lot of people won't say anything because they fear being seen as a jerk, being disliked, or hurting another person's feelings.

Assertiveness is a social skill that you can learn. Typically, when people get better at being assertive, the overall quality of their relationships improves. They no longer feel that they can't say what they really think or that they have to keep quiet for the sake of friendships. When people learn how to communicate assertively, they awaken to a whole new realm of possibilities in communication.

TIP

Want to be more assertive? *Basic assertions* are expressions such as "No, I don't like that movie" or "Thank you, but I've had enough fruitcake." *Empathic assertions* are statements used to convey that you understand the other person's position even if you're not going along with it. "I understand that you prefer fast food over Italian, but I'm really craving spaghetti."

When someone begins with a basic assertion and then progresses into more straightforward statements with little ambiguity, she engages in *escalating assertiveness.* This is a good skill to use with pushy salespeople, as this example demonstrates:

> **Salesperson:** Can I help you find something?
>
> **Customer:** No thanks.
>
> **Salesperson:** Well, we've got these great deals in women's apparel today.
>
> **Customer:** Really, I'm not interested.
>
> **Salesperson:** How about . . .
>
> **Customer:** For the third time, can you please leave me alone? I don't want your help.

TIP

A particularly useful tool in assertive language is the "I statement" — using a personal position rather than pointing out the other person's behavior and using the "you" word. Instead of telling my boss that he's been hounding me and he's starting to tick me off, I may say, "I get the sense that you're putting unfair pressure on me, and I'm feeling frustrated." Easier said than done, I know, but it works pretty well. Try it!

TIP

The following is a quick list of verbal defense strategies that you can use against manipulative and rude people:

>> **Broken record:** Simply repeating oneself over and over again. "I said no! What part of *no* don't you understand? I'll say it again. No! No!"

>> **Fogging:** Agreeing with what someone is saying but not changing one's position. "You're right, I should watch what I eat. I have gained a few pounds." All the while thinking to yourself, "I'm going to eat whatever I feel like eating. When can I get away from this jerk?"

>> **Meta-level:** Taking a conversation to a more abstract level than the original conversation. "I think this is a good example of how hard it can be to get one's point across. I've often wondered how we can get past this." I like to call this the old therapist switch-a-roo! "What is the ideal weight anyway? Being heavy used to be a sign of beauty and prosperity. I'm beautiful and prosperous, not fat."

Chapter **11**

Getting Along . . . or Not

'll never forget the time I saw news video of two groups of Buddhist monks fist-fighting for control over a monastery. I was shocked to see people whom I stereotypically perceived as peaceful acting so violently — toward each other! The image was disturbing, but it was also a potent demonstration of how a situation, or the influence of a group, can fuel individual behavior. These typically peaceful individuals seemingly were overcome by a situation that triggered them to engage in behavior that they themselves probably could not explain if asked.

It may be true that an individual is pushed and pulled by the dynamics of his personality and acts instinctively based on genetic makeup. Behavior also seems to vary as a function of thinking. However, psychology would be incomplete without considering the social influences on behavior and mental processes.

Social psychology is the study of the social causes of and influences on behavior.

REMEMBER Social psychologists have long suggested that many of the answers to questions about human behavior lie in understanding social influences such as group norms, conformity, and group pressure. This chapter explores these and other social influences on behavior and highlights the powerful impact of being around other people. The influence of social forces on individual behavior cannot be underestimated.

The study of social influences completes the biopsychosocial model of human behavior. (See Chapter 2 for more on the biopsychosocial model.)

Playing Your Part

Unless you're a hermit and you live by yourself in a shack in the middle of the desert, you exist within a *social matrix* — a multilayered configuration of social relationships that range from the parent-child bond to your co-worker–co-worker interactions. Picture yourself in the middle of a huge multi-ringed circle with each ring representing a level of social organization.

REMEMBER

Each of these circles carries a set of expected behaviors — rules that dictate what each individual is supposed to do. Each social group's rules or behavioral expectations are called norms. Cultures have norms, families have norms, and even subcultures have norms.

A subculture may consist of a small social group, often organized around a recreational activity. A gang may be considered a subgroup within its own subculture. Gangs have their own language, clothing styles, and rituals that delineate clear rules for the behavior of each individual member. That social structure is what I'm talking about when I use the term *norm*.

Americans typically like to see themselves as rugged individualists, wincing at the idea of blindly following norms. But norms are not all that bad. They simplify complex social situations, allowing people to think about things other than how to act and what to say in a particular situation. Norms serve as "mental shortcuts," and social situations operate more smoothly when norms are clear.

Some norms seem to be universal. Psychologist Roger Brown in 1965 found that people almost universally speak more respectfully to others of higher status and more casually to those of lower status. This manner of addressing others is built into the very structure of some languages, including Spanish and French. The appropriate way to conjugate a verb depends on how well you know the person you're speaking to.

Certainly, universal norms exist, but some variations exist as well. If you're a Palestinian Christian, it is customary and normative to firmly resist any food offered to you while visiting someone's home and only to accept after much counter-insistence by the host. Americans on the other hand may even ask for something to eat or drink when visiting someone's home without thinking twice. Another common variation in cultural norms relates to waiting in line. Some cultures don't seem to appreciate the orderliness of waiting in a single-file line when ordering food at a fast-food establishment, but others do. The norm of *personal space* (the physical space or area around us) too can vary by culture. Some cultures seem to value personal space more than others.

GETTING CARRIED AWAY

Role definitions are a powerful determinant of behavior, and the definitions sometimes overpower individual personalities and preferences. In 1972, Phil Zimbardo, psychologist and professor emeritus of psychology at Stanford University, conducted a famous experiment known as the *Stanford prison experiment* that illustrated the power of roles. College students were recruited to participate in a mock-prison situation in which they were randomly assigned to be either guards or inmates. The experiment took place in a makeshift prison in the basement of the psychology building at Stanford University.

The experiment revealed that people seem to naturally know what the roles of both inmate and guard entail, and Zimbardo had to discontinue the experiment within a week because of what he saw happening. The otherwise normal and healthy college students began to take their roles far too seriously. The guards treated the inmates inhumanely and with harsh disdain, and the inmates began to truly hate the guards and focus only on the circumvention of the "prison" system and survival.

In other words, the students got caught up in their roles and forgot about the reality of the situation.

REMEMBER

A *role* is a specific type of norm that defines how a person should act in a specific situation. Each individual has certain roles to play (student, employee, brother, sister, parent, and so on) that dictate different behaviors for different situations. Typically, individuals have clear roles to play in specific situations.

Ganging Up in a Group

In a classic episode of the *Twilight Zone*, everyone gets plastic surgery when they reach adolescence, and everyone picks the same transformation so that everyone looks the same — a sort of Ken Doll for the men and a Barbie face for the women. In the episode, one girl decides to keep her natural-born look and is subsequently tormented and ridiculed for wanting to do so. She was under enormous pressure to conform, to give into group pressure, and to go along.

This dynamic is a very real part of everyday life in a community. Groups exert all kinds of pressure on their individual members. Sometimes groups have very clear and explicit rules that keep people in line; in other cases, the rules or pressures are more subtle.

In this section, I point out the group and social influences and determinants of an individual's behavior. This includes a discussion of how individuals conform and react to group pressure and influence an effort on tasks, as well as how people treat each other and "police" each other's thinking.

Conforming

Conformity is a change in behavior that results from real or perceived group pressure. Most people are surprised to realize how much individuals conform. I mean, how many purple houses are on your block? Not many I bet.

In a study from 1937, Muzafer Sherif, one of the founders of social psychology, looked at how people would change their judgments based on knowing how other people answered certain questions. Subjects were asked to estimate how far a light moved across a dark room. Sherif found that when other people were present and offered a different estimate, the subject would change his or her answer to be more in-line with what the others' answers were. Knowledge of the other people's answers influenced the subjects' answers.

In 1955, Solomon Asch, another pioneer in social psychology, found the same thing when he put people in a group and asked them to estimate the lengths of lines. Subjects changed their answers to go along with the group consensus. Both of these experiments are good examples of how an individual may conform under group pressure, even if the pressure is subtle.

Obedience is an extreme form of conformity and often involves going against one's better judgment or truest intentions. When I think of obedience, visions of dog-obedience school pop into my head — me standing there with a collar and leash around my neck, jumping up to get my treat for performing the requested trick. Sounds extreme, doesn't it?

REMEMBER

I would like to think that I'd walk out of an experiment in which I had to torture someone with electric shocks, but the majority of subjects in one famous study followed orders and didn't stop applying shocks. (See the nearby "Shocking, no?" sidebar.) Why?

There are eight factors that seem to increase conformity and obedience:

>> **Emotional distance:** The more personal contact someone has with an individual, the less likely he is to act without compassion against that person. It's harder to be cruel to another person when the victim has a face.

- >> **Proximity and legitimacy of authority:** When an authority figure is close by, obedience is more likely. The authority's legitimacy also matters. You are more likely to be obedient to an individual that you think has genuine authority than someone you perceive to be a poseur.

- >> **Institutional authority:** When an authority figure is part of an accepted institution, obedience is more likely. In other words, I'm more likely to comply with the suggestions of a court-appointed judge than some guy sitting next to me at the bus stop (assuming he's not a judge). Recognized institutional authority has a powerful effect on obedience.

- >> **Group size:** Groups of three to five people have a maximum effect on conformity pressure; groups containing fewer than three and more than five people have a less powerful effect.

- >> **Unanimity:** When groups are in complete agreement, it's more difficult for a single individual to resist conforming.

- >> **Cohesiveness:** The more a group feels that it is bound together and tightly organized, the more power the group has over its members. As an example, I used to play softball on a team without uniforms, and it just didn't feel right. We needed uniforms to be a real team. Uniforms are one way to increase cohesiveness because looking the same as others in a group strengthens a sense of unity.

- >> **Status:** People with a higher status than you tend to have more influence over your obedience/compliance.

- >> **Public response:** People conform more when their behaviors are made public. It's easier to disagree privately or anonymously.

Although conformity and obedience are not necessarily bad things, learning how to resist both may be important — just in case. One needs only to think of Nazi Germany, perhaps the most horrific example of the dangers of conformity, to understand why maintaining a certain degree of individual diversity is important in any social group.

The best way to prevent conformity may be to maintain a sense of and respect for human uniqueness. Freedom of speech and religious tolerance are also good protections against conformity. As long as people feel comfortable being themselves and can freely speak their minds, conformity is a little more difficult. (See the "Birds of a Feather . . . or Not" section later in this chapter for more on prejudice and stereotypes.)

SHOCKING, NO?

Harvard University psychologist Stanley Milgram in 1965 conducted an obedience experiment that bordered on the extreme. In fact, it was so extreme that the same experiment would not be allowed today, because it would not pass the required ethics review. Subjects were seated at a control panel with a switch for delivering electrical shocks to a "subject" on the other side of a partition. The subjects were actually experimenters pretending to be participating as real subjects.

The premise: The subject is to be shocked each time that he or she gets a question wrong. With each subsequent wrong answer, the shock gets stronger and stronger. The shocks start at 75 volts and go up to 450 volts.

At some point, the subject is yelling and pleading with the real subject to stop administering the shock. An experimenter stands next to the real subject with a clipboard and a white lab-coat insisting that the real subject continue with the experiment and continue to administer shocks, despite the pretend subject's protests and obvious pain.

In reality, the fake subjects did not receive any shock at all; they only pretended to get shocked. But ask yourself, "When would I have stopped giving the shocks?" Maybe you think that you would have stopped the second the subject started yelling and asking you to stop. I'm sure the subjects in Milgram's study thought the same thing.

However, the shocking outcome (sorry about that one; couldn't resist) was that 63 percent of the real subjects went all the way to 450 volts in compliance (or obedience) with the experimenter! That's enough voltage to potentially cause death.

Doing better with help

"There's no I in TEAM!" A lot of coaches use this line in their pep talks, trying to convey the idea that the better a team plays together, the better their results will be. And social psychologists have found that this idea is true to a certain extent. When we're in the presence of others, people are more physiologically aroused and energized, and dominant behaviors are strengthened. This phenomenon is called *social facilitation*.

Robert Zajonc, professor emeritus at Stanford University, found that when a person does something relatively simple and routine, being in the presence of others improves her performance. But when a task is complex, having others around can hinder performance. So it may be a good idea to conduct that calculus contest somewhere other than Madison Square Garden. Although, folding laundry in the Garden is probably okay.

Kicking back

When I was in junior high school, teachers often asked me to participate in group projects. It usually went something like this: Four less-motivated students would pair up with the "smart" kid and let the "smart" kid do all the work. The motivationally challenged pupils would then ascribe their names to the project in order to get the credit.

REMEMBER

This is an example of *social loafing* — the tendency for people to exert less energy and effort when engaged in a group task that ignores individual accountability.

In 1979, psychologists Latane, Kipling, Williams, and Harkins found, for example, that when people were put in groups of six and instructed to clap as loudly as they possibly could, the amount of noise produced was less than that of one person clapping alone. People loaf when engaged in activities as groups. Loafers are *free riders,* people who rest on the efforts of other people in the group, like those kids who just mouth the words in the school choir.

Hey, if nobody can tell if I'm singing or not, then why should I exert myself? I'm not getting credit for my individual effort anyway.

Remaining anonymous

Ever wonder why groups of people who do really awful things often wear uniforms? Take the Ku Klux Klan, for example. What's with the pointy hats? Researchers have found that diminishing individual identity and diffusing individual responsibility reduces people's inhibitions. Uniforms reduce the individual member's uniqueness as well as inhibitions. This dynamic can result in people doing things that they may not do if they were alone or more easily identifiable. When this happens, people become *deindividuated.*

A certain amount of freedom seems to accompany blending into a crowd or being anonymous. Maybe people are less afraid of getting caught doing something bad in this situation. Children, for example, have been found to steal more when they are deindividuated.

It seems that anonymity and a lack of unique identification can facilitate antisocial behavior — something to think about when you consider how anonymous American society can be. Some people don't even know their next-door neighbors. Then again, with social media and the Internet becoming ever more pervasive, living anonymously is getting harder and harder.

Thinking as one

Groups can have both positive and negative effects on individual behavior. You may perform some tasks better when working within a group and get lazier while performing others.

In 1971, Irving L. Janis, a research psychologist at Yale University and professor emeritus at the University of California, Berkeley, introduced a concept related to a potentially adverse effect of group participation: a phenomenon known as *groupthink*. When groups work to suppress disagreement and dissent in order to maintain group harmony, they are engaged in groupthink.

Dissent can sometimes threaten the cohesiveness of a group. When people start expressing ideas that are contrary to the group's views, the group sometimes reacts negatively. Galileo was one of the most famous victims of groupthink in history. He discovered evidence related to the solar system that challenged the prevailing thought of the day. Did he receive high praise and honors? Hardly! He was locked away in prison for being a heretic, a dissenter.

Groups work hard, both consciously and unconsciously, to prevent dissent. Janis identified eight symptoms of groupthink that can exist in a group:

>> **Illusion of invulnerability:** When groups think they are untouchable, they're more likely to squash dissent.

>> **Belief in the group's moral superiority:** When a group thinks it is ultimately moral, it ignores its own immorality.

>> **Rationalization:** A group becomes more closed-minded as it collectively justifies its actions.

>> **Stereotypes regarding the opposition:** When an opponent is viewed in biased or prejudiced terms, his statements that contradict the group's views are easier to ignore.

>> **Conformity pressure:** Strong pressure on individuals to go along with the group's will and to not disagree minimizes dissent; non-conformers are cast out.

>> **Self-censorship:** Group members keep their dissenting opinions to themselves rather than rock the boat in some cases.

>> **Illusion of unanimity:** Internal dissent can sometimes be kept out of sight and away from the full group's view; therefore, dissent appears not to exist.

>> **Mind guards:** Some group members take an active role in protecting the group from dissent or contrary information. They're like the "thought police" in George Orwell's book *1984*.

Groupthink can cause a lot of problems. Alternatives to the status quo may go unexamined, thus preventing a complete survey of any problem that the group faces. Risks may be ignored. And ultimately, the group makes decisions that can be compromised.

REMEMBER

Here are some ways to avoid groupthink:

>> Encourage everyone in a group to express his own opinions and viewpoints.

>> Invite external people into the group to provide alternative viewpoints.

>> Ask individual group members to play the devil's advocate role to work through conflicting ideas.

Persuading

I often wish I had a bit more power of persuasion. The greatest example of this power comes from the movie franchise, *Star Wars*. Jedi warriors have the ability to influence the thoughts of others by using "The Force" for what's called the "Jedi mind trick." In fact, I'm pretty sure that the guy who sold me my last car used the Jedi mind trick on me — the dark side of The Force, I think. But I digress.

Persuasion is a powerful force in all social interactions and arrangements. People don't just use it to sell products. There are two paths to persuasion:

>> **Central route:** The central route occurs when the "persuadee" actively processes the potentially persuasive information. In 1991, Bas Verplanken, a professor of social psychology at the University of Bath, found that when people think deeply about something, any associated change in attitude or opinion is more likely to stay changed.

>> **Peripheral route:** This approach involves getting someone to associate an intended message with certain images, sometimes positive and sometimes negative. It relies on the mind's natural ability to associate things. Remember classical conditioning? (If not, check out Chapter 8.) Examples of persuasion via the peripheral route include using showing hard-bodied models to sell gym memberships.

REMEMBER

Psychologists Petty and Cacioppo warn that if you're going to try to persuade people, don't warn them that it's coming. Distracting the people you hope to persuade helps because they won't be able to mount a strong counterargument to your claims.

In addition, four key components make up any persuasive argument: credibility of communicator, delivery approach, audience engagement, and age of audience. I cover these components in the following sections.

Credibility of communicator

A message is more likely to be persuasive if someone perceived as credible delivers it.

>> **Expertise is often a powerful indicator of credibility.** People listen to experts. One thing to keep in mind, though: Just because someone says that she's an expert doesn't mean she necessarily is. When in doubt, always check credentials, including education, training, and experience.

>> **People are more likely to be persuaded by someone seen as trustworthy.** Such as an actor in a white doctor's coat pitching an herbal supplement for example.

>> **Attractive people's messages are more persuasive.** The term *attractive* can relate to a person's physical appeal or personality and charisma.

>> **Similarity plays a role.** The more someone is like you, the easier it is for her to persuade you.

Delivery approach

Should a persuader appeal to someone's emotion or to reason and critical thinking? Here's a breakdown of these and other message-delivery options:

>> **Reasoned approach:** In 1983, John Cacioppo and others found that when trying to persuade highly educated or analytical people, a reasoned approach is best. These individuals seem to like to think things over, analyzing information before making a decision. They're not necessarily smarter, but they are typically more aware of recent information.

>> **Emotional approach:** Those who don't have the time or inclination to read every consumer review when going to buy a new car are more likely to trust other people and get swayed by emotional appeals. The thought process is "My sister said she loved her new car. I think I'll get one."

>> **Fear factor:** A lot of persuasive messages use fear to scare people away from harmful or unhealthy behaviors. (Find examples in Chapter 18.) These messages work. Fear-evoking ads are all around — telling you to stop smoking, to avoid abusing drugs, to vote for so-and-so and definitely not the other option, for

example. There's only one catch. If you're going to scare people in order to persuade them, you need to provide concrete information on how to deal with or change their behavior; otherwise, the audience may freeze up or fail to act at all in the face of the fear.

>> **Two-sided argument:** A two-sided argument is one that acknowledges the other position, giving the impression of fairness and objectivity. Advertisers have been using this technique for years, conducting "taste tests" and other comparative challenges with their rivals. You know what they're up to!

Audience engagement

The best way to present persuasive information is to get your audience to play an active part in processing your argument. Active engagement captures the other person's attention and carries an expectation that he will comprehend the message, remember it, and then take action. As the amount of energy that a person invests in mentally processing a message increases, so does the likelihood that it will stick. Passive reception of a message, like listening to a lecture, is less likely to have an impact.

Age of audience

Research has found that older people are less likely to change their attitudes and opinions than people who are younger. The early twenties are years in which people are particularly vulnerable to persuasion. This is a time in many people's lives when choices abound and information is exchanged at a rapid rate. Many people in their early twenties are in college, entering the work force, and expanding their social networks. They're exposed to a whole new world of information, and this can make resisting persuasion more difficult.

TIP

Want to know how to resist persuasion? With the daily barrage of persuasive messaging that you may encounter, it helps to know how to stay committed to your own beliefs and attitudes. Psychologist William McGuire proposed that a good way to resist persuasion is through the process of *attitude inoculation*, which involves exposing yourself to weak, or weaker, arguments against your position in order to inoculate, or firm up, your resistance to counterarguments. This process gives you practice and confidence in refutation. It's like warming up before a big game. And if you need to inoculate someone else's attitude or position on an issue, try presenting him with weak opposing arguments.

EASY AS PIE

There's a great rock video out by a band named Cake that demonstrates the influence of persuadee participation perfectly. In the video, a man walks around a beach, asking real people to put headphones on and listen to the new song. They're encouraged to comment on the song. This is a much more powerful advertising technique than if the man just walked up with a sign that read, "Check out Cake's new song. In stores now!" The persuadees are participating in their own manipulation. It's beautiful. I don't know whether the video makers were thinking this way, but if they were, they hit on a great persuasion technique!

Being Mean

Most people probably think of themselves as civilized, but it's hard to ignore all the violence and rage that seems so prevalent in today's world. Some of the most horrific acts of human brutality have been committed in recent years — not in some savage society of the remote past. And, unfortunately, most people have experienced some form of violence and aggression. Mass atrocities affecting whole nations as well as smaller-scale heinous acts among individuals indicate that aggression and violence are unfortunate facts of human life.

Why do people act in a way that harms other people? What triggers a person's violence? Psychologists have searched for answers to these questions by studying *aggression*, a form of violence. *Aggression* can be defined as any behavior that is directed at and intended to hurt another person or persons.

Two types of aggression exist:

>> **Hostile aggression** is driven by anger and is an end in itself.

>> **Instrumental aggression** is used to serve some other purpose, such as intimidation or extortion.

Most of the theories about aggression focus on determining why hostile aggression is committed.

Acting naturally

One idea is that some people are born with a violent instinct and a genetic predisposition to act aggressively. It does seem that some children are naturally more aggressive than others, and research supports the natural-born killer theory:

>> Freud proposed that people are born with aggressive instincts, and genetic studies show that identical twins are more likely to be more equally aggressive than fraternal twins (Rushton and others, 1986).

>> Some research also shows higher levels of the hormone testosterone in both men and women who've been convicted of violent crimes when compared to those convicted on nonviolent crimes (Dabbs, 1988).

The brain may have something to do with it as well. Specific centers in the brain seem to be implicated in producing and inhibiting aggressive behaviors. Individuals with severe damage to the frontal lobes of the brain have long been observed as having more difficulty controlling their aggressive impulses than people without this damage because this inhibition is seen as one of the functions of the frontal lobe. This difficulty with controlling aggression is a disinhibition process.

Being frustrated

Or maybe violent and aggressive people are just frustrated. I'm one of those drivers who gets angry when I'm stuck in traffic and other drivers are rude. Now, I don't curse out my window at people or get into fistfights, but I sure do get frustrated.

In 1989, social psychologist Leonard Berkowitz, known for his research on human aggression, found that sometimes frustration leads to aggression, and sometimes it doesn't. When someone does get frustrated, she can get angry, and when a person feels angry, she's predisposed to act aggressively. It's like the body and the mind are poised, on alert, to act with aggression. This trigger comes from a cognitive evaluation of a situation and usually a conclusion that the person who is ticking you off did so on purpose. This scenario is likely to produce an aggressive response. So if you step on someone's toes, you'd better hope she realizes it was an accident.

Doing what's learned

Maybe the violence comes down to people being a product of their environment. An aggressive person may have learned to act aggressively by watching other people do it.

Albert Bandura, professor emeritus at Stanford University, would agree. *Social learning theory* holds that aggressive behavior is learned by observing others and by seeing aggressive people rewarded for such behavior. Little boys are often rewarded for being "tough." Boxers and MMA (Mixed Martial Arts) fighters are paid big money to beat people up. Some may say that aggressive acts are rewarded on a regular basis in our society, too. What child wouldn't see the benefits of aggression in such an environment?

Violence on television and in video games has come under fire in recent years because of its perceived connection to the dramatic increase in youth violence. Americans watch a lot of TV. American kids, in particular, spend a ton of time in front of different kinds of screens.

Even as far back as 1972, Gallup polls reported that Americans were watching an average of seven hours of TV a day. In 2012, that number was about the same, 6–7 hours per day. Regardless of your opinion on the connection between violence and television, the fact is that there's a lot of violence on the tube.

In 1990, George Gerbner found that seven out of ten programs contain violent scenes, with primetime programming containing five violent acts per hour. No doubt about it, TV doles out a heavy dose of violent images. A United States Senate Committee in 2006 found that an average American child sees 200,000 violent acts and 16,000 murders on TV by age 18.

BLAMING MEDIA

I've watched violent television all my life, and I don't consider myself a violent person. Most research concludes that there is a modest positive correlation between exposure to violence in the media (film, television, music, Internet, and video games). That is, the more violent a child's media viewing is, the higher chance a child will engage in aggressive behavior.

The American Academy of Pediatrics states, "Extensive research evidence indicates that media violence can contribute to aggressive behavior, desensitization to violence, nightmares, and fear of being harmed" in children.

My question is, why is there so much violence in our media anyway? Does it offer viewers something valuable? Is it an emotionally arousing persuasion technique used by corporations to sell their goods? I don't know, but it may be worthwhile to examine the reasons behind the inclusion of so much violence in the entertainment industry.

Lending a Helping Hand

I've always marveled at people like Mother Teresa who devote their entire lives to helping others. Mother Teresa's sacrifice was unquestionable. What drives people to help in this way? It certainly wasn't money for the saint. I never saw Mother Teresa driving around in a Rolls-Royce.

A favorite topic among social psychologists is *altruism,* having concern for and helping other people without asking for anything in return. Maybe these psychologists study altruism with such zeal because it's an integral part of everyday life. People are constantly presented with situations in which someone needs help, even if it's a sad, late-night commercial showing starving children in other nations.

I think most people like to see themselves as helpful people. Or, if not particularly helpful, then at least willing to help in certain situations or when the need is severe. A great deal of research by social psychologists investigates why, when, and who people actually help. Some of the findings are surprising, even shocking.

In New York City in 1964, a woman named Kitty Genovese was brutally murdered outside of her apartment by a man with a knife. She struggled with the attacker and screamed for help for nearly 35 minutes. No one came to her aid. Later reports by 38 of her neighbors stated that they had witnessed the crime and heard her screams, but they did nothing to help her.

What happened here? Why didn't anyone help? As you're reading this, you may be telling yourself that you would have helped. When I first heard this story, I thought, "What was wrong with those people?" Think about it, though. It's not likely that all 38 people were cold, callous individuals who didn't care about a woman being murdered within earshot. Instead, they were influenced by social psychological principle in which social situations have a powerful influence on individual behavior. The Kitty Genovese story illustrates the main point of social psychology — the power of a situation is a major factor in determining an individual's behavior.

Why help?

Before I introduce you to some of the main theories of why people perform altruistic acts, I want to conduct a little test.

TIP

The next time you're in a public place, try one of these experiments:

>> **Experiment #1:** Drop five coins on the floor near a group of people and act like you don't notice. Time how long it takes for someone to help you. Try to remember as much about them as you can.

>> **Experiment #2:** Pretend to trip and fall in the public place. Make the same observations. (This may make an interesting YouTube video, but it is not recommended for safety reasons.)

If you performed these experiments, what happened? Who helped you? How long did it take to receive help? Do you know why a person decided to help you? I know — it was probably because of your stunning good looks! Actually, believe it or not, attractiveness does make a difference. I cover this later in the chapter.

Theories about why people actually help others are all over the map. Here are some of the popular ones:

>> **Social exchange theory:** Helping is a type of trading process.

>> **Selfishness theory:** Helping someone may lead to rewards.

>> **Genetic theory:** Helping is a genetic impulse.

Exchanging social goods

Researchers E. B. Foa and U. G. Foa introduced *social-exchange theory,* the idea that helping is part of a reciprocal process of giving and receiving social "goods" such as love, support, and services. Individuals try to minimize personal costs and maximize benefits, just like any good businessperson does. In helping situations, if the benefit of helping is higher than the cost of not helping, a person is more likely to help. This kind of makes sense if you consider that sometimes helping people involves putting ourselves at physical risk or serious inconvenience.

Also supporting this theory is A. W. Gouldner's *reciprocity norm,* which holds that a cultural norm tells people they should return help to those who help them. You scratch my back, and I'll scratch yours. In turn, people don't hurt those who help them out. Never bite the hand that feeds you! There's only one catch to this theory: Sometimes, people can get offended if you offer them help. If they can't return the favor, they may feel demeaned by the offer. Reciprocity works best when it's between equals.

EMPATHIZING ABOUT SYMPATHY

Some people get confused between empathy and sympathy. *Empathy* involves a personal understanding of someone's suffering, and *sympathy* is distant and impersonal concern about another person's suffering. Imagining being in someone else's shoes is a type of empathy, and feeling sorry for a person who's actually wearing uncomfortable shoes is the gig with sympathy.

Looking out for number one

In the 1950s, Ayn Rand wrote *Atlas Shrugged,* a famous philosophical novel that promoted the "virtue of selfishness." If each person looks out for "numero uno," all will be well, the theory goes.

Rand was not alone in thinking that selfishness isn't all that bad. Similar to social-exchange theory, the selfishness theory argues that helping behavior is driven by a person's *own* best interests. Do you give in order to receive? Some rewards are external, like praise and notoriety, and others are internal, like reducing negative feelings such as guilt.

Motivated by the love inside

In 1991, social psychologist Daniel Batson came to the rescue of humanity's sense of goodness with his theory that people help others because individuals have a natural *empathy* for other people, especially those they are attached to.

Psychologist and professor emeritus at New York University Martin Hoffman found that even infants seem to possess a natural ability to "feel for" others. They cry when they hear another baby cry. Are they just crying because the sound of the other baby's crying is hurting their ears? Probably not; it's more likely that they cry because they are in touch with the other baby's pain. People can relate to feeling upset at the sight of another person's misfortune. This natural empathy may encourage helping behavior.

How often do you help those people who stand on the side of the street holding the "Will work for food" signs? Do you feel a responsibility to help them? They're hoping you do. The *norm of social responsibility* holds that people should help others who need it. Bernard Weiner at UCLA in 1980, however, found that people typically apply this norm only in situations in which we perceive the person needing help as not having caused the situation due to her own negligence or fault. If I think that the person only needs help because she "did it to herself," I am less likely to adhere to the norm of social responsibility.

Do you think that the guy standing with the sign on the side of the street made some bad choices or somehow screwed up? Ask him; you never know until you ask. You may be eschewing your social responsibility if you don't offer some help.

Richard Dawkins also supports the genetic theory in his book *The Selfish Gene* (1976), in which he proposed that people are altruistic because their genes compel them to be. The idea of *kin protection* states that genes promote altruistic behavior toward kin or family in order to ensure the survival of the group's genetic makeup. Following this line of reasoning, I'm much less likely to help someone I don't know. Why would I? They don't share my genes.

REMEMBER

The more genetic material I share with someone, the more likely I am to help him or her. That's it. Nothing fancy.

When to help?

One of the most remarkable findings in altruism research is the idea that people are less likely to help when they're in the presence of others than when they're alone. This sounds strange, doesn't it? I may think that the fear of appearing cold and uncaring in front of others may encourage people to help more.

But research shows otherwise. When someone is in a crowd, he is actually less likely to notice that other people need help. In New York City, for example, people are always surrounded by other people. It's a crowded place, and most people can't take the time to notice everything and everyone around them simply because of the sheer volume of information; it's easier to fade into a crowd.

Strangely enough, when others are around, people are also less likely to interpret someone's behavior as indicative of needing help. Bystanders look to others for a sign as to how they should respond in a situation. If the other people don't act alarmed, then an individual typically won't be alarmed (or react) either. If the situation is ambiguous, not a clear-cut helping situation, a person's interpretation of the event in the presence of others is likely to be that intervention is not required. This is especially true if the other people are strangers.

A final problem with helping in the presence of others is called *diffusion of responsibility*. People usually just assume someone else will take care of whatever needs doing. If no one else is around, then I'm the only one left; I've got to help. But if others are around, it's easy to assume they'll do it. What happens when everyone assumes that everyone else is going to offer assistance? Help doesn't happen.

That's exactly what two researchers, psychologists Latane and Darley, found in a 1968 study in which experiment subjects were witness to a victim of a feigned seizure. Persons who were led to believe they were alone reported the emergency to authorities more quickly than those who believed they were just one among other witnesses.

It's not all bad news when it comes to groups, though. Research has found that when someone in a group takes action, others are more likely to jump in. Helpful people in this scenario serve as *prosocial models* and are a strong influence on altruistic behavior. The problem is getting someone to make the first move. Until someone does, the negative forces of the bystander effect are active. The *bystander effect* or *bystander apathy* is the dynamic of not getting involved in a situation when there are too many people standing around; you're likely to just stand there, too. So go ahead and be a hero. Make the first move — someone has to.

Who gives and receives help?

In my personal life sometimes I feel like helping people and sometimes I don't. Sometimes I would rather watch television than help my friend move that new couch. Still others seem to always have help available when they need it (unlike my couch-purchasing friend). Are certain people more helpful or "help-able" than others?

What about how helping affects feelings? I've always wondered about the origins of the tradition of buying cigars for friends when a baby is born. I still don't know where it comes from, but altruism research shows that happy people tend to be more helpful or giving (happy dad, cigar as gift). Does that mean that sad people aren't helpful at all? It actually depends on how rewarding helping others is to the person experiencing sadness. If sad people aren't too self-absorbed and self-focused, altruistic acts can be very rewarding for them. Feeling good, doing good! Feeling bad, doing good! Sounds good, especially if I'm feeling bad.

Pious people are often viewed as helpful. Many nonprofit organizations are operated by religious denominations. But are religious people really more helpful than their non-religious neighbors? Here's what research shows: When people indicate that religion is very important in their lives, they have been found to give 2.5 times as much money to charity as those who indicate that religion is not very important. The verdict: Religious individuals are definitely generous, and, in some research findings, they're more generous than non-religious individuals.

Researchers Eagly and Crowley in 1986 found that women get helped more often than men, and attractive women get helped more often than unattractive women. I guess the ugly men out there are out of luck. Luckily for them, similarity to the helper seems to be a factor. The more someone looks like or dresses like me (or you), the more likely I am to help them out. So you better cross your fingers and hope that the next time you're in of need help, someone thinks you're looking good.

Birds of a Feather . . . or Not

Airports, particularly international airports, are amazing places, I think. The diversity in these places is amazing. People of all colors, shapes, sizes, cultures, and nationalities all under one roof. But this diversity provides fertile soil for discrimination. Whenever people with differences are together, there is the potential for prejudice.

In this section, I introduce you to prejudice, stereotypes, and discrimination and describe how you can respond to these social dynamics.

Examining isms

Prejudice is a negative and disrespectful attitude, thought, or belief about a person based on his membership in a particular group. Some law enforcement agencies have been accused of using a prejudicial and controversial practice that's known as *racial profiling* in which officers can assume that certain individuals are potentially involved in criminal activity simply because they belong to a particular "race" or ethnic group.

A well-known example of potential racial profiling has been in play at airport security checkpoints following the terrorist attacks in New York, Washington, and over Pennsylvania on September 11, 2001. As a result of that attack, airport security may be more inclined to stop and more thoroughly and intensely question individuals of perceived Middle Eastern descent. If that's indeed happening, then airport security is guilty of racial profiling.

Psychologist Lynne Jackson proposes that prejudice is, in part, based on *stereotypes*, beliefs that most members of a group possess the same characteristics, traits, and behavioral tendencies. White men can't jump or dance. Arabs are terrorists. Asians can't drive. These blanket statements are offensive, right? That's the point of prejudice based on stereotypes; these conclusions about individuals based on their affiliation to a certain group are disrespectful.

Moreover, people often see what they expect to see. So if a person in the target group happens to perform the behavior our stereotype predicts — boom! Stereotype strengthened. The other people in that same group who don't behave according to our stereotype are often not noticed.

Some common forms of prejudice include the following:

>> **Racism** centers on a person's perceived "race" or ethnicity.

>> **Sexism** is based on a person's gender.

>> **Ageism** focuses on a person's age.

>> **Ableism** is based on a person's disability.

>> **Nationalism** centers on a person's national origin.

>> **Sanism/Mentalism** relates to a person's mental abilities or mental illness.

Religious intolerance (negative attitudes about a person based on his spiritual beliefs) and homophobia (fear of people with a homosexual orientation) are also common forms of prejudice.

What about *psycholigistophobia?* That irrational fear of a person's occupation being a psychologist and the belief that all psychologists are crazy, have a beard (if they're male), and love to offer free advice at cocktail parties. Okay, I made this one up and I shaved my beard. But psychologists have a rep!

Stereotypes can be conscious or unconscious. I can be aware of my stereotyped beliefs or not. But where do stereotypes and subsequent prejudice come from? From a social learning theory perspective, prejudices may be learned. People can certainly be taught specific beliefs by parents, the community, peer groups, and culture.

Some theorists propose that prejudice is a consequence of human evolution, that the mental process is an inherent part of the human mind that evolved to help humans identify who's part of "their" group and who's not, who poses a danger or is a potential competitor for resources.

Yet many psychologists propose that, ultimately, prejudice is a cognitive evaluation process that's essentially a consequence of the mind's tendency to "chunk" information together for the purpose of making vast amounts of information more manageable. Prejudice is a mental shortcut. Research shows that in situations in which people are distracted, tired, or unmotivated, they are more vulnerable to prejudicial and stereotypical thinking. Lynne Jackson likens this dynamic to a sort of "lazy process" that emerges when people lack the resources to carefully process social information.

Understanding discrimination

The human mind may have a tendency to group people in the form of prejudice, and this is often not an innocuous process. Prejudice can lead to *discrimination* — differential treatment of a person or group based on prejudicial attitudes and beliefs. Prejudice, although perhaps seemingly natural, is often deployed by advantaged groups and individuals against groups and individuals who enjoy lower levels of social advantage.

Here are two common forms of discrimination:

>> **Interpersonal:** Individual acts of discrimination such as not picking the short-statured kid for the basketball team (He may be quite good!)

>> **Institutional:** Policies, procedures, rules, laws — voter ID laws that prohibit the poor or elderly from voting because they don't have proper identification, for example — or a culture within an organization that systematically disadvantages one group in comparison with others

Making contact

The seemingly automatic bias in human thinking, fortunately, can be addressed through an approach known as *contact,* which was formally studied by the psychologist Gordon Allport. Contact holds that when a group of diverse people get together to collaborate on reaching a common goal or project, positive attitudes toward each other increase and negative attitudes decrease. This does not mean that you can just throw a block party and invite all your diverse and prejudiced friends, and they'll learn to get along. To work, contact encounters must be structured to support equality, cooperation, and safety.

Psychologists Pettigrew and Tropp analyzed hundreds of studies and proposed the following key ingredients of a successful "contact" encounter:

>> **Reduction in anxiety** occurs through exposure to others without threat or harm.

>> **Increased empathy** is a result of learning from and about others.

>> **Increased knowledge** about others decreases stereotypes.

A person can also reduce his stereotypic and prejudicial attitudes simply by having friends and associates who are friends with or associated with people of the other group. This is a vicarious contact situation and works to reduce prejudice and stereotypes because a person you already trust is showing trust in another person, which means you can in turn trust that person as well.

For example, if your best childhood buddy befriends a colleague who belongs to a group you have a prejudice against, you're more likely to become less biased toward that person and group after learning your trusted friend enjoys their company.

REMEMBER

Research also suggests that clear, well-communicated cultural and group norms *against* prejudice can have a big impact. Often, prejudice in individuals is the result of group pressure to conform and adopt prejudicial attitudes. Flipping that around, the same pressure to conform can be a powerful influence as well.

IN THIS CHAPTER

» **Getting started**

» **Exploring and mastering**

» **Experimenting**

» **Building and connecting**

» **Aging**

Chapter **12**

Growing Up with Psychology

Have you ever wondered what it would be like to have a psychologist as a parent? What if both parents were psychologists? Would that be a good thing or a bad thing? You may imagine that the typical dinner-table conversation would sound something like this:

Parent: How was your day today?

Child: Fine.

Parent: Fine, huh? That's funny; somebody doesn't look like he had an all right day. What about it honey? How was your day, really?

Child: I got into a fight with that big, stupid bully at school again. Well, I didn't really get into a fight. He just took my lunch pail and threw it into the trash can.

Parent: How did that make you feel? Frustrated? Angry? What role did you play in the situation?

Child: You know, just once I'd like to hear you say that you'll do something about it or protect me somehow. Maybe you could teach me how to defend myself. I'm tired of being in therapy at the dinner table. I'm going to my room.

Parent: Well, I guess I messed that one up. How does that make me feel?

I don't know if having a psychologist as a parent is necessarily a good thing or a bad thing. Some people seem to think that it would scar a kid because everything she does would be overanalyzed. But that's not really fair. If a parent is a pediatrician, would people expect her to leave her medical knowledge at the door and not treat her own children if they became ill? Of course not. But anything can be overdone.

One of the largest areas of psychological study is psychological development. Although many people think of children when they hear the term, developmental psychology covers the entire span of human life. *Lifespan psychology* is the study of human psychological development from conception until death.

I describe some of the areas traditionally covered in lifespan psychology in other chapters in this book. Personality development, for example, is the focus of Chapter 11. Self-development and the development of relationships are explored in Chapter 10. Therefore, this chapter focuses on physical and motor development, cognitive development, and social development.

Beginning with Conception and Birth

The process of psychological development begins with conception. Genetic processes, which play a big part in the future development of behaviors and mental processes, originate with the union of a woman's egg and a man's sperm. Each coupling creates a new genetic combination called a *genotype* — the genetic makeup of an individual.

Through a complex process that's best understood by geneticists and biologists, genes express themselves in what's called the *phenotype* — the actual manifestation of genetic codes in observable biological and psychological processes as shaped and impacted by our environment. So this means that I may have the genotype for being tall and muscular, but if I suffer from malnutrition and never exercise, I may be letting myself fall short of my genotype potential.

In this section, I introduce you to pregnancy and the process of fetal development.

Xs and Ys get together . . .

Sperm and eggs are specialized cells in the body that contain half of the genetic material necessary to make a whole person; they're called *sex cells* because they are involved in sexual reproduction.

Human beings contain 46 chromosomes. You get 23 chromosomes from your mother and 23 from your father. Non-sex-related cells contain a full set of genetic material with 46 chromosomes. A person's chromosomes determine the unique aspects of his biological and psychological makeup. They are the genetic building blocks of cellular construction.

The 23rd pair of chromosomes, the sex chromosomes, determines the sex of the child. Sex chromosomes can be either the X or Y variety. Sperm cells can carry either an X or a Y chromosome, but an egg can only carry an X. When the sperm and the egg get together, their unique combination determines the sex of the child.

Boys have a 23rd chromosome pair that contains one X and one Y (XY) chromosome. Girls have two Xs (XX). Because the mother can only give an X chromosome and the father can give either an X or a Y, the father's sex-chromosome contribution plays the deciding role.

The role of genetics in human behavior and mental processes has been part of the decades-long dispute known as the *nature versus nurture* debate. Proponents of the nature argument believe that behavior is genetically determined. Biology is destiny, so to speak. The nurture advocates believe that the environments in which a person grows up determine his psychological makeup.

REMEMBER

This debate has been basically squashed in the last 25 years by the middle-ground position that both biological and environmental factors are involved, with different weight being given to one or the other depending on the psychological process in question.

Uniting and dividing all in one night

Biological development begins with the process of sexual reproduction. So it goes that psychological development begins as well as behavior; mental processes are intrinsically tied to biological development. For more on the relationship between psychology and biology, flip to Chapter 3.

The development process begins after a man and woman have sexual intercourse:

Germinal stage (conception to 2 weeks)

1. **The sperm and egg meet, combining their half-sets of chromosomes.**

    This is *fertilization,* and it occurs in the *fallopian tubes.*

2. **Twenty-four to 30 hours pass as a one-celled *zygote* (the fertilized egg) begins to divide itself.**

   This occurs in the fallopian tube as well. Through a process called *mitosis,* each chromosome makes a copy of itself and contributes the copy to the formation of a second cell. Cells continue to divide and multiply, repeating this process throughout fetal development. Fetal development is underway!

3. **Three to four days pass while the fertilized egg travels to the uterus.**

   Upon reaching the uterus, *implantation* occurs. During implantation, the fertilized egg rests against the wall of the uterus and eventually merges with and becomes implanted in the lining of the uterus.

4. **The *embryonic period* begins.**

   This period occurs about 14 days after the *pre-embryonic stage,* or the *germinal period* starts. The *embryonic period* lasts until the end of the eighth week of pregnancy.

Embryonic stage (3rd week through 8th week)

5. **Cells continue to divide.**

   The beginnings of a recognizable human take shape. The rudiments of the nervous system and other bodily systems are beginning to take shape.

Fetal stage (9th week through birth)

6. **The *fetal period* begins and lasts until birth.**

   This begins in the third month of pregnancy. This final stage is an extremely delicate process. Psychological difficulties can sometimes be traced to problems in fetal brain and nervous system development. Intellectual disability, learning disabilities, and other cognitive disorders are sometimes linked to fetal difficulties.

REMEMBER

It's extremely important for expecting mothers to maintain proper nutrition, avoid infectious diseases, and eliminate drug, alcohol, and tobacco use. These behavioral changes won't guarantee the birth of a healthy child, but they certainly increase the odds.

The biological developments of each period are highlighted in Table 12-1.

TABLE 12-1

Fetal Development by Stage of Pregnancy

Germinal (Weeks 0–2): What's There?	
Amniotic sac	Placenta
Embryo	Umbilical cord
Embryonic (Weeks 3–8): What's There?	
Buds (arms and legs)	Heartbeat
Eyes and ears	Nervous system
Fingers and toes	Spinal cord
Fetal (Weeks 9–36): What's There?	
Organ systems working	Sex organs
Red blood cells	White blood cells
Fetus is very active	Fetus is sleeping like a newborn

Going from Diapers to Drool

About 36 weeks after conception, some lucky woman has just given birth to a healthy child. Infancy is an exciting time in which both physical and psychological developments occur at an unprecedented rate. One minute, children do nothing but sleep, and the next minute they're playing peek-a-boo.

In this section, I describe early child development including motor and cognitive development and language development.

Survival instincts

For approximately nine months as a fetus, a child relies almost exclusively on his mother for survival. This dependence doesn't end with birth. Although the infant's basic biological systems are functioning on their own, the maintenance of those systems requires the attentive care of a parent or primary caregiver. Sometimes, new parents can get overwhelmed with the responsibility of caring for an infant. The good news is that infants are born with a pretty impressive set of basic skills to help them survive.

In fact, nearly all of the most basic human survival skills are present at birth. When I say *basic*, I mean really basic — breathing, sucking, swallowing, and eliminating. Babies need to breathe to get oxygen. They need to swallow and suck to eat.

They need to eliminate in order to cleanse their systems. You nervous parents-to-be out there can rest assured that you won't have to teach your infant how to suck on a bottle or a breast. It's natural and automatic. It's reflexive.

These skills are part of a broader list of innate reflexes infants are born with that aid in their survival. Here are a few more:

>> **Rooting reflex:** Turning their heads in the direction of a touched cheek in an attempt to suck

>> **Moro (startle) reflex:** Stretching out their arms and legs and crying in response to a loud noise or a sudden dropping motion

>> **Grasping reflex:** Grabbing on to things, such as someone's finger

Motoring about

One of the most anticipated areas of infant development for a lot of parents is a child's motor development. Parents can't wait to watch their child gain more and more prowess in her physical abilities. Infants have very little control over their limbs and head when they're born. It takes time for the central nervous system (brain and spinal cord) and the peripheral nervous system (nerves outside the brain and spinal cord) to get things coordinated.

The progression of control begins with control of head movements and then turns to control of the limbs and torso, which usually begins around the age of 6 months. Eventually, greater fine motor control kicks in around the 8- to 12-month mark. For example, children may begin to grab things with just two fingers when they are 9 months old. Table 12-2 shows this progression.

TABLE 12-2   **Synopsis of Motor Development in Infancy**

Age in Months	Abilities Present
1–3	Lifting head and sitting up with support
4–8	Holding head still and balancing it; looking around; using thumb to grasp; sitting up briefly without support
8–12	Coordinating hand activities; controlling trunk and sitting without support; crawling; beginning to favor the use of one hand over the other; sitting to standing position while holding on to something; walking with help, taking simple steps
14	Standing alone and walking alone without difficulty
18	Running and tumbling

As infants turn into toddlers, their motor behavior becomes more sophisticated. They can run, kick, throw, ride tricycles, and perform a variety of other complex motor-behavior sequences. *Fine motor skills,* increased dexterity, and control over the use of their fingers and hands continue to develop as children figure out how to manipulate small objects like cups, crayons, and little toys.

Flexing their muscles

While infants are beginning to rely on their reflexes and developing more control over their muscle movements, their brains are developing at an extremely rapid rate. Actually, brain development begins during pregnancy and continues throughout childhood and adolescence. The progression of brain development begins with the motor areas of the brain. Without the necessary brain development in these areas, infants would not be able to respond reflexively and gain control over their bodies.

The next stop on the brain-development express is the *somatosensory* areas of the brain, the areas involved in sensation and perception (the olfactory, taste, pain, auditory, and visual areas). Infants are born with a good sense of hearing. They can discriminate between their mothers' voices and strangers' voices, for example, which may be a result of hearing their mothers' voices throughout pregnancy. Their senses of smell and taste are also keen. Visual acuity is less developed at birth and gradually develops over the course of the first year of life.

Scheduling time for schemata

Like a road map or template, children use what Swiss psychologist Jean Piaget called *schemata,* or mental modes of thinking, to represent, organize, and integrate experience. *Schemata* are basic ways of thinking about the world. Rather than sit passively by as the world presents them with information, children actively construct an understanding and mental representation of the world. There are three basic schemata:

>> **Sensorimotor schemata:** These organized patterns of thought are generated from a child's direct interaction with and manipulation of the objects in their environment.

For example, when a 1-year-old takes everything off her plate and drops it on the floor, she's not just trying to annoy her mommy and daddy. According to Piaget, she's developing a sensorimotor schema to understand the relationship between cause and effect. It's a simple representation of a basic mechanical relationship: "I drop food. Then, Mommy and Daddy turn red. This is fun!"

>> **Symbolic schemata:** With the development of these schemata, a child begins to symbolically represent earlier sensorimotor relationships. He can think about the objects in his world without having to directly interact with them.

>> **Operational schemata:** These internal, mental activities involve the manipulation of the symbolic representations of objects. Operational schemata involve the ability to think abstractly and to solve problems without actually having to physically attempt a solution. So, instead of jumping in front of a car to see if it hurts, the child can imagine jumping in front of a car and decide whether it would hurt.

Basically, the three schemata begin with concrete interactions with the world and progress to a more symbolic and abstract thinking process. This is a hallmark of Piaget's work; remember that you start out with the concrete and then graduate to the abstract. Now that I think about it, maybe that's why I never did well in Sunday school. I couldn't get past the idea that clouds didn't seem strong enough to support heaven. Wouldn't everything fall right through? I still haven't figured that one out.

REMEMBER

People are born with two processes that help further develop thinking:

>> **Organization:** Organization involves combining the different schemata already developed with new and more complex schemata. You're basically constantly shifting your understanding of the world to create a better and more complete picture.

>> **Adaptation:** Adaptation is a process of getting adjusted to the demands of the environment. Adaptation is accomplished by two distinct subprocesses:

  • **Assimilation:** Little kids use assimilation all the time. When little Jimmy calls a horse a "doggy," that's assimilation in progress. Children attempt to understand novel objects in their environment by drawing upon what they already know and applying that to new objects and situations. It's kind of like using a template; the child tries to fit everything into that one template. If the child only knows one type of four-legged animal with a tail, then even a horse is a "doggy."

THINKING THINGS THROUGH

Cognitive developmental theory is the study of the development and maturation of thinking. A Swiss psychologist named Jean Piaget is the father and reigning king of cognitive developmental theory. Piaget began thinking about thinking as he watched his own children grow up, analyzing their behavior and theorizing about the thoughts running through their little heads. I guess having a psychologist for a parent really can be kind of scary.

Piaget is considered to be a *mentalist* because his theory holds that a person's overt behavior is due in a large part to how she thinks about the world. Piaget emphasized how you think, instead of what you know. After all, a dictionary contains a lot of information, but can it solve the equation 2 + 2? Piaget defined intelligence as the collection of mental abilities that help an organism adapt. He also suggested that intelligence involves seeking *cognitive equilibrium* — a harmonious balance between an individual's thinking and the environment. You constantly encounter novel situations and stimuli from your environment. These new experiences challenge the human mind, which leads to an imbalance. Thinking is the process that restores the balance.

- **Accommodation:** Accommodation is essentially the opposite process of assimilation; instead of adding new experiences to old *schemata*, existing schemata are altered to fit the new information. The child may split a current category in half ("doggy" turns into "big dog" and "little dog") or create a new category (doggy becomes "dogs" and "horses") for remembering experiences. Cognitive growth, then, is the ongoing and persistent process of children applying (assimilating) their understanding to the world and making accommodations for new information. This is the overall process of adaptation, which allows for the maintenance of cognitive equilibrium between thinking and the environment.

Getting your sensorimotor running

The *sensorimotor stage* is the first stage of cognitive development, and it lasts from birth to 2 years of age. During the sensorimotor stage, the problem–solving abilities of an infant grow beyond simple reflexes. Infants extend reflexive behaviors to novel objects in their environment. An infant may suck on a little toy in addition to his mother's nipple or the nipple of a bottle. It can take some babies a few tries to get used to sucking on a pacifier until they are able apply their natural sucking knowledge and ability to other objects.

Almost accidentally, babies discover that they can have a physical effect on the objects in the world. They gradually build on these accidental discoveries and develop intentional and coordinated responses on a simple scale. Eventually, babies progress to a type of experimentation or trial-and-error learning in which they do things to the objects around them just to see what kind of impact they can have on these objects.

The ability to imitate people also develops during the sensorimotor stage. Babies often smile when you smile at them. One of the most common forms of imitation is cooing. When an infant develops the ability to imitate, she often coos back at people who coo at her. That's so cute!

A final key development in this stage is the development of a skill called *object permanence*. If you hide something from a baby who has not yet developed object permanence, he forgets about it. But, when babies achieve object permanence, they remember that the object is still around even if it's not in plain sight — they try to look for the object when you conceal it. So, if you're going to hide things from your children, do it before object permanence develops.

Learning within the lines

Sometimes, when I'm playing with toddlers, I catch myself quizzing them and testing the limits of their knowledge. I may read them a book and ask them to point things out on each page, "Where's the ball?" This sort of toddler homework is perfectly okay, as long as I don't overdo it, which I have a tendency to do.

A lot of parents begin to teach their children some of the rudiments of knowledge that serve as a foundation for future school learning. Recognizing objects and categories of objects such as shapes, colors, animals, numbers, and letters are basic skills that all children need to possess. Although some level of preexisting skill is present, a child's ability to recognize objects increases around the ages of 18 months or 2 years. Children love to learn stories, songs, and nursery rhymes at this time in their lives.

Play is a very important part of a toddler's discovery experience. By the age of 2½, most children can play alongside their peers in both cooperative and independent activities for a sustained period of time. Prior to this age, children may engage in short sessions of independent play or interactive physical play (like patty-cake) with adults or older children. Toddlers and preschoolers prefer more natural toys such as sand, mud, and water. They invent their own games but still don't do too well with rules and regulations.

REMEMBER

Some parents expect their children to learn how to recognize and write letters before they get to kindergarten. But, for most toddlers and preschool-aged children, these skills are too advanced, and very little retention can be expected prior to kindergarten. By the age of 5, children do begin to form letters.

Drawing, however, is a related skill that toddlers and preschoolers do demonstrate some ability in. Most 2- and 3-year-olds can scribble, and by the end of this period, they can easily create straight lines, curves, and loops. Four- and 5-year-olds begin to draw representations and pictures with simple designs. They can easily color within the lines.

Saying what you think

A lot of parents remember their child's first words. When their little one utters the words *momma* or *dada,* their hearts usually melt. *Ball* usually doesn't get the same reaction.

REMEMBER

The dominant position in psychology on the development of language is that language is innate and gradually unfolds as the child's brain develops. This doesn't mean that children are born with a language, but that they're born with the innate mental capacity to learn and grasp the rules of the language community they're born into. Parents can facilitate language development by providing a supportive and stimulating environment and prompting children to use their words to communicate their needs and desires.

Children aren't born speaking in sentences or giving speeches. Well, at least none of the children I've ever met. Children learn to talk little by little. Language develops in stages over the course of the first two to three years of life. Here's a quick overview of language accomplishments that make parents so darn proud:

>> **0 to 4 months:** Infant speech begins with *cooing.* For the first few months, infants make sounds that come naturally from the movements of the mouth (feeding, breathing, and sucking) and from crying. Making a "raspberry" sound or humming are good examples of sounds that come from natural mouth movements.

 The vocal behaviors associated with crying are experimented with and the use of voice begins. These sounds occur both spontaneously and in response to interaction with others. A baby may coo in response to a mother's cooing, for example. These interactions often serve as a basis for future social development as well as parent and child engaging in sound-making games, taking turns, and getting a feel for each other's interaction style.

>> **5 to 8 months:** Infants slightly refine their basic sounds. Around the seventh or eighth month, infants begin to form sounds that resemble syllables. In English, some syllable sounds are easier to utter than others, such as *ma* or *ba*. It's pretty hard to get a 6-month-old to utter a *th* or *l* sound. This stage of experimenting with sounds is called "babbling."

>> **12 to 18 months:** Around the one-year mark, infants begin to use simple monosyllabic words. Early consonant and vowel sounds are then combined to produce early polysyllabic words like *momma* or *boo-boo* or *bye-bye*. This process continues for the next few months, as new words occasionally emerge and mastered words serve as a foundation from which to generalize.

>> **18 months:** Language development explodes around the time infants reach the 18-month mark. Building upon their ability to generalize, children begin to form simple two-word sentences (called "telegraphic speech"), and then three-word sentences, and on and on. The next thing you know, you're answering more "why" questions than you ever thought possible.

Children learn new words at the approximate rate of one word every two hours. That's staggering! I've taken Spanish at different points throughout my life, and I felt super productive if I could learn one word every two weeks. Pretty sad, I know.

This explosion in language development continues until children are about 3 years old. Their language skills expand beyond using one word for many things — *ball* is no longer every round object, *doggy* is no longer anything with four legs, and so on.

Most children have learned the greatest portion (the structures, rules, and a great deal of vocabulary) of their native language by the age of 4. By the time they're ready to enter kindergarten, kids have acquired approximately 8,000 words and learned to use language in a variety of social situations. They can also ask questions and make negative statements. At this point, the rudiments of language are solidly in place, and it's simply a matter of continued learning and increased sophistication, building upon the existing foundation.

Blooming social butterflies

The earliest relationships infants have are with their primary caregivers. A parent and a baby often engage in simple visual and touching games with each other. Infants also make facial gestures at strangers. The interactions between an infant and her primary caregiver have been likened to a dance in which each partner takes cues from the other in a scene that almost seems choreographed. This process of using feedback from each other to gauge social interaction has been called *reciprocal interaction*, and it often depends on the primary caregiver's ability to respond to the cues given by the child.

A good connection between an infant and primary caregiver is often the result of something called the *goodness of fit* — the fit between a child's and a caregiver's temperaments and styles. I've often heard parents say that each of their children had a different temperament and that learning to respond differently to each child was a challenge at times. Some children may be very outgoing and seek social stimulation, but others can be shy and may require a lower-key style of interaction. I think part of the art of parenting is knowing how to match up with a child's temperament; this often represents a significant challenge in therapy with children.

An infant's social circle gradually expands to include siblings, and she begins to show signs of *separation anxiety* (fear of being left by a primary caregiver) between the ages of 7 and 9 months. From 16 to 24 months, infants are able to spend time playing and interacting with others without too much significant involvement from their primary caregivers. From the beginning of 3 to 4 years of age, children's social worlds continue to expand. Sometimes quarreling occurs as they encounter the limitations of dealing with other children. Sharing and taking turns become more important, and simple friendships and fondness for specific children also begin to emerge.

Getting on the Big Yellow Bus

Most children enter kindergarten around the age of 5. This marks a significant turning point in child development — learning, cognitive, and social skills become increasingly important. Children leave their parents and the protective and facilitative environment of the home to begin interacting with a larger and more complex world. School-related skills, such as writing, reading, spelling, and simple mathematics, begin to occupy a great deal of their mental energy and time.

Mastering the crayon

During kindergarten, children learn to use tools and writing-related materials with greater skill. Some children may be exposed to such things as scissors, glue, or paint for the first time in kindergarten. They're also expected to learn how to write letters, their names, and a few simple words during this year in school as well as acquire the basics of reading, including letter recognition and beginning phonics. As children progress through school, these skills are expected to expand with the ability to read and write larger pieces of information.

Mathematical skills begin with counting. By the age of 4 or 5, most children can count with one-to-one correspondence. *One-to-one correspondence* is when a child can count each object she is presented with. So, if I put five apples out, children at this age will count ("One, two, three," and so on) for each apple. As children progress from kindergarten through the school system, they develop concepts of addition and subtraction, and eventually they develop more sophisticated operations that extend to advanced multiplication, division, and sometimes, even fractions.

Being preoperational doesn't mean you're having surgery

The sensorimotor stage of cognitive development is followed by the preoperational and operational stages. Thinking continues to become more sophisticated, using the gains from earlier stages and applying these to more difficult problems.

The *preoperational stage* (ages 2 to 7) marks the development of symbolic thought. A child now possesses the ability to allow one object, a symbol, to represent another object. A hallmark of this is pretend play. How can a stick become a sword, or a bathroom towel be a superhero's cape? Symbolic representation!

The most striking features of preoperational children's thought processes, however, are the abilities that they don't possess. Kids at this age have a hard time classifying objects into two or more categories. For instance, if you ask them if there are more total balls or more red balls in a collection of four red balls and three green balls, they usually answer "red balls." They've locked onto one prominent feature of the collection of balls and cannot think abstractly to solve the problem. How much does 50 pounds of feathers weigh? A preoperational child may give some figure less than 50 pounds as his or her answer.

REMEMBER

A classic development that sharply marks the difference between a preoperational child and a concrete operational child is called *conservation* — the ability to understand that something remains the same even though its appearance or surface properties may change.

Get a tall glass of water and an empty short glass. With the child present, pour the water from the tall glass into the smaller short glass. Now, ask the child which glass had more water in it. The child will always say the tall one; it's bigger. However, after the child gets older and progresses to the concrete operational stage, she can solve this problem.

The *concrete operational stage* marks the development of a child's ability to mentally represent a complex series of actions and perform relational logic. At this stage, children use a skill called *seriation*, which allows a child to arrange objects in a series on some dimension, like bigger to smaller, smaller to bigger, taller to shorter, and so on. Believe it or not, most children can't do this until they're about 7 years old.

A concrete operational child still gets hung up on more abstract problems, or problems that are hypothetical. If a problem has no basis in reality, the concrete operational child has a very hard time answering the question. They balk at "what if" questions because these questions require them to abstract concrete knowledge to situations that have never happened. Luckily, they get there in the formal operations stage, which comes in adolescence.

In the zone

Cognitive development does not occur in a social vacuum. At least that is what the famous Russian psychologist L. S. Vygotsky emphasized. Vygotsky proposed that a child's social and cultural environment determined the types of and extent of the cognitive skills and abilities that get developed. The demands of the social and cultural environment emphasize what is necessary and important cognitively.

For Vygotsky, cognitive development is particularly shaped by the "teachers" a child encounters during development. A child will adjust to the expectations of those teachers and cognitive mentors, learning from and internalizing their cognitive processes. These "teachers" are referred to as the *more-knowledgeable-other (MKO)*, the person in a learning situation who has more knowledge, cognitive skill, and understanding. Keep in mind that these "teachers" don't have to be actual teachers or even adults; they can simply be other people who are MKOs, such as other children.

When a child is developing cognitively, there will be gaps between what he can do and what is expected. For instance, a child may be expected to know his times tables up to five but only knows them for 1 and 2. But, with guidance and help, a child may be able to perform above the level achievable independently. The gap between what can be done and what cannot but can be facilitated by a MKO is what Vygotsky called the *zone of proximal development*. He believed that the zone of proximal development is where instruction should be most focused and intense, to push cognitive development along.

Becoming even more social

The primary social-development issues for school-aged children are peer relationships and social functioning outside the home. By the time children enter school, their relationships with their parents are pretty well solidified. These relationships continue to develop, but relationships outside of the home are the primary focus between the ages of 5 and 12.

During these years, expectations of a child's social ability grow dramatically. Parents no longer tolerate tantrums and less sophisticated social problem-solving techniques, such as hitting other children. Children are expected to follow rules and instructions, especially in the classroom. Their affiliations with other children increase, and they start to develop a small, core group of friends.

If a child has social difficulties, these problems show up when she enters school. Problems related to getting along with the other children, joining in games, and cooperating with the routines expected of them when they're away from their parents can sometimes lead to peer rejection, emotional difficulties, or school failure.

Agonizing over Adolescence

Perhaps one of the most significant events in a child's life is his or her experience with puberty. Puberty is marked by an increase in the sexual hormones of progesterone, testosterone, and androgens. Development of secondary sexual characteristics, such as pubic hair, maturation of the genitalia, menstruation and breast development for girls, accompanies puberty. Interest in sex is markedly increased as boys begin to take interest in girls, and vice versa. Adolescents no longer think that members of the opposite sex have cooties or are gross.

Along with these wonderful physical changes come some pretty profound changes in thinking. By the time children reach the ages of 11- or 12-years-old, they can solve the "what if" problems they are faced with because they reach the cognitive-developmental peak of formal operations. This period is called *formal operations* because the concrete thought processes of childhood are combined into more advanced concepts such as abstractions.

Children can now reason based on hypothetical questions. They don't need concrete examples or demonstrations like they did during the earlier stages of cognitive development. They've become little scientists, able to conduct mental mini-experiments instead of having to tackle problems by using trial and error.

REMEMBER

Keep in mind that just because kids and adolescents can ask and answer these questions doesn't mean they actually do. When I was a teenager, I repeatedly failed to ask myself, "What if I get caught lying to my parents?" I should have used my formal operational thinking a little more.

Pining over puberty

Exactly when puberty begins is a questionable matter. It can come at different times for different children. But researchers have noticed that the age of onset for puberty has been gradually decreasing. On average, kids are entering puberty at younger ages. This development has been dubbed the *secular trend,* and researchers believe that it's due to better childhood nutrition.

The average age of onset for puberty in Western countries is showing a decline of three months per decade.

The timing of puberty can have serious repercussions, depending on when it comes. Boys who develop later than others sometimes suffer from peer ridicule and social setbacks related to popularity and dating. Girls who develop too early sometimes find themselves in situations that they're mentally and emotionally not prepared for because their bodies make them look older than they really are.

What about sex? A great deal of variation in sexual norms exists across societies, but whether or not a society puts strict limits on adolescent sexual behavior, sexual desire is a primary issue for members of this age group. Most of the time, teenagers learn about sex from their friends and from the media. The old birds and the bees talk doesn't come up as often as people may think.

Moving away from parents

One striking difference between childhood and adolescence is the diminished importance of parents in a teenager's life. Prior to adolescence, parents and the home occupy center stage in a child's life. During the teen years, adolescents begin to express their independence and autonomy by making friendships their top priority.

Social functions that involve parents take a back seat to teen-exclusive functions, such as dances, parties (without chaperones), and outings at this stage in a child's development. Hanging out, texting, going on Facebook, and staying overnight at friends' houses are commonplace.

Peers are a major source of self-esteem, and fitting in is often more important than parental acceptance. Teenagers experiment with identity and social roles. Relationship skills and patterns laid down in childhood grow in sophistication at this stage. Romantic relationships become extremely important. Being the star of the household gives way to desires for being popular or well-liked among friends.

Existing as a Grown-Up

Although many teenagers beg to differ, there is life after adolescence. In fact, the majority of a person's years on this planet take place in what is referred to as *adulthood*, defined as the years between 18 and death. Adulthood is often divided into three periods:

>> **Young adulthood:** Ages 18 to 39

>> **Middle adulthood:** Ages 40 to 64

>> **Late adulthood:** Ages 65+

In adulthood people keep growing, changing, and developing. These years are just as packed with life as the previous 18, simply in different ways. In this section you will be introduced to the developmental tasks of adulthood including marriage, work, and retirement.

Looking at you

Young adulthood covers a wide range of ages; a great many of the impactful experiences of a person's life happen during these years, including starting and finishing college, beginning a career, getting married, and starting a family. All in all, these can be very busy and productive years. A lot is going on.

Physically, people peak in strength, reflexes, and stamina in their mid-20's; upon entering middle adulthood they become more and more aware of the changes in their bodies and how their bodies are less resilient, more susceptible to disease, and overall less youthful than in young adulthood. Women enter *menopause* sometime in their late 40s to early 50s, in which they stop menstruating, are no longer fertile, and experience hormonal changes that can sometimes lead to very unpleasant experiences such as hot flashes and even panic attacks.

Connecting and working

Relationships in adulthood continue to develop. Intimacy is typically sought, sometimes resulting in marriage. Although the divorce rate for first marriages in the United States is about half of all marriages, people still get married. However, people are getting married at later ages — not in their early 20s as much — and nearly half (47 percent) of the United States adult population is unmarried according to the US Census Bureau in 2012.

Having and raising children can be a large part of young adulthood, although not all adults choose to have children. This is another trend throughout the United States that suggests that cultural and societal mandates to "get married and have kids" is less prevalent than in previous decades.

A significant portion of modern adulthood involves working and achievement. Middle adulthood sparks questions that consider the wisdom of decisions made in young adulthood. If a person goes to college right after high school — or enters the workforce right away — she will likely reflect back and wonder if it was the right choice. Am I doing what I wanted to do? Does my daily life have meaning? Have I met my goals? Did I do what I wanted to do?

As late adulthood approaches, one begins to prioritize what is important in life and what is less important. As people transition to this final phase, they begin to see themselves as old.

Aging and Geropsychology

If old age is upon you, you're not alone. The population of 65+ has grown by 74 percent between the years 1990 and 2020. By contrast, the under 65 set has grown 24 percent during this same period.

Perhaps most obviously, bodies have and continue to age, which means many physical changes occur at every stage of life, especially late adulthood. Hair and skin thin and may gray. Bones become more brittle, and muscle tone decreases. Energy and stamina decrease, and sensory capabilities decline with less acute vision, sight, hearing, and even taste.

Physical decline in aging has been looked at from at least two explanatory models:

>> **Genetic programming theories of aging:** Aging is the result of genetic programming in which cells stop dividing and growing and begin a "self-destruct" course toward eventual death.

>> **Wear and tear theories of aging:** With time, bodies break down from use, the buildup of waste and toxins take their toll, and the body wears out, like an old shoe.

Of course the body is not the only thing about a person that's aging. Cognitive changes in late adulthood include some minor changes such as slightly slower processing speeds and less effective and efficient memory. On the upside, people in this stage experience stable and, in some cases, improved problem-solving strategies and information.

Memory, however, remains one of the main concerns for the aging and aged population and their families. Am I inevitably going to lose my memory? The data and research in this area spell out a much more complex picture than one may expect. For some people, memory loss and impairment does not occur. For others, mild forms of memory loss may occur for specific domains such as episodic memory (memory for events) while other forms of memory, such as memory for general knowledge and facts, remains relatively untouched by age. (For more about memory, see Chapter 6.)

For some, aging comes with an increased risk for actual diseases that leads to cognitive decline and memory impairment generally referred to as the *dementias*. One of the most prevalent dementias is *Alzheimer's disease*. Although not fully understood, Alzheimer's is a progressive brain disease that results in gradual and irreversible cognitive decline. Prevalence is estimated to be about 20 percent of people 75 to 84 and almost 50 percent of people over the age of 85. Medication treatments have been shown to help with some cognitive improvement for some people, perhaps slowing the progression of the disease, but there is currently no known cure for Alzheimer's.

Socially, late adulthood can be filled with grandchildren and friendships and, despite the clichés, it does not have to include loneliness. Of course, the specter of death is there and seeing friends and peers die is an inevitable stressor. Some people age quite gracefully; some do not, but is there really a good way to age?

I live in a community that is considered a retirement and resort community for the most part. I see what I refer to as "positive models" of aging around me every day — people in late adulthood exercising (more than me, by the way), working, volunteering, socializing, and looking pretty darn good doing it all. I can only hope to follow their model.

Older adults being social and active is known as the *activity model of aging*; psychologists postulate that people who age best are those who maintain their interests, activities, and social interaction, and continue to live their lives in line with middle adulthood in most respects.

Chapter **13**

Psychology in the Digital Age

What would shock a time traveler from the 1700s if he were to show up in New York City tomorrow? Certainly the giant metal and glass buildings, flying machines, horseless carriages, and countless other technological marvels would astonish him. Yep, the world has changed and continues to change rapidly, sometimes, it seems, right before my eyes. My 2-year-old plays on and actually operates an iPad. Wow, I could barely manipulate Tinkertoys (an antiquated non-digital form of entertainment from the mid-20th century).

Something called "Moore's Law" states that computing power essentially doubles every two years, making it an exponential force. Machines, computers, and technology are all around. They seem as pervasive as food, air, and clothing. Massively complex and high-powered technologies are an integral part of people's lives. I didn't get my first computer until college. Before that, a fancy typewriter with a little digital readout was all I thought I needed. I had to actually go to the library to research something. I had to use a payphone to call somebody and I didn't even get a pager (what's that you say?) until my mid-20s. By the way, my first computer was a 33-megahertz machine. It took 15 minutes just to turn on and boot up. Oh yeah, we turned our computers off back then.

Consider the following scene from the movie *Terminator Salvation* (2009):

> **John Connor:** The devil's hands have been busy. What is it?
>
> **Kate Connor:** It's real flesh and blood, though it seems to heal itself quickly. The heart is human and very powerful. The brain, too, but with a chip interface.
>
> **Marcus Wright:** What have you done to me?
>
> **Kate Connor:** It has a hybrid nervous system. One human cortex, one machine.
>
> **Marcus Wright:** Blair, what have they done?
>
> **John Connor:** Who built you?
>
> **Marcus Wright:** My name is Marcus Wright.
>
> **John Connor:** You think you're human?
>
> **Marcus Wright:** I am human.

Yes, Marcus Wright is a cyborg, a combination of human biological parts and machine and computer technology. I have news for you, you and me, we're cyborgs too. But don't go digging into your skull for your computer interface. Your biological life is interfaced with technology as you drive around in a car, sit in front of a computer, talk to others through smartphones, have your medical health monitored by devices in the hospital, and watch people on the television screen. Okay, that's a little odd, I'll admit, but the point is that computers, the Internet, mobile phones, and massive computing power have fundamentally changed how people live, how they view themselves, how they interact with each other, how they interact with their environments, how they learn, how they play, and how they spend their time. The context of human life has been changed dramatically by digital technology, and it is critical to understand how all of this influences human psychology, development, and perhaps even the brain.

Cyberpsychology is the branch of psychology that is dedicated to the study of the intersection of psychology and all facets of technology, particularly digital and computer technology. In this chapter, I discuss how digital technology is impacting people socially and how computers and related technology might be changing human cognition. I also cover the less positive sides of technology, such as cyberbullying.

Love and Robots

Humans are social beings, some more than others, some hardly at all, and some extremely so. However, human evolution has occurred within the context of being together, and survival of the species through sexual reproduction depends on it after all. Socializing assumes communicating. Although much of human history has been dominated by communicating through speech (such as talking, story-telling, oral traditions in religion), there has and continues to be a simultaneous use of "technology" to connect through communication ranging from cave paint-ings, carrier pigeons, written text, books, telegraphs, and on up to telephones, smartphones, and of course the Internet and its various social media. Computer and digital technology has become a dominant form of communication with email, text messaging, and videoconferencing in real time. Computers, mobile phones, and the Internet are many things to many people, but they are most certainly social and communication tools.

Talk to the box

Strange sights abound in public spaces: people walking down the street talking to themselves; rooms full of people not talking but staring at little rectangles in their hands, or bigger rectangles on their laps, or even bigger rectangles on the tables in front of them. Their hands are moving frantically, rhythmically, and with pur-pose. People talk to people through devices. This looks strange, even feels strange, or does it? After all, they are "talking" to other people, or reading other people's thoughts and ideas, or writing their own thoughts and ideas. They are communi-cating and socializing in effect. Scientists who study these phenomena refer to these types of communications as *computer-mediated-communication* (CMC) and their corresponding social dimensions as the study of *online social networks* (to broadly include mobile networks mediated through the Internet).

The reasons people connect through digital technology and Internet are not all that different from the reasons they connect through flesh and bones and analog technology. People want to gossip, keep tabs on each other, catch up, get roman-tic, look for help, give help, show off, brag, and so on. However, although the motives between the "two worlds" of communication (online versus offline) remain very much the same, it is interesting to note that *social networking sites* (SNSs) are considered the preferred mode of social networking for many people. So, although the need to network socially remains constant, the preferred medium has shifted. This is a rapidly changing scenario. Consider that some research has shown that the once ubiquitous, pervasive, and massive use of email has declined and is being replaced by Facebook-based communication, Twitter, Snapchat, Ins-tagram, and other services.

SNSs are used by billions of people. So everyone is online and using SNSs, right? Well, not everyone. Cyberpsychologists have wondered if there is a difference between people who use SNSs and those who do not or a difference between those who use them a lot or just a little. Research has shown that the popularity of SNSs use can be predicted by an individual's sense of how effective he or she is at using the Internet (called *Internet self-efficacy*), the need to belong, and what is called "collective self-esteem," or how a particular individual's social network feels about itself as a whole. Extraverts are also more likely to use SNSs, but extraverts are more likely to be social offline as well. Interestingly, not only do people use SNSs to meet their social needs, but over time, maintaining the online social network becomes a goal in and of itself.

Me and my friends

I can be anybody I want online, right? Are people's online identities drastically different than their offline ones? Research has shown that with the exception of outright deception, there tends to be consistency between online and offline identities. The only caveat is that my online persona tends to be just slightly exaggerated in the positive direction as I put forth my slightly idealized version of myself. Also, although I can put up any profile I want on any website I want, SNSs like Facebook have some degree of "social policing" in that my profile gets connected to other people's, and as this process happens several times over, the "truth" sort of emerges. In other words, it is relatively easy to lie about who I am, but it is way harder to lie about who I am and who all my friends are when a person can simply just look at all my online friends and see for themselves. My online self and offline self merge, depending on how much is shared. Some people take steps to ensure some degree of separation or anonymity, and others are way, way more open. Sometimes there are negative consequences to this, such as losing a job because of bad behavior displayed on a Facebook page. So unless everybody is lying en masse, there tends to be a fair amount of *persona bona fide* online.

One of the more common criticisms of CMS and SNSs are that they are making people and society more isolated and less sociable, to which the users say the exact opposite. What does the science say? Research has shown that the CMC and SMSs are like the transformational chemical "potion" from the 1980s movie the *Swamp Thing,* directed by horror movie master Wes Craven and starring Ray Wise and Adrienne Barbeau. The potion simply makes you "more of what you already are." CMS and SNSs are used to strengthen and solidify offline and already existing relationships. People build, rebuild, rekindle, and maintain relationships online. Online socializing can be used to avoid feelings of loneliness and build feelings of connection, but research has shown that individuals with "weak" or thin social networks offline will not necessarily gain or create "strong" or dense networks online. Those who struggle socially do not necessarily gain from going online.

But wait, I've got 1,000 online friends and we're all super close. Right?! Research shows that a person's network size is more a function of how much time he or she spends online, although, once again, extraverts tend to have larger networks. However, SNSs users appear to have a built-in sense of how many friends is too many friends, and the larger a person's network gets, the more observers mistrust the intimacy of that network. Social popularity as measured by online friends doesn't look that much different than it does offline, and it's kind of shallow. The more physically attractive you are and the more physically attractive your online friends are, the more friends you'll have, for example.

That perfect someone

Say I write a note looking for love, for a beautiful, smart, and nurturing person to spend the rest of my life with, put it in a bottle, cork it, and send it off through the waves and into the wide ocean. Has this ever worked? There is one story floating around on the Internet about a Swedish man and a Sicilian woman who met this way and got married, and of course, Kevin Costner and Robin Wright Penn found each other this way in the 1999 movie *Message in a Bottle*. Online dating is almost the exact opposite of the "message in a bottle technique," but the motive may be the same: to find someone. Online dating involves putting oneself "out there" to a massive "ocean" of people as opposed to a massive "ocean" of water. That is, the odds can go way up with online dating.

Online dating is widely popular and some statistics show that nearly one fifth of all marriages in the United States began as online relationships. It's a billions of dollars industry. There are many critics of online dating, some of them coming from a safety perspective and others from a perspective that you can't really get to know anybody well enough online. But there are just as many supporters. Is online dating really that different?

Research has shown that online dating is different from offline dating in some important ways. To begin with, the "getting to know you" phase and even the courtship phase of relationships is altered. Offline dating begins more slowly as people meet in less deliberate ways (unless you are "set up" by someone) through your typical social circles or daily activities such as church, work, or classmates. Offline dating tends to be a function of proximity, a "girl next door" effect of sorts. But online dating can connect you to potential mates from anywhere in the world; there is no proximity limitation.

In offline dating information about a potential mate is gathered more slowly as it emerges or comes up during casual conversation. There really isn't anything more awkward than going on a date and feeling like you are being interrogated or interviewed. This is also true for getting a sense of how you "get along" and interact with each other. A few dates can give a person a lot of data of how a potential romantic partner "is" among people and in social situations. Online dating can connect you to "just the facts" and the salient and nitty-gritty aspects of a person in just a few lines of a profile on a dating website. Information gathering is sped way up. Online data doesn't, however, afford you the ability to see the person in social action. For that you have to go offline.

The main thrust of online dating services' marketing is that these sites can connect you to an extremely large number of potential mates. The premise is that this facilitates finding "Mr. Right" because you've conducted an exhaustive search. A criticism of this aspect of online dating is that because of the sheer numbers of people a seeker might come in contact with, he or she might resort to "quick and dirty" or shallow "rule out" strategies and make snap judgments based on more obvious (but perhaps less important) features in a person's profile.

Researcher Eli Finkel and his colleagues also warn online daters against what they call the "assessment mindset" in which other people are seen as "commodities" or objects to be "consumed," as this may lead to a more dehumanizing tendency. You might see someone as a "means to my end" rather than as a real person. This is a stark warning, but research lends some credence to this notion. It has been shown that the more dating profiles a person has access to, the more he or she will engage in searching for the "ideal mate" or the "soulmate." This mindset is seen as problematic because basic social psychological and relationship research has shown that when a person expects a mate to be "ideal" for him or her, that relationship is less likely to succeed when stress or challenge arrives. And arrive it always does! It is even thought that online daters might also doubt current romantic "selections" because, in the back of their mind, they think there might be somebody better out there, waiting among the yet-to-be explored profiles, almost a perpetual "grass might be greener" phenomenon.

But does it work? There is no scientific data to support the assertion that online dating is either more or less effective than offline dating. Online dating certainly exposes you to more people. And it can lead to some interesting problems such as the "assessment mindset" or the never-ending search for the perfect mate. As is true with online friendships and social networks, it would seem that the online world is not all that different from the offline world, albeit in perhaps a more exaggerated or amplified form.

Digitized (d)evolution

Fill in the blank:

People sit in front of (A)_____ screens for hours at a time!

All my kids ever do is play (B)_____ and they're always on that dang (C)_____.

If I get one more (D)_____ I'm going to throw this (E)_____ in the trash!

Some of the possible answers:

A. television or computer

B. LEGOs or videogames

C. phone or tablet

D. message or email

E. phone or computer

Your answers to these fill-in-the-blank questions might depend on the era you grew up in. Technology changes, but some of the complaints don't. But some critics of modern technology have issued dire warnings about how the devices and networks you and I use are changing us for the worse. Author Nicholas Carr warns that the Internet is making us inattentive and shallow-minded fools. Mark Bauerfein thinks the digital generation is the "dumbest generation." Although both of these claims are likely to be more provocative than realistic, it does beg the question: How are people's minds, ways of thinking, and perhaps brains changing in response to digital technology and the Internet?

To begin with, the answer to that question remains a very fertile "it's too soon to tell" anything definitive. Research has been conducted, but much more needs to be done. Some findings so far, however, actually contradict the critics. Some studies have shown that surfing the net, as opposed to making people "shallow" or allowing them to "shut off their brains," actually stimulates the brain in a way that people use a greater proportion of their neural circuitry than when offline. Brain circuits involved in decision making and complex reasoning have been shown to be stimulated in particular. Other research has shown that even playing violent video games (the scourge!) has a positive impact on cognitive performance, as does playing nonviolent video games.

Certainly those digital kids can't pay attention though. They all have ADHD, right? Multitasking is a way of "being" for many digital people. On the phone, surfing the net, and downloading a movie all while listening to the psychology professor in Introduction to Psychology class. Research in this area actually leans toward the critics to some degree. There is no credible data or evidence to suggest that attention capacity or ability is better in this digital population as they claim to have "learned" to multitask. In fact, research has shown that attention *suffers* in these situations, and as a consequence, so does overall performance. The evidence so far suggests that it is still better to focus on one specific task than to divide one's attention across a variety of tasks.

What goes hand in hand with attention span is oftentimes impulsivity or impatience. The digital generation gets information fast, faster than any time in history. Nonetheless, there is once again no scientific evidence that digital technology and the Internet are making people more impatient.

Consider author Andrew Keen's warning as captured in the title of his 2008 book, *The Cult of the Amateur: How blogs, MySpace, YouTube, and the rest of today's user-generated media are destroying our economy, our culture, and our values.* This is a huge claim and a compound question that would have to be investigated by sociologists, anthropologists, perhaps historians, and, of course, psychologists.

Researchers have looked at this issue at a smaller level by exploring whether the digital generation sees information from peers' expressions on the Internet as being more credible than information from authority figures. Sorry, Mr. Keen, there is no evidence to support this assertion. Not yet anyway. Although peer opinions found on social networking sites (SNSs) do seem to be valued more when it comes to entertainment and preference purchases, other studies have shown that when it comes to learning and getting information for academic assignments, for example, even the digital generation still values the authority of teachers, parents, and textbooks.

The Dark Side of the Digital World

It would seem that digital technology, computers, mobile phones, iPads, iPhones, the Internet, and the like have turned out to be less harmful than helpful. There are, however, examples of the "dark side" of these technologies. Cybertheft and crime is a multibillion dollar industry. How many obviously fraudulent emails land in your Junk mailbox every day? How often do you hear about people having credit card numbers or even their identities stolen online? Unfortunately, there are numerous news stories of children and adolescents being lured into dangerous (offline) situations by online predators through chat rooms, emails, and other online ploys. In some ways, the power, reach, speed, and anonymity of digital technology and the Internet have made it much easier to commit certain types of crimes and offenses, and they have also expanded the realm of application for other offline problems such as addiction and bullying.

Say that to my face

Anonymity can make it much easier to lie and can lower a person's inhibitions. Digital technology in general and the Internet in particular make anonymity much easier. Have you ever noticed how rude, cruel, and downright nasty some of the comments on YouTube can be? What about book reviews on Amazon? There is an appearance that computer-mediated-communication (CMS) has a tendency to facilitate less inhibited communication. Cyberpsychologist John Suler calls this type of unrestrained communication *toxic disinhibition*.

Dr. Suler outlines several factors that contribute to the rude and unrestrained verbal behavior sometimes encountered online:

> **Anonymity:** A person's actions or words cannot be directly traced to him or her, making it easier to act or speak in ways that he or she would not otherwise do so.

> **Asynchronicity:** Online communications oftentimes do not occur in "real time," so the emotional impact of a "heated" situation may not factor in to someone's thinking.

> **Minimization of status and authority:** Online, everyone is an equal, or so it seems that way in cyberspace.

Unfortunately inappropriate and potentially damaging behavior doesn't stop with name-calling and verbal insults. Deception has become a somewhat ubiquitous online phenomenon. People pretending to be completely different people, online financial scams, and outright fraud occur everyday online. After a 2010 movie titled *Catfish*, a documentary about online dating and romance scamming, the term "catfish" is now synonymous with this type of behavior. Essentially, deceptive individuals set up fake dating or SNSs profiles, lure unsuspecting suitors in, and then engage in sometimes very long online relationships with the victims, all the while being somebody completely different.

Is the online environment just full of sociopaths? Cyberpsychologists Avner Caspi and Paul Gorsky call this behavior *identity play*. Their research found that frequent Internet users are more likely to deceive than less frequent users and that in contrast to face-to-face deception, online deception is viewed as enjoyable in its own right by some perpetrators. They propose the existence of an altered "online morality" that perpetuates this behavior.

Hooked on the Internet

Comedian Aziz Ansari takes a humorous jab at himself for being what appears to be addicted to the Internet. He tells the story of how in the middle of working at his computer, he will at times, stop what he is doing and decide he needs to know everything there is to know about the actor Joe Pesci. This can take hours, and at some point, he realizes he has to get back to work, but not before he keeps looking up more and more and more and more.

Internet addiction is not recognized by the American Psychiatric Association as a formally diagnosed mental disorder. However, it is recognized as a problem that people experience, suffer from, and oftentimes need treatment for. It can be understood as obsessive and compulsive Internet overuse that interferes with functioning (like Aziz's work).

M. Griffiths lists the following criteria for determining if an individual can be considered addicted to the Internet:

>> **Salience:** Being on the Internet is most important activity in the person's life.

>> **Mood change:** Mood changes substantially in response to use or non-use (for example, flying into a rage if something takes too long to load).

>> **Tolerance:** Higher "doses" of the experience are needed to achieve the same result.

>> **Withdrawal symptoms:** Negative feelings and sensations occur if individual cannot be online.

>> **Conflict:** Relationship problems and decline in school or work performance occur due to Internet use.

>> **Relapse and reinstatement:** There is a tendency to return to addictive behavior even after periods of control.

Risk factors for becoming addicted to the Internet include being male, alcohol consumption, dissatisfaction with family life, and recent stress. Notably, similar factors are found for all addictions.

REMEMBER

Because Internet addiction is not viewed as necessarily different from other addictions, it is believed that it is not the properties of the Internet itself that are at issue but rather an individual's seeking refuge from stress in the online universe. Fortunately, there are treatment programs both in the United States and internationally.

Bullying moves from the schoolyard to the desktop

A controversial headline has shown up in United States newspapers:

Teen Commits Suicide Over Cyberbullying

There have been lawsuits and even criminal charges. There is really no question that cyberbullying is a problem. Researcher P.K. Smith and colleagues define *cyberbullying* as an aggressive, intentional act carried out by a group or individual, using electronic forms of contact, repeatedly and over time against a victim who cannot easily defend him or herself. Cyberbullying can occur in chat rooms, through email, in SNSs, and through any other CMC medium. It can be repetitive or happen only once. It can take the form of making verbal threats, posting of pictures or video, or using any other verbal (textual) behavior that fits the definition (such as lambasting someone's reputation, for example, or spreading lies).

Julian Dooley, Jacek Pyzalski, and Donna Cross conducted a review of research exploring the question of whether cyberbullying differs from face-to-face bullying. An obvious difference can be that physical power differences are less relevant online. Motives to inflict harm and fear appear to be similar, however. Another difference is that with face-to-face bullying, the perpetrator may gain some form of reinforcement in the immediate moment, whereas with cyberbullying, this form of reinforcement may be delayed or experienced more indirectly. With face-to-face bullying, males tend to be the vast majority of perpetrators. However, with cyberbullying, some studies have shown that females and males engage in the same rates of perpetration, and others have shown only slightly higher rates for males. Another similarity between the two are the underlying motivations to bully: social control, dominance, and entertainment.

TIP

What can you do? First of all, bullying of any kind should never be ignored by witnesses. However, there are instances where a single case of cyberbullying could be ignored in order to wait and see if the bully just moves on. Sameer Hinduja and Justin Patchin of the Cyberbullying Research Center provide the following additional coping tips:

>> Tell someone else and talk about it.

>> Never retaliate because doing so just might feed into the bully's motivation.

>> Tell the bully to stop unequivocally.

>> Save the evidence and document incidents.

>> Block the bully's access to you through security settings on SNSs, messaging apps, and email.

>> Report the bullying to the content provider or network administrator.

>> Call the police.

Can Technology Make Us Better at Being Human?

Technology, the Internet, social media, video games, iPads in the highchair, and phones in the hands all can get a pretty bum rap. But there's got to be some benefit, right? Of course there is. I was talking to my two teenagers one night about their use of technology. I was going on about how they don't interact anymore, don't talk to me, and don't have any social skills. They gladly pointed out that my binge-watching of *Game of Thrones* wasn't any different. In fact, they pointed out that at least they are communicating with people, sharing pictures and videos, and telling jokes. They also pointed out that they see the benefit in people posting videos on platforms like TikTok because they are expressing themselves, showing pride, making people laugh, and so on. "Okay," I said. (But secretly I still don't buy their argument.)

How then has all this technology made us better or at least helped us? Technology has been at the center of humanitarian-driven revolutions in the Middle East as activists and protestors coordinated ad hoc rallies through text messages and social media. Video chat and social media have allowed people to stay in touch with loved ones and friends on the other side of the world. Telehealth connects people who may otherwise not get healthcare from their doctors and therapists. Grassroots capitalists have access to audiences without huge corporations taking their pound of flesh. Massive amounts of information is available to anyone with an Internet connection that might have only been available to the privileged with advanced degrees or access to university libraries. Information has been democratized. Massive cloud-based computing helps us understand complex phenomena that baffled us before. People find husbands, wives, and partners. People find long-lost relatives or friends. We can trace our ancestry like never before. We can look for jobs more easily. We can work from home more often (if we are afforded the privilege), which cuts down on our carbon footprint. We can buy things, more things, and even more things really easily. Well, maybe that's not such a benefit — unless you are the one selling those things. Customer service is more accessible. Wow, I think I went a little too far with that one. But you get the point, I hope.

5
Adapting and Struggling

Find out about the growing field of health psychology and its approach to stress, illness, coping, and human psychological strength and resilience.

Explore what it means to struggle psychologically.

Discover how mental health professionals understand "disorder."

Get a closer look at some of the more common mental health issues.

Chapter **14**

Coping When Life Gets Rough

Under pressure? Most of us can identify with the song by Queen. When I was in college, I could stay up all night studying, take exams the next day, and then go to work as a busboy in the evening — without even thinking about breaking plans with my friends at night. I could just keep going and going. When I hit the work world, I could work as a prison psychologist during the day, teach community college at night, and do mental disability testing on the weekends. I must have worked more than 100 hours every week. Then I got married and had kids and got a mortgage. The pressure mounted, and I felt like I was swimming in syrup and barely keeping my head above its sweet grasp. I couldn't "handle it." I couldn't do it!

"Life" was happening around and to me, and I came to know stress in new and sometimes-upsetting ways. I found myself looking for sources of energy, strength, replenishment, and an inner reserve.

I realize that all of this may seem rather tame to some. I mean, come on: work, kids, blah blah blah. Well, as you see in this chapter, the subjective experience of pressure and strain is part of what defines *stress* for all of us. But beyond the traffic, the long lines at the store, the barking dog, the irritating or insensitive social media post, and the dreaded spinning wheel of buffering, there are also *extreme stressors* associated with psychological *trauma*. Facing the potential for death in situations of war, natural disaster, or pandemic has the potential to be traumatic. Experiencing serious physical or psychological harm, as in cases of domestic violence, sexual assault, or child abuse, can be traumatic. Losing someone you love can be traumatic. Is that dark enough?

This isn't an autobiography, so I'll spare the details, but I've experienced both mundane and extreme stressors. Struggle seems inherent to all living organisms, and few (or none) are exempt, so learning something about dealing with stress and trauma might be helpful. Thankfully, however, psychological science has something to offer and say about these issues. In this chapter, I introduce and discuss the concepts of stress, crisis, trauma, grief, coping, and resilience.

Stressing Out

Every year around the same time I get sick. It never fails. Come October, I've got a cold. Is it the weather? Is it a cosmic curse? At some point I made a connection between my getting sick and stress. In school, it was the stress of midterms. Now, it's the stress of the holidays. Everyone gets stressed about different stuff, and sometimes the stress makes people become physically ill.

REMEMBER

What is stress? There's a two-part answer:

>> When most people talk about stress, they refer to the things or events that cause worry, anxiety, and strain — work, money, bills, kids, bosses, and so on. These are *external pressures*. The strains and pace of modern life seem to get the best of most people at one time or another. That's the first part.

>> Stress can be defined as a person's *mental and behavioral responses to and subjective experience* of external pressures.

Ways to think about stress

Psychologists and researchers from other fields have expanded on the definition of stress mentioned above. Some have developed models that view stress as the process of balancing mental and physical tension. Others have approached stress from the cognitive perspective. In this section, I discuss three of these models.

Homeostasis

Formal definitions of stress range from descriptions of bodily reactions to cognitive models. In his 1997 book *Stress and Health: Biological and Psychological Interactions*, William Lavallo defined stress as a bodily or mental tension to something that knocks people off balance, either physically or mentally. Conversely, when a person has *equilibrium*, he's maintaining a balance between the external world and his internal world. Walter Cannon, an American physiologist at Harvard Medical School, in 1939, called this concept *homeostasis*. So basically, people feel stressed when they're out of homeostatic balance.

Hans Selye, an endocrinologist at the Université de Montréal and Nobel Prize nominee, gave one of the most famous theories of stress. His theory was based on something he called the *general adaptation syndrome (GAS)*. The idea is that when someone is confronted with something that threatens either her physical or mental equilibrium, she goes through a series of changes:

>> **Alarm:** The initial reaction to the stressor. The brain and hormones are activated in order to provide the body with the necessary energy to respond to the element causing stress.

>> **Resistance:** The activation of the body system best suited to deal with the stressor. If the stressor requires that you run — if you're being chased by a pack of wild dogs — then your nervous system and hormones make sure that you've got enough blood pumping to your legs to get the job done. Plus, extra energy is provided to your heart so it can pump blood faster. It's a beautifully designed system.

>> **Exhaustion:** The final stage. If the bodily system activated in the resistance stage gets the job done, your trip down GAS lane ends. If the stressor continues, you enter this final stage. When you're exhausted, your body is no longer able to resist the stress, and it becomes vulnerable to disease and breakdown.

Appraisal

The body is not the only thing at work when you're stressed. Numerous cognitive (thinking) and emotional responses are also going on. Arnold Lazarus, a South African psychologist known for his work on behavior therapy, stated that during times of stress, an individual goes through a process of emotional analysis. It's kind of like having a little psychologist inside your head. You ask yourself to determine the current significance of the problem and its importance for the future. How does this stress work? You make two important *appraisals,* or evaluations — known as *primary* and *secondary appraisals.* An appraisal is an assessment or estimate of the value of something.

In most stressful situations, something important is at stake, or at least you think it is; otherwise, you wouldn't be stressed about it. The evaluation of what is at stake is the primary appraisal of the situation. At this stage, situations are classified into one of three categories:

>> **Threat:** An example of a threatening situation is a situation that requires a response. If I'm standing in line at the grocery store and someone cuts in front of me, I'm not forced to respond. But if a guy grabs me by the shirt and threatens to kick my butt if I don't let him in front of me, I have to respond in one way or another. Like run!

>> **Harm-loss:** A harm-loss situation may involve getting hurt in some way — physically, mentally, or emotionally. A blow to my pride may be seen as a harm-loss situation. It's relative.

>> **Challenge:** I can also look a threatening person straight in the eye and see the perceived threat as a challenge. Instead of seeing the situation in dangerous terms, I may see it as an opportunity to try out those judo lessons I've been taking.

After figuring out what's at stake, I take stock of the resources I have available to deal with the situation. This is secondary appraisal. I may take a look at my previous experience with this type of situation. What did I do when this happened before, and how did that turn out? Most people also take a look at how they feel about themselves. If you see yourself as a capable person, then you're likely to become less stressed out than someone who thinks less of their capabilities.

Stress can be viewed as something more than the actual situation; a person's reaction depends on how he looks at the stressor. Stress is not a situation; it's a consequence of how a situation and a person's response to that situation interact. I can react differently to the same situation. For example, If I'm called on to pitch for the final out in the bottom of the ninth inning in the World Series I could get all stressed out because I dread failing, giving up the game-losing home run. Or, I could look at the situation with excitement because I have the opportunity to pitch for the last out and the win. The situation didn't change, but my reaction to it did. One leads to the experience of stress, one does not.

Stress can also be a product of how much control a person thinks she has over events and situations. Stress arises when people lack an adequate response to a situation, and the consequences of failure are important. Seeing yourself as having little or no control can have negative psychological and physical consequences.

TIP

On the other hand, feeling like the "master of your domain" may help keep stress at bay. I remember a cartoon from my childhood called *He-Man and the Masters of the Universe*. He-Man had this phrase that he yelled out when he was getting ready to kick butt: "I have the power!" It would be nice if I could just yell that out and be ready to take on the world. In 1982, George Mandler, professor emeritus at the University of California, San Diego, defined *mastery* as the thought or perception that things in an individual's environment can be brought under her control. Sounds like He-Man to me.

Allostasis

Surprise! Gotcha! Think fast! Look out! Sudden, unpredictable events or situations are stressful, even when they're good. Some of us can roll with it and some of us can't, but we all have our limits. Think about having a "surprise" everywhere you went, with people jumping out at you. Maybe they're just saying "Good day!" or maybe they're yelling "Move it!" Either is stressful. So it's nice to know what's coming as it helps us prepare and potentially respond and cope better.

Some theorists and researchers believe that the concept of homeostasis was too focused on the "reaction" side of the stress response. These scientists proposed that the dimension of efficacious adjustments and changes to mental processes and behaviors in response to stress was just as critical to understanding it, and this gave rise to the concept of *allostasis*.

Allostasis consists of all of an organism's abilities to respond to homeostatic challenge, make adjustments in mental processes and behavior, and prepare to be more "ready" next time. So we're not just reacting; we're adapting! We're not just coping; we're adjusting and continuing to adjust on an ongoing basis.

According to researcher Jay Schulkin, as the environment constantly changes around us, we evoke mental processes, behaviors, and biological processes to promote continuity, stability, and predictability. We need things to be stable and predictable, and some of the hallmarks of extreme stress, for example, are unpredictability and the experience of it coming from "out of nowhere." If you've ever been rear ended in your car while just sitting at an intersection minding your own business, you know what this feels like. It's a shock that can be very upsetting and intense. At least if you saw the car coming in your rearview mirror, you avoid surprise. Jay Schulkin states it well:

> . . . [allostasis] is about adapting to change to achieve the goal of stability in the face of uncertain circumstances, something all of us know about early in life and continue to experience throughout life; it is not a very abstract concept, it is up close and personal and pervades our experiences.

Allostasis is an adaptive process, not simply a reactive process. However, similar to homeostasis and Selye's concept of exhaustion, chronic strains (allostatic loading) or massive and immediate strains can lead to pathology. (For more on such pathology, see the sections about trauma later in the chapter.)

The causes of stress

So stress isn't just a situation. It's an evaluative process and a result of how you think and feel about a situation. That explains why some stimuli are stressors and some are not, and why some people get stressed out by certain things that don't affect other people. However, some situations are pretty stressful for nearly everyone. Here are some things that most people find stressful:

» **Extreme stressors:** Events that occur rarely and that have a severe and dramatic impact on routines and access to normalcy, such as natural disasters, human-made disasters (such as an oil spill), war, terrorism, migration, and watching others get hurt

» **Developmental and psychosocial stressors:** Events that occur as you grow and change, including marriage, childbirth, raising children, caring for a sick person, and being a teenager

» **Common stressors:** Things you deal with in daily life — urban living, daily hassles (like driving to work), job pressure, and household chores

Psychologists Holmes and Rahe in 1967 created a list of stressful events called the *social readjustment rating scale.* They took different stressful events and assigned a point value to each of them — the higher the point value, the more stressful the event is. Here are the top five:

Event	Point Value
Death of a spouse	100
Divorce	73
Marital separation	65
Jail sentence	63
Death of a close family member	63

If you're wondering what the bottom-five stressful events are, they are (in descending order of stressfulness): change in number of family get-togethers, change in eating habits, vacation, Christmas, and minor violations of the law.

Bringing this research on stressors up to date, the American Psychological Association reported in 2011 the following list of what stresses Americans out the most:

1. Money
2. Work
3. The economy
4. Relationships
5. Family responsibilities
6. Health problems of family
7. Personal health problems
8. Job stability
9. Housing costs
10. Personal safety

The impact of stress

Stress can have an impact on all areas of our biopsychosocial function. Some of these effects can reach the point of severity that they actually cross over into a full-blown diagnosable disorders. (For more on diagnosis and disorders, see Chapter 15.)

The psychological impact of stress has long been of interest to researchers and practitioners. We know that the experience of stress at varying levels is at the very least correlated with negative emotions and behaviors such as increased irritability, anger, hostility, nervousness, anxiety, sadness, depression, reduced motivation, and helplessness. Finding the exact connection between stress and its relationship to these negative emotions and behaviors is an ongoing endeavor as researchers look for links between the two in several areas: biology, neuropsychology, cognition, emotions, and personality.

One link, for example, involves the concept of *rumination*, which is constant, persistent, chronic, overthinking. Playing negative scenarios over and over again in one's mind is clearly linked to an increase in negative emotion. Debbie Downer thinks too much! How someone regulates or "manages" his or her emotions has also been cited as a moderator. The *Dynamic Fit Model of Stress and Emotional Regulation* proposes that individual differences between people's reactivity to emotional stimuli play a big part. Researchers Sarah Myruski, Samantha Denefrio, and Tracy Dennis-Tiwary state that being too overreactive is a problem, but so is being too underreactive. This model also states that our ability to use positive appraisal is a moderator, as are positive self-affirmations and the ability to employ relaxation strategies when we need them. Emotional expressiveness is also good; suppression is not so good.

Based on the work of Selye and others, it's been discovered that stress can lead to physical health problems or illness in several ways. An indirect link between stress and physical health problems may involve people who engage in potentially physically harmful behaviors as a means to cope with stress. A lot of people drink alcohol when they're stressed. Drinking alcohol can be harmful to your health, especially if you drink and drive. Another dangerous behavior often associated with stress is increased cigarette smoking. I've heard plenty of patients talk about smoking as a way to relax. But it's so unhealthy!

REMEMBER

Another link between stress and physical illness comes from the new and exciting field of *psychoneuroimmunology*, the study of the connection between psychology and the immune system. Researchers have long suspected that there's a connection between the two systems, and there actually is. High levels of stress and intense emotions can suppress nervous system functioning. There isn't a clear-cut diagnosis of all the ins and outs, but the suspicion is that the cost of the body's coping reactions to stress is paid in part by the immunity department.

Ever heard of the flight-or-fight response? Walter Cannon showed that exposure to extreme stress causes people to decide whether they're going to take off running or stand their ground and fight. It sounds animalistic, but you can also look at it as a choice between walking away or yelling at someone. Either way, these protective actions require energy. Arguing and running from someone can be tiring! So the brain sends signals to the heart and the hormone system that causes blood pressure to increase. The heart races, respiration quickens, and sugar levels in the blood rise. When these changes occur, all of the body's vital resources are devoted to the moment. Resources from other areas are used for the immediate purpose of fighting or fleeing.

The hormones that kick in when you're in fight-or-flight mode are epinephrine and cortisol — both have immunosuppressive effects. If higher-than-normal levels of epinephrine and cortisol are present in the blood stream, then the immune system doesn't work as well. It kind of makes sense, if you think about it. If a bear is chasing you, probably the last thing on your mind is getting the flu. Forget the flu; you can't get the flu if that bear rips your head off! Save the head, and you can deal with the flu later.

A RISK TO THE HEART

People with the *Type A personality* — a personality pattern characterized by an aggressive and persistent struggle to achieve more and more in less and less time — are the real go-getters of the world. They're the corporate executives who build a Fortune 500 company from the bottom up in a matter of years, the millionaire workaholics, and the hyper-competitive college students driven by perfection. Type A people tend to be very impatient and view almost everything as urgent.

You may be thinking, "So what? These people can be very successful, right?" Yes, but they also generally have a higher risk of suffering from *coronary heart disease* — hardening of the arteries, angina, and heart attacks. But before you quit school and make relaxing walks on the beach your full-time job, remember that the relationship between Type A personalities and developing coronary heart disease is not one-to-one. The research shows an *increase* in *risk;* developing these health problems is not inevitable.

Risk means that these folks need to take precautions and be aware of contributing factors and warning signs. Read up on coronary heart disease if you're worried; check out *Heart Disease For Dummies* by James M. Rippe, MD (Wiley, 2004). And if you're really worried, go see your family physician.

Relationships between stress and specific diseases seem to exist. Strong negative emotions such as anger, chronic hostility, and anxiety are associated with hypertension, ulcers, rheumatoid arthritis, headaches, and asthma.

Crisis: Accumulated or overwhelming stress

There's a great scene in the movie *The Doors (1991)* starring Val Kilmer as the famed singer Jim Morrison. Jim walks into a room full of people after just getting sentenced to hard labor for public exposure. He's bombarded by bad news of cancelled gigs, the women in his life calling, one is pregnant, not getting invited to Woodstock, and so forth. He starts to have flashes of horrible scenes: Charles Manson, bodies in Vietnam, bombs, the assassination of Martin Luther King Jr., and on and on. Doors music is playing over the scene, with gunshots, bombs, and screams, and then the sounds all stop and he says with a shaky calm and a tear running down his face, "I think I'm having a nervous breakdown."

"Nervous breakdown" is not a term we hear very often anymore. It used to be used a lot more in common parlance and in the media. Nowadays, we talk about celebrities going to rehabilitation because of "exhaustion." Nervous breakdown?

Psychologists don't use that language either; instead we talk about *crisis*. Psychologist Lawrence M. Brammer identified three types of crises:

>> **Normal developmental crises** like graduating from high school

>> **Situation crises** like being dumped by the love of your life

>> **Existential crises** like when you realize that the money you earn doesn't allow you to afford housing, or you feel isolated and you think of hurting yourself

A crisis can result from the accumulation of stress or a sudden event of overwhelming stress. It is defined by Richard James as "the perception or experience of the event by the person as an intolerable difficulty that exceeds the individual's resources and coping abilities."

It just so happens that I did my doctoral research on crisis, and I quote from my work:

> A crisis is a temporary disorganization and inability to cope with customary methods, a breakdown in adequate problem solving and coping, and emotional disequilibrium.

People in crisis can experience disorganized thinking, racing and intrusive thoughts (depicted well in the film mentioned above), confusion, fear, anger, tension, impulsivity, and even suicidality and violent lashing out.

Crises are by definition temporary but they can linger. Resolution of a crisis depends on its severity, one's personal and social resources, effective coping, changing the situation, getting help, breaking down the problem into manageable parts, pacing one's efforts, and having basic optimism.

There are two kinds of *crisis intervention*, first-order and second-order.

>> **First-order crisis intervention** is often referred to as *psychological first aid* and involves an intervener communicating with a person, helping him or her explore what is happening or has happened, coming up with possible solutions, taking action on those options, and developing a plan for following up. The main goals of psychological first aid are to provide support, reduce lethality (keep people form hurting themselves or others), and link the person to helping resources.

>> **Second-order crisis intervention** is often referred to as crisis therapy, and it's for someone whose crisis is not yet "over." This therapy involves ongoing intervention over a period of weeks.

Posttraumatic stress disorder

Suffering breaks our world. Like a tree struck by lightning — splintered, shaken, denuded — our world is broken by suffering, and we will never be the same again.
—Nathan Kollar, Professor Emeritus of Religious Studies, St. John Fisher College

Sometimes, a stressor can be so big, so hurtful, so scary, so sudden that it overwhelms our ability to cope, manage, and function. When this happens, psychologists refer to this as *traumatic stress* — stress that is so extreme that it is traumatic. One of the most well known psychological results of exposure to extreme stress (trauma) is *posttraumatic stress disorder (PTSD)*. PTSD can occur when a person is exposed to a life-threatening situation or a situation that may involve serious injury. War, car accidents, plane crashes, rape, and physical assault are all examples of situations that may cause PTSD. The symptoms include emotional numbing, guilt, insomnia, impaired concentration, intrusive experiences such as flashback, avoidance of trauma-related events and memories, and excessive physiological arousal (hyperactivity due to fear). Many Vietnam War and Iraq War veterans returned home with PTSD. During World War I, PTSD was called *shell shock*.

The National Center for Posttraumatic Stress Disorder (part of the US Department of Veterans Affairs) defines PTSD as a mental health problem that some people develop after experiencing or witnessing a life-threatening event, like combat, a natural disaster, a car accident, or sexual assault. It's normal to have upsetting memories, feel on edge, or have trouble sleeping after this type of event.

It is important to keep in mind that there always is a *subjective component* to traumatic stress. Anna Freud (Sigmund Freud's daughter) advocated for an individualized definition of trauma: "I shall always remember not confuse my own with the victim's appraisal of the happening." That is, not everyone experiences the same events as traumatic. I remember conducting a psychological evaluation for PTSD with a young man who was a war veteran. I initially assumed that his trauma was related to being in combat, but it turned out that it was actually from a vehicle accident he was in while in Iraq. So just like Anna Freud warns, don't get confused, and don't assume!

So if there is so much room for subjectivity, how can we diagnose someone as having PTSD? The *Diagnostic and Statistical Manual of Mental Disorders, 5th Edition* attempts to address this issue by listing criteria that "qualifies" as a traumatic event or stressor:

Exposure to actual threatened death, serious injury, or sexual violence in one (or more) of the following ways:

1. Directly experiencing the traumatic event(s).

2. Witnessing, in person, the event(s) as it occurred to others.

3. Learning that the traumatic event(s) occurred to a close family member or close friend.

4. Experiencing repeated or extreme exposure to aversive details of the traumatic event(s) (for example, first responders collecting human remains . . .).

So once we have established that a traumatic event has occurred by these criteria, what kinds of reactions can occur? Intrusive memories, dreams, flashbacks, distress when exposed to reminders of the event(s), physiological reactivity, avoidance, thinking and mood impairment, exaggerated fears and beliefs, diminished interest in activities, feeling detached or estranged, and an inability to experience positive emotions, irritability, angry outbursts, reckless behavior, and sleep disturbance.

Traumatic stress/PTSD is certainly an extremely distressing and disruptive experience. The bad news is that there seems to be no shortage of the types of experiences that trigger it. The good news is that there are some very effective treatments out there, including Cognitive-Behavioral Therapy, Eye Movement Desensitization and Reprocessing Therapy, and Prolonged Exposure.

The stress of loss

Losing someone you love can be extremely stressful, even traumatic. John Bowlby, famous developmental psychologist and psychoanalyst, proposed that understanding the stressor of loss makes the most sense within the context of attachment. (For more on attachment, see Chapter 10.) It is because we are attached that loss can be so difficult. Grief can be profound and touch every part of a person's being. Psychologist Joanne Cacciatore writes of her grief from her daughter's death in her book *Bearing the Unbearable: Love, Loss, and the Heartbreaking Path of Grief:*

> I wanted to scream at the cars driving past the cemetery. I wanted to yell at the birds in the trees casting shadows on her headstone. . .. It felt like a physical dying, repeated every day upon the opening of my eyes on the rare occasions that sleep had actually come. Breathing hurt, and a global pain emanated from the tips of my hair to the tips of my toes.

Although grief is a powerful stressor, it is not always traumatic. Dr. William Steele, founder of the National Institute for Trauma and Loss in Children (TLC), states that there are over a dozen different terms for grief and mourning. Here are a few:

>> **Bereavement:** An experience from the death of a loved one which may include emotional pain and distress

>> **Grief:** A powerful emotional experience after a *significant loss* that may include anxiety, yearning, extreme sadness, and confusion

>> **Mourning:** The *process* of feeling and expressing grief over time

>> **Traumatic/complicated grief/bereavement:** Persistent and problematic grief that impairs functioning

TIP

These terms can be confusing, so think about it like this: I am bereaved because someone I love died. I feel grief. I am engaged in mourning. I can't emerge from mourning, so I'm experiencing complicated grief.

Lets be clear: Grief and bereavement are not disorders! But sometimes the loss can be so devastating, the grief so intense, and the mourning so prolonged that the sufferer may qualify for a diagnosis of "other specified trauma- and stressor-related disorder: *persistent complex bereavement disorder.* At the time of this writing, this "disorder" can be diagnosed under a classification system in the *DSM-5* considered the "other x,y,z" category. There are all kinds of "other" diagnoses in the *DSM-5*, designed to capture presentations in which symptoms are present that cause "clinically significant distress or impairment in social, occupational, or other important areas of functioning" but do not meet the full criteria for any of the disorders in a particular class.

It is notable that the committee of experts and professionals that get together to put the *DSM* revisions together are considering adding this as an official diagnosis with criteria such as reactive distress to the death and social/identity disruption that lasts at least 12 months for an adult and 6 months for a child.

Coping Is No Gamble

Stress, stress, stress — everyone's got it. So what can you and I do about it? This question brings me to the concept of *coping*, the response to stressful and upsetting situations. Sometimes a person's coping strategies can make things better (as in getting healthy from exercising) and sometimes they can make things worse (if your way of coping is to blow your paycheck at a casino). There are many different ways of coping with stress; some are good and some are bad.

Even though bad coping skills can lead to problems, having no coping skills can lead to vulnerability and, sometimes, more problems. That's why on occasion, using bad coping techniques is better than not coping at all.

Learning how to cope

Most psychologists classify coping behaviors into two big categories, *approach processes* and *avoidance processes*. Approach coping is more active than its avoidance cousin; approach processes resemble a take-charge kind of response to stress.

REMEMBER

Common approach coping responses include:

>> **Logical analysis:** Looking at a situation in as realistic terms as possible

>> **Reappraising or reframing:** Looking at a situation from a different perspective and trying to see the positive side of things

>> **Accepting responsibility:** Taking charge of your part in a situation

>> **Seeking guidance and support:** Asking for help (see the next section "Finding resources")

>> **Problem solving:** Coming up with alternatives, making a choice, and evaluating outcomes

>> **Information gathering:** Collecting additional information about the stressor so you can more easily cope

Avoidance coping strategies are less active and involve coping in less direct ways. Here are some common avoidance coping strategies:

>> **Denial:** Refusing to admit that a problem exists

>> **Avoidance:** Evading possible sources of stress

>> **Distraction or seeking alternative rewards:** Trying to get satisfaction elsewhere like watching a funny movie when feeling sad or enjoying recreational activities on the weekend to cope with having a bad job

>> **Venting or emotional discharge:** Yelling, getting depressed, worrying

>> **Sedation:** Numbing oneself to the stress through drugs, alcohol, sex, eating binges, and so on

Finding resources

Coping is more than just the actions that a person takes in response to stress. The way an individual copes also depends on the resources available to him. After all, a billionaire who loses her job may experience a lot less stress than a suddenly unemployed day laborer who makes $30 a day and has a family of five.

CHILL OUT!

There all kinds of proposed "stress management" approaches out there. Some of them are evidence-based and some are not. (For more on evidence-based therapy, see Chapter 17.) We all get stressed. That's a given, so what can we do about it? Here are some proven and researched stress management techniques that actually work:

Autogenic training, biofeedback, cognitive behavioral therapy, diaphragmatic breathing, emotional freedom technique, guided imagery, mindfulness-based stress reduction, progressive muscle relaxation, relaxation response, and transcendental meditation.

A person's response to stress is a complex reaction that depends on her coping skills, environmental resources, and personal resources. Any life event that a person encounters is influenced by the interaction of the person's ongoing life stressors, social coping resources, demographic characteristics, and personal coping resources. Further, the person's cognitive appraisals of the stressor influence her health and well-being in both positive and negative ways.

An *integrative approach* considers three factors when attempting to predict the health outcome of a particular stressor:

>> The resources an individual possesses prior to encountering a stressor or stressful event

>> The event itself

>> The appraisal of the event

An individual's ability to resist stress is called *resilience* — the outcome of the interaction between an individual's *personal* and *social resources* and his coping efforts. Personal coping resources include stable personality traits, beliefs, and approaches to life that help us cope:

>> **Self-efficacy:** Your belief in yourself and that you can handle a situation based on your experience

>> **Optimism:** Having a positive outlook on the future and expecting positive outcomes

>> **Internal locus of control:** Your belief that certain things are within, not out of, your control

REMEMBER

One type of environmental resource that is helpful in coping is *social resources*, which aid in coping by providing support, information, and problem-solving suggestions. Good social resources include family, friends, significant others, religious and spiritual organizations, and sometimes even co-workers and supervisors. Other environmental resources include money, shelter, health services, and transportation. These things can make all the difference in the world when someone's attempting to cope with stress.

Chapter **15**

Modern Abnormal Psychology

A fictional Mr. Smith is a 30-year-old married man with two children who lives in a quiet suburban neighborhood. He works as a shipping manager for a local trucking company. Mr. Smith has been in relatively good physical health and is considered by most people to be a pretty average guy. About three months ago, Mr. Smith approached his wife with the idea of getting a home security system. She agreed, and they installed an alarm system. Mr. Smith then told her that he wanted to install cameras around the perimeter of their home. She reluctantly agreed and soon after began waking up in the middle of the night to find Mr. Smith peeking out of their bedroom curtains with binoculars. He became very agitated when she questioned him about his behavior.

Mr. Smith's actions continued for several weeks, and he wouldn't tell his wife what was going on. Then one day she found a gun as she was cleaning out their closet. She'd never known her husband to own a gun, so she confronted him about it out of concern for their children's safety. When she approached him, he told her that he bought the gun to protect them from the neighbor next door. Mr. Smith said that he had been watching the neighbor for a few months, and he was convinced that the neighbor was involved in a real-estate scheme to get their home. The plot involved the neighbor hiring some criminals to break into their home and rob them in order to scare them into moving and selling their home at a really low price. The neighbor could then buy the house for next to nothing, tear it down, and expand his own home onto the property.

Do you think there's anything strange about Mr. Smith's behavior? Should his wife be worried, or is he being adequately protective? The answers to these and related questions are part of the field of *abnormal psychology* — the psychological study of abnormal behavior and mental processes. Another term for abnormal psychology is *psychopathology.* But what is abnormal about certain mental processes and behaviors?

In this chapter, I introduce you to the concept of psychopathology, how professionals go about deciding or figuring out if some is experiencing it, different systems of understanding it, and the various disorders that characterize modern abnormal psychology such as schizophrenia, bipolar disorder, depression, and anxiety.

What Is" Abnormal" Anyway?

Like much of this book, I am going to ask you to think and behave like a psychologist. For this chapter, you are going to play the part of a "psycho-diagnostician" However, there really isn't a role in psychology called "psycho-diagnostician." But one of the most common and important functions psychologists engage in is performing diagnostic evaluations, often called *psychodiagnostics evaluations.* The point of these evaluations is to arrive at a *diagnosis* or a *diagnostic formulation.* The *APA Dictionary* tells us that a diagnosis is "the process of identifying and determining the nature of a disease or disorder by its signs and symptoms, through the use of assessment techniques (for example, tests and examinations) and other available evidence."

A diagnosis is also "the classification of individuals on the basis of a disease, disorder, abnormality, or set of characteristics."

The "process" of gathering information for diagnosis is discussed in detail in Chapter 16, so I'm not going to get into the details of how we gather information. I will be focusing on what a diagnosis is according to psychological science and what goes into defining it.

To get to a diagnosis, we have to decide if the information we've gathered tells us if something is "wrong" based on the norms of the tests and still other "norms." Like it or not, your job now is to make a determination of whether what you are seeing is outside those norms. More specifically, is what is presenting to you outside the mental processes and behavioral norms and mental health norms.

Every society in the world has standards of thought and behavior and conduct that delineate what are normal or abnormal mental processes and behavior. Individuals, families, and groups have these standards. When people act outside those norms, their mental process (for example, a delusion or a hallucination) and/or the behavior may be labeled "abnormal." There are at least four different theories or models that can be used to define normal versus abnormal behavior:

>> **Normative criterion:** People act abnormally when they do things contrary to what the majority of people do or act very differently than what is expected. Individuals are expected to live up to societal norms; when that doesn't happen, people suspect something is amiss. Sometimes statistics are used by professionals and researchers to figure out who's outside the norm. If nine out of ten people act a certain way, then the behavior of the one person who doesn't conform is statistically abnormal. The non-conforming behavior is considered rare.

>> **Subjective criterion:** Sometimes a person senses his feelings may be different from those of most other people or that he may be doing things differently from how most others do it. In this very limited sense, the person is "abnormal." If I feel like something is wrong with me because of my awareness of my being different, then I may consider myself a suitable subject of abnormal psychology. This is a case of judging one's own behavior as abnormal.

>> **Maladaptive criterion:** Does my behavior help me survive and successfully function in my society? If not, according to this criterion, maladaptive behavior is abnormal. If I have a difficult time adapting and adjusting to life's demands, my behavior is maladaptive. This may include my engagement in a pattern of risky or otherwise harmful or destructive behavior that would make it more likely I would not survive or function well in society.

>> **Unjustifiable or unexplainable criterion:** Sometimes people act in ways and do things that can't be explained. People often assume that there must always be a reason why someone acts in a certain way. If a reasonable explanation for certain actions doesn't exist, people may label the behavior as abnormal.

Who decides what's normal?

I've never taught a psychology course without at least one student raising a protest against the concept of abnormal behavior. "Who gets to decide what's normal and what's not?" he tends to ask. This is an excellent question. Who gets to say what's abnormal? Who has the final say on this matter? There are two ways to look at it: what I call the *professional authority* approach and the *subjective authority* approach.

Like it or not, clinical psychologists and psychiatrists have been "designated" or deemed by society (at least at lot of societies) as "authorities" on making these normal/abnormal mental process and behavior determinations. This vested *professional authority* is "given" or "entrusted to" socially validated healthcare professions, psychologists, and psychiatrists. If this endowment of authority is acceptable to people, then they are likely to avail themselves of what these professionals have to offer. However, although this sounds like a simple "take it or leave it" approach, there is always the empirical test of whether diagnoses of abnormal mental processes and behavior actually do anyone any good. It would be naïve to take the position that psychological and psychiatric approaches to human problems is a panacea. But to fully reject it would be irresponsible toward and dismissing of those who have been helped by this approach.

When someone goes to a professional for help and gets slapped with an "official" diagnosis, there can often be an experience of disappointment, of feeling objectified, of feeling like the whole thing was downright impersonal. Any time we start talking about people in terms of categories, particularly categories of normal versus abnormal, this is a dicey proposition. Being labeled by someone other than yourself doesn't always feel right. That's where the concept of *subjective authority* or experience comes in. After all, who knows you better than you? Who knows what feels "right" or "wrong" better than you?

In my practice, parents will bring their child in for an evaluation because they are concerned about them and worry that they may "have" a particular mental disorder. Although they never say, "I think my child has a mental disorder," they do say things like, "I think my child has ADHD, or autism, or something!" They want to be sure. Okay, I can help with that because of my professional authority.

But let's say I do the evaluation and the child doesn't meet criteria. Do I just send the family on their way? What about their concern, distress, and the reason they came in to begin with? Shouldn't I factor in their experience of what is going on at least a little? Some psychologists and psychiatrists propose that the patients' subjective experience should be taken as authoritative and play at least a partial, if not a substantial, role in making diagnoses. Additionally, some clinicians see official diagnoses as "necessary but insufficient evils" but not necessarily useful tools for working with their clients and patients. They instead put more weight on their own theoretical orientations and on the client's experience to guide their work together.

Ryff's Psychological Well-Being Model

In line with privileging a person's sense of how they are doing relative to mental health, psychologists offer up the concept of *subjective well-being*. How do you feel? Are you satisfied with your life? People suffering from Major Depressive Disorder may say they feel like "S!@t" and they "hate" their lives. These are certainly experiences we should take into consideration. Psychologist Carol Ryff at the University of Wisconsin–Madison gives us an excellent list of experiences that contribute to our sense of well-being. Imagine the opposite of these as indicators that we are not feeling well, or that we are experiencing subjective un-well-being.

>> **Self acceptance:** A positive attitude toward the self, acknowledging and accepting both the positive and the negative aspects, and positive feelings about one's past

>> **Positive relations with others:** The sense of having the ability to cultivate and to have warm, trusting, intimate relationships with others, a concern for others, and the ability to cooperate

>> **Autonomy:** A sense self-determination and independence, following one's own conscience and honoring one's own values

>> **Environmental mastery:** One's self-assessment of the ability to handle day-to-day affairs, make use of opportunities, choose activities that resonate with oneself, and the general sense of having the ability to play an active role in their environments

>> **Purpose in life:** The sense of having an aim, goals, objectives, and a sense of direction

>> **Personal growth:** The sense of continuous striving to be better, realizing one's talents, and fulfilling one's potential

Defining Mental Disorders

Let's just say that any debate, discussion, or disagreement around the definitions of normal and abnormal/mental health or mental disorder is welcomed and a sign of a healthy society that can openly work these issues out. As the debate will no doubt continue on, I propose that we take a very pragmatic view of abnormal psychology and its symptoms, diagnoses, and disorders. One significant pragmatic approach comes from process called *taxonomy* — the science of classification. Over the years, psychiatrists and psychologists have worked to delineate the abnormal behaviors that suggest the presence of a mental illness by developing a taxonomic system that has culminated into the most widely used classification system for determining the presence of a mental disorder: the *Diagnostic and Statistical Manual* published by the American Psychiatric Association. The first *DSM* was published in 1952 and has been through seven revisions and updates. The latest version, published in 2013, is called the *Diagnostic and Statistical Manual of Mental Disorders, 5th Edition*.

The *DSM-5* defines a mental disorder this way:

> . . . a syndrome characterized by clinically significant disturbance in an individual's cognition, emotion regulation, or behavior that reflects a dysfunction in psychological, biological, or developmental processes underlying mental functioning. Mental disorders are usually associated with significant distress or disability in social, occupational, or other important activities. An expectable or culturally approved response to a common stressor or loss, such as the death of a loved one, is not a mental disorder. Socially deviant behavior (e.g., political, religious, or sexual) and conflicts that are primary between an individual and society are not mental disorders unless the deviance or conflict results from a dysfunction in the individual, as described above.

Let's examine this definition from the perspective of some of the things we talked about previously. There are aspects of both professional ("disability in . . .") and subjective authority ("distress" and "important activities"). There is also an exclusion for "problems in living" and conflict with society. Again, despite the critics of the *DSM* who view it as a tool for maintaining hierarchies in a society, the definition provided above is pretty solid.

The *DSM* is full of disorders, 297 at last count. It is full of *symptoms* and clusters of symptoms identified as *disorders*. Let's take a closer look at those two terms for a minute.

>> **Symptom:** A behavior or mental process that is a sign or signal of a potential disorder. Symptoms are usually found within the following categories:

- Thinking or thought processes

- Mood or *affect* (referring to how someone feels emotionally, such as depressed, angry, or fearful) and vegetative symptoms (concerning eating, sleeping, and energy level)

- Behavior (such as violence, compulsive gambling, or drug use)

- Physical signs (such as muscle or joint pain, headaches, excessive sweating)

>> **Disorder:** A collection of symptoms that indicate the presence of a *syndrome* (co-occurring groups of symptoms). In developing a taxonomy of abnormal psychological disorders, psychiatrists, psychologists, and other researchers look for specific groups of symptoms that tend to occur together, distinguishing one set of co-occurring symptoms that are distinct from other sets of co-occurring symptoms.

The *DSM* divides all 297 disorders into the following 22 categories:

Neurodevelopmental Disorders	Schizophrenia Spectrum and Ot[...]chotic Disorders
Bipolar and Related Disorders	Depressive Disorders
Anxiety Disorders	Obsessive-Compulsive and Related Disorders
Trauma-and Stressor-Related Disorders	Dissociative Disorders
Somatic Symptom and Related Disorders	Feeding and Eating Disorders
Elimination Disorders	Sleep-Wake Disorders
Sexual Dysfunctions	Gender Dysphoria
Disruptive, Impulse-Control and Conduct Disorders	Substance-Related and Addictive Disorders
Neurocognitive Disorders	Personality Disorders
Paraphilic Disorders	Other Mental Disorders
Medication-Induced Movement Disorders and Other Adverse Effects of Medication	Other Conditions That May be a Focus of Clinical Attention

I want to make a couple of final points before getting into a few of the specific mental disorders most commonly observed by mental health professionals today. First, it's important to realize that psychologists view all behavior on a continuum of normal to abnormal. For example, crying is a normal behavior, but crying all day, every day for more than two weeks is abnormal. Second, everyone has experienced a symptom of mental disorder at one time or another. But simply having a symptom does not mean a person has the actual disorder. Remember, disorders consist of specific groupings of symptoms that define a particular syndrome. The rules for determining what symptoms constitute a disorder are complex and include specific time frames and degrees of severity.

WARNING

So don't get carried away and start diagnosing everyone you know just because you see a symptom or two. It's not that simple; a symptom does not a disorder make!

In the next sections, I take a closer look at some disorders in the *DSM*. These were selected for a more in–depth look because of being more well known and common (such as major depression).

Psychotic Disorders: Grasping for Reality

One of the most well-known signs of mental disorder is losing touch with reality. When someone loses touch with objective reality and begins imagining things and acting on those imagined things, he may be suffering from a class of illness known as *psychotic disorders.*

Psychotic disorders are considered by mental health professionals but also by many a layperson (particularly family members of those who suffer from psychotic disorders) to be the most severe of all mental disorders. In addition to losing touch with reality, people who are suffering from a psychosis often have severe functional deficits related to basic self-care (eating, shelter, and personal hygiene), social and occupational functioning, and thinking.

Schizophrenia

The most common form of psychosis is *schizophrenia.* Psychiatrist Eugene Bleuler used the term schizophrenia in 1911 to describe people who exhibited signs of disorganized thought processes, a lack of coherence between thought and emotion, and a state of disconnection from reality. It may be easy to think that "schizophrenia" stands for "split-personality," but that's a mistake. In schizophrenia, the different components of personality (thoughts, emotions, behaviors) are inconsistent — for example, a mother laughing when her son breaks his arm because the bone poking through his skin looks funny.

Today, the *DSM-5* criteria for schizophrenia include:

» **Delusions:** A delusion is a firmly held belief that a person maintains in spite of evidence to the contrary. One common type of delusion is a *paranoid* or *persecutory delusion,* which involves intense fear that you're being followed, listened to, or otherwise threatened by someone or something. Check out the vignette in the introduction to this chapter. Mr. Smith appears to be experiencing a paranoid delusion. He "knew" that the neighbor was out to get his house!

Another common form of delusion is the *grandiose delusion,* in which a person experiences an extremely exaggerated sense of worth, power, knowledge, identity, or relationship. Someone who is grandiose may believe he can speak to supernatural beings or that he is a supernatural being himself! Or, he may just think that he's the smartest, most attractive person alive.

» **Hallucinations:** A hallucination can be defined as a perception that occurs without external stimulation that is experienced as very real. Hallucinations can be auditory (hearing voices or sounds), visual (seeing people who are not there, demons, or dead people), olfactory (smells), gustatory (tastes), or somatic (experiencing physical sensations within the body). Most hallucinations are auditory and often involve someone hearing a voice or voices commenting on his or her behavior.

Command hallucinations are a potentially dangerous form of auditory hallucination because they involve a voice or voices telling the sufferer to do something, often involving violent or suicidal behavior.

» **Disorganized speech and thought:** If you've ever had a conversation with someone, and you had no idea what she was talking about, you may have witnessed disorganized speech and thought, which are characterized by extremely tangential (mostly irrelevant), circumstantial (beating around the bush), or loosely associated (jumping from one unrelated thought to another) speech. These abnormal styles of communicating may be evidence of a *thought disorder.* An extreme form of thought disorder is called *word salad* — when a person's speech is so incoherent that it sounds like another language or nonsense. Sometimes people even make up words that don't exist, called *neologisms.* For example, "I think the glerbage came by and sluppered the inequitised frames from me."

» **Grossly disorganized or catatonic behavior:** When a person behaves in a disorganized manner, she may act extremely silly or childlike, easily get lost or confused, stop caring for herself and her basic needs, do strange or bizarre things like talk to herself, or be extremely socially inappropriate. Catatonic behavior involves complete immobility, absolute lack of awareness of one's surroundings, and sometimes being mute.

>> **Negative symptoms:** A negative symptom refers to the absence of some usual or expected behavior. The absence of the behavior is what is abnormal. Three negative symptoms are often associated with schizophrenia:

- **Flat affect:** When a person exhibits no emotionality whatsoever

- **Alogia:** Indication that a person's thought processes are dull, blocked, or generally impoverished

- **Avolition:** When a person has no ability to persist in an activity; looks like an extreme lack of motivation

When a person experiences these symptoms, he may be suffering from schizophrenia. I say *may* because a person may exhibit these symptoms for different reasons: drug use, sleep deprivation, or a physical disease. Making the diagnosis of schizophrenia is a complex and very serious task. Specific time frames and *rule-outs* are involved. Rule-outs involve eliminating other possible or plausible explanations.

REMEMBER

Schizophrenia is diagnosed in about 4 to 5 of every 1,000 people. Generally the condition is diagnosed in individuals between the ages of 18 to 35. Sometimes, but rarely, it's diagnosed in childhood. Schizophrenia typically begins in the late teens and early twenties and is fully present by the mid- to late twenties. It can develop rapidly or gradually, and there can be periods of less severe symptoms. Some sufferers are chronically and persistently ill. Periods of illness can be characterized by a marked inability or diminished capacity to function in everyday life, often leading to school failure, job loss, and relationship difficulties.

Don't be fooled by how easy it is to list the symptoms of schizophrenia and describe them; they are very serious. Individuals with schizophrenia often face enormous challenges in society and sometimes end up in jail, in hospitals or similar institutions, or living on the streets because of their illness.

Schizophrenia's causes

Determining the causes of psychological disorders constituted part of the old nature-versus-nurture debate. Are the causes of schizophrenia organic (biochemical/physiological) or functional (resulting from experience)? At the moment, perhaps because of the wide array of newly developed brain-scanning techniques, the organic explanations are far more prominent. However, the best answer may lie in a synthesis of the two points of view. This is still a very difficult topic to tackle because numerous theories for the cause of schizophrenia exist, each with varying degrees of scientific support. The main theory in practice today is the *diathesis-stress model*, which merges two different areas of research.

First, some definitions. A *diathesis* is a predisposition to a particular disease. *Stress* can be defined as any number of psychological and social factors. So the diathesis-stress model holds that schizophrenia is the consequence of a stress-activated diathesis or predisposition.

Proposed biological diathesis for schizophrenia includes problems with brain chemistry and/or development. Researchers have found malformed parts of the brain in people with schizophrenia. These biological abnormalities can lead to problems with thinking, speech, behavior, and staying in contact with reality.

For the stress component, psychological factors address the reality distortion associated with schizophrenia. Why do schizophrenics make a break from reality? Some experts propose that the world experienced by someone with schizophrenia is so harsh, and its conflicts so intense, that the person needs a vacation from it. Research supports that psychic trauma, such as child abuse, can be related to psychotic breakdowns, and it certainly constitutes a harsh reality that inspires an escape. The research, however, does not state that child abuse causes schizophrenia in all or even a majority of cases, but it's a potentially overwhelming stressor. Trauma is a form of extreme stress, regardless of the source. This stress may interact with the diathesis, the predisposition, and lead to psychotic symptoms.

A social factor related to schizophrenia that has shown promise in recent research is a phenomenon known as *expressed emotion.* Expressed emotion (EE) refers to negative communication by family members directed at the person suffering from schizophrenia. EE often consists of excessive criticism. Family members may comment on the patient's behavior, "You're crazy!" for example. EE also includes emotional over-involvement of family members that can overwhelm the patient. Let me be perfectly clear, though: I am not saying that criticism and over-involvement cause schizophrenia, but only that these factors may contribute to the stress component of the diathesis-stress model, as may many other stressors.

WARNING

You may think that you've developed schizophrenia after reading about its causes. Don't get too caught up in the detail. The bottom line is that a lot of the research out there about schizophrenia is inconclusive. What's known is that brain abnormalities in schizophrenics may interact with certain kinds of stress in a way that triggers the disorder. The devastating effects of schizophrenia keep researchers working hard to figure out this disorder. Research has come a long way, but there's still an awful long way to go.

Treating schizophrenia

Schizophrenia is one of the most difficult mental disorders to treat. Its effects are often debilitating for both the individual with the disease and his family. Approaches to treating this illness range from medication to helping individuals develop important functional skills such as money management or social interaction methods.

>> Antipsychotic medications such as Haldol and Zyprexa are typically the first line of treatment for people suffering from schizophrenia or related psychotic disorders. Although they are extremely beneficial, these medications are known as *palliatives* because they don't cure disease; they just lessen the intensity of symptoms.

>> Psychosocial treatment and rehabilitation have also shown promise in managing schizophrenia. Patients learn social and self-care skills that can help reduce the number of stressors they face.

>> Although seemingly out of fashion in recent years (too labor-intensive and therefore too expensive), psychotherapy, specifically cognitive therapy, has been used in recent years to teach patients to challenge their delusional belief systems and become better "consumers" of reality.

TIP

Most recent research agrees that a combination of medication and talking therapy is the most effective treatment intervention for schizophrenia. Early intervention and solid social support are also factors associated with a favorable prognosis. With medication, psychotherapy, and support from family and friends, many people suffering from schizophrenia can lead productive lives.

A core problem is that the symptoms of schizophrenia are often so severe that people with this condition often have a difficult time achieving levels of emotional and behavioral consistency necessary to maintain jobs and effective relationships. In addition, perhaps because of damaged self-esteem, poor self-image, and ambivalent attitudes about relating and succeeding, schizophrenics are notorious for inconsistent medication compliance, which only intensifies unpredictable behavior and well-being.

Other types of psychoses

In addition to schizophrenia, two other forms of psychosis are *delusional disorder* and *substance-induced psychotic disorder*.

>> **Delusional disorder:** Characterized by the presence of fixed false beliefs, not particularly bizarre, that are held despite evidence to the contrary. Moreover, these beliefs are not particularly functional or helpful. For example, a husband may be obsessed with the idea that his wife is having an affair but unable to prove it or find any evidence. This belief would be classified as a delusion if it

persisted for at least one month. In a different scenario, someone may think that the water in his home is poisoned, contrary to evidence that it is not. The key thing about a delusional disorder is that the delusional person has no other signs of psychosis, such as those found in schizophrenia.

>> **Substance-induced psychotic disorder:** Exists when prominent hallucinations or delusions are present as a result of being under the influence of a substance or withdrawing from a substance. People under the influence of LSD or PCP often exhibit psychotic symptoms, and it's not unusual for people who have used cocaine or amphetamines to experience psychotic-like symptoms when they "come down" — an experience that mimics psychotic symptoms. This problem can be very serious, and anyone considering using drugs, including cannabis or alcohol, should know that they may experience psychotic symptoms as a consequence of this decision.

WHAT CAUSES MENTAL DISORDERS?

There are many researched, theoretical, hypothetical, and proposed models of causes, or *etiologies,* of mental disorders ranging from genetics, cognitive, social, and stress related. In the sections of disorders covered in more depth in this chapter, I include information about their etiology. Etiologies for mental disorders are not as cut and dry as finding a virus or a "broken" part of the brain. Again, like everything else related to people, finding what causes mental disorders is a complex endeavor. Here is a list of some of the most common approaches to mental disorder etiology:

- Behavioral Genetics: Genetic risk and gene-behavior associations

- Neurological and Neuropsychological: Cognitive, neurological, and neuropsychological dysfunction

- Sociocultural: Cultural and political factors that contribute to pathology

- Stress-Diathesis: Biological risks impacted by stressors

- Cognitive: Distortions in the cognitive interpretation of situations, events, and experiences

- Behavioral: Disorders as learned responses to stimuli and reinforcement

- Developmental: Failures of or disruptions in the normal developmental process

Feeling Funky: Depression

I wonder if blues music would be around if all those musicians were psychotherapy patients. Those songs don't seem particularly sad though; they just seem a bit pitiful to me. Nevertheless I sometimes ask new patients if they've ever been depressed; some of them reply, "Sure, doesn't everyone get depressed?" Not exactly.

Sadness is a normal human emotion typically felt during experiences of loss. The loss of one's job, lover, child, or car keys may trigger sadness. But that's just it — this is sadness, not depression. *Depression* is an extreme form of sadness that includes a number of specific symptoms. Being dumped by a boyfriend or a girlfriend at one time or another is a fairly universal experience. How does it feel? Sad. Most people feel fatigued, unmotivated, and sleepless when they get dumped. But all of these feelings eventually go away. People get over it and move on. The same kind of response is normal when a loved one dies. This is called *mourning* or *grief.* Again, grieving is not depression. Depression is something different.

In this section, I discuss major depressive disorder, how it manifests, and some of the theories and explanations behind it.

Staying in the rut of major depression

When someone is depressed to the degree of needing professional attention, she experiences a majority of the following symptoms of *major depressive disorder over a minimum of a two-week period* (because anybody may experience these on occasion or for a day or two, or hours):

>> Depressed mood for most of the day and for most days

>> *Anhedonia* (marked disinterest or lack of pleasure in all or most activities)

>> Significant weight loss or weight gain, without trying, and decreased or increased appetite

>> Difficulty sleeping or excessive sleeping

>> Physical feelings of agitation or sluggishness

>> Fatigue or lack of energy

>> Feelings of worthlessness or excessive guilt

>> Difficulty concentrating and focusing

>> Repeated thoughts of death or suicide

Hopefully, most people who ask, "Don't we all get depressed?" won't have that same response after seeing all of these symptoms. If you are experiencing three or more of these symptoms or if you have any doubts, get thee to a doctor!

WARNING

Sometimes, depression can become so severe that the sufferer may think about committing suicide. Many dangerous myths about suicide are floating around. One is that people who talk about suicide don't do it. This is false! In fact, talking about suicide is one of the most serious signals that someone may actually do it. All talk about suicide or self-harm should be taken very seriously. If you're worried about someone or having suicidal thoughts yourself, contact a mental health professional or call a local crisis or suicide hotline immediately.

REMEMBER

Depression is one of the most common forms of mental disorder in the United States, occurring on average in about 15 percent of the population. Major depressive disorder can occur just one time in a person's life or over and over again, lasting for months, years, or even a lifetime. Most people who suffer from a recurring major depressive disorder have periods of recovery in which they don't experience symptoms, or they experience the symptoms in a less intense form. Depression can occur at any point in a person's life and doesn't discriminate against age, race, or gender.

Depression's causes

Depending on whom you ask, the search for the causes of depression can be divided into two camps:

>> **Biological:** Biological theories of depression place blame on the brain and the malfunctioning of some of the chemicals that comprise it.

>> **Psychological:** The psychological theories of depression focus mostly on the experience of loss.

The *biogenic amine hypothesis* is the most popular theoretical explanation of the biological underpinnings of depression. According to this hypothesis, depression is a function of the dysregulation (impaired ability) of two neurotransmitters in the brain, norepinephrine and serotonin.

Neurotransmitters are chemical substances in the brain that allow one neuron to communicate with another neuron. The brain contains many different neurotransmitters, each with varying functions, in specific regions. Specific neurotransmitters help certain brain regions do the work of particular human activities. The parts of the brain seemingly most affected in depression are those involved with mood, cognition, sleep, sex, and appetite.

Psychological theories of depression come from several sources:

>> **Object Relations Theory:** Melanie Klein in the early 20th century proposed that depression was the result of an unsuccessful child developmental process that may result in a difficult time coping with feelings of guilt, shame, and self-worth.

>> **Attachment theory:** John Bowlby's mid-20th-century theory, which argues that all of a person's relationships with other people originate from the initial attachment bonds he forms with primary caregivers as an infant. A disruption in the attachment relationship may prevent a healthy bond from forming, thus making the child vulnerable to depression when faced with future losses and relationship difficulties.

In infancy, many factors — a drug-addicted parent or an unloving foster home are just two examples — can disrupt bonding and attachment. Children with poor attachment relationships are often left feeling helpless. Helplessness is a hallmark of depression.

>> **Learned helplessness theory:** Martin Seligman in the 1960s worked with people's experience of and with failure or an inability to achieve what they desire at some point in their lives. Under normal circumstances, most people can keep on keeping on; they don't give up or develop any serious sense of pessimism about the likelihood of future successes. But some people, because of adverse circumstances or a general tendency to view their efforts as worthless, may become depressed in the face of disappointing experiences and come to see insurmountable odds in their path.

>> **Cognitive theory:** Aaron Beck's 1960s theory has become extremely popular and is well supported by research. Beck proposed that depression is a type of thinking disorder that produces the emotional outcome of depressed moods and the other related symptoms. Several cognitive "distortions" may be involved:

- **Automatic thoughts:** Automatic thoughts are statements people make secretly to themselves that produce depressive experiences. For example, if you get in your car in the morning and it doesn't start, you may consciously say, "Dang, just my luck." But unconsciously, you may be having an automatic thought (that you're not even aware of having), "Nothing ever goes right for me."

- **Mistaken assumptions and self-other schemas:** The assumptions and self-other *schemas* (beliefs about who you are in relationship to others) that you assume to be true — as well as your views of the world, yourself, and the future — greatly influence how you move in the world. Beck introduced the *cognitive triad*. Each point in the triangle contains a set of beliefs that reflect a negative evaluation of oneself, a hopeless view of the future, and a view of the world as excessively harsh.

- **Cyclical thinking:** A final component of the cognitive view is the cyclical nature of depressive thinking. For example, if you believe that you can't do anything, then you won't exactly be fired up when you approach a task; your motivation is affected by your belief about your abilities. Then, you probably make minimal (if any) effort because of your lack of motivation, and, in turn, "prove" to yourself that you really can't do anything right. This twisted and self-confirmatory bias in thinking often leads to depression.

Treating depression

Several effective treatment approaches for depression exist. Antidepressant medication, including famous medications as Prozac and Paxil, works for some people. Psychotherapy, specifically cognitive-behavioral therapy and interpersonal psychotherapy, is also helpful for many people. Research also indicates that "activity" — staying physically active and generally busy — makes an effective antidote to depression. Some studies even indicate that regular physical exercise can be as effective as medication in alleviating symptoms of depression according to the self-reports of subjects, but more research needs to be done before this is considered a mainline treatment. The common standard of practice is to utilize both medication and psychotherapy.

Bipolar Disorder: Riding the Waves

Bipolar disorder used to be known as *manic-depression* can be characterized as a disorder of severe mood swings involving both depression and *mania* — a state of excessively elevated or irritable mood lasting for approximately one week and co-occurring with the following symptoms:

>> Inflated self-esteem or grandiosity (coming up with a solution to end starvation and creating peace on Earth, all before tonight's dinner reservation)

>> Decreased need for sleep (feeling rested with three to four hours of sleep a night or feeling of not needing sleep at all; there's just too much to do!)

>> Extreme need and pressure to talk

>> Racing and rapid thoughts

>> Extremely short attention span

>> Drastically increased activity level (engaging in a lot of projects or mowing the lawn at 2 a.m.)

» Excessive engagement in pleasurable activities that have potentially damaging consequences (gambling your house payment, spending sprees, sexual excursions)

An accurate diagnosis of bipolar disorder requires a person to experience at least one episode of mania in his life and currently be experiencing a manic, depressed, or mixed episode (both depression and mania). A person needs to experience both depression and mania — hence the concept of severe mood swings — to earn his bipolar stripes, so to speak.

People suffering from bipolar disorder usually have several recurring episodes over the course of their lifetimes. Manic episodes can be particularly damaging because when someone is in the throes of mania, it's not uncommon to amass extremely large debts, incur broken relationships, or even engage in illegal or criminal acts.

Bipolar disorder is akin to being on a roller coaster of extreme emotion (sometimes sad, sometimes happy) beyond all proportion, but these mood swings do not occur within a day or even within a week. Bipolar disorder refers to extreme mood swings that occur over a long period of time — such as four mood episodes (either depression, manic, or mixed) within a ten-year period. An episode can last anywhere from one week to multiple years.

Some people have what's called *rapid cycling* — they may experience four or more episodes within a one-year period. Rapid-cycling individuals have an especially tough experience because each bipolar episode can be quite disruptive, and there's no time to get their life back together between episodes.

WHAT'S THE DEAL WITH DEPRESSION DRUGS?

Antidepressant medication is one of the most widely prescribed medications in the United States. What's the story with that? Is everyone in the U.S. depressed? I think it comes down to a great deal of public awareness about depression — and television advertising for these drugs doesn't hurt either. But it's important to remember that certain forms of psychotherapy can be just as effective as medication in the short-run and perhaps more beneficial to a person's long-term well-being than medication. In other words, the best "drug" for depression may not be a drug at all.

Bipolar disorder's causes

The most popular theories on the causes of bipolar disorder — specifically, mania — are biological. Research has implicated neurochemical abnormalities in the specific parts of the brain that involve the neurotransmitters dopamine and serotonin. There is little other conclusive evidence.

Long before biological studies, however, psychoanalysts offered their explanation: Mania is a defensive reaction to depression. Rather than feeling overwhelmed with depression, a person's mind makes a switch of sorts, turning that extreme sadness into extreme happiness. The symbolic equivalent to this idea is laughing when someone you love dies. It's a severe form of denial. When a manic patient is seen in psychoanalytic-oriented psychotherapy, the main focus is this defensive hypothesis.

REMEMBER

Stress, too, is thought to play a role in intensifying the mood episodes within bipolar disorder. Stress doesn't necessarily cause mania or depression, but it can make matters worse or speed up the arrival of an approaching mood episode.

Treating bipolar disorder

Currently, the first line in treating bipolar disorder is medication. A class of drugs known as *mood stabilizers* is used to stabilize a person's mood and reduce the likelihood of future episodes. Common mood stabilizers are Lithium and Depakote.

Supportive psychotherapy can also be part of treatment, mainly to help people deal with the negative consequences of manic behavior and come to terms with the seriousness of this illness. Cognitive-Behavioral Therapy (CBT) is being used increasingly to help people with bipolar disorder manage their behavior and identify early warning signs of an upcoming mood episode.

For more information on bipolar disorder, read *Bipolar Disorder For Dummies* by Candida Fink and Joe Kraynak (Wiley, 2012).

Panic Disorders

Euphemisms abound when it comes to the most common class of mental disorders, the *anxiety disorders.* "Stress," "worry," "nerves," "nervousness," and "fear" are all everyday terms for this condition. *Anxiety* is a sense of generalized fear and apprehension. When someone is anxious, he is generally fearful. Fearful of what? That depends. Identifying what scares a person helps psychologists determine what kind of anxiety disorder he may have.

REMEMBER

Normal worrying aside, anxiety disorders are probably the most common type of mental disorder. But is worrying actually a mental disorder? Remember, all behavior and mental processes exist on a continuum of normalcy. Worry can be so intense or bothersome to the worrier that it reaches the level of a disorder in need of professional attention. Worried about being a pathological worrier yet? Relax, take a deep breath, and read on. There's more to cover before you start jumping to conclusions and running for help.

Some of the most common anxiety disorders include:

>> **Generalized anxiety disorder:** Excessive and persistent worry about many different things

>> **Posttraumatic Stress Disorder (PTSD):** Reexperiencing traumatic events that were life threatening, hyper or excessive physiological arousal and avoidance of trauma-related places and people

>> **Obsessive-compulsive disorder:** Obsessions (recurring thoughts) and compulsive behavior (driven to repeat an activity like hand-washing)

In this section, I focus on one of the most common anxiety disorders; it's known as *panic disorder.*

If you live in a bad neighborhood and you're afraid to leave your home at night, that's not a phobia; that's realistic (or rational) anxiety! On the other hand, some people are afraid to leave their homes, and it's not because they live in a bad neighborhood. The people I'm referring to suffer from a phobia of large, open, or crowded places called *agoraphobia.* Agoraphobia is typically associated with a major anxiety disorder known as panic disorder — a condition in which a person experiences recurring panic or anxiety attacks and a fear of future attacks.

The *DSM-5* definition for a panic attack is "a discrete period of intense fear or discomfort, in which four (or more) of the following symptoms developed abruptly and reached a peak within 10 minutes":

>> Palpitations, pounding heart, or accelerated heart rate

>> Sweating, trembling, or shaking

>> Shortness of breath, feeling of choking, or chest pain

>> Nausea, dizziness, or lightheadedness

>> Feelings of unreality or being detached from oneself

>> Fear of losing control or going crazy or dying

>> Numbness, tingling, chills, or hot flashes

A person who has recurrent panic attacks may be suffering from panic disorder if he worries incessantly about having more attacks, has unrealistic fears of the implications of the attack, or has significantly changed his behavior as a result of the attacks. A hallmark of panic disorder is fear that the panic attacks are a signal of some major illness, such as a heart attack, losing one's mind, or dying. This symptom can be very serious because it can lead to excessive stress. Worrying about dying can be pretty stressful and may well be a factor in triggering the very illnesses a person is actively dreading.

REMEMBER

The most common change in a person's behavior is the development of agoraphobia. This state involves an intense fear of being in places or situations in which it may be difficult to get away or to get help if needed. Common examples of situations associated with agoraphobia are riding in elevators, standing in a large crowd, traveling on a crowded subway car, or even driving in thick traffic.

This is only the first half of agoraphobia, though. The other part involves the person avoiding these potentially trapping situations and, often, confining himself to his home. This symptom can be extremely stressful for the person suffering from panic disorder and for his family members as well. What kind of life can you have if your spouse or parent won't leave the house? Severe marital strain is not uncommon for people with panic disorder.

SCARED SWEATERLESS

People can fear or worry about all kinds of things. When someone is extremely afraid of a particular thing or situation, even if she knows it poses no real danger, it's called a *phobia*. There are different types of phobias. Social phobia is the fear of people. Agoraphobia is the fear of being outdoors, away from home, or in crowded places. Angoraphobia is fear of sweaters and heavy winter coats. Just kidding about the last one, but hundreds of phobias are out there. Here are a few notables:

- **Acrophobia:** Fear of heights

- **Claustrophobia:** Fear of closed spaces

- **Nyctophobia:** Fear of the dark

- **Mysophobia:** Fear of germ contamination

- **Zoophobia:** Fear of animals or a specific animal

Panic disorder's causes

At least two excellent explanations of panic disorder exist; there's David Barlow's *biopsychosocial approach* as well as the *cognitive model.*

Barlow's main idea is that panic attacks are the result of a hyperactive fear response within the brain under stress. Certain individuals possess a physiological vulnerability in which their nervous systems overreact in some situations. This biological vulnerability is paired with the psychological vulnerability that's caused by exaggerated beliefs about the dangerousness of certain bodily sensations and the world in general.

The cognitive model (Beck, Emery, & Greenberg, 1985) is similar to Barlow's model, but it puts more emphasis on the person's beliefs. The basic idea of the cognitive model is that panic attacks are the result of a misattribution of normal bodily sensations that leads to increased fear, which in turn exacerbates the sensations, which leads to more misattribution. It's a vicious cycle. A person interprets something that he feels is life threatening or dangerous, and this makes him worry, which intensifies both the feeling and his fear of it.

Treating panic disorder

Panic disorder is treated by mental health professionals with both medications and various forms of psychotherapy. Antidepressant medications known as tricyclics can reduce the occurrence of panic. Benzodiazepines, a class of "relaxing" drugs, are also used for some people to reduce the likelihood of anxiety symptoms getting "out of control" and blossoming into full-blown panic.

Behavior therapy is usually an important part of treatment for panic patients. It sounds kind of cruel, but behavior therapy basically involves teaching relaxation techniques and then, in small-step increments, exposing patients to situations that formerly triggered panic. The exercise teaches participants how to endure a panic attack until it subsides. More importantly, it works. Patients become calm in situations that initially triggered strong anxiety.

Cognitive therapy can teach sufferers to change their thinking in ways that reduce their tendency to misperceive or misinterpret bodily sensations and blow them out of proportion. The intent of cognitive therapy is to change "what if thinking" to "so what thinking" through education about physiological processes and available sources of help.

Mental Disorders in Young People

Mental disorders affect children and adolescents at rates similar to adults, which is about 1 in 5, or 20 percent, according to the United States Surgeon General. Kids are not exempt from mental problems; they experience many of the same disorders that adults do, in slightly different numbers. For example, rates of depression in people under the age of 18 years old are similar to adults, but the occurrences of schizophrenia in the under–18 set are much lower than for adults. Schizophrenia is considered fairly rare in children. Anxiety disorders, on the other hand, may be the most common disorder of childhood; incidences among kids are similar to occurrence rates for adults.

Although children and adults can experience the same mental disorders, there are some disorders that are more likely to show or "turn up" during childhood; they're typically recognized in a person before she reaches adulthood:

>> **Intellectual disability:** Characterized by abnormally low intellectual and adaptive skills such as self-care and communication abilities

>> **Learning disorders:** Problems related to acquiring, manipulating, and using information, including dyslexia and mathematics disorder

>> **Motor skills disorders:** Insufficient development of coordinated physical activity

>> **Communication disorders:** Difficulties with expressive and receptive speech

>> **Oppositional defiant and conduct disorder:** Characterized by behavior that violates the rights of others, such as aggression, criminal behavior, and bullying

>> **Feeding and eating disorder of infancy and early childhood:** Abnormal eating in terms of amount, intake method, or some other feature, such as ingesting nonnutritive substances, known as the disorder *pica*

>> **Tic disorders:** Involves the presence of involuntary vocal or motor movements and includes Tourette's disorder

>> **Elimination disorders:** Includes encopresis (the soiling of clothing with feces) and enuresis (same problem only with urine)

>> **Attention deficit/hyperactivity disorder:** Characterized by abnormal levels of activity and deficits in concentrating, attending, and impulse control

>> **Pervasive developmental disorders:** Involves disorders of severe deficits in communication, social functioning, and behavior, including autism

Dealing with ADHD

Are you always on the go, unable to sit still, constantly messing with things, struggling to think before acting or doing something foolish, spacing out frequently, and having a hard time finishing things? These are common examples of behaviors and symptoms of *Attention Deficit/Hyperactivity Disorder* or ADHD.

REMEMBER

ADHD used to be called *ADD* or Attention Deficit Disorder, but it's been officially recognized as ADHD for at least 20 years. The actual diagnostic symptoms of ADHD are divided into two categories: symptoms of hyperactivity and impulsivity and symptoms of inattention. Individuals can display predominant symptoms in one of the two categories and meet criteria for the diagnosis. Or, they can have symptoms in both and be considered a "combined type."

Here's a rundown of the symptoms associated in each of the two categories:

>> **Hyperactivity and impulsivity:** Fidgety, squirmy, can't stay seated, runs and climbs excessively, can't play quietly, always on the go, talkative, can't wait, interrupts, and is intrusive

>> **Inattention:** Difficulties with paying close attention to details, making careless mistakes, difficulty sustaining attention, not appearing to listen, poor follow-through and finishing things, loses things, is distractible, and forgetful

ADHD can range in severity from very mild to severe and is not typically diagnosed before the age of 4 years old. Boys are more likely to have ADHD, but it shows up in girls too. The most common treatment is medication, typically in the class of psychostimulants (such as Ritalin or Straterra), but behavior modification and psychosocial interventions are also important parts of treatment. Specifically, the approach popularized by Russell Barkley and in the work of Dr. Arthur D Anastopoulos uses psychosocial interventions that include behavior modification components, parent education, child education, and counseling, if necessary.

Wondering why psychostimulants are part of treatment? The medication used to treat ADHD functions as a brain stimulant. It's the concept of adults using coffee to stay up and work or study. People tend to concentrate a little better when they're a little wired.

REMEMBER

Although it seems counterintuitive, the underlying neuropsychological deficits of ADHD are consistent with the use of a stimulant medication. Essentially, the symptoms of ADHD are the result of the less-than-optimal functioning of the frontal lobe of the brain, deficits in its functions known as *executive functions*, such as planning and organizing. The frontal lobe and its executive functions play a critical role in inhibition and impulse control, organization, attention, concentration, and *goal-directed behavior*, which is knowing how to stay on target to meet a goal, even if that goal is simply picking up your socks.

For people with ADHD, the frontal lobe is "underpowered" and not up to its tasks, thus leaving the rest of the brain disorganized, impulsive, overly active, and prone to a bit of wandering. Stimulant medications address the power shortage, give the frontal lobe a boost, and slow down Joe ADHD to focus him and increase his impulse control.

The cause of this frontal lobe power deficit has yet to be fully identified but research shows a strong genetic component and the role of some sort of negative developmental event or exposure that results in underdevelopment of the frontal lobe and executive functions.

Autism: Living in a world of one's own

I am much less autistic now, compared to when I was young. I remember some behaviors like picking carpet fuzz and watching spinning plates for hours. I didn't want to be touched. I couldn't shut out background noise. I didn't talk until I was about 4 years old. I screamed. I hummed. But as I grew up, I improved.

— TEMPLE GRANDIN

Temple Grandin is a relatively famous adult woman who has *autism,* a neurodevelopmental disorder characterized by deficits or abnormal language development, abnormal social skills and development, and repetitive and restricted behavior. Actress Claire Danes starred in a TV movie about Temple Grandin made in 2010 that featured her life, her struggles, and her success. Ms. Grandin, who holds a PhD in animal science, is considered by many as a spokesperson and advocate for those with autism and engages in numerous speaking engagements every year to increase awareness of this condition.

Autism, usually recognized by the age of 3 to 4 (although signs and symptoms can manifest and show up earlier) consists of symptoms and deficits the following three areas:

>> **Impairment in social interaction:** Deficits in nonverbal social behavior such as eye contact and gestures; failure to develop peer relationships appropriate to age level; a lack of spontaneous seeking to share enjoyment, interests, or achievements with other people; and lack of social or emotional reciprocity

>> **Impairments in communication:** Delay in, or total lack of, the development of spoken language or, in individuals with adequate speech, impairment in the ability to initiate or sustain a conversation with others; stereotyped and repetitive use of language or idiosyncratic language such as repeating incessantly or odd intonation or word usage; and deficits in varied, spontaneous make-believe play or social imitative play

> **» Repetitive and stereotyped patterns of behavior, interests, and activities:** Intense preoccupation with one or more stereotyped and restricted patterns of interest that is abnormal either in intensity or focus; inflexible adherence to specific, nonfunctional routines or ritual; stereotyped (persistent repetition of a behavior with no obvious purpose) and repeated motor mannerisms (such as hand or finger flapping or twisting, or complex whole-body movements); and persistent preoccupation with parts of objects

Autism is a complex neurodevelopmental disorder that can range from mild (often called *high-functioning autism*) to severe. A cause for the disorder has yet to be identified, but research findings are promising. For example, genetic research is progressing. No "autism gene" has been identified, but much has been learned about the underlying cognitive and neuropsychological aspects of autism. Two areas in particular stand out: *neural connectivity models* and *theory of mind* models.

It is thought that the brain in individuals with autism develops and is organized differently from the brain in children with typical development (see Chapter 3 for content on how the brain is organized and works). Research findings are complicated, showing that autistic people have some underdeveloped areas as well as some overdevelopment — and even larger brain volume. Taken as a whole, researchers propose that the brain in autism interacts and communicates with itself in unique and disordered ways that differ from activity in typical individuals. From this perspective, autism can be considered a disorder of neural organization and integration.

Thinking that someone you're looking at or talking to has a "mind of his own" is known as "theory of mind" (abbreviated TOM). Most people believe that other people have a mind just like their own, which helps them understand the world from another person's point of view. Consistently, research and clinical work show that individuals with autism have deficits in TOM. In other words, people with autism do not assume the existence of an "other's mind" and, as a result, display social and communication deficits. Their difficulties with understanding facial expressions and gestures, anticipating the actions of others, engaging in conversation, and showing social and emotional reciprocity may be a consequence of TOM deficits. But, as with genetics, TOM deficits have yet to come through as the "silver bullet" of underlying deficits that account for or produce the entire syndrome of autism.

One thing is for certain; in many respects, autism is a lifelong disorder. Yet there's significant hope for those who get early and intensive intervention. As a neurodevelopmental disorder, the course of autism can likely be altered in a significant and positive direction. A comprehensive intervention approach that broadly addresses a child's neurodevelopment and development has been developed, researched, and shows encouraging results. These approaches use a "teaching" approach of sorts to facilitate the normal development of children and address developmental delays. Here are four of the most well-researched and exciting intervention approaches for autism:

>> **Applied behavior analysis — Discrete trial teaching (DTT):** DTT is a specific teaching technique in which the principles of operant and classical conditioning are used to present children with massed learning trials that are very intensive (find details on ABA in Chapter 16 and information on operant and classical conditioning in Chapter 8). DTT is most associated with the work of Dr. Ivar Lovaas [1927–2010]).

>> **Pivotal response treatments (PRT):** PRT is considered an ABA intervention, but it differs from DTT in that it tends to be more play-based, uses naturalistic reinforcement within the operant conditioning paradigm, and focuses on increasing the motivation of the participant to optimal levels. PRT is associated with the work of husband-and-wife psychologist team, Drs. Robert and Lynn Koegel of University of California, Santa Barbara, who first developed their work in the 1970s.

>> **Early start Denver model:** Developed by psychologists Sally Rogers and Geraldine Dawson in the early 2000s, the early start Denver model combines the PRT approach and a "developmental model" in which experiences identified as critical in child development are used to guide the intervention and its curriculum.

>> **Verbal behavior approach:** Dr. Mark Sundberg developed the VB approach in the early 2000s to help children with autism learn how to communicate and speak. Although not considered a comprehensive intervention approach for all developmental areas, the verbal behavior approach is widely respected as a sophisticated and well-designed intervention for communication and language development.

Let's Talk about Stigma

No discussion about mental disorder would be complete without addressing the issue of *stigma*, which the APA dictionary defines this way:

> The negative social attitude attached to a characteristic of an individual that may be regarded as a mental, physical, or social deficiency. A stigma implies social disapproval and can lead unfairly to discrimination against and exclusion of the individual.

The experience of having a mental disorder can be a very painful experience for the individual and the people around him or her. Although not always, people can feel lonely, isolated, confused, helpless, and even experience despair. People's freedom can be taken away as they are held involuntarily because of being a danger to themselves or others due to a mental disorder. Jobs can be lost. Relationships damaged. The disorder itself presents a challenge to happiness, well-being, and functioning. Additionally, people diagnosed with a mental disorder can experience discrimination, prejudice, and bias in their daily lives, at the workplace, school, or even within their own families. Psychologist Patrick Corrigan tells us, ". . . the prejudice and discrimination that often accompany illness can be as limiting as the condition itself." He reminds us that stigma can impact a person's self-esteem and self-efficacy. Stigma marks an individual or an entire group of individuals as "deviant" and facilitates their marginalization.

Stigma doesn't just "feel" bad; it has very real-world consequences. People may avoid getting help for not wanting to be labeled. Stigma is not about the individual; rather, it is about the society and the people around that individual. However, this stigma can be internalized in the form of shame, embarrassment, and even despising oneself.

Why does stigma even exist? There are many theories and studies that have attempted to address this question. Sociologists have proposed that stigma serves the function of establishing and maintaining power hierarchies in a society. Psychologists have examined stigma in terms of negative stereotypes and valuation of ingroup members and devaluation of outgroup members. Common negative stereotypes for those with a mental disorder include dangerousness, notions that they "brought it on themselves," and incompetence.

Needless to say, the reduction of or even the eradication of stigma for mental disorder is a necessary course of action. There have been some strides over the last 30 years in this regard. The Americans with Disabilities Act of 1990 was established to protect the rights of individuals in the public sphere, including work, school, and business. In 2007, the United Nations developed the Convention on the Rights of Persons with Disabilities to codify the rights of individuals with disabilities in international relations. However, even with these legal and human rights advances, still work needs to be done. Psychologists suggest that such actions as protests, public service announcements, education, and increased contact with persons with mental disorders can all help to reduce stigma.

Ultimately, the goal is *empathy*. Empathy for fellow human beings. Empathy for their struggles. Yet another goal is empowerment so that individuals with mental disabilities aren't pitied or patronized but seen in their totality as persons, not diagnoses.

6
Repairing, Healing, and Thriving

Dig deep into psychological evaluation, testing, assessment to find out how psychologists apply psychological science to human abilities and difficulties.

Get familiar with the differences among traditional "talk" psychotherapies: Behavior therapy, cognitive therapy, and other popular forms of psychological treatment.

Explore what is "positive" in psychology.

Chapter **16**

Testing, Assessment, and Evaluation

Psychologists do therapy, right? Yes. But so do other professionals such as marriage and family therapists and clinical social workers. But they provide treatment for mental disorders, right? Yes, but so do psychiatrists. So what's different about a psychologist, you might ask? The answer: psychological testing, assessment, and evaluation.

Ever seen the television show *House, M.D.* featuring a curmudgeonly, stubborn medical doctor named Dr. Gregory House? He specializes in figuring out medical cases that other doctors and providers have been baffled by. He "solves" many a medical mystery, and it makes for excellent viewing. But that's fiction, right? Well, Dr. Lisa Sanders of the Yale University School of Medicine, who serves as a technical advisor for the show, says that such specialists do actually exist in the real world. I propose that the testing, assessment, and evaluation skills of psychologists are similar to those on display on that show. So psychologists are a bunch of Dr. Gregory Houses? That would be grandiose, but kind of. We do specialize in getting to the root of problems and issues with the use of highly developed instruments, tools, and procedures. I don't believe it's overstating the case that the solid use of psychological science goes into the development and use of psychological tests and assessment procedures.

But let me come down a little bit off the high horse. Yes, psychologists specialize in *psychological assessment* and use tests and instruments. No, they don't have all the answers. People, their minds, behavior, problems, and abilities are complicated. Sometimes the unaided eye, or viewpoint, or interview isn't quite enough to get a handle on things. That doesn't mean that our methods are an "X-ray" to the psyche, but they're pretty good! As mentioned previously, psychologists do a lot of things that other professionals do. But testing, assessment, and evaluation is our particular specialty (like Dr. House). We get called in, referred to, and consulted because of our expertise in these methods. Psychological assessment is in our wheelhouse, so to speak. It's our strong suit and maybe our strongest suit working as *applied psychologists*. Although other psychologists may disagree, assessment may be what we are best at in the applied branch of psychological science.

In this chapter, I introduce and discuss psychological assessment, testing, and evaluation. I explore its purposes, the science behind it, and survey a few specific areas of assessment, as covering it all would be well beyond the scope of this book.

Answering the Call

I get at least two to three calls per week when a parent or patient needs help and has been exploring all options without making any progress. Again, a mantra of this book is that people are complicated, and sometimes it takes a complicated process to get to the bottom of things. Psychologists are asked to "answer" all kinds of questions, such as

> What is this person's diagnosis?
>
> What are this person's cognitive strengths and weaknesses?
>
> Is this person fit to do job X? (For example, police officer, special forces soldier)
>
> What are this parent's strengths and weaknesses?
>
> Can this person make medical and legal decisions for him- or herself?
>
> Was this person criminally insane at the time of the crime?

So how do we define testing, assessment, and evaluation?

Testing is simply the administration and scoring of psychological tests. This can be done by a *psychometrist*, defined by the National Association of Psychometrists as a technician responsible for the administration and scoring of psychological and neuropsychological tests under the supervision of a clinical psychologist or clinical neuropsychologist. Psychologists don't practice psychometry; they assess and evaluate.

Assessment and evaluation can be viewed as a problem-solving and decision-making process. *Assessment* is the process by which results from different sources of information including interviews and tests are "put together" and integrated into a meaningful picture of a person.

Evaluation is the process in which testing and assessment results are put together to answer the specific question that a person was referred to the psychologist for, such as, for example, "Will this person be a risk to society if released from prison?" or "Can this person perform well as an astronaut?"

What kinds of tests and instruments are there?

There are psychological tests and instruments for almost anything psychological. If you survey a standard catalog of psychological tests and instruments, you'll find over 350 instruments from just one publisher alone!

It is important to point out that different kinds of psychologists use different kinds of tests. Clinical psychologists use clinically oriented tests such as diagnostic instruments, personality tests, cognitive tests, and adaptive skills inventories. Counseling psychologists may use aptitude tests. Forensic psychologists may use violence risk assessment instruments.

The following is a list of the different categories of tests and instruments:

Development	Speech, Language, Communication
Adaptive Behavior	Cognitive
Intelligence	Neuropsychological
Achievement	Learning
Social	Emotional
Behavioral	Occupational
Sensory	Health
Motor	Personality

What kind of evaluations do psychologists do?

As with the different kinds of tests and instruments, the different types of evaluations psychologists do depends on their specialty, be it clinical, forensic, or otherwise. Here is a list of the different kinds of evaluations applied psychologists may conduct:

Clinical/Diagnostic	Mental Disability
Forensic	Civil Capacity
Competence to Stand Trial	Criminal Insanity
Learning Disability	Educational
Aptitude	Fitness for Duty
Custody	Mental Injury
Employment	Job Performance
Violence Risk Assessment	Pre-Surgical

So that's a broad overview of the tools and process. In the following sections, I cover specific techniques and the nuts and bolts of testing instruments in general and introduce you to some tests under specific categories mentioned in the preceding lists.

The Interview and Evaluation Process

The first step toward any solution is to recognize and clearly define the problem. Psychologists use specific tools and techniques for that very purpose. There should always be a clear *referral question*. Sending someone to a psychologist for a fishing expedition, so they can dig around in their heads, so to speak, is not good practice on the part of the referring party and borders on being unethical. Once the referral question is clarified and the *audience,* or recipient of the information, is identified (such as patients themselves, an employer, or a court), then the process can begin.

Here's how it typically goes: A person visits a psychologist, and the conversation begins with an exploration of the patient's reason for referral, which is the reason the person is there for assessment, and evaluation for the *presenting problem,* which is the issue that motivated the patient to seek assessment. The discussion then gets into a more thorough information-gathering process:

Psychologist: Tell me, Mr. Smith, what seems to be the problem?

Smith: How am I supposed to know? You're the doctor.

The "What's the problem?" question sometimes annoys patients because they often don't know what's going on. After all, they're seeking help from a professional and expect the psychologist to have the answers. But without a thorough investigation of the patient's history, current functioning, and concerns, a psychologist can only perform expensive guesswork. The process may take 1 to 2 hours or even 12 hours of assessment, depending on the referral question or presenting problem.

Interviewing and observing

There may be as many interview techniques in the psychological world as there are individual psychologists out there. Everyone has a different way of getting at the relevant information. It really depends on the type of referral question. So a clinical evaluation may ask different questions than a fitness-for-duty evaluation. For the purpose of this section, I will focus on the most common form of interview that people encounter when referred to a psychologist: the *clinical interview*.

Psychologist John Sommers-Flanagan is not overstating when he says that the "status of clinical interviewing as a fundamental procedure is almost universal." Although clinical interviews can vary between theoretical orientations, Dr. Sommers-Flanagan has identified some universal characteristics, including overall goals and objectives, such as balancing information gathering and "therapeutic helping." It may sound strange, but oftentimes a psychological evaluation can be very therapeutic by itself. Someone may have wondered for most of her life why she loses jobs and flies off the handle at the smallest provocation, for example. She may be relieved to find out she has bipolar disorder. Disclaimer: Not everyone who loses jobs and flies off the handle has bipolar disorder. That was just an example.

Clinical interviewing shares many of the same characteristics as other interviewing approaches. Interviewers engage in exploration of the present problem or referral question. I like to start off with questions like, "How can I help you? Tell me why you're here." Sometimes it helps to offer some comfort because it's kind of weird and not a typical experience to go tell a complete stranger about your problems, how you feel, and all that is going on in your life and mind. Sometimes even stating that the whole situation seems awkward can help: "I know this is weird. . .." This is particularly helpful with adolescents who are often reluctant attendees at this event.

Observing mental status

The psychologist engages in attentive listening and observation, trying to get as complete a picture as he or she can about what the interviewee is saying, how they are acting, what they are talking about, what they are not talking about, what they are focused on, how forthcoming they seem to be, and how comfortable they are. These are just a few things that we attend to and observe. A useful tool to gather this information is the *Mental Status Exam*, in which the psychologist observes these 11 mental status areas:

>> **Appearance:** Grooming, hygiene, physical characteristics, and unusual features are observed. If someone has an unusual appearance — severely underweight, disheveled, or bizarre or inappropriate grooming, for instance — outside of cultural or subcultural norms, it may be worth discussing.

>> **Behavior:** Some of the most striking signs of disturbance come from the way people act.

- *Body movement:* Body movements such as fidgeting, fast movements, slowed movements, or strange gestures may be relevant. Nervous individuals may fidget a lot. Depressed patients may sit slumped in their chairs. Someone with a paranoid delusion that the CIA is following him may get up and peek out the curtains every five minutes.

- *Facial expressions:* Facial expressions can sometimes reveal how a person is feeling. A sad, mad, immobile, or frozen expression, for example, can indicate specific moods.

>> **Speech:** Two disorders in particular, schizophrenia and bipolar disorder, include disturbances in speech:

- *Schizophrenia:* A patient's speech may be disordered, jumbled, or difficult to understand. He may seem to be speaking a foreign language, using words and phrases that don't seem to make sense. For example, I once received an anonymous phone call while volunteering at a homeless shelter. When I asked the caller if I could help him, he replied, "Stick the pin in the cushion. You called me. What do you want? The letters make me crazy . . . light bulb . . . beat the drum . . . stick the pin in the cushion . . . what do you want?" This is an excellent case of disordered speech.

- *Bipolar disorder:* The rate and pace of speech can be abnormal in people with bipolar disorder. Patients in a manic episode, for instance, can speak very fast and act as if they physically need to keep talking. They may jump from one topic to another.

>> **Mood and affect:** *Mood* describes the predominant emotions being expressed by the patient. Is she sad, happy, angry, euphoric, or anxious? *Affect* refers to the range, intensity, and appropriateness of a patient's emotional behavior. Is she mildly sad or intensely sad? Does she feel anything other than sadness, or does she seem to have a full range of emotions? Another common observation of affect is called *mood lability*. How often and easily does mood change? Is she hot one second and cold the next?

>> **Thought content:** What people think about is relevant to any clinical evaluation. Bizarre thought content, such as delusions, can be telltale signs of the presence of a mental disorder. Less bizarre but sometimes equally disturbing thoughts, such as obsessive preoccupations and intrusive ideas, can also be signs of severe anxiety. Thoughts of death and violence are relevant to assessing suicidality and violence potential.

>> **Thought process:** Different ways of thinking can sometimes be clues to a mental disorder.

- *Tangential thinking:* Often a sign of thought disorder, tangential thinking is characterized by a wandering focus and the tendency to go off on tangents that are only minimally related to the topic currently being discussed.

- *Clang associations:* These are serious indicators of thought disorder. When someone ends a sentence with a word, and the sound of that word triggers another thought, related to the conversation only by the sound of the last word uttered, the thought process is known as a *clang association*. "I came home from work the other day, and the car was in the driveway . . . highways are crowded. Loud noises bother me . . . tree." This type of disordered thought is unorganized and hard to follow; it doesn't make sense.

>> **Perception:** Perceptual problems consist of hallucinations. Patients can experience auditory hallucinations (voices), visual hallucinations, olfactory hallucinations (smells or odors), gustatory hallucinations (tastes), or somatic hallucinations (strange bodily sensations, such as feeling like bugs are crawling under the skin). A very serious auditory hallucination is when patients hear a voice or voices telling them to hurt themselves or someone else. These are sometimes called command hallucinations.

>> **Intellectual functioning:** This status can be casually observed by paying attention to the patient's vocabulary, general quantity of knowledge and information, and abstract thinking ability. However, trying to figure out someone's intellectual functioning based on observation alone is highly subjective and should only be used as a starting point for further assessment.

>> **Attention/concentration and memory:** Pay attention to whether a patient is distracted during the interview and struggling to concentrate on the task at hand. Short-term memory can be checked by asking the individual to

remember a few things and checking with her a few minutes later. How well she recalls her history and provides historical information offers a measure of long-term memory. Many disorders present attention problems and memory deficits.

>> **Orientation:** Does the patient know where she is? The season? The time? Ascertaining whether a patient knows where she is in time and space is an important part of the MSE. Many serious medical conditions and neuropsychological disorders manifest signs of disorientation.

>> **Insight and judgment:** Does the patient understand that she may be mentally ill? Does she understand the relationship between her behaviors and mental processes and a psychological disturbance? Insight is important for assessing how motivated a patient is going to be during treatment and whether compliance issues are likely to interfere with illness management or recovery. Addressing a patient's judgment involves looking at the soundness of the decisions she makes and the degree of impulsivity and planning that goes on before she takes action. Judgment is especially important when assessing for dangerousness, violence potential, or suicide risk.

Asking questions and developing rapport

Psychologists can ask different types of questions and use a variety of techniques such as open-ended questions (How did that feel?) or close-ended questions (Have you ever heard a voice speaking to you but no one was around?). Questions can be directive or non-directive.

Other techniques include paraphrasing, asking *presuppositional* questions (a question to "lead" in order to rule something out or steer the conversation), or *projective* questions (designed to get at information in a less direct or confrontational manner).

Developing good *rapport* (mutual understanding) is a key to getting accurate and thorough information. Psychiatrists Ekkehard Othmer and Sieglinde Othmer (yes, psychologists borrow from psychiatry) provide a good list of rapport-building techniques:

>> Put the patient (and yourself) at ease

>> Show compassion and address the "suffering"

>> Become an ally

>> Show expertise

>> Establish leadership

>> Balance the roles of interviewer and therapist

History taking

Does the psychologist want an autobiography? In a way, yes, except that only specific areas are covered. Formats for taking a history are also extremely varied, but most of them include the following elements:

>> **Presenting problem:** When did it all begin? The most relevant aspect in a psychological interview is the history of the presenting problem. What is the concern? Is it your behavior, mood, relationships, thinking? When did these problems begin? Have they been stable and consistent or have they come and gone? What have other people said about this? This can sometimes be presented in the form of a *problem checklist*.

>> **Home environment and family history:** Who do they live with? Parents, siblings, children. Health history and mental health history in the family.

>> **Developmental history** (for children and adolescents): Developmental milestones (walk, talk, potty trained).

>> **Health and medical history:** Illnesses, general health, medication, hospitalizations, accidents, surgeries.

>> **Educational and occupational history:** Highest level of education, learning issues or delays, special education, jobs.

>> **Legal history:** Arrests, jail, child custody.

>> **Social history:** Dating, marriage, friends, groups, organizations.

>> **Cultural and religious information:** Languages spoken, primary language, secondary language, did they immigrate, relevant questions about religious affiliation.

>> **Substance use and abuse:** Drinking, illicit drug use, recreational drug use, rehabs, 12-step groups.

>> **History of mental health and treatment:** Trauma, abuse, previous evaluations, therapy, medications, hospitalizations, suicide attempts, violence, aggression.

REMEMBER

A prudent professional always takes the time to assess the most serious aspects of a case first, and no issues are more serious to a psychologist than suicide or a patient's potential for violence.

Checking under the Hood with Psychological Testing

Psychological testing is part of the entire psychological assessment process. Psychologist Anne Anastasi (1908–2001), a past president of the American Psychological Association and a distinguished researcher in psychological assessment, defines a psychological test as an objective, standardized sample of behavior or mental processes. Tests can formalize data based on observations.

Testing formats include surveys, pencil and paper tests, exercises and activities (like putting a puzzle together), interviews, and observation. Testing in psychology is not much different from testing in other fields. A blood test is a means of measuring an individual's T-cell count, for example. A personality test is a way to measure some specific aspect of a person's personality. Psychological testing uses the same idea; it just focuses on the subject matter of psychology, behavior, and mental processes.

REMEMBER

A test is objective if it meets acceptable standards in three important areas: standardization, reliability, and validity.

Standardization

Anne Anastasi considers a test properly *standardized* if it has a uniform procedure for administering and scoring. Control of extraneous variables allows for maximum accuracy. In other words, if I give a test differently to two different people, then I can't very well trust the results because I've violated the principle of control in science.

Establishing a norm for a test is another step in standardization. A *norm* is a measure of the average performance for a large group of people on any given psychological test. For example, the average score on the Wechsler Adult Intelligence Scale, 4th Edition, is 100. This average score establishes a point of comparison for the test taker's scores to be referenced to. This is called *a norm* and is a standard by which to compare people. Norms are established by administering the test to a large group of people, or several groups, and measuring the average performance and range of performances, something called *variability.* So, if I develop a test to measure problem solving, I would establish a norm or comparison group by going out and giving my test to thousands of people and documenting their performance and the range of performances. This comparison group is used to compare the scores of any individual taking the test to the thousands of other people who took the test and allows me to determine how well or how poorly any one individual test taker did in comparison to all the other people who took the test.

Reliability

Reliability is consistency across different testing occasions, test providers, settings, or circumstances. A reliable test should give the same result regardless of the circumstances. An inconsistent test is not reliable and therefore not very helpful for psychological testing. If I give the same person the same test on two or more occasions, will he get the same or comparable score? If the answer is yes, then the test is reliable. If I test a person, and another psychologist uses the same test on the same person, the results should be comparable; this is called inter-rater reliability.

A test needs to prove reliable before being put to use by professionals. In fact, psychologists are ethically bound to use reliable tests and instruments because they are being entrusted to provide accurate and useful information. An unreliable test is not able to deliver in that regard. A psychologist wants to know if a person's test performance is due to their own characteristics and not to the setting, circumstances, or situation. The psychologist would not be measuring what he thinks he is measuring if a test weren't reliable.

An example of reliability used in test development is *test-retest reliability*. This involves giving a test and then giving it again later (not too soon, of course, because you don't want practice effects) and then seeing if the scores are close or similar.

When it comes to psychological testing, I've often had patients object that a test was unreliable and that it didn't prove or measure a darn thing. They may have had a point, but only if the test was unreliable.

Validity

How do you know that a test you're using is really measuring what it claims to measure? You may think that you're measuring intelligence when you're really measuring English-language aptitude. This actually happens quite often when tests are improperly used with people for whom the test has not been *normed* — which means that its statistical properties haven't been established with a large population of individuals similar to the people to whom it will be applied. Tests used with people who were not part of the group the test was normed on are highly suspect and most likely invalid.

When a test measures what it claims to measure, it's considered *valid*. The validity of a test is established by comparing the test with an outside measure of the psychological topic in question. If I have a test that claims to measure depression, I must compare my test findings with an already established measure of depression such as the Beck Depression Inventory.

REMEMBER

Keep in mind that many, if not most, psychological tests measure things that are unobservable in the way other factors in other fields are. T-cells can be physically seen and counted under a microscope. But intelligence cannot be viewed in the same manner. Intelligence is presumed to exist as it manifests itself in a measurable form on a psychological test. Therefore, the scientific basis on which psychological testing is formed is of utmost importance.

Psychological testing is a little more sophisticated than asking a few questions and counting up someone's responses. It's a scientific endeavor. Because of the complexity of psychological testing, most professionals argue that use of tests should be controlled — only qualified examiners should use them. The risk for potential oversimplification or misinterpretation is just too high when an untrained administrator attempts to diagnose a person's mental status through testing.

Plus, if the tests are spread around indiscriminately, people may become too familiar with them and be able to manipulate their responses; thus the tests would lose their validity. Instead of measuring someone's intelligence, for example, the psychologist may end up measuring a subject's skill at remembering the test questions and answers that reveal the traits he wants to show.

More Detail on Testing Types

Numerous types of psychological testing exist. Five of the most common are clinical testing, educational/achievement testing, personality testing, intelligence testing, and neuropsychological testing. Each of these different types of tests looks at a different type of behavior and/or mental process.

Clinical testing

Clinical psychologists (psychologists who work with mental disorders and abnormal behavior) typically use clinical testing as a way to clarify diagnoses and assess the scope and nature of a person's or family's disturbance and dysfunction. Specific tests are designed to assess the extent to which a patient may or may not be experiencing the symptoms of a particular disorder. These are *diagnostic tests.* A popular example is the Beck Depression Inventory, which is designed to assess a patient's level of depression.

Behavioral and adaptive functioning tests are two types of clinical tests that determine how well a person is doing in her everyday life and whether she exhibits specific problem behaviors. A common instrument used with children is the Child

Behavior Checklist, which is designed to assess the extent of a child's behavior problems. Another commonly used clinical test is the Conner's Parent Rating Scale, which detects attention deficit/hyperactivity disorder (ADHD) symptoms.

In addition to disorder-specific inventories and tests, a wide variety of tests designed for other purposes lend themselves to the diagnostic process. Intelligence tests are designed to measure intelligence, but they can also show signs of cognitive dysfunction and learning disabilities. Personality tests are designed to measure personality, but they can also provide helpful insight to the types of psychological problems an individual is experiencing.

Educational/achievement testing

Educational and achievement tests measure an individual's current level of academic competence. Glen Aylward, chair of the Division of Developmental and Behavioral Pediatrics at the Southern Illinois University School of Medicine, identifies three major purposes of this type of testing:

>> Identify students who need special instruction.

>> Identify the nature of a student's difficulties in order to rule out learning disabilities.

>> Assist in educational planning and approach to instruction.

A typical educational/achievement test assesses the most common areas of school activity: reading, mathematics, spelling, and writing skills. Some tests include other areas such as science and social studies. A popular achievement test in wide use today is the Woodcock-Johnson Psychoeducational Battery, Revised. The test consists of nine subtests, measuring the standard areas of instruction but in more detail (mathematics is broken down into calculation and applied problems, for example).

Educational/achievement testing is widely used in the school systems in the United States and Western Europe. When a child or older student is having a hard time in school, it's not unusual for her to take an achievement test to get a closer look at her basic skill level. Sometimes, students have a difficult time because they have a learning disability. Part of identifying a learning disability is assessing the student's achievement level. Other times, a student struggles because of non-academic difficulties such as emotional problems, substance abuse, or family issues. An achievement test sometimes helps to tease out these non-academic problems.

Personality testing

Personality tests measure many different things, not just personality. Numerous tests are designed to measure emotion, motivation, and interpersonal skills as well as specific aspects of personality, according to the given theory on which a test is based. Most personality tests are known as *self-reports*. With self-reports, the person answering questions about herself, typically in a pencil-and-paper format, provides the information.

Personality tests are usually developed with a particular theory of personality in mind. A test may measure id, ego, or superego issues, for example, if it originates from a Freudian view of personality development.

Getting down with MMPI-2

Perhaps the most widely used personality test in the United States is the MMPI-2, The Minnesota Multiphasic Personality Inventory, 2nd Edition. Almost all American psychologists are trained to use the MMPI-2, which is considered to be a very reliable and valid instrument. A patient's results from a MMPI-2 test provide rich information about the presence of psychopathology and level of severity, if present. The test's results also reveal information about the emotional, behavioral, and social functioning of the test taker. A lot of psychologists use the MMPI-2 as a way to check the accuracy of their observations and diagnoses.

The MMPI-2 test consists of 567 individual items and produces a score on nine clinical categories or scales. If a score is over a specific cutoff, it usually gets the attention of the psychologist administering the test. Psychologists consider such scores to be of clinical significance. The MMPI-2 covers a wide variety of areas, including depression, physical complaints, anger, social contact, anxiety, and energy level.

Projecting to the deep stuff

Projective personality tests are a unique breed of test. When most people think of psychological testing, these kinds of tests come readily to mind. The stereotype involves sitting across from a psychologist, looking at a card with smeared ink or a picture of somebody doing something on it, and answering questions like "What do you see here?"

REMEMBER

Projective personality tests are unique because they're based on something called the *projective hypothesis,* which states that when presented with ambiguous stimuli, people will project, and thus reveal, parts of themselves and their psychological functioning that they may not reveal if asked directly. It's not like these tests are trying to trick people, though. The idea is that a lot of folks can't exactly put words to or describe what's going on mentally and emotionally because of psychological defense mechanisms. Some people are not conscious of their feelings. Projective tests are designed to get past the defenses and penetrate the deep recesses of the psyche.

Perhaps the most popular projective personality test and maybe even the most popular psychological test of all time is the Rorschach Inkblot Test (RIT). The RIT consists of ten cards, each with its own standard inkblot figure. None of these inkblots are a picture or representation of anything. They were created by simply pouring ink onto a sheet of paper and folding it in half. The only meaning and structure the cards have are provided by the projections of the test taker himself.

Intelligence testing

Intelligence tests may be the most frequently administered type of psychological test. They measure a broad range of intellectual and cognitive abilities and often provide a general measure of intelligence, which is sometimes called an *IQ* — intelligence quotient.

Intelligence tests are used in a wide variety of settings and applications. They can be used for diagnostic purposes to identify disabilities and cognitive disorders. They're commonly used in academic and school settings. Intelligence tests have been around since the beginning of psychology as an established science, dating back to the work of Wilhelm Wundt in the early 20th century.

The most commonly used tests of intelligence are the Wechsler Adult Intelligence Scale, 4th Edition (WAIS-IV) for adults and the Wechsler Intelligence Scale for Children, 4th Edition (WISC-IV) for children. Each of these tests contains several subtests designed to measure specific aspects of intelligence such as attention, general knowledge, visual organization, and comprehension. Both tests provide individual scores for each subtest and an overall score representing overall intelligence.

Neuropsychological and cognitive testing

Although not a new field, tests of neuropsychological functioning and cognitive ability, related specifically to brain functioning, are rapidly becoming a standard part of a psychologist's testing toolset. Neuropsychological tests have traditionally been used to augment neurological exams and brain imaging techniques (such as MRIs, CT scans, and PET scans), but they're being used more widely now in psychoeducational testing and other clinical testing situations.

REMEMBER

The technology of scanning techniques picks up on the presence of brain damage, but neuropsychological tests serve as a more precise measure of the actual functional impairments an individual may suffer from. Scans say, "Yep, there's damage!" Neuropsychological tests say, ". . . and here's the cognitive problem related to it."

Neuropsychological testing is used in hospitals, clinics, private practices, and other places where psychologists work with patients who are suspected of neuropsychological impairment. People suffering head trauma, developmental disorder, or other insults to the brain may need a thorough neuropsychological examination.

A popular neuropsychological test is actually not a test at all but a collection of tests called a *test battery*. The Halstead-Reitan Neuropsychological Test Battery includes numerous tests that measure neuropsychological constructs such as memory, attention and concentration, language ability, motor skills, auditory skill, and planning. The battery also includes an MMPI-2 and WAIS-IV test. Completing the battery requires several hours, and it's never done in one sitting, so going through a neuropsychological evaluation can take several weeks and be costly. However, when conducted by a competent professional, the testing can yield a tremendous amount of helpful information.

Many neuropsychological instruments are available; some are comprehensive, like the Halstead-Reitan, and some are designed to measure a specific function such as language or attention. Whether a neuropsychological evaluation is conducted using a comprehensive instrument or a collection of individual instruments to create a profile of neuropsychological strengths and weaknesses, the following areas of neuropsychological functioning are typically assessed:

>> **Executive functions:** Focusing, planning, organizing, monitoring, inhibiting, and self-regulating

>> **Communication and language:** Perceiving, receiving, and expressing self with language and nonverbal communication

>> **Memory:** Auditory memory, visual memory, working memory, and long-term memory

>> **Sensorimotor functions:** Sensory and motor functions, including hearing, touch, smell, and fine and gross muscle movements

>> **Visual-spatial functions:** Visual perception, visual motor coordination, visual scanning, and perceptual reasoning

>> **Speed and efficiency:** How fast and how efficient thinking is

Keeping Them Honest

An important tip that a psychologist doesn't typically find out about in graduate school is that not everybody coming in for an evaluation or assessment is honest. What? No way! Hard to believe, maybe, but it's true. Unfortunately, some people who seek a psychological assessment and evaluation, or have been ordered to get it, engage in what psychologists call dissimulation and malingering.

Dissimulation in assessment occurs when a client conceals, distorts, and alters his true abilities, concerns, and other characteristics for various motives. Dissimulation is deception. Within the assessment context, a person may dissimulate by concealing or distorting some deficit or disorder by "faking good" or "faking bad." *Malingering* is a "faking bad" process in which a person deliberately feigns, fakes, or exaggerates symptoms or deficits.

Why would someone want to "fake good" when getting a psychological assessment or evaluation? This most often occurs when the results of the psychological assessment are being used for some sort of selection or screening process such as employment, background check, parenting evaluation in a divorce proceeding, or risk assessment.

When I worked in forensics, one of the duties I performed was to assess the violence risk of prison inmates convicted of serious violent crimes who were approaching a parole evaluation. My job was to estimate how likely it was that an individual would commit more violent crimes or offenses if freed. My evaluation played a big part in whether an inmate was granted parole, so these people had plenty of incentive to present themselves as a low risk and "fake good."

On the other side, why would anybody want to make herself seem to be mentally ill? Plenty of reasons exist for presenting such a picture, but most often it's for money. A common "faking bad" scenario is when a person tries to demonstrate an inability to hold down a job and therefore qualify for compensation without working (such as Social Security benefits) during an employment disability evaluation.

It's not all just about money, though. When someone's arrested and accused of a crime, she can sometimes get away with a lighter punishment — or even be found not guilty — if a mental disorder is to blame. This is a gamble that some accused people are willing to make, and "faking bad" is the road to take.

REMEMBER

The bad news for the dissimulators and malingerers out there is that psychologists have tools, methods, and specialized techniques of evaluation and assessment that are specifically designed to sniff out deception, poor effort, exaggeration, and dishonesty. Many test instruments themselves have built-in components and scales to measure dishonesty factors. Special interview techniques and lines of questioning can help with this as well. In fact, in the business of forensic assessment, there is good money to be made on being an expert in picking out the fakers, and these professionals pride themselves on being able to detect deception.

Chapter **17**

We Can Help!

Think of those commercials for substance abuse treatment programs or mental health programs:

Are you struggling, suffering, feeling challenged, and needing to change?

We can help!

Our special approach to your (fill in the blank) will accomplish (fill in the blank).

Well, admittedly, that's pretty much the same message I have for you in this chapter. There *is* help out there for our struggles, suffering, and challenges, but there's a big but! The type of "help" that is outlined and discussed in this chapter is considered founded and based on psychological theory and science. It is professional help.

Did you know there is a program on the web that is a slogan generator? I didn't use it and came up with one on my own:

We can help with your suffering, struggles, challenges, and needs to change your mental processes and behavior through the professional use of psychological intervention/treatment/therapy based on psychological theory and science.

Not so catchy, is it? Maybe I should have used the slogan generator!

How can I make such a claim? It's not spurious! It can be backed up with decades of thoughtful theory development, research, evaluation, and analysis. If one was to conduct a search of the American Psychological Association's Database *PsycInfo* using the keyword *psychology*, one would find a repository of almost 2,000,000 papers, studies, and reviews spanning a period of approximately 200 years. Compare that to the database of physics, which includes over 6,000,000 papers, studies, and reviews. That's not even close, right? But remember, psychology is a significantly younger science. Modern scientific physics, beginning with Copernicus and Galileo, began around the mid 1500s. That's a head start of over 250 years! When you look at the rate of production per year, psychology is progressing at the rate of 9,800 papers, studies, and reviews per year. Compare that to physics, which has a rate of approximately 13,600 per year. Not bad for such a young science, I think!

Directly relevant to this chapter, when you conduct a search of the American Psychological Association's Database *PsycInfo* using the keywords *treatment* or *therapy*, one can find a catalog of over 300,000 papers, studies, and reviews spanning a period of over 100 years. I think that's a pretty good basis for the "we can help" claim. It's tantamount to an army of thinkers, investigators, and practitioners fulfilling their altruistic, Good Samaritan roles. We've tried and experimented with different forms of "help" and have some ideas about what works and what doesn't. So I think we've done a pretty good job considering that our subject matter is the messy and complicated world of people and their problems.

REMEMBER

Does that mean we've got it all figured out? Not by a long shot. However, over those years and all that work, theorists, researchers, and practitioners have developed some fairly solid ideas about what actually works in the area of professional psychological help.

In this chapter, I cover general factors in using psychological science to help people in the forms of *psychological intervention, treatment,* and *therapy.* I also look at broad models of intervention and some of the different types of intervention. Finally, I discuss the "crown jewel" of psychological intervention: psychotherapy.

Is It Time for Professional Help?

Let me tell you a story. A tenant calls his landlord because there is a big leak in the ceiling. The landlord rushes over, assesses the situation and says, "I can fix this." He rushes to the local big-box home improvement center and gathers his supplies: duct tape, a plastic trash can with a lid, a small tarp, and plastic tubing. He sets up an ingenious contraption that he tapes to the ceiling around the leak that works to funnel the water into the trash can. He's impressed with himself and believes his inventiveness will buy him some time before he has to call in a professional.

About an hour after he leaves, the tenant calls him again. "The ceiling caved in!" he yells. What? The contraption didn't work? He then calls a professional. (Yes, this is true story, and I'll give three guesses who the landlord was.)

One of my favorite movies is *Nacho Libre* (2006) where Jack Black (Nacho) and Hector Jimenez (Steven) play fledgling wrestlers in a small town in Mexico. There's a great scene following another loss after a long string of losses for Nacho and Steven:

> **Nacho:** Those eggs were a lie, Steven. A lie! They gave me no eagle powers! They gave me no nutrients!

> **Steven:** Sorry.

> (Man walks in and hands Nacho an envelope of money.)

> **Nacho:** I don't want to get paid to lose. I want to win! (Leans back and sighs.) I need professional help.

Yes, both the landlord and Nacho came to a point when they decided they needed professional help. We've all got problems, right? (For more on what those might look like, see Chapter 15.) The psychologist Ronald Miller states that psychologists attempt to offer "practical solutions to the pressing problems of human suffering." Have you ever said any of the following:

> I feel like crap!
>
> I'm depressed.
>
> I can't stop getting angry and flying off the handle.
>
> My relationships are broken.
>
> I can't concentrate.

Whatever the specifics, we've all "been there" and may need professional help. We may want to feel better, act or behave better, think better, relate better (be a better wife, parent, son, employer), and do more of the good stuff we do and less of the bad stuff. Of course, what does "better" mean? Do I want to be happier, healthier, more productive, have better habits, be more skilled, cope better, and be more resilient?

It's a complex question and there are many different ways to determine "better" and whether professional help is warranted. The American Psychological Association (APA.org) offers the following suggestions on when someone might want to consider seeking professional help from a psychologist (paraphrased):

>> Having a prolonged sense of hopelessness and of being "stuck."

>> Your problems haven't gotten better by you own efforts, or by the efforts of friends, family, or other resources (like the Self-Help section of the local bookstore).

>> You are not functioning at work, home, or school.

That's a pretty short list, and it may sound like everyone should get professional help. But hold on. That's not what I am saying at all. Some problems and issues are just "life," with its ups and downs and all arounds. Other problems might be too difficult to fix, overcome, or get past, and those might be the ones that require the advice Nacho gives himself: "I need professional help."

Really, no one can decide for someone else when he or she should get professional help although there are circumstances where the "choice" is more compelled than suggested, as in situations where a boss says you'll lose your job, a spouse says they'll leave you, a child says "I hate you," or a court orders it.

Types of help

If someone has decided to seek help, what kind of help would they seek, where would they seek it, and from whom would they seek it? There are numerous types of help out there with various definitions floating around, from "treatment" to "psychotherapy" to "intervention" to "counseling." Let's explore some of them.

Treatment

The American Psychological Association provides an excellent definition of *treatment:*

> . . . in the context of healthcare . . . any process in which a trained healthcare provider offers assistance based upon his or her professional expertise to a person who has a problem that is defined as related to "health" or "illness". . . . In the case of "mental" or "behavioral" health, the conditions which one may seek "treatment" include problems in living, conditions with discrete symptoms that are identified as or related to illness or disease, and problems of interpersonal adjustment. The treatment consists of any act or services provided by a bona fide health provider intended to correct, change, or ameliorate these conditions or problems.

So treatment is essentially the professional act or service provided for the purpose of change.

Psychotherapy

Treatment can come in the form of therapy, intervention, or counseling. Psychologist John Norcross defines *psychotherapy* as

> . . . the informed and intentional application of clinical methods and interpersonal stances derived from established psychological principles for the purpose of assisting people to modify behaviors, cognitions, emotions, and/other personal characteristics in directions that the participants deem desirable.

Let's unpack that a bit. "Informed and intentional" means that psychotherapists are professionally educated and trained, know what they are doing, and are doing it on purpose. They've been to school, have had practicums, internships, have taken and passed licensure exams, and have gone on to continue their training, honing their skills, and sometimes getting advanced, postgraduate certifications. The use of "clinical methods and interpersonal stances derived from" means that they are using specific models for helping that involve interacting person to person (could be individual or group) that are based on scientific research and validation. "The purpose of assisting people" and "that the participants deem desirable" means that they aren't just fiddling around in your head and tinkering with your emotions, relationships, and behaviors for the heck of it. They are working to effect change in mental processes and behavior toward the desired change of the person seeking help.

Treatment and psychotherapy go hand in hand. Many people, however, may never actually participate in psychotherapy. They may instead find themselves in counseling, receiving pharmacotherapy, engaged in psychoeducation, or skills training.

Counseling

Dr. David S. Doane draws a distinction between counseling and psychotherapy: Counseling is typically shorter in duration and focused on more immediate management of target issues and adjustment, whereas psychotherapy is more long term and focuses on more broader and more "core" issues. In some ways, the differences come down to length, breadth, and scope. Both can be provided by Master's-level and Doctoral-level practitioners.

Of course, this distinction is not without contention and has spurred many a spirited debate in the professional community as therapists and counselors fight over the turf of changing, intervening, and treating problems and issues around mental processes and behavior. That's an entire book in and of itself.

Pharmacotherapy

Pharmacotherapy involves the treatment of human suffering using the medical model and typically focuses on mental disorder specifically. (For more on pharmacotherapy, see Chapter 3.) Pharmacotherapy involves the use of medications by a medical doctor (psychiatrist, family physician, neurologist) to alleviate symptoms such as depressed mood, hallucinations, and agitation. It is important to point out that in today's society, many more people take medications than receive psychotherapy.

Psychoeducation

Psychoeducation involves the teaching and learning of psychological principles to individuals and groups to help them without engaging in actual psychotherapy. It's like attending a class that might involve learning more about relationships, parenting, managing children's behavior, and so on. This book is in part an attempt by me, at psychoeducation, in hopes that the information presented might help someone somewhere.

Although not typically seen as such, psychological evaluation and assessment can be viewed as another form of psychoeducation and may have its own therapeutic value or serve a therapeutic function. Learning about one's issues, strengths, weaknesses, and abilities can be a powerful intervention. Look up any number of quotes online and they'll be any number of people claiming that "information is power" or "knowledge is power." Information about ourselves and our relationships can help us make informed decisions about what to do, how to do it, what to change, and what not to change. I can tell you that a when a parent sees their child struggling academically, it is extremely helpful to understand he has a learning disorder. When a person is struggling at work, it can be extremely helpful to know what social skills or the lack thereof may be at play.

Skills training

Skills training overlaps with psychoeducation but has the extra feature of participants actually practicing what they are learning about. Examples of skills training programs are social skills training for people with social difficulties, anger management, emotional regulation skills training, and assertiveness training.

TIP

Where can someone find these different forms of help? Therapists and counselors can be found in nearly all communities. They can be found in private practice offices, private clinics, public and government clinics, university counseling centers, employee assistance programs, substance abuse treatments centers, hospitals, and even online!

There are lot of self-help resources out there. Self-help can mean a lot of things, but essentially it refers to any therapy, intervention, or behavior change activity that does not involve professional help, except indirectly through the writings, films, or other sources from professionals. I don't know how many self-help resources are out there because there are too many to count. I do know that the self-help section at the local bookstore is at least three to four times larger than the psychology section. (I think it's labeled "self-improvement" now.) Sources of self-help include books, workbooks, videos, films, podcasts, and seminars.

So are these resources going to put professional helpers out of business anytime soon? Maybe, because some of this stuff actually helps! Despite the criticisms, there is evidence that at least some of it can work. (Whew, that's good because I own a lot of self-help books!) If you are interested in finding out if that $25 investment in self-improvement is going to actually help, then check out colleague John Norcross's book, *Self-Help That Works: Resources to Improve Emotional Health and Strengthen Relationships* (Oxford University Press, 2013).

The Crown Jewel of Therapy: Psychotherapy

There may be no other activity more representative of the field of psychology than therapy, or more accurately, *psychotherapy*. I think when most people think of psychologists, they think of them as therapists. I've often wondered how many therapists' kids invite their parent to speak at career day at their school. "My mom is a therapist. She helps people, I think. She sits around with people, and they talk about their problems. Sometimes they cry, and sometimes they get mad." Yeah, that's basically it in a nutshell. Actually, there's way more to it than that, which I cover in the next few sections.

Remember the definition of therapy from John Norcross earlier in the chapter? It's pretty technical sounding, so I want to give you two others:

>> Lewis Wolberg, a prominent psychoanalyst from New York, defined psychotherapy as a form of treatment for emotional problems in which a trained professional establishes a relationship with a patient with the objective of relieving or removing symptoms, changing disturbed patterns of behavior, and promoting healthy personality development. The symptoms addressed are assumed to be psychological in nature.

>> J. B. Rotter of the University of Connecticut gives another good definition: "Psychotherapy . . . is planned activity of the psychologist, the purpose of which is to accomplish changes in the individual that make his life adjustment potentially happier, more constructive, or both."

I think a good conversation with friends over a pizza can promote a happier life, so what's all the fuss about? Psychotherapy is more than just a conversation between two people; it's a professional relationship in which one of the participants is an acknowledged healer, helper, or expert in psychological, interpersonal, or behavioral problems.

Good ethics is good therapy

To do any job well, there needs to be a set of rules or guidelines. Being good at therapy is no exception. The rules in this case are essentially the ethics of psychotherapy. They lay down the basic behaviors that a good therapist can or should engage in.

REMEMBER

Good therapy is ethical therapy. It may sound like an oversimplification but unethical therapy can't be good for you! There is some debate as to what ethical therapy is and isn't, but that is an advanced subject beyond the scope of this book.

In keeping it simple, I want to lay out what ethical therapy looks like. There are a lot of principles, and here are the highlights:

>> **Informed consent:** Except in some circumstances, participation in psychotherapy is voluntary. Essentially, therapists enter into an actual contract to do therapy with an individual and inform them of various important features of the therapy process and relationship. Then the client agrees to consent to the therapy based on this shared understanding. In family therapy, it can be a little different. If a therapist can get consent from everyone involved, great, but at the very least, they should get "assent," or the agreement by someone not of age or ability to consent. For example, it would be hard to get a 5-year-old to consent to family therapy.

>> **Confidentiality:** Therapists have a duty to protect the information gathered from and during therapy. This includes the appropriate storage of records. They cannot disclose a client's information without the permission to do so by the client. There are some exceptions to this rule, however, in cases of child abuse, elder abuse, or dependence adult abuse. And there is a duty to warn if an individual threatens to harm another person.

>> **Boundaries:** Psychotherapy never involves sex! Therapists will not have sex with their clients. They also do not engage in relationships with clients outside the professional relationship, such as business partners, friends, and so on. And they also do not engage in these relationships with another person closely associated with or related to the client.

>> **Competence and scope of practice:** Therapists must have the requisite training and education to engage in the type of therapy they are providing. If they have no experience or training with children, they should not be providing therapy to children unless there are no other options around, such as in areas with no or few therapists in general. If that is the case, they proceed with full consent of a guardian.

>> **Personal problems:** Psychotherapists should refrain from activities and behaviors that result in personal problems that would interfere with their work activities. If problems do occur (because they are human after all), they should seek consultation, get their own help, and limit what they do until they are ready to go again.

The common factors model

There are dozens of models/modalities of therapy, and there are definitely too many to cover in this chapter. Each of them has unique approaches to problems, mechanisms of change, what the therapists do and say, and what the role of the client may be. Research over the years, however, has identified some common or universal features of effective psychotherapy. These are the ingredients of effective therapy that cut across all modalities. Way back in 1936, psychologist and therapist Saul Rosenzweig began the discussion of these common factors, and research has continued ever since. Psychologist Bruce Wampold tells us that at the center of the common factors model is the *collaborative relationship* between the therapist and the client:

> . . . there is focus on the therapist, the client, the transaction between them, and the structure of the treatment . . .

The common factors found in the research can broken down into *client factors*, the *therapeutic relationship, therapist factors, contextual factors*, and *monitoring of treatment and outcomes.* We'll take a look at the two most significant factors from psychotherapy research: client factors and the therapeutic relationship.

TIP

For more on these and the other factors, check out the books *The Heart and Soul of Change: Delivering What Works in Therapy* (APA books, 2009) and *How and Why Are Some Therapists Better Than Others?* (APA books, 2017).

There is a clear finding from psychotherapy research that is summed up in the following statement by psychologists Arthur Bohart and Karen Tallman:

> Yet the fact is that clients' active involvement in the therapeutic process is critical to success.

Client factors

Therapy is more likely to work when a client's *self-righting* and *self-healing* capacities are emphasized and fostered. This sounds counterintuitive, but the basic notion is that people get "better" on their own and without professional therapy all the time by engaging in the same actions as a therapist without the help of a therapist. For example, a person with a social phobia might just work up the nerve to approach people little by little. This is akin to systematic desensitization therapy!

Bohart and Tallman list the following client factors that contribute to successful therapy:

>> **Client involvement and participation:** Clients are willing to engage in the tasks of psychotherapy and have cooperation with the therapist, making treatment a collaboration.

>> **Client perception of psychotherapy:** When clients view their therapist as high on empathy and more collaborative versus directive, therapy gets better. Also, it has been shown that clients enter therapy with their ideas as to what they need and use this as a filter or lens to what the therapist offers.

>> **Client agency, activity, reflexivity, and creativity:** It helps for clients to see themselves as agents of change, to value their own contributions to the therapy, and attribute their own efforts to success (as opposed to the therapist's efforts). Creativity in problem solving helps too. Coming up with their own ideas and solutions enhances the process.

The therapeutic relationship

Just in case you were thinking it's all on the client, psychotherapy research reminds us of the critical importance of the relationship between therapist and client. This is often referred to as the *therapeutic alliance*. Therapists' intent listening to clients, putting the client's experience before their own, asking for feedback on the relationship, avoiding being critical, and asking clients what they think is most helpful are all powerful factors.

It may be hard to imagine therapists acting any other way, but you'd be surprised. Imagine someone going to a therapist because his dog died and the therapist tells him that his marriage is the "real" problem. That may very well be the case, but the client came because his dog died. Sounds pretty invalidating, doesn't it? This is a true story, and no, I wasn't the therapist.

This is an example of *gaslighting,* and it is interesting contrast to the helpful approaches listed earlier. Essentially, a therapist gaslights their clients when they make them doubt themselves by suggest that their perceptions are inaccurate, that they don't "really know" what's going on, and that the therapist "knows" better. This is patronizing at best, manipulative and damaging at worst.

REMEMBER

Clients and therapists should have the same goals, reach consensus on how to get there and what to work on, and feel bonded in the process.

The therapeutic relationship is enhanced by *empathy.* Empathy is like a powerful glue for human connection. It can take a person from isolation to connection. It's a bridge. Carl Rogers, the famous psychologist, defines empathy as "the therapist's sensitive ability and willingness to understand clients' thoughts, feelings, and struggles from their point of view." Therapists should work to really understand their client and communicate their attempts to do so, even if they don't understand at a particular time. This doesn't mean that they "fake it"; it means that therapists should try to understand and show that they're striving and making an effort.

Some people imagine a therapist just sitting there, nodding, pen in hand, scribbling notes and saying, "Uh huh. Uh huh. Tell me more." That's fine and all, but research shows that therapists who provide feedback to their clients by pointing out their behavior and the effects of their behavior have a stronger therapeutic alliance.

Therapists can provide effective feedback by preparing the client to receive feedback (like "Can I give you some feedback?"), explaining the goal of the feedback, giving positive feedback along with negative feedback with support, and going at an appropriate pace. I had a therapy supervisor state it this way: "It's all about tact, dosage, and timing."

Major Schools of Therapy

As I state earlier in this chapter, there are a lot of therapies out there. James Prochaska and John Norcross, in their book *Systems of Psychotherapy – A Transtheoretical Approach,* 9th Edition (Oxford University Press, 2019), identify 15 different "schools" of therapy with various individual approaches under each category.

The main trend, it seems, is to get away from a "one size fits all" approach. Some "sizes fit all," like ethical therapy and common factors. But then the sizing needs a more custom fit. This requires that therapists become more flexible in their approaches to clients but also leads to specialization in doing therapy for specific problems. It's really about a good match.

Some therapists have a lot of tools in their tool chest for a lot of problems. Think of this therapist as a "master" of sorts (this therapy for that problem, that therapy for this problem). Some therapists may have fewer tools overall, but their focus is sharp and effective for a specific problem. Think of this therapist as a "specialist." There also a third option. Some therapists may have fewer tools or even one tool for a broad range of problems. Think of this as a "jack of all trades" approach. I realize that the "jack of all trades" label may have a negative connotation and that I may be suggesting that this is a therapist to avoid, but this assertion couldn't be more untrue. Such therapists may be extremely effective for a range of problems even though they may not be "masters" or "specialists." In fact, one could argue that "masters" don't really exist. A "master" of all disorders and all therapies is like a unicorn. We want them to be real, but nobody's found one yet. Most therapists are probably either "jacks" or "specialists" or somewhere in between.

In this section, I discuss therapies from some of the major schools of psychotherapy. Think of these as the tools for the broad-based "jack approach." These therapy approaches are used to address a wide range of problems, from depression, to anxiety, to relationship issues. Most people who see a therapist are going to see a "Cognitive Therapist" or an "Interpersonal Therapist" and not a "Therapist Specializing in Problem X." In that way, the practice of psychotherapy is different than the practice of medicine. Most psychotherapists have a "school" they ascribe to first and then they specialize. In medicine, the "school" is medicine itself and specialties are represented by specific problems or categories of problems focused on body systems, such as heart disease, endocrinology, or neurological diseases. Of course, there are specific therapies for specific problems that have been identified by research, but even these cluster under a major school or overall approach.

Psychodynamic therapies

Psychoanalyst Harry Stack-Sullivan introduced an *interpersonal* focus to Sigmund Freud's classic psychoanalysis in the 1920s that emphasized the real relationship dynamics between patient and analyst. Freud emphasized what was going on inside the patient's deep unconscious, but the interpersonally oriented analysts instead began to focus on what happens in the real relationship. This interpersonal approach has come to be known as *psychodynamic psychotherapy*. (For more on classic psychoanalysis, see the sidebar "Let's analyze it!")

Psychodynamic therapy is built on the foundations of *psychodynamic theory,* providing a theoretical basis for understanding a client's problems, issues, symptoms, and determining how to work with those.

Foundational to psychodynamic therapy is the existence of the *unconscious,* which is that part of our minds that lay outside of our awareness but nonetheless exerts control over our behavior. This is critical to the therapy because a therapist can help a client gain access to those unconscious thoughts, feelings, and memories in order to help them neutralize their influence on their behavior.

Another foundational theoretical concept is that human life is fraught with *conflict.* From conflict, psychological problems manifest as *symptoms,* which are defined as signs or indicators of the presence of an internal and unconscious conflict. Stress can lead to symptoms as events trigger unresolved conflicts from a person's early development or childhood. Certain events can also stimulate the use of *defense mechanisms,* or ways of coping that can also lead to problems (more on defense mechanism in a few).

There is a focus on childhood experiences and, according to Jacques Barber and Nili Solomonov, conflicts between balancing the needs and desires for dependence and independence. The *self* in relation to *others* (mom, dad, and so on) are critical players in this drama, and in therapy, there is a focus on this drama being played out between client and therapist known as *transference.* Transference occurs when a client begins to relate to the analyst in a way that's reflective of another (typically earlier) relationship. It's a distortion of the real relationship and interaction between the patient and analyst. In other words, we don't leave our relational baggage at the door; we bring it right in and play it out with the therapist.

These acted-out conflicts reveal all kinds of strategies that clients use to manage and cope. As I previously mentioned, these are known as defense mechanisms. It is important to point out that defense mechanisms are not in and of themselves "bad" or maladaptive. Some start out as natural and creative attempts to deal with life's conflicts. However, they can become entrenched and their use rigid and over generalized, and that's a problem. Some defenses are more problematic from the start and lead to dysfunction almost immediately.

Generally, defense mechanism are broken into essentially two categories: *primary* and *secondary.* Primary defenses are considered more pathological and "primitive" in nature and are reflective of conflict that occurred more early in a client's life and are more problematic. Secondary defenses are more "mature" and aren't necessarily problematic unless the client is rigid in their use. Here is a short list of primary and secondary defensive processes:

Primary:

>> **Extreme withdrawal:** Pulling way from the outside world, shutting it out, and oftentimes retreating into fantasy.

>> **Projection:** Attributing thoughts, wishes, fears, and so forth onto another person. Clients "project" what is going on inside their own minds. This leads others to feel misperceived and can result in a lot of conflict. Some theorists propose that extreme projection can lead to paranoia, where extreme aggression within oneself is projected onto another, and the other person is seen as extremely hostile.

>> **Acting out:** Enacting or behaving with the direct expression of an unconscious impulse or desire without having to consciously acknowledge feeling a particular way.

Secondary:

>> **Regression:** This is state of a psychological return to an earlier stage of development. When clients regress, they act younger, often childish. Temper tantrums, ignoring reality, and living in a fantasy world are examples of regression. Do you stick your fingers in your ears and repeat "La la la la la la" so that you can't hear someone talk? Regression!

>> **Repression:** This involves keeping impulses and desires out of your awareness so that you don't act on them and they don't destroy your life. Repression requires a great deal of mental energy.

>> **Rationalization:** I didn't like her anyway! Oh, you mean she rejected you. When something negative happens or we do something we regret, we may explain it away by minimizing its effect on us.

We're in conflict. We aren't aware of it. We're acting in problematic ways, with dysfunctional thinking and feeling. We are "defensive." Our relationships are the stages for this drama. Now what? Psychodynamic therapists are not intimidated by any of this. They dive right in and get to work. How? Jonathan Shedler of the University of Colorado Denver School of Medicine breaks it down very clearly. He summarizes the mechanisms and techniques of psychodynamic therapy into seven steps:

1. **Focus on affect and expression of emotions.** Therapists help clients get in touch with their emotions and express them, particularly the painful or aversive ones.

2. **Exploration of attempts to avoid distressing thoughts and feelings.** Clients are encouraged and helped in not avoiding or escaping these emotions and not to engage in defensive maneuvers when they come up.

3. **Identification of recurring themes and patterns.** Clients and therapists explore thoughts, feelings, behaviors, and relationship patterns that seem to come up over and over again without resolution.

4. **Discussion of past experience (developmental focus).** Nobody can escape their childhood! Not according to psychodynamic therapists. This aspect of the therapy is designed to help the client see the connection to early life experiences and their current thoughts, feelings, behavior, and relationships.

5. **Focus on interpersonal relations.** Therapists assist clients in focusing on their current relationships and how they can be improved through the therapy process and engagement in Steps 1 through 4.

6. **Focus on therapy relationship.** Clients are engaged in a real-time, real-life relationship with the therapist that serves as a space for reenacting and enacting old themes, patterns, and defensive maneuvers.

7. **Exploration of fantasy life.** Therapists encourage clients to let their minds "roam free" in a manner of speaking. Clients think aloud and aren't expected to edit. This facilitates self-reflection, which serves as the basis for growth and positive development.

REMEMBER

Ultimately, psychodynamic therapy's goals are to reduce symptoms but also to foster a client's capacity for a more full life, better relationships, experience a wider range of emotions, and be better at facing life's challenges. Sounds pretty good actually.

LET'S ANALYZE IT!

No discussion of therapy would be complete without discussing the *couch*. The image of a patient lying on the couch is one of the most popular images of therapy. I actually own a psychoanalysis couch, but it's in storage and I don't have it in my office. The use of the couch is in fact how therapy was done when Freud was practicing *classic psychoanalysis*. In this well-known scene, the analyst sits upright in a chair, out of the patient's line of sight, for technical reasons related to the task and goals of the therapy itself. The client talks. They're doing psychoanalysis! Not really, but kind of.

The problem is, almost nobody does this anymore. In fact, almost nobody practices classic psychoanalysis anymore! Classic psychoanalytic theory is still around, but it has mostly been transformed over the years and is now more of a foundation for newer theories and therapy models. It may have all started with Freud and classic psychoanalysis, and we should thank him for that. But it became time to move on from our primitive attachment to this form of therapy a long time ago, and it should now be left to the historians.

Behavior therapy

Behavior therapy emphasizes the current conditions that maintain a behavior, the conditions that keep it going. This form of therapy focuses on the problem, not on the person. A psychology professor who I once had, Elizabeth Klonoff, likened behavior therapy to a weed-pulling process. She stated that psychoanalysts attempt to pull the weed up by its roots so that it'll never come back, but behavior therapists pluck the weed from the top, and if it grows back, they pluck it again. Of course, this makes behavior therapy sound more inefficient than it actually is. The idea is that in behavior therapy, the developmental or childhood origins of a problem are not necessarily as important as the conditions that keep it going. In that sense, if you change the maintaining conditions of a behavior, then you have in essence "uprooted it," as long as those conditions don't recur. For example, who cares how you started smoking? The important part is the factors that keep you smoking.

Behavior therapy treats abnormal behavior as *learned* behavior, and anything that's been learned can be unlearned. A key feature of behavior therapy is the notion that environmental conditions and circumstances can be explored and manipulated to change a person's behavior without having to dig around their mind or psyche and evoke psychological or mental explanations for their issues.

The simplicity of the behavioral approach to psychological problems is made possible with an equally simplified (but not easy) set of practices. Behavior therapists put a lot of emphasis on the scientific method and its focus on observable changes and measurement. The therapy techniques and activities are well planned out, highly structured, and systematic. The therapist is viewed less as a holder of some divine truth and more as a collaborative partner in the behavior-change process. The patient is expected to pull his own weight outside of therapy, as well as in the therapy session itself, by completing homework assignments designed to change behavior in the real world and to further the progress made during each session.

Behavior therapists begin by conducting a thorough assessment of the patient's problem. Here's a simple outline of the basic steps of *behavioral assessment:*

1. Identify the target behavior.

Step one involves taking a thorough look at the problem the patient originally presents to the therapist. Behavior therapists use a special technique called an *ABC analysis* to analyze the initial problem. The ABC analysis is an evaluation of the events that happen before, during, and after a *target behavior* (the patient's problem behavior).

A. stands for the *antecedents* of a particular behavior, the things or events that happen just prior to the target behavior, including time, place, people involved, circumstances.

B. stands for behavior, as in the target behavior. In the case of the bickering couple, the target behavior is the act of arguing, itself.

C. stands for the *consequences* of the behavior, or the events and general circumstances that occur after and are a direct result of *B*. In the case of the arguing couple, the *Cs* may be that both individuals get mad and stomp off, the man goes out for a drive, or the woman leaves the house to take a long walk.

2. **Identify the present maintaining conditions.**

Spiegler and Guevremont define the *present maintaining conditions* as those circumstances that contribute to the perpetuation of the behavior. They identify two specific sources:

- **Environment:** Conditions from the environment include time, setting, reactions from others, and any other external circumstances. This would be the who, what, when, where, and how of our arguing couple.

- **Patient's own behavior:** The patient's contribution includes his or her thoughts, feelings, and actions. This would be what each partner is thinking, feeling, and doing before, during, and after the arguments.

3. **Establish the specific goals of therapy in explicit terms.**

The original therapy goal may be to stop arguing. However, this description is a little too vague for a behavior therapist's liking. A more precise measure of the target behavior may consist of identifying specific numbers, occurrences, or lengths of time of the arguments. So, instead of the couple simply trying to stop fighting, a more fitting target behavior is to reduce their fighting to once a week.

Exposure-based therapies

There are several different types of therapy known as *exposure-based therapies* that involve "exposing" a target behavior to new conditions in order to reduce its occurrence. *Exposure* is another word for reassociating or relearning a target behavior with another behavior that results in the cessation of the target behavior.

One of the most popular forms of exposure therapies is *systematic desensitization (SD)*. SD is most commonly used to treat phobias, like fear of public speaking, social phobia, or some other specific phobia. Therapists have also used it to successfully treat panic disorder accompanied by agoraphobia. There are several types of exposure-based therapies based on the systematic desensitization principle:

>> **Covert sensitization (imaginal exposure):** The "learning" or associating is only occurring in the patient's mind and not in real life. The procedures that

Wolpe and Jacobsen developed are very similar. Therapists teach patients how to enter a state of deep relaxation. Then they ask the patients to imagine themselves in the fear-producing, phobic situation, while maintaining their state of relaxation. When a patient's anxiety level gets too high, the therapist asks the patient to let go of the image and continue to just relax.

When this process is repeated over and over again for several sessions, the fear response to the situation is diminished because the state of relaxation is competing with the original fear of the situation or object. Instead of fear, the patient now associates relaxation with the fear-inducing situation or phobic object.

>> **Graduated-exposure therapy:** When a patient learns to perform his feared behavior in a real-life situation, he or she is engaging in *in vivo sensitization*. Usually, this form of desensitization is done gradually, hence its name. If I'm afraid of flying, my therapist may start with me watching movies about flying (of course these should be movies about flying that don't include a crash or some kind of airline disaster). Then I'd go to the airport; then I'd sit in the terminal; then go on an airplane. There's a gradual move toward the eventual goal of flying, but not until I've done a lot of preparatory work and discovered how to relax during subsequent stages.

Cognitive therapy

The power of thought should never be underestimated. *Cognitive therapy* is a popular and well-researched form of psychotherapy that emphasizes the power of thought. From the perspective of cognitive therapists, psychological problems such as interpersonal difficulties and emotional disorders are the direct result of maladaptive thought processes or distorted thinking. Maladaptive thinking can go something like this:

A (losing my job) → **B** (my thoughts about getting fired) → **C** (my emotions and subsequent and more exaggerated thought processes about the event)

Sometimes thinking can be biased or distorted, and this can get people into trouble. Cognitive therapy approaches reality from a relativistic perspective: An individual's reality is the byproduct of how he or she perceives it and thinks about it. However, cognitive therapists don't view psychopathology as simply a consequence of thinking. Instead, it's the result of a certain kind of thinking. Specific errors in thinking produce specific problems.

Aaron Beck, considered to be one of the "inventors" of cognitive therapy (along with Albert Ellis), identified some specific cognitive distortions that lead to psychological problems:

- **Arbitrary inference:** This distortion occurs when someone draws a conclusion based on incomplete or inaccurate information.

- **Catastrophizing:** My grandmother used to refer to this distortion as "making a mountain out of a molehill." Beck defined it as seeing something as more significant than it actually is.

- **Dichotomous thinking:** Thinking only in terms of black and white, without considering the gray areas, can get us into trouble.

- **Overgeneralization:** When someone takes one experience or rule and applies it across the board to a larger, unrelated set of circumstances.

- **Personalization:** When someone thinks an event is related to him or her when it actually isn't.

REMEMBER

The theory underlying cognitive therapy is beautiful in its simplicity. If psychological problems are the products of errors in thinking, therapy should seek to correct that thinking. This is sometimes easier said than done. Fortunately, cognitive therapists have a wide range of techniques and a highly systematic approach at their disposal.

The goal of cognitive therapy is to change biased thinking through logical analysis and behavioral experiments designed to test dysfunctional beliefs. Many thinking errors consist of faulty assumptions about oneself, the world, and others. Cognitive therapy usually goes something like this:

1. **The therapist and patient perform a thorough assessment of the patient's faulty beliefs and assumptions and how these thoughts connect to specific dysfunctional behaviors and emotions.**

TIP

Christine Padesky and Dennis Greenberger, in their book *Mind Over Mood* (Guilford Press, 1995), provide the patient with a system for identifying these thinking errors, which cognitive psychologists commonly call *automatic thoughts* — thoughts that occur automatically as a reaction to a particular situation. The patient is asked to keep track of specific situations that occur between therapy sessions and to identify and describe in detail his reactions to those situations.

2. **The therapist and patient work together, using the automatic thought record, to identify the cognitive distortions mediating between the situations and the patient's reactions.**

This often-difficult process can take anywhere from several weeks to several months, but at the end of the process, the distortions have been thoroughly identified.

3. **The therapist and patient work collaboratively to alter the distorted beliefs.**

The therapist and patient collaborate in a process of logical refutation, questioning, challenging, and testing of these faulty conclusions and premises. This effort attempts to make the patient a better thinker and break him of the habit of poor information processing.

Playing together nicely: Behavior and cognitive therapies

Albert Ellis was the founder of a combined form of therapy that borrows from both behavior therapy and cognitive therapy. *Rational emotive behavior therapy*, or REBT, is built on the premise that psychological problems are the result of irrational thinking and behavior that supports that irrational thinking; therefore, they can be addressed by increasing a patient's ability to think more rationally and behave in ways that support more rational thought.

REMEMBER

Ellis is a charismatic psychologist whose style and personality accentuate the main ideas of REBT. Rational emotive behavior therapists believe that most of our problems are self-generated, and that people upset themselves by clinging to irrational ideas that don't hold up under scrutiny. The trouble lies in the fact that many people don't scrutinize their thoughts very often. People make irrational statements to themselves on a regular basis:

"I can't stand it!"

"This is just too awful!"

"I'm worthless because I can't handle this!"

These are examples of irrational thinking. Rational emotive behavior therapists define these statements as irrational because they argue that people can actually handle or "stand" negative events. These events are rarely, if ever, as bad as people think they are. Also, people often hold themselves to rules of "should" that increase their guilt for being overwhelmed, sad, anxious, and so on. "I shouldn't get angry." "I shouldn't care what she thinks." "I shouldn't worry about it." Ellis used to call this "shoulding all over yourself." REBT therapists vigorously challenge statements like these.

REMEMBER

The challenging posture of REBT should not be taken as harsh or uncaring. REBT emphasizes the same levels of empathy and unconditional acceptance as many other therapies. REBT therapists are not necessarily trying to talk patients out of feeling the way that they feel. They're trying to help patients experience their emotions in a more attenuated and manageable fashion. There are healthy levels of emotion, and then there are irrational levels of emotion. The goal of therapy is to help the patient learn how to experience her emotions and other situations in this more rational manner.

The behavior-therapy aspects of REBT involve the patient engaging in experiments designed to test the rationality or irrationality of his beliefs. A therapist may ask a patient who is deathly afraid of talking to strangers to approach ten strangers a week and strike up a conversation. If the patient originally thought that he was going to die from embarrassment, the therapist may begin their next session with, "Nice to see you. I guess talking to strangers didn't kill you after all, did it?"

REBT takes the position that two approaches can bring about changes in thinking: talking with a therapist and rationally disputing irrational ideas, and engaging in behaviors that "prove" irrational ideas wrong. Ellis states that people rarely change their irrational thinking without acting against it. Their thinking won't change unless their behavior changes.

Acceptance and mindfulness-based therapies

Therapy is certainly about change. Change your behavior. Change your thinking. Behavior and cognitive therapies are consistent with this notion. But change is hard, right? I've failed at change, and I'm pretty certain you know somebody who has as well. Change is a multibillion dollar industry. Just peruse the "Self-Help" section of the local bookstore. But what do you do with all this failure to change? How can you change your failure to change? This is exhausting to write about let alone live with.

Luckily, a group of therapies classified broadly as "acceptance and mindfulness-based" therapies have been developed that put the issue of change front and center. At the core of these therapies is the concept of *acceptance*, defined within the therapies as helping patients stop struggling with the change process and helping them experience their lives, emotions, thoughts, and behavior in a direct, non-judgmental, open-minded, and accepting manner. Two well-researched and popular forms of acceptance- and mindfulness-based therapies are *ACT (acceptance and commitment therapy)* and *MBCT (mindfulness-based cognitive therapy)*.

According to these therapies, a patient's lack of acceptance of his life, emotions, history, and so on is part of the problem; it is part of the pathology for which he visited a therapist in the first place. Rather than change behavior (as in behavior modification) or thoughts (as with cognitive therapy), there is an emphasis on changing the way a patient approaches his behavior and thoughts. A patient is changing the way he views and interacts with his issues, history, and problems. It's kind of like stepping back, or stepping away, for a different and nonjudgmental perspective.

The *mindfulness* component involves being aware of the real and present moment and staying open to the ongoing thoughts, sensations, and feelings without trying to change, alter, or modify them. Facing these things with acceptance and mindfulness is therapeutic.

But it isn't all about acceptance. A key decision point for therapists is whether and when to help patients accept or change at any given point or with any given situation. This decision is based on evaluating situations or circumstances using two criteria: changeability and justifiability.

>> **Is the situation changeable?** If something is not changeable, such as the death of a loved one, then focusing on changing that situation would not lead to psychological health. If a situation is changeable, such as whether or not you can stop drinking soda, then it should be a focus of change. Change what can be changed, accept what cannot. Can anyone say *Serenity Prayer*?

>> **Is the reaction justifiable?** The "justifiable" aspect of a patient's thinking, emotions, or behavior involves an analysis of whether or not a patient's reactions are in proportion to and related to an actual event or situation or if they are out of line or overreactions. If a reaction is not justified, then solving the problem that triggered the reaction doesn't make sense because there was no real problem to solve, just an overreaction. If the situation or circumstance is changeable, then change it; if not, then adopt an accepting attitude toward it. If your reaction is justifiable, then accept your reaction or change your reaction. If it is not a justifiable reaction, then just accept the reaction, non-judgmentally and mindfully.

Dialectical behavior therapy

Dialectical behavior therapy, the brainchild of Dr. Marsha Linehan, is a therapy approach that combines the behavioral, cognitive, and mindfulness approaches. DBT was originally developed for individuals diagnosed with borderline personality disorder who were engaging in self-injurious behavior (such as cutting themselves) and who were at high risk for suicide. Since its inception, however, DBT has been used with a much wider range of problems and patients and is considered one of the most well researched and empirically based therapies in clinical psychology.

DBT is considered a very comprehensive intervention that includes individual therapy and a range of consultative approaches to a client's problems and skill-building approaches (such as social skills training). In many of its behavior and cognitive approaches, it's not necessarily all that unique from other behavior and cognitive approaches. One aspect that certainly sets DBT apart, however, is the inclusion and centrality of acceptance and mindfulness components.

A key acceptance and mindfulness feature of DBT is found in the name of the therapy itself, *Dialectic*. Dialectic refers to the broad concept that reality is interconnected, made up of opposing forces and forms, and dynamic and constantly changing. A dialectic view of things would hold that something can be two seemingly contradictory things or in two contradictory states at the same time. A patient can both want to change and not want to change at the same time. The central dialectic in DBT is focused on the opposing forces of acceptance and change. Patients are taught how to change and are expected to change but are also taught how to and are expected to work on acceptance of themselves, their past, and the world.

DBT respects and responds to the all-too-often reality that people coming to therapy can feel pushed too hard to change and as a result will drop out of therapy early. Focusing too much on change may be emotionally overwhelming, feel invalidating, or even feel shaming. It is critical to strike a balance between acceptance and change. This balance is sought and achieved with a variety of techniques including training in mindfulness. Dr. Linehan outlines the following key components of mindfulness:

>> **Observing:** Simply experiencing the present moment, thoughts, emotions, bodily sensations, and so on

>> **Describing:** Describing the present moment without judgment

>> **Participating:** Throwing oneself into an activity without self-consciousness

DBT mindfulness involves paying attention to the current, moment-by-moment reality and in a non-reactive manner, responding to the facts rather than the patient's own thoughts, emotions, or other reactions. This engenders acceptance, facilitates effective problem solving, and reduces avoidance. The patient has to be willing not to resist reality and to resist engaging in "as if" or "it shouldn't be this way" thinking, or insisting something is true or real when in fact it is not. This willingness then facilitates more effective problem solving and reduces reactivity over time.

Client-centered therapy

Take a minute to do a little exercise. Get a piece of paper and a pen and make a list of all the people you admire and hold in a positive light. Who's on the list — teachers, spouses, celebrities, parents? What about yourself? Are you on your list of people you positively regard? Would you be a member of your own fan club?

In this big, chaotic world of billions of people, sometimes it seems like I don't matter, like my individual identity is so small, so insignificant. Yet I walk around with the sense of being an individual. Sometimes I feel so independent that I actually feel lonely and isolated, like no one cares about me. "What about me? Don't I matter?"

Carl Rogers cared. Rogers (1902–1987) is perhaps one of the most famous psychologists of all time, nominated for the Nobel Peace Prize and considered on par with Sigmund Freud. His influence on psychotherapy has been profound. He put the person back into the process, attempting to understand and value each of his patients as unique individuals with real problems and not just as abstract theories and models. You can say one thing for sure about Carl Rogers's *client-centered therapy* — it placed great value on the *humanness* of each and every patient. Rogers believed that all humans inherently strive toward the fullest development of their capacity to maintain an optimal level of survival. It's kind of like the U.S. Army slogan, "Be all you can be."

Growth is a big buzzword for client-centered therapists. A patient's personal growth is foremost in the therapist's mind and central to the therapy process. Every time I read something from a client-centered perspective or something that Carl Rogers wrote, I start reflecting and asking myself, "Am I growing?" If you count my waistline, the answer is definitely yes. As far as that personal growth and expanding abilities stuff . . .

What does Carl Rogers's belief in the inherent worth of each of his patients have to do with helping them get better? Are client-centered therapy patients paying for someone to like them, to value them? Maybe, but that would be a gross oversimplification. It's more than an "I'll love you until you can love yourself" therapy or "I'll accept you until you can accept yourself."

REMEMBER

The healing or helping mechanism in client-centered therapy is found in the process of the therapist working to understand the patient's unique experiences, thoughts, behaviors, and feelings. As the therapist strives to understand where the patient is coming from, the patient learns to experience herself in a new, and more productive, life-enhancing way.

Understanding theory of the person

Why would Carl Rogers think that making a genuine connection with his patient and really trying to understand what it's like to be that particular individual has a helping or healing effect? The answer to that question may seem obvious: All of us like to feel understood. (See Chapter 10 for more on the importance of relationships.) Having people get what you're about seems to give you a sense of well-being, a feeling of being more alive and present against the backdrop of a dark and uncaring world.

WANTING TO BE UNDERSTOOD

Although he's not considered a client-centered therapist, Eric Fromm introduced a concept that attempts to explain why being understood is so important to everyone. Fromm believed that people all make constant attempts to check their perceptions and experiences against the perceptions and experiences of others, particularly people whose opinion is of value. You may have heard of the concept of a *reality check* — like asking someone if she just saw the UFO land in the field next to the highway. "Did you just see what I just saw?" If the other person saw it too, you experience something Fromm called *validation*. Validation is the experience of having someone concur or support your experience of reality. Validation brings a sense of presence; it makes you feel like you *exist*. According to Fromm, without validation, people would feel as if they didn't exist.

Have you ever talked to someone when she wasn't getting what you were trying to say, like she didn't understand you? This type of experience can feel pretty bad. In situations like this and many others, you can feel disconnected and, in extreme cases, isolated.

Why is being understood or understanding others so difficult at times? Rogers believed that each and every person has a unique frame of reference from which he experiences the world. Think about it. Someone else in this world may look just like you, have the same name, and be exactly like you in almost every other way. Biologically, identical twins even share the same genetic code. But even identical twins are not exactly alike. They are, in fact, two separate people.

I like to look at it this way: No other person can occupy the same physical space that I occupy at the same time I occupy it. And they can't occupy the same mental space either! In the abstract, people can "walk a mile in my shoes," but in the literal sense, only when I'm not wearing them.

DEVELOPING A SENSE OF SELF

You're unique! Our individual experience is specifically separate from others', and as you differentiate your experience from the experiences of others, you begin to develop a sense of self, a sense of who you are. A sense of self depends first, however, on how other people see you and relate to you. As children, experience is intertwined and merged with the experiences of parents, families, and caregivers. They serve as an experiential guide of sorts, providing the first models of understanding and experience in the world. Later, you begin to differentiate your experience from the experiences of others.

REMEMBER

This *experience-differentiation process* is only possible, however, within an environment of positive regard and support from those around you. If I see a UFO, and the other person doesn't, he may still support me in my experience by saying that he doesn't see the UFO, but that doesn't mean I didn't see it. If he wasn't supportive, he may say, "You're crazy! You don't see a UFO!" More realistically, I've often witnessed a young child who gets hurt or upset and goes to a parent for comfort only to have the parent say, "You're not hurt. You're okay." This situation is the opposite of validation; it's an *invalidating* experience. The child may get confused, thinking, "I feel hurt, but Daddy says I'm not. Am I really hurt or not?" Pretty confusing stuff for a kid.

Dealing with differences in self-perception

Rogers called the experience of oneself, as it depends on the views of others, the *conditions of worth*. As long as people continue to meet the conditions of worth set up by others, they'll do fine. But when they don't receive unconditional acceptance, they can get into trouble and experience distress. They may then start seeking the *conditional acceptance* of others because they've yet to experience their own *unconditional acceptance*.

When seeking conditional acceptance, a person lives a lie of sorts, adopting a confusing and undifferentiated experiential approach to living. If her experiences are different than the experiences of those around her, she may distort her own thinking, feelings, or behavior in order to be in line with those of others. She may walk around with a belief that, if she thinks, feels, and behaves in accordance with the people around her, she'll get the positive regard she is longing for.

Even if people don't receive unconditional acceptance, they still have this underlying sense of individuality and uniqueness. When there's a disconnection or inconsistency between your experience of yourself and your experience of yourself as you distort it to be in line with others' views, you're *incongruent*. This involves having two views of yourself: how you actually are, and how you think others think you are. Rogers believed that what lies at the core of psychological maladjustment is the incongruity between your total experience and your distorted self-concept. This incongruity leads to feeling estranged, disconnected, and not whole. You're then only living out part of your full being and therefore not fulfilling your basic need to experience, enhance, and expand your being.

As a person travels along this compromised path, he may use different defense mechanisms to keep up the act. He may selectively process information about himself, others, and the world so as not to overturn the apple cart of reality. For example, a lot of families have a "black-sheep" member who stands out. At times, this person may deliberately do something that goes against the grain in order to stay in line with his family-derived self and the image that everyone has of him. Sometimes, he can stick to this plan in such a rigid manner that he may actually lose touch with reality.

Reconnecting in therapy

One of the main goals of client-centered therapy is to help the patient reintegrate different versions of the self: how the patient sees himself and how he thinks others see him. At the center of this process is perhaps Rogers's most important contribution to psychotherapy — *unconditional positive regard.* This involves accepting the patient as a person without judging his experiences, feelings, thoughts, or behaviors in a moral sense. The therapist does not want to repeat the invalidating experience that the patient probably went through growing up or continues to go through.

Client-centered therapists engage in what Rogers called *reflection* — communicating to the patient that they hear what the patient is saying and that they're trying to understand where the patient's coming from. Rogers emphasized *accurate empathy.* Therapists who adopt this concept stay away from imposing their own understandings and structures on the patient's experience. This helps patients begin to see how they've distorted their own experiences without introducing any new distortions in relation to the therapist's expectations.

The therapist *reflects* you back to yourself by being attentive and describing to you the self that you're presenting to him. During this process, your self-awareness increases, and you start to see yourself in a way that you've never been able to before. The client-centered therapist is kind of like a mirror or a *self-amplifier.*

REMEMBER

Another huge contribution Rogers made to psychotherapy was the introduction of his six *necessary and sufficient conditions* that must be in place for therapy to be helpful:

>> A professional, respectful, and accepting relationship formed between the client and therapist.

>> A patient's willingness to be vulnerable and to experience strong feelings, such as anxiety, and the therapist's ability to motivate the patient to seek and stay involved in the therapy relationship.

>> Genuineness: The client is expected to be "freely and deeply" himself, not distorting how he feels or what he thinks.

>> Unconditional positive regard.

>> Accurate empathy.

>> Perception of genuineness: The therapist has to be a real person (with feelings, thoughts, and behaviors of his own), not just a person playing a role, acting, or pretending for the sake of the client.

Rogerian, or client-centered, therapy has been around in one form or another for about 60 years now. The ultimate question for any form of psychotherapy, psychological intervention, or medication is whether it works or not. Research into the effectiveness of client-centered therapy has typically investigated the specific "necessary and sufficient" conditions.

Most studies, including one conducted by Beutler, Crago, and Arezmendi, have shown that three of the six conditions, empathy, genuineness, and prizing (unconditional positive regard), are valuable but not necessary or sufficient (on their own) to bring about therapeutic change. That is, a therapist doesn't have to possess or do these things in order to be helpful. Orlinsky and Howard, however, found that warmth, empathy, and genuineness facilitate the therapy process. In other words, therapy may go a little better if the therapist creates these conditions. It doesn't seem to hurt, so why not?

Emotion-focused therapy

Can an emotion be unbearable? Can it cause problems in someone's life? What about not having "any" emotions, sometimes referred to as *alexithymia*, which according to the *APA Dictionary of Psychology* is "an inability to express, describe, or distinguish among one's emotions." I can't tell how often the concept or notion of "emotional regulation" comes up in my clinical work. Parents, clients, and other professional are constantly evoking the idea that if the identified client (the person everyone is looking to help, change, or get along with better) was better at "regulating" their emotions, they would benefit as would those around him or her.

But whether we like them or not or acknowledge them or not, emotions are critical, and psychologist Leslie Greenberg developed a model of psychotherapy called *emotion-focused therapy (EFT)* to help people "use" their emotions to improve their lives. EFT represents an excellent example of how the application of psychological science and methodology can lead to better therapy. By intensely studying therapy sessions in fine detail, through a process known as *task analysis,* Dr. Greenberg investigated what actually happens during therapy sessions to improve outcome for clients.

EFT is built on the foundation that emotions are what motivates us to do what we do. They are adaptive and help guide us toward what is good for us and not good for us. Emotions tell us that if we're sad, for example, then we have lost someone or something (like a job). Dr. Rhonda Goldman states, ". . . emotions act as a kind of compass, guiding people as to what is important and what needs are being met or not."

EFT holds that every emotion reflects a need and being aware of our emotions is being aware of our needs. That's kind of important. Emotions guide or drive our mental processes and behavior. Clients get into trouble when they are not aware of or ignore emotions because this means they are not aware or ignoring their actual needs.

EFT helps people change their emotional processes. Does that mean that when someone feels sad they should "change" that sadness into happiness, like, "Hey, put a smile on that sad face"? Not at all. EFT therapists help clients change how they process and use emotion in the service of better living. Dr. Greenberg states that the goals of EFT are to engage in a collaborative relationship that helps clients ". . . better identify, experience, accept, tolerate, regulate, explore, make sense of, transform, and flexibly manage their emotions. As a result, clients will become more skilled in experience emotion and . . . live vitally and adaptively." This is the exact definition of that emotion regulation stuff parents, clients, and other professionals are always talking about.

Therapists working with the EFT approach help clients learn when to *activate* and when to *regulate* their emotions. Emotions should be activated if clients are avoiding them, disavowing their emotional experience, engaging in dysfunction behavior because of this lack of awareness or disavowal, and inhibiting appropriate adaptive behavior. Emotions should be regulated when they overwhelm, don't lead to adaptive behavior, interfere with functioning, and confuse the client. They should also be regulated (or down-regulated really) when they lead to aggression and maladaptive coping such as drug use, overeating, and self-harm.

REMEMBER

EFT has been found to be effective for a wide range of problems and fits nicely into the "jack of all trades" category of psychotherapy models. It has been found to be helpful with depression, anxiety, and couple difficulties. It has also been integrated into many other schools, including psychodynamic therapy, cognitive-behavioral therapy, and other humanistic therapies.

Empirically Supported Treatments for Specific Problems

The debate between "one size fits all" and specific approaches for specific problems is reflected in the literature. Some articles and books talk about "effective therapies for problem X," and some literature covers "evidenced-based practices with therapy Y." It can be very confusing. How does one know or pick? Fortunately, researchers have been asking these same questions and have come up with a way of determining if a therapy is effective. It's known as the *empirically supported treatments/therapies* model (ESTs).

It is critical to point out however that the ESTs designation is not assigned to schools of therapy like the ones discussed previously in the chapter. The ESTs label is assigned to specific therapy approaches for specific problems. Again, compare it to medicine. Of course, one thinks of medical treatment as a whole as generally effective, at least when compared to no medical treatment. Analogously, we can say that psychotherapy is effective. But medical research goes on to say that "treatment X" is effective for "condition Y." Similarly, the ESTs approach to psychotherapy is stating that "psychotherapy alpha" is effective for "condition/problem/diagnosis beta."

According to psychologist John Sakaluk and colleagues, therapies that fall under the ESTs category are considered to be the best of the best. They work. They are "clinically efficacious."

But I have to give a little disclaimer: The following lists are not meant to be comprehensive, and just because a treatment is not listed here does not mean it is not effective. There are just too many to cover, so I thought I'd give you a little appetizer before you go off and eat a full meal of the ESTs research and literature. Bon appétit!

ESTs for depression

>> **Interpersonal psychotherapy for depression:** Therapists help clients in improving their relationships' contributions to their current depression.

>> **Behavioral activation for depression:** Therapists help clients engage in more rewarding experiences, reduce isolation, and recognize and persist in experiences they would normally avoid.

>> **Cognitive therapy for depression:** Therapists help clients develop more accurate and helpful beliefs with regards to depressive thinking and behavior.

>> **Acceptance and commitment therapy for depression:** Therapists help clients learn to accept thoughts, feelings, memories they have avoided and teach psychological flexibility in striving for their valued goals.

>> **Emotion-focused therapy for depression:** Clients learn to be more aware of, regulate, and use their emotions in more adaptive ways.

ESTs for anxiety and trauma

>> **Exposure therapy for specific phobias:** Clients are gradually exposed, little by little, to fear-inducing stimuli while utilizing adaptive coping mechanisms until they no longer avoid those stimuli.

>> **Eye movement desensitization and reprocessing for PTSD:** Therapists use a combination of eye movements or alternating bilateral physical stimulation (such as a vibrating pad in one's hand) and a cognitive processing approach to help clients more fully process traumatic memories and experiences.

ESTs for disorders in children

>> **Cognitive-behavioral training program for parents of children with ADHD:** Using a behavioral management approach, parents are trained to use positive reinforcement for non-ADHD positive behaviors and to not reinforce behaviors they wish to reduce or eliminate.

>> **Parent-child interaction therapy for oppositional children:** Parents are trained to reduce in themselves behavior that "triggers" a child and to engage their child in a more effective manner of interacting and relating.

>> **Applied behavior analysis for autism spectrum disorders:** Children are taught a wide range of developmental skills using the principles of operant conditioning such as positive reinforcement as well as those principles being used to reduce negative behavior such as aggression and self-injury.

>> **Pivotal response interventions for children with autism:** Operant conditioning is used to teach children "pivotal" skills such as motivation and social initiations with the use of naturalistic positive reinforcers.

Chapter **18**

Be Positive! Fostering Wellness, Growth, and Strength

t's not all doom and gloom when it comes to psychology. In fact, that's quite a misperception. As should be pretty apparent by now, psychological science has a lot more to offer than just diagnoses and digging into people's troubled psyches. We study brains, development, thinking, relationships, and so on — all the topics covered from Chapter 1 to Chapter 17. But we aren't done yet. Psychologists are working hard to research and apply findings to the areas of health and performance.

In this chapter, we explore the psychological sciences of health behavior, positive psychology, and optimal performance.

Going beyond Stress: The Psychology of Health

Psychologists don't stop at the intersection of stress, disease, and coping. They're also attempting to apply what they know about human behavior and mental processes to the problems of health in general. They're looking for ways to keep people physically well and trying to find out how people's behavior contributes to illness. Psychology researchers work in the field of *health psychology*, the psychological study of health and illness.

Health psychologists work in many types of settings, ranging from universities (conducting research) to clinics and hospitals, which involve the direct care of patients. Their main activities include preventing illness, helping people and families cope with illness, and developing programs for health-related behavior change and maintaining a healthy lifestyle.

Preventing illness

Health psychologists engage in three types of illness prevention:

>> **Primary:** Preventing an illness from occurring in otherwise healthy people. Examples of primary prevention programs are childhood immunization, condom use, and HIV-awareness campaigns.

>> **Secondary:** Focusing on the early identification and treatment of a developing illness or disease. Secondary prevention programs include breast cancer awareness campaigns and the promotion of self-examinations for testicular cancer.

>> **Tertiary:** Helping people cope with already developed diseases and preventing them from getting worse. Tertiary prevention programs include helping people reduce high blood pressure, quit smoking, and treat obesity.

Making changes

Have you ever kept a New Year's resolution to start doing something healthy — exercise more often, take a yoga class, eat better, get more rest, wear your seat belt? Why not? If you're being honest, I bet you're thinking it was harder than you thought it would be. Take a minute to think about what keeps you from doing what's most healthy.

A common problem with health-related behavior is people not sticking to the course they know is right. Part of this problem falls under the heading of *compliance* — whether or not someone follows through with a physician's recommendations and treatment or his own health-related plans. But what determines whether or not someone engages in health-promoting behavior to begin with? Some people make it look so easy. They go to the gym regularly. They eat right consistently. They don't smoke — ever.

Some people do unhealthy things than others for numerous reasons. For starters, a lot of people won't start or stick with a health-related behavior if substantial barriers are in the way. It's too easy to give up if something or someone makes it hard. Perhaps you don't go to the gym because it's too expensive, or you don't sleep enough because you don't have a nice set of pajamas. Money is a commonly cited barrier to engaging in healthy behavior. Another reason people don't *just do it* is that the health-related behavior may cut into something more fun or necessary. If I go to the gym, I'll miss my television programs. If I eat right, I'll have to go to the grocery store, and then I'll have to cook, and then I'll never finish any of my other household duties.

Commitment to change is most often brought about when a person believes that he can make a difference. A lot of people have a *fatalistic* attitude toward their physical health — the "you go when you go" philosophy. They don't see their behavior as contributing to their health and, therefore, don't bother to change.

REMEMBER

This mind-set is also known as having an *external locus of control* — thinking that control over something rests outside of oneself. Having the belief that the power to change a situation or event resides inside yourself, that it's under your control, is called an *internal locus of control*. When someone feels that he can control something, he's more likely to try and do something about it.

After you've changed, either because of external rewards or because of your belief that you can make a difference, how do you maintain those changes? It's easy to quit smoking, for example, but staying smoke-free is another story. You can maintain a commitment to healthy behavior by first examining the pros and cons of changing and not changing. Your ability to develop an accurate tally depends on having access to reliable information. Confusing or conflicting health messages don't quite do the job.

A number of factors influence people's tendencies to listen to and believe a particular source of information. Research on *persuasion* — getting somebody to do something he may not do on his own accord — has supplied psychologists with much of their knowledge in the area of source believability. Who do people believe?

For a message to be persuasive, it must grab your attention, be easy to understand, and be acceptable and worthwhile. You also have to be able to remember it. If you don't remember the message, who cares what it said? Persuasive arguments tend to present both sides of an issue, making the arguments look fair and unbiased. Fear-inducing messages work best when attainable steps are mentioned along with the scary stuff.

Decisions to engage or not to engage in healthy behavior are based on many factors, including your beliefs about the behavior and your locus of control. Researchers Hochbaum, Rosenstock, and Kegels, working in the US Public Health Services in the 1950s, came up with the *health belief model* to demonstrate the psychological processes someone goes through when making health-related decisions. The model is based on beliefs about the following:

>> **Severity:** How bad can the illness or disease get if I don't do something about it?

>> **Susceptibility:** How likely am I to get sick if I don't engage in healthy behavior?

>> **Benefits outweighing costs:** What's in it for me, and is it worth it?

>> **Efficacy:** How effective will my attempts at change be? I don't want to work for nothing.

The answers to these questions play a role in determining the likelihood that a person will do the healthy thing. If I arrive at a high severity, high susceptibility, high benefits-over-costs, and high-efficacy conclusion, then the likelihood that I'll choose the healthy option goes up. Otherwise, the healthy path may not seem to be worth the sacrifice and effort.

Intervening

What's the next step after you decide to do something about your unhealthy lifestyle? What can you actually do to get the ball rolling? A health psychologist or other health professional can design *interventions* that help you change and then maintain that change.

Behavior modification is a powerful method of behavior change. The most basic, yet very powerful, form of behavior modification is to use punishments and rewards for either not engaging or engaging in the target behavior. For example, if I schedule myself to run three times a week at 5:30 p.m. and I don't do it, then I have to clean the kitchen and bathroom, and do the laundry that night. If I comply, I get to treat myself to a nice dip in the spa. The trick with this technique is to enlist a partner to keep you from cheating on your rewards and punishments. I may decide to skip the laundry and go in the spa even if I don't run. A partner helps keep you honest.

REMEMBER

Cognitive change is a process by which I examine the mental messages I give myself that may prevent me from changing a behavior or maintaining a change. Everyone has *automatic thoughts* — thoughts that they don't realize automatically go through their minds in certain situations. I may tell myself that I really want to run three times a week, but I also may be having the automatic thought, "You'll never do it; you never follow through with anything." Well, thanks for the positive reinforcement, me!

The good news is that automatic thoughts can be replaced with positive self-statements. This process takes a lot of practice and encouragement from other people, but the conversion is usually worth the hard work.

This section only begins to scratch the surface of health psychology and stress-related issues, but I hope this overview of the subject whets your appetite for more knowledge about living a less stressful and healthier life. Remember to relax, believe in yourself, and don't avoid things. And reward yourself when you follow through with this advice!

Harnessing the Power of Positivity

Again, some people criticize psychology as "negatively focused" with all its focus on therapy and pathology and learning disabilities; they say it's always trying to fix people and groups. Well, a group of psychologists in the late 1990s and early

2000s, headed by the well-known psychologists Martin Seligman and Mihaly Csikszentmihalyi, introduced an essentially new branch of psychology known as *positive psychology*. Positive psychology is defined as a science of positive subjective experience, positive individual traits, and positive institutions that improve quality of life and prevents pathologies.

Positive psychology as a science of human strength covers a range of topics:

Emotional intelligence	Creativity
Optimism	Self-efficacy
Wisdom	Compassion
Gratitude	Altruism
Courage	Toughness
Meaning	Humor

Since its inception, research programs have taken positive psychology into the realms of business, sports, the military, and stress and illness. The military has sought the help of positive psychologists to alleviate stress and bolster the hardiness of its troops. Patients with terminal illnesses seek help in finding hope and courage in the face of death. Creative professionals want to be more innovative.

A central organizing concept in positive psychology is the idea of optimal living, characterized by two opposing poles of success: *flourishing* and *floundering*.

Flourishing (and its opposite, *floundering*) is synonymous with positive mental health as opposed to mental illness or disorder. Imagine going to a psychologist for a mental health check-up or wellness visit instead of the traditional "what's wrong with me?" focus. This can happen on a yearly basis the same way some people visit a medical doctor for an annual physical — not because they're sick but because they want to get a checkup. Call it a *mentacal* (ment-*uh*-cull). Okay, so I need to work on the name, but you get the point.

Psychologist C. L. M. Keyes, professor of sociology at Emory University in Atlanta, Georgia, identifies the following dimensions of flourishing/mental health:

>> **Positive affect:** Emotional well-being

>> **Avowed quality of life:** Satisfied with life

>> **Self-acceptance:** Positive attitude toward oneself

>> **Personal growth:** Seeking challenges

- » **Purpose in life:** Meaning

- » **Environmental mastery:** The ability to select, manage, and mold one's environment

- » **Autonomy:** Guided by one's own standards

- » **Positive relations with others:** Calm, trusting relationships

- » **Social acceptance:** Positive attitude toward others and human differences

- » **Social actualization:** Belief in people's potential for growth

- » **Social contribution:** Seeing one's daily activities as useful to others

- » **Social coherence:** Interest in society and social life

- » **Social integration:** Belonging

Flourishing as a concept is used by some psychologists in therapy as a guide in determining broad, more lifestyle-oriented goals for therapy clients or patients as they set goals for themselves in life. It can be used as an informal metric of client well-being, pointing therapist and client toward areas in need of improvement. However, it is not a formal component of therapy and is not considered part of formal diagnosis. That is, therapy focusing on flourishing, as opposed to treating a mental disorder, is not typically reimbursed by third-party payers such as insurance companies. Professional therapy provided by a psychologist would not necessarily focus on flourishing as a primary goal in therapy but could include, interweave, and use the concept within therapy in providing direction for personal growth to a client in a general manner. This crosses over a bit into the realm of *life coaching* or advice giving, roles that therapists typically do not engage in. However, if a client asks for this service and consents to it, understanding the psychologist's training and expertise in this regard, then what happens between two consenting adults can be considered generally acceptable.

Stepping Up!

Generally, when we do something we like to do, we do it well and to the best of our ability. If our ability is enough, then great. If not, then maybe we work harder to get better. Researchers and practitioners in the area known as *performance psychology* address the mental processes and behaviors that go into performing at our *peak performance level* when we engage in activities that we wish to excel at. Much of this research and work comes from the area of sports psychology, but many, if not most, of its findings and applications can be extended to any practice, activity, or job in which one wishes to "be their best," such as the performing arts, high-stress occupations, and teaching.

High-performance skills

Psychologist Mark Anderson identifies what he calls the "Canon of Psychological Skills" for enhancing performance: relaxation, self-talk, imagery, goal setting, and concentration.

>> For the relaxation component, a performer performs best when her or she is able to relax and stay calm under performance demands. Anxiety, fear of failure, and apprehension hinder performance.

>> Self-talk can involve mental statements or even verbalizing tactics that counter anxiety and fear. (For example, "You've got this!") You can use imagery to rehearse and see yourself performing in a desirable way, and you can build confidence by succeeding in low-risk situations.

>> Dr. Andersen calls the goal setting component the "workhorse of the mental skills canon." He distinguishes between outcome goals (like winning) and process goals that involve running through a routine that moves a performer toward his or her outcome goal. (For example, you win a swim race one stroke at a time.)

>> Finally, there's concentration, which helps a performer stay on point, on target, and aware of when he or she is off target.

Choking versus being clutch

Certainly, we would all like to be peak performers, but sometimes we fail, we fall short, and we *choke!* Psychologists Mark Frame and Sydney Riechin define choking as a suboptimal performance under pressure conditions. Maybe I'm old but, who could forget the legendary game with basketball star Reggie Miller's end-of-the-game performance against the New York Knicks in Game 1 of the 1995 Eastern Conference Finals of the NBA? Well, it's not unforgettable for the reason one might think. It's famous (or infamous if you're a Knicks fan) because as Miller won the game singlehandedly in the closing minute, at the end, he made a choking gesture toward the bench and crowd at Madison Square Garden, putting both hands around his throat. Ouch! Bad sportsmanship? Sure. But choke the Knicks did. Sorry, New York.

Choking is always a possibility, but we'd all like to imagine that we could be the Michael Jordan hitting the game-winning shot. (Or is that just me?) The opposite of choking is referred to as being *clutch*, which is improved and enhanced performance under pressure. When the pressure's on, one steps up, comes through, and pulls it off.

Research in this area has identified six primary factors that seem to improve our chances of being clutch:

>> Complete and deliberate focus that involves fully concentrating through will and intent is critical.

>> Our effort must be intense; we must "give it our all" and "buckle down."

>> Our awareness becomes amplified, and we are consciously thinking about what we are doing, and we experience a sense of control over it. Sometimes performers talk about being "unconscious" and not thinking about what they are doing. This is the opposite; they are thinking intensely and intentionally.

>> Heightened physiological arousal and being "pumped up" are important.

>> We should be free of negative thoughts and doubts, and we should fear nothing.

>> Finally, although we are deliberately thinking about what we are doing, the skills that we have trained so hard to master become automatic and happen without having to focus on those. We are focused on performing, but not on the individual steps. Ever think about walking while you're walking? Yeah, it's *not* that.

So once you've got these peak performance and clutch skills, look out Michael, Reggie, or Tom (Brady, that is).

Acquiring the Bionic Brain

Something happens to me nearly every day at around two in the afternoon. After a busy morning of report writing, therapy sessions, emails, phone calls, testing, and other doings of a psychologist, I "hit a wall." That is, I slow way down, have trouble concentrating, and become much less productive. After doing some reading, I realized that maybe my brain glucose levels are lower at this time and my brain isn't firing on all cylinders. I started eating a little protein snack and hydrating a little better, which seems to perk me up. My brain needed a boost, I guess.

Athletes train to get stronger, faster, and more agile. Musicians practice to get more fluid and precise. But what if you want to get mentally quicker, more agile, stronger, more precise, or just plain smarter? This is an area of psychology known as *cognitive* enhancement, defined in 2008 by psychologists Nick Bostrom and Anders Sandberg as the amplification or extension of core capacities of the mind through improvement of external information-processing systems.

Many forms of cognitive enhancement are being researched, and some have been around for a very long time. In essence, education is a form of cognitive enhancement. Other forms include mental training, medications, transcranial magnetic stimulation (TMS), relaxation techniques, neurofeedback, and biofeedback.

Some techniques that are being investigated in animals (not on humans) include genetic and prenatal and perinatal processes such as gene replacement and fetal supplementation in mice.

Before you go out and buy that *Baby Einstein* DVD collection for your unborn genius, know that there has been absolutely no data to support that any "make your baby smarter" program has ever actually made a baby smarter.

Doing smart drugs

I once had a gig doing learning disability and psychological assessments for a local university, and I witnessed something interesting. A whole bunch of students were actually looking for me to diagnose them with ADHD! It didn't take me long to figure out why. The doctors over at the university health center would not prescribe a psychostimulant to a student without an official diagnosis of ADHD. Now, these students weren't looking to get "high" off Ritalin or Strattera, and they weren't necessarily looking to sell the pills. But they were looking to boost their attention and concentration skills so that they could excel academically.

REMEMBER

In these modern times, medications and pharmacology are an integral and widely accepted part of life. Medications that are designed and used for cognitive and neuropsychological improvement and/or enhancement are called *nootropics*.

Many ethical and moral objections exist to using drugs to enhance mental performance, and some people see them in the same way they think of using steroids or performance-enhancing drugs in sports: It's cheating. That's a huge discussion. But, for a moment, consider that a person with a learning disability, brain injury, or other cognitive deficit could take a medication to improve his mental functioning. Is this any different than taking medicine for other types of ailments?

The fact is, this is already happening — sometimes in overt ways and often in indirect ways. An indirect way of using medication to improve thinking comes from the use of antidepressant medication. Anyone who's ever been severely depressed can attest that the condition comes with a mental fog of sorts (something professionals call *pseudodementia*) that accompanies the depressed mood and feelings of guilt and lack of pleasure and motivation. Antidepressants help ease this cognitive dullness.

Medications that enhance or otherwise assist in cognitive processes include the following:

» **Stimulants:** Used for increased attention and short-term memory and includes such drugs as Adderall, Vyvanse, Atomoxetine (Strattera), and good old-fashioned caffeine

» **Cholinergics:** Used as memory enhancing-drugs; examples are Aricept and medical cannabis

» **Dopaminergics:** Used to increase attention and alertness and includes such drugs as methylphenidate (Ritalin, Concerta) and modafinil (Provigil)

The list of known or suspected nootropic drugs is much larger and expanding. However, I must point out that the number of prescriptions written for these drugs for actual nootropic purposes is still fairly limited. It would seem that physicians may be somewhat hesitant to go down the rabbit hole of drug-induced or assisted cognitive enhancement.

Hitting the limits of the skull

Just as mental training, neurofeedback, and drugs can enhance cognitive processes, so to can devices such as cochlear implants, computers, smartphones, and even sticky notes. The field of technological devices that enhance cognitive processes is known in some circles as *cognitive prosthetics* or *neuroprosthetics*.

Many scientists show incredible interest in the promise and possibility of the field of cognitive prosthetics. Some fairly well-established devices are already available, including *speech production devices*, mobile phone or mobile technology software programs that "talk" for individuals who cannot or do not speak, *memory aide* software programs, and even voice-activated and voice-prompted GPS route and guidance systems.

Perhaps one of the most interesting approaches to cognitive prosthetics comes from work being done with *brain-computer-interfacing* in which external computer and/or other digital devices are directly wired into the brain and controlled directly by brain activity. Studies reveal that when electrodes are inserted into the brain of a primate or human, even those with fairly profound neurological damage, control of a computer cursor is possible. This technology doesn't sound like much at first, but think about it: Controlling a computer interface with your brain is downright telepathic almost — and pretty cool!

7

The Part of Tens

Chapter **19**

Ten Tips for Maintaining Psychological Well-Being

There's no magic formula — and no standard — for being a psychologically "well" or a healthy person. Is psychological well-being simply the absence of mental disease or mental illness? If so, a lot of people are perfectly healthy from a psychological standpoint. Is the absence of physical disease the same thing as being physically healthy? Some people think that there's more to being healthy than being disease-free. Unfortunately, this chapter doesn't give you all the answers to these questions. In fact, it probably creates more questions than answers.

Psychologists are not necessarily in the business of deciding the values of a society. A lot of scientists think that values are beyond the scope of science, that values and morals are too subjective and personal to be reduced to scientific analysis. But some psychologists believe that psychological health is as close to a universal value as any. After all, who doesn't want to be healthy?

Psychology has uncovered a lot about human thinking and behavior over the years, and it would be a waste not to try to apply some of that knowledge to the human quest for well-being, happiness, and health. I agree that psychologists may be overstepping their bounds when they advocate a particular set of values.

But, as a professor of mine once said, "That's an empirical question, isn't it?" What he meant is that opinions can be evaluated empirically, and one opinion can be judged with respect to another as long as agreed-upon criteria for evaluating the opinions are in place. In other words, researchers may actually be able to evaluate the "good life" with psychological science as long as they can all agree upon a definition of what the good life is. For example, I may agree that a good life is one in which my needs are met without much effort and I'm relatively free to do what I please. With that, researchers can scientifically evaluate circumstances, behaviors, and thought processes that lead to such conditions. If researchers can agree upon a standard, they can investigate what contributes to the achievement of that standard.

REMEMBER

Because this chapter is providing tips for psychological health, I need to set a standard. So here it is: I define psychological health broadly as *optimal living*. This is a safe position because individuals can tweak the meaning of optimal living to fit their own values.

My use of the term optimal living in this chapter takes a *subjective* view of psychological health. For years, psychologists have studied the concept of *subjective well-being*. This concept refers to my sense of personal well-being and happiness without reference to the views of anyone else. It represents my personal values, and it may or may not be in harmony with others around me.

Some philosophers have argued that it is morally preferable to hold values that correspond with the values of others or, at the very least, to hold values that don't impinge upon or impact the values of others. Subscribing to a value system that doesn't impact the values of others is the "different strokes for different folks" approach.

Another definition of psychological health is perhaps more objective. This definition holds that psychological health centers on behaviors and mental processes that lead to the ability to adjust and function well in one's life. This view can also be subjective to some degree. For example, you may adjust quite well to prison, but this adjustment may involve behaviors that can be considered quite unhealthy in other contexts. But, for most people and societies, the norms for good adjustment and functioning often involve surviving within the typically acceptable rules and boundaries of a community.

At the very least, psychological health involves being happy. I've never met a person who didn't want to be happy, even if being happy to him meant being miserable. You can't escape the desire to be happy. That reminds me of a joke:

"Hit me, hit me!" says the masochist.

"No!" says the sadist.

Enough of the philosophical. Let's get down to practical suggestions. The following ten tips for maintaining psychological health are equally important. No one is more important than the others; that's why they are not numbered.

Accept Yourself

A lot of popular psychology and self-help books tell us to "love ourselves." It's not a bad idea. Severe dislike for oneself is often associated with extreme guilt, shame, and depression. Don't underestimate the power of believing in your abilities and valuing your uniqueness.

Too often, people lead inauthentic lives that are defined by others as they strive for acceptance. Self-acceptance is a crucial ingredient for motivation and positive emotion, and accepting yourself even leads to more acceptance by others. Accepting yourself is not the same as thinking you are perfect.

Strive for Self-Determination

When I feel like the captain of my own ship, I'm more interested in life, more excited about life, and more confident. My motivations are a complex mix of the things I truly want for myself and things I've adopted from significant others over the years.

Feeling as if I have some control over the decisions that affect me is crucial to psychological health. When I'm in controlling, punitive, or dominating environments, my sense of importance and freedom suffers.

Sometimes you need to adapt to the desires and values of others. In these situations, you can still retain a sense of self-determination if you agree even slightly with what you're adapting to. What if you want to paint your house bright purple, but the city won't let you? Well, if the officials can agree to lavender, then you probably don't feel so pushed around. It's rarely (if ever) a good thing for people to feel like they're being told what to do when they don't agree with the directive.

Stay Connected and Nurture Relationships

Sometimes it seems like modern lives are lonely. Everyone speeds around in their cars or stares into computer screens all day, isolated from other people and busy with the details of their own lives. I've often felt like I have to sacrifice productivity at work in order to socialize. I hear people make similar comments all the time, "I just don't have time for friends and family." Here's a tip: Make time!

In these times of mega-cities and super-suburbs, it can be hard to stay close to friends and family. The age of the small town filled with extended family is all but gone. Small towns are out there, but most people don't live in them. Despite these conditions, there is a benefit in working to maintain closer proximity to people who matter. The huge growth in mobile phone, Internet, and social media use may reflect both the desire to stay connected and an attempt to do so in a fragmented and fast-paced world.

Having friends and family around is nice, but it's only a good thing if the relationships are good. Some people can't wait to get as far away from certain people as possible. Feeling emotionally connected and supported by your relationships is just as important, if not more important, than simple proximity. People need intimate relationships that they can count on when times are hard. They need trustworthy romantic partners who value the same things.

Here are some other helpful hints for maintaining good relationships: Practice forgiveness, be tolerant, communicate honestly, express yourself, balance independence with dependence, and act responsibly toward others — and nurture their values, desires, feelings, and wishes.

Lend a Helping Hand

When you reach out to others in need, you often get a sense of mastery over my own circumstances, and you're working to foster positive social conditions. Lending a helping hand helps the intended beneficiaries, and it also helps the individuals who offer the assistance.

Find Meaning and Purpose and Work toward Goals

Feeling like life is meaningless is a hallmark of depression. One of the drawbacks of modern society is the sense of alienation that can come from working day in and day out with only the next workday or the next paycheck as a reward.

It's crucial to have meaningful personal goals. Research consistently finds that the process of working toward goals is as important as the goals themselves. At times, goals can be too lofty, and people can set themselves up for disappointment because they can't reach them. This defeats the purpose of setting goals in the first place. Realistic and meaningful goals are helpful. Having goals is not the same as being perfectionistic. Perfectionists set themselves up to fail because no one is perfect. Being a little kind to yourself and understanding that you're going to make mistakes in life is part of accepting yourself, and it's good for your psychological health.

Find Hope and Maintain Faith

Research has consistently shown that having a deep sense of spiritual faith can be a protective measure for dealing with loss, illness, and psychological disorders. When things seem dark, it really helps to have a sense of hope and optimism about the future and a belief that goals can eventually be achieved.

Having a *positivity bias* helps to override fear and maintain motivation. Being biased in this way is kind of like seeing the world through rose-colored glasses. Pessimists may claim that they're more in touch with reality, but a little positive illusion never hurts.

Find Flow and Be Engaged

Professional athletes talk about "being in the groove" when they've had a good game. *Flow* is the experience of feeling totally engaged, involved, engrossed, and focused in an activity or experience. Living a happy life is a matter of learning to maximize and control inner experiences in order to feel harmoniously engaged in the activity for its own sake.

I once heard a piece of Buddhist wisdom: If you are thinking about resting while sweeping the floor, you are not truly experiencing life as it exists. When you sweep, sweep. When you rest, rest. Find flow!

Enjoy the Beautiful Things in Life

The ability to appreciate beauty is *aesthetics*. There's a lot of negativity and ugliness in the world — wars, disease, violence, and degradation are all around. Depressing, right? Being able to appreciate the beautiful things is a saving grace in a world that's so often unattractive.

The experience of beauty is personal and one that no one else can define for another person. You may see the beauty in a famous painting or the sun shining through the clouds. When I see a well-executed play in football, it brings tears to my eyes. "That's beautiful, man!" Sniff, sniff.

Even things that are imperfect and incomplete can be beautiful, particularly if you are a practitioner of the "wabi-sabi" worldview derived from Buddhism. Finally, an excuse not to clean the house!

Struggle to Overcome; Learn to Let Go

Challenge and adversity are undeniable facts of life. Being able to effectively cope with challenges is crucial to maintaining psychological and even physical well-being. Each person has a variety of skills and techniques used to cope with stress and adversity. Here's the best general advice for coping with adversity: Cope actively within situations that you have some measure of control over, and cope passively within situations that you don't have control over.

Active coping involves taking actions to improve a situation such as looking for a job when you're fired instead of just saying, "Oh well, I guess I just wasn't meant to have a job." In situations that you can control, such as many health-related problems, taking action consistently leads to better outcomes and better psychological functioning.

Passive coping involves processes of psychological and emotional acceptance. When a person you love dies, you may run yourself ragged trying to shake or diminish the feelings of loss and sadness. But eventually, you have to accept the reality of the situation. Accepting reality when you cannot change it is a good example of passive coping. Forgiveness is another one.

Don't Be Afraid to Change

Morihei Ueshiba, founder of the martial art aikido, wrote a book called *The Art of Peace*. His secret to living a peaceful life was the core principle of Judo: Go with the flow! When you are rigid and inflexible, you are more likely to experience resistance and strain yourself in trying to maintain your posture. When you are flexible and willing to change a behavior that is not working, you are more adaptable and better adjusted. It takes courage to change your ways, but it is vital for health and well-being.

Chapter 20

Ten Great Psychological Movies and Shows

So what makes a good psychological movie or show? I think a good psychological film or show makes the viewer feel, act, and think like a psychologist. It's a lens (literally and figuratively) that affords you the gaze of the psychologist. Could good psychological films and shows really just be another form of data collection and analysis, even research, or even therapy? That sounds so dry and analytical, doesn't it? But we all know a good movie or show can be therapeutic. They can be investigatory explorations and qualitative looks into and from a psychological perspective and viewpoint. They don't necessarily have to have a psychological theme or be about psychologists. They can represent the "acts" of a psychologist in all the ways "they" are: researchers, therapists, consultants, people with things to say about things that they see people do, feel, and think.

We get to "be" psychologists for 90 minutes or 10 episodes as we analyze the characters and the story from the viewpoint of our own minds and the minds of the creators. They may depict a person suffering or experiencing a mental disorder. They may show what it's like to receive or give psychological treatment. They may just take us so deep into the experiences of the characters that we can't help but feel like we are seeing into their minds. Of course, if you put ten psychologists in a room, you'd probably get 100 different movies or shows that would qualify using my criteria. These are my picks, and because of that, there's no rating system. They're good and I like them. Watch them.

One Flew Over the Cuckoo's Nest

One Flew Over the Cuckoo's Nest was released in 1975 and based on Ken Kesey's book of the same name. The film, directed by Milos Forman, stars Jack Nicholson as Randle P. McMurphy, a man who is involuntarily committed to a mental hospital.

This movie is poignant because it raises the question of whether Nicholson's character is really mentally ill. The film is a commentary on the mental health system during the time period within which the movie is set and how the system was used as a means of social control. Is Nicholson's character mentally ill, or is he just a pain in the neck who has a problem with authority? There's no doubt that Jack stands out and bucks the system every chance he gets, but does that make him sick? Maybe he just has a real zest for life.

Excellent acting, social commentary, and existential angst. Who gets to decide what's real and what illness is? Maybe it's the one's with the keys to the cell? Definitely check this one out, and for more discussion of the issues brought up by this film, check out Chapter 3's sections on medication and Chapter 15 on abnormal psychology.

A Clockwork Orange

A Clockwork Orange, based on the book by Anthony Burgess and directed by Stanley Kubrick, was made in 1971 and stars Malcolm McDowell as Alex DeLarge, a young troublemaker and delinquent. McDowell and his gang of three friends engage in various crimes and shenanigans, such as fighting, vandalism, skipping school, and the like. One night, they steal a car and go for a joy ride. They commit a horrific home invasion, raping a woman and brutally beating her husband. McDowell gets caught.

This is where the psychologically interesting part begins. McDowell is put through a rigorous behavior modification program that utilizes a technique called *aversion training*. After learning takes place, every time McDowell's character is exposed to violence, he becomes violently ill. Therefore, he is compelled to avoid engaging in violence in order to avoid getting sick.

The film seems to pose a number of questions: Do we really want to resort to such tactics in reforming our criminals? Are we doing more harm than good? Is the level of violence in a society a function of a collective aversion to it or more a matter of the strong preying on the weak?

This move made my list because of its macabre nature and its use of behaviorism, not to mention the social commentary on violence in society. (For more on behavior therapy check out Chapter 17.)

Ordinary People

Ordinary People (1980), directed by Robert Redford and starring Timothy Hutton, Jud Hirsch, Donald Sutherland, and Mary Tyler Moore, is about a teenage boy recovering from depression and a suicide attempt following a boating accident that took his older brother's life. This is an excellent story about how complex grief and depression can be and yet how much can be accomplished by taking things slowly and making them simple.

The acting is superb. The depiction of a mental disorder is excellent. But the emotion, the pain, the sadness — these elements are what put this film on my list. Doing therapy with real people and real pain and real loss is heartbreaking sometimes, and this movie will break your heart, but perhaps open it up as well.

Girl, Interrupted

In *Girl, Interrupted,* a 1999 film directed by James Mangold, Winona Ryder plays a depressed and suicidal young woman who's admitted to a mental hospital. She's reluctant about being there and resists many of the efforts by the staff to help her "get better." The movie contrasts the characters' lives and afflictions as a way to demonstrate that middle-class suburban angst is small potatoes when compared to other more "serious" illnesses. At the same time, the film doesn't minimize Ryder's difficulties, but instead it appears to place them in perspective. Developing a new perspective is a turning point for Ryder's character; her life is simply being *interrupted.* She won't let her life end in the institution due to a failure to deal with her problems.

I think the moral of the story is that Ryder's character was fortunate to have made it out alive, merely taking a detour into mental illness instead of permanent residence. It's a very personal story. It's a story about hope and the harsh reality of some people's lives (For more about life's "issues," check out Chapter 18.)

The Silence of the Lambs

This is the movie that made everyone want to go out, join the FBI, and become a profiler. Directed by Jonathan Demme, this 1991 film stars Jodie Foster and Anthony Hopkins in a psychological thriller that gets you inside the mind of a serial killer. Foster's character, Clarise Starling, is an FBI agent who must deal with a famous psychiatrist/serial killer named Hannibal Lecter, played by Anthony Hopkins. The movie centers on their interactions and the psychological games they play with each other in order to get what they both want. Hopkins plays doctor with Foster's psyche, and Foster asks Hopkins to look inside and use his self-knowledge to help her catch a serial killer.

The movie's strength is not so much in its portrayal of a mentally ill psychiatrist, but in its insight to how the human mind works and how we become who we are. The tragedy of Foster's childhood makes being a profiler her destiny. The serial killer's (Buffalo Bill) quest for transformation into his true self drives his horrendous murders. The real anomaly is Hopkins's character. He seems to represent both the good and the bad aspects of the human psyche. He helps Foster, both as consultant and as healer, but he also demonstrates depravity and demonic insanity through acts of murder. It's as if he is both the giver and the taker of life. His powerful knowledge of the human mind easily turns into a tool for murder. Hannibal Lecter represents what a lot of us fear — that those we trust to help us can also hurt us.

TIP

If Hannibal Lector interests you, then you'll love the television series *Hannibal* (2013–2015) starring Will Dancy as Will Grant, Mads Mikkelsen as Dr. Hannibal Lector, and Laurence Fishburne as Jack Crawford. It's a great show that's dark, twisted, stylized, and maybe better than *The Silence of the Lambs.* Check it out!

Sybil

Sally Field stars in this classic 1976 made-for-TV movie, directed by Daniel Petrie, about multiple personality disorder (nowadays known as Dissociate Identity Disorder). Field, playing Sybil, is a reclusive young woman who appears to be shy and quiet, but under the surface a chaotic tangle of personalities swirls out of control. She ends up in the care of a doctor who begins to treat her for multiple personality disorder.

The scenes in which Field and her doctor are in therapy together are very dramatic and disturbing. They're intense! Sally Field's performance is super powerful. It's actually pretty hard to watch someone act so strangely. It gets a ten on the "Hair on the Back of My Neck Standing Up" scale. It gives me the willies! As Sybil switches back and forth between personalities, the therapist begins to gain some insight as to how Field's character could have become so ill.

Field's character was horribly sexually and physically abused as a child. The film presents the professionally popular idea that MPD is the result of the personality splitting off from itself in order to defend the core personality from the reality of the abuse. It does a good job of respecting this notion and stays a true course, not yielding to the temptation to get too "Hollywood."

The strength of *Sybil* rests on three pillars: Sally Field's acting, the emotional intensity of the therapy scenes, and the portrayal of a deeply wounded woman.

The Matrix

The Matrix (1999), directed by Lana and Andy Wachowski and starring Keanu Reeves, Laurence Fishburne, and Carrie-Anne Moss, is an apocalyptic film in which a "master computer" has taken over the world and the minds of all humans and created an alternative reality. Humans are kept alive in a farm of sorts, where the energy from human bodies keeps the technology powered.

The master computer has taken over the minds of all humans by linking them into a virtual reality "matrix" in order to sustain their minds and mental functioning after finding out that without the matrix-derived mass delusion the human body would die, thus eliminating its power source. However, a group of people have managed to "break free" from the matrix and "come back" to reality, waking up to a world in which most humans are fuel and the master computer hunts them down.

Are you surprised to see this movie on this list? Some critics and viewers consider *The Matrix* to be a good "action" film, and some say it is quite mediocre. But this movie explores the concepts of virtual reality, artificial intelligence, machine intelligence, consciousness, and human-machine/human-technology relationships. The matrix itself is suggestive of the Internet and how it is often mistaken for reality. Are people becoming disembodied minds in this Internet age? Is this a form of mental slavery in which human minds and desires are subject to manipulation by more powerful, massive, and complex intelligences such as corporate marketers and spin masters?

The Matrix is thought-provoking and taps into some very contemporary and complex areas of psychological study and research.

Black Mirror

Black Mirror (2013–2019) is a multi-episode show with free-standing episodes, each telling a strange, sometimes dark, and definitely thought-provoking tale of humanity's complicated relationship with technology. One episode tells the story of a man who finds out about his wife's infidelity by reviewing her "memory" program implanted in her eye and brain. Another one is about two women who fall in love in a simulated world created by a "brain storage" facility of sorts for people who have died. Yet another episode shows how the world of "likes" and social media posts and profiles can go haywire. This show, like the *Matrix*, takes current issues around technology, blows them up, puts them on steroids, and forces us to look at them. This sounds like a form of Flooding Therapy, or a good therapist confronting you with your issues. You know, like a black mirror!

True Detective (Seasons 1 and Season 3)

True Detective Season 1 (2014) stars Matthew McConaughey as Detective Rust Cohle and Woody Harrelson as Detective Marty Hart. This show, like some others on the list, is about murder, but it made the list for so much more. The torment of Rust Cohle is palpable. You can feel it, and you empathize with his drive and his anger. He is a "savant" of sorts, being able to "feel" things and draw conclusions that make him an excellent detective. He is wild, unruly, unorthodox, but not dangerous, and somehow you feel reassured and safe with him. Marty Hart, on the other hand, seems very orthodox, nor particularly invested at first, a serial adulterer who seems to be just waiting to retire. He's not particularly likable at first. But when these two get together, they fuel each other. They don't match, but they're on a mission.

Season 3 (2019) does not disappoint either. Starring Mahershala Ali as Detective Wayne Hays and Stephen Dorff as Roland West, it's another story of partners working together, not particularly liking each other, but driving each other. Wayne Hayes is full of regret about a crime he could never solve and walked away from years earlier. He's haunted by ghosts and suffering from mid-state dementia. The show is filmed in an interesting way as well, cross-cutting across different time periods and keeping the viewer disoriented. The detectives are complicated people (like all of us) trying to solve a complicated crime. They're looking to redeem themselves for past mistakes. Who isn't?

You might be wondering about Season 2. Well, it wasn't horrible but nowhere near as good as 1 and 3. Each season is independent from each other, so my advice would be to watch Season 2 if you're in a show hole.

Psycho

No list of great psychological movies would be complete without Alfred Hitchcock's 1960 film *Psycho*. Anthony Perkins stars as a depraved psychopath with a strange delusion that involves dressing up like his mother. Perkins's character appears to suffer from a "split" personality in which part of his personality is his mother. How weird is that? The "psycho" in *Psycho* only kills one person in the entire movie, small potatoes by today's standards, but Hitchcock's use of suspense and surprise are superb.

Psycho introduced the American public to the idea of a psychopathic killer, a man with a warped mind. On the outside, Perkins's character is meek and socially awkward, a boy in a man's body. The suggestion is that underneath that calm exterior is a deranged killer waiting for his opportunity. But the key psychological component in *Psycho* is Perkins's twisted relationship with his mother. He is the quintessential "momma's boy," unable to go out into the world on his own and enjoy the pleasures that he fantasizes about. Classic!

Index

Numbers

16pf (16 personality factors), 172

A

ABC analysis, 342
ability of consciousness, 74–75
ableism, 227
abnormal psychology. *See* psychopathology
absolute threshold, 69
acceptance and commitment therapy (ACT), 347–348
accessibility, 195
accessory structures, 61
accurate empathy, 353
acetylcholine, 46
achievement testing, 321
acoustic energy, 60
acquisition phase, 163
ACT (acceptance and commitment therapy), 347–348
acting out, 340
action potentials, 44
active engagement, 217
activity model of aging, 248
actor-observer effect/bias, 201
A-delta fibers, 66
ADHD (attention deficit/hyperactivity disorder), 57, 302–303
adolescence
  mental disorders, 301–305
  puberty, 244–245
adrenaline, 119–120
adulthood, 246–247
aesthetics, 377–378
affect, 131
affective science, 130
age, 217
ageism, 227
age-related norms, 21

aggression, 218–220
  frustration leading to, 219
  genetic predisposition, 218–219
  social learning theory, 219–220
aging, 247–248
agoraphobia, 298–299
alcohol consumption, 41
allostasis, 267–268
Allport, Gordon, 171, 228
Alpert, Richard, 83
alpha activity, 76
altruism, 119–120, 221–225
Alzheimer's disease, 49, 248
American Academy of Pediatrics, 220
American Psychological Association (APA), 18–19, 35, 131, 269, 330
American Society of Anesthesiologists, 77
Americans with Disabilities Act of 1990, 306
amplitude, 65–66
amygdala, 135
analytical intelligence, 111
Anastasi, Anne, 318
anatomical organization, 43
Anderson, Mark, 366
anesthesia, 75
anesthesia awareness, 77
anger, 138–140, 162
anhedonia, 292
anonymity, 256–257
anterior cingulate cortex, 135
antidepressants, 55, 296, 368
antipsychotic medications, 55
anxiety disorders, 297–299
  ESTs for, 357
  psychopharmacology and, 56–57
anxiolysis, 75
anxiolytic medications, 56
APA (American Psychological Association), 18–19, 35, 131, 269, 330

appeal, 195
applied psychologists, 17–18, 309–326
appraisals, 265–267
approach processes, 276
architecture of thought, 92
Ariely, Dan, 103–104
Aristotle, 60
Aron, Arthur, 197
The Art of Peace (Ueshiba), 378
Asch, Solomon, 210
assertiveness, 205–206
assessment. *See* psychological assessment
assessment mindset, 254
asynchronicity, 257
atoms, 43
attachment, 188–190, 274
attachment behavior, 188
attachment figure, 188
attachment figures, 139
attachment styles theories, 189
attachment theory, 53, 294
attainability, 196
attention deficit/hyperactivity disorder (ADHD), 57, 302–303
attention processes, 93–94
attitude inoculation, 217
attraction, 195–197
auditory cortex, 66
authoritarian parenting style, 192
authoritative parenting style, 192
authority, 29
autism, 303–305
automatic thoughts, 345, 363
autonomous motivation, 122
availability heuristic, 103
avoidance processes, 276
awareness, 75–76
axons, 44
Aylward, Glen, 321

B

backward conditioning, 154–155

balance, 68

Bandura, Albert, 173, 219

Barlow, David, 300

Baron-Cohen, Simon, 62

Barrett, Lisa Feldman, 137

basal ganglia, 50

basic assertions, 206

basilar membrane, 66

Batson, Daniel, 223

Bauerfein, Mark, 255

Baumrind, Diana, 192

Be Here Now (Dass), 83

Bearing the Unbearable (Cacciatore), 274

Beck, Aaron, 294–295

behavior, normal vs. abnormal, 280–283

behavior modification, 362

behavior therapy, 300, 342–343

behavioral genetics, 52

behaviorism, 20, 115

bell curve, 112

benzodiazepines, 56, 300

bereavement, 274–275

Berkowitz, Leonard, 219

Berridge, Kent C., 128

beta activity, 76

Big Five personality traits, 172

binocular cues, 65

biofeedback, 368

biogenic amine hypothesis, 293

biological metatheory, 20

biological psychology, 39–57
  brain, 49–52
  cells, 44–49
  DNA, 52–53
  nervous system, 42–43
  overview, 39–42
  psychopharmacology, 53–57

biological reductionism, 40

biopsychosocial approach, 300

biopsychosocial model, 24–27, 39–57

bipolar depression, 57

bipolar disorder, 295–297

Bipolar Disorder For Dummies (Fink and Kraynak), 297

bipolar I disorder, 55

Black Mirror (film), 384

Bleuler, Eugene, 286

Bobo Doll study, 173

body, biopsychosocial model, 24

body awareness, 180

Bostrom, Nick, 367

bounded rationality, 103

Bowlby, John, 188, 274, 294

brain, 49–52
  early child development, 235
  emotions in, 133–135
  forebrain, 50–51
  hindbrain, 51
  midbrain, 51
  peripheral nervous system (PNS), 52

"Brain in a Vat" experiment, 107

brain-computer-interfacing, 369

brainstorming, 105

Brammer, Lawrence M., 272

Brand, Jay, 16, 105

Bransford, John, 104

Brazelton, T. Berry, 235

British Psychological Society, 19

broad theoretical perspectives. *See* metatheories

Broadbent, Donald, 93–94

Brooks-Gunn, Jeanne, 179

Brown, Roger, 208

Bruner, Jerome, 200

Buddhism, 83

bullying, 259

Burger, Andrea, 122

Buss, Arnold, 182

bystander effect, 225

C

C fibers, 66

Cacciatore, Joanne, 274

Cannon, Walter, 265, 270

Cannon-Bard theory, 136

cardinal traits, 171

Carlson, Neil, 40

Carr, Nicholas, 255

Carroll, John, 109

Caspi, Avner, 257

catfishing, 257

Cattell, Raymond, 109, 172

Cattell-Horn-Carroll Theory of Cognitive Abilities (CHC Theory), 109

causal relationship, 33

causation, correlation vs., 33

CBT (Cognitive-Behavioral Therapy), 297

cell membrane, 45

cells, 44–49
  activating brain change, 47–49
  networks, 47
  neurotransmitters, 45–47

central nervous system (CNS), 42

central traits, 172

cerebellum, 51

cerebral cortex, 50

certified therapists, 356

Chabris, Christopher, 93

challenge, 266

Chalmers, David, 74

characteristic feature, 98

CHC Theory (Cattell-Horn-Carroll Theory of Cognitive Abilities), 109

cheat sheet, for this book, 3

chemical energy, 60

child development, 241–244
  cognitive development, 243
  early child development, 233–241
  kindergarten, 241–242
  mental disorders, 301–305, 358
  preoperational stage, 242–243
  social development, 243–244

choking, 366

cholinergics, 369

Chomsky, Noam, 114–115

chromosomes, 230–233

chunking, 95

classic psychoanalysis, 341

classical conditioning, 20, 149–157

D

Damasio, Antonio, 75, 76, 134

Darley, John, 224

Darwin, Charles, 26

Davidson, Richard, 143

Dawkins, Richard, 119, 224

daydreaming, 81

DC: 0–5 (Diagnostic Classification of Mental Health and Developmental Disorders of Infancy and Childhood), 286

De Becker, Gavin, 134

Deak, Anita, 135

deception, 257

Deci, Edward, 122

decision making process, 101–104

Deckers, Lambert, 118

deductive reasoning, 101

defense motive state, 134

defining feature, 97

degenerative diseases, 49

deindividuated, 213

deliberate actions, 76

delta activity, 77

delusional disorder, 290–291

delusions, 287

dementias, 248

dendrites, 44

dependent variables, 33

depression, 292–295

   causes of, 293–295

   ESTs for, 357

   feeling anger, 139

   medications for, 56

   as psychological pain, 129

   psychopharmacology and, 55

   symptoms, 292–293

   treating, 295

depth, sight and, 65

descriptive research, 30

descriptive statistics, 32

desires, 127, 139

developmental psychology, 17, 21

Diagnostic and Statistical Manuel, 5th Edition (DSM-5), 273–274, 275, 283–285

Diagnostic Classification of Mental Health and Developmental Disorders of Infancy and Childhood (DC: 0–5), 286

dialectical behavior therapy, 348–349

DIAMONDS classification system, 178

diathesis-stress model, 288–289

Dickson, David, 203

Dictionary of Psychology (APA), 131

The Dictionary of Psychology (Reber), 1

Diener, Ed, 140

difference threshold, 69

diffusion of responsibility, 224–225

discrete trial teaching (DTT), 305

discrimination, 154, 166, 227–228

disorders, 284. See also mental disorders

dissimulation, 325–326

distances, sight and, 65

divided attention, 93

divorce, 192

DNA, 52–53

Doane, David S., 331

Dodson, John Dillingham, 124

Dooley, Julian, 259

dopamine, 46, 55, 128

dopamine dysregulation hypothesis, 55

dopaminergics, 369

dreams, 79–80

drive reduction theory, 120–121

drowsiness, 75

drug use

   altering consciousness with, 81–82

   opponent-process theory, 125

DSM-5 (Diagnostic and Statistical Manuel, 5th Edition), 273–274, 275, 283–285

DTT (discrete trial teaching), 305

dualism, 107

Dylan, Bob, 127

dynamic cues, 199

Dynamic Fit Model of Stress and Emotional Regulation, 269

dyssomnias, 78

E

early start Denver model, 305

eating disorders, 23

EC (embodied cognition), 99, 106–108

echoic memory, 94

ecological perception, 68–69

educational testing, 321

educator psychologists, 18

EE (expressed emotion), 289

Einstein, Albert, 110

elaborative rehearsal, 95

electrochemical system, 42–43, 61

electroencephalogram (EEG), 76

electromagnetic energy, 60

electromagnetic radiation, 63

electrophysiological activity, 76

Ellis, Albert, 346

embodied cognition (EC), 99, 106–108

embodied simulation (ES), 99

embodied social cognition theories, 202

embryonic period, 232

emergent self, 182

Emotional Intelligence (EQ), 142–143

Emotional Intelligence (Goleman), 142

The Emotional Life of Your Brain (Davidson), 143

emotional regulation (ER), 143–145

emotional style, 143

emotion-focused therapy, 354–355

emotions, 130–145

   anger, 138–140

   in brain, 133–135

   defined, 131

   Emotional Intelligence (EQ), 142–143

   emotional regulation (ER), 143–145

   evolutionary psychology, 132–133

   expressing, 137–138

   happiness, 140–142

   order of, 135–137

empathic assertions, 206

empathy, 223, 306, 337

empirical method, 16, 27–28

groups, 209–215
  conformity, 210–211
  deindividuated, 213
  groupthink, 214–215
  social facilitation, 212
  social loafing, 213
groupthink, 214–215
Grudin, Jonathan, 10
guided search theory, 94
gustation, 67

H

Half a Brain Is Enough (Battro), 48
hallucinations, 55, 287
Halstead-Reitan Neuropsychological Test Battery, 324
Hamilton, N. Gregory, 187
happiness, 140–142
  PERMA, 141–142
  psychological well-being approach, 141
  subjective well-being (SWB), 140–141
Hargie, Owen, 203
Harlow, Harry, 189
harm-loss situations, 266
Hartup, Willard, 194
health belief mode, 362
health psychology, 360–363
hearing, 65–66
The Heart and Soul of Change (Duncan et al.), 335
hedonic hotspots, 128
hedonic principle, 128
hemispheres, 49
Heraclitus, 21
heuristics, 102–103
Hierarchical Taxonomy of Psychopathology (HiTOP), 286
hierarchy of needs, 121
Higgins, E. Tory, 128
high, state of being, 81–82, 125
high-functioning autism, 304
hindbrain, 51
Hinduja, Sameer, 259

HiTOP (Hierarchical Taxonomy of Psychopathology), 286
Hobson, Alan, 80
Hoffman, Martin, 223
Hofmann, Wilhelm, 127
homeostasis, 120, 264–265
Horn, John, 109
How and Why Are Some Therapists Better Than Others? (Castonguay and Hill), 335
How the Mind Works (Pinker), 43
Hull, Clark, 120, 156
humanistic metatheory, 22
hypersomnia, 78
hypnosis, 84
hypnotic induction, 84
hypothalamus, 50
hypotheses, 27

I

IASP (International Association for the Study of Pain), 129
ICBM (International Consortium for Brain Mapping), 47
iconic memory, 94
icons, used in this book, 2–3
identity, 181–186
  online identity, 252–253
  personal identity, 182–183
  self-esteem, 185–186
  social identity, 184–185
identity play, 257
illusionists, 72
Imitation Game, 89
inattentional blindness, 93
incentive theory, 124
incus, 66
independent variables, 33
indifferent permissive parenting style, 193
individual differences, 171
inductive reasoning, 100
indulgent permissive parenting style, 193
inference, 203
inferential statistics, 32

Information Age, 363
information-processing approach, 90
informed consent, 334
inhibitory neurotransmitters, 45
insomnia, 56, 78
insula, 135
integral expanded consciousness, 81
intellectual disability, 112
intellectually gifted, 112
intelligence, 108–113
intelligence quotient (IQ), 323
interactionist theory, 115
internal locus of control, 361
International Association for the Study of Pain (IASP), 129
International Consortium for Brain Mapping (ICBM), 47
internet addiction, 257–258
internet self-efficacy, 251
interoception, 134
interpersonal communication, 203
The Interpretation of Dreams (Freud), 79–80
interval schedule, 164
interventions. *See* psychological intervention, treatment, and therapy
interview, psychological, 312–317
introspection, 88
intuitive decision making, 102
invisible audience phenomenon, 181
iodopsins, 63
IQ (intelligence quotient), 323

J

Jackson, Lynne, 226
Jacobsen's organ, 67
James-Lange theory, 136
Janis, Irving L., 214
Johnson, Mark, 108
just-noticeable difference (JND), 69

K

Kahneman, Daniel, 102
K-complexes, 77

Minnesota Multiphasic Personality Inventory (MMPI-2), 322

mirror test, 179

Mischel, Walter, 123, 175

mitosis, 232

MKO (more-knowledgeable-other), 243

mnemonics, 95

monism, 40, 107

monocular cues, 65

monosodium glutamate (MSG), 67

mood, 131

mood stabilizers, 297

Moore's Law, 249

morality, 186

more-knowledgeable-other (MKO), 243

moro (startle) reflex, 234

motivation, 117–145

  adrenaline, 119–120

  defined, 118

  emotions, 130–145

  expectancy theory, 124

  needs, 120–121

  opponent-process theory, 125

  optimal level of arousal theory, 123–124

  pleasure and pain, 127–128

  psychological pain, 128–130

  self-determination theory (SDT), 121–123

  social-cognitive theory of motivation, 125–127

motor development, 234–235

mourning, 275, 292

movement, sense of, 68

MRI (magnetic resonance imaging) scans, 50

MSG (monosodium glutamate), 67

multiple intelligences, 111–112

N

"N of One" problem, 33

narcolepsy, 78

National Center for Posttraumatic Stress Disorder, 273

National Center on Sleep Disorder Research, 79

National Council on Aging, 247

National Institute for Trauma and Loss in Children (TLC), 274–275

nationalism, 227

nationality, 185

nativist theory, 114–115

natural selection, 53

nature vs. nurture debate, 26, 231

Nazi Germany, 211

NE (norepinephrine), 47, 55

needs, motivation and, 120–121

negative punishment, 161

negative reinforcement, 159

negative-afterimage effect, 64

nerves, 42

nervous breakdowns, 271

nervous system, 42–43

Nesse, Randolph M., 133

neural network, 106

neurocomputational approach, 43

neurofeedback, 368

neurogenesis, 48

neurons, 42, 44

neuroplasticity, 48

neuroprosthetics, 369

neuropsychological testing, 323–324

neuropsychology, 20

neurotransmitters, 42–43, 45–47, 293

Newell, Allen, 104

nightmares, 78

nootropics, 368

Norcross, John, 331

Nordgren, Loran F., 127

norepinephrine (NE), 47, 55

norm of social responsibility, 223–224

normal consciousness, 75

normal distribution, 112–113

nurture vs. nature debate, 26, 231

O

obedience, 210

object permanence, 238

Object Relations Theory, 23, 294

obsessive-compulsive disorder, 56, 298

occipital lobe, 50

Olds, James, 127

olfaction, 67

olfactory bulb, 67

One Flew Over the Cuckoo's Nest (film), 380

one-to-one correspondence, 241

online dating, 253–254

online identity, 252–253

online morality, 257

online resources

  American Psychological Association, 35

  cheat sheet for this book, 3

  sleep disorders, 79

online social networks, 251

open-head injuries, 49

operant conditioning, 20, 157–158

operational schemata, 236

opponent-process theory, 64, 125

optic nerve, 63

optimal level of arousal theory, 123–124

optimal living, 373–378

orbitofrontal cortex, 135

order of emotions, 135–137

  Cannon-Bard theory, 136

  constructivist theory, 137

  James-Lange theory, 136

  two-factor theory, 136–137

Ordinary People (film), 381

P

pain, 66, 127-128. *See also* psychological pain

panic disorders, 56, 297–300

parallel distributed processing approach (PDP), 106

parallel processing, 47

parasomnias, 78

parenting, 192–193

parietal lobe, 50

Parks, Rosa, 122

rote rehearsal, 95
Rotter, J. B., 334
rules of thought, 92
Rumelhart, David, 106
rumination, 269
Ryan, Richard, 122
Ryff, Carol, 141, 283

S

sample size, 32–33
sampling bias, 32
Samuels, Richard, 90
Sandberg, Anders, 367
sanism, 227
Saunders, Christine, 203
Schacter, Stanley, 136
schedule of reinforcement, 163–165
schemas, 98, 174–175, 294
schemata, 235–237
schizoid personality disorder, 188
schizophrenia, 55, 129, 286–290
Schneirla, Theodore, 128
schools of therapy, 337–355
Schulkin, Jay, 267
Schunk, Dale, 126
science, 15–16
scientific method, 29–30
scripts, 175–176
SD (systematic desensitization),
    343–344
SDT (self-determination theory),
    121–123
secondary defenses, 339–340
secondary drives, 120
secondary reinforcers, 160
secondary traits, 172
second-order crisis intervention, 272
secular trend, 245
secure base, 189
sedation, 75
selective serotonin reuptake
    inhibitors (SSRIs), 55
Self Comes to Mind (Damasio), 134
Self Psychology, 23
self-acceptance, 375

self-consciousness, 179–181
self-destructive behaviors, 129–130
self-determination, 375
self-determination theory (SDT),
    121–123
self-efficacy, 173
self-esteem, 185–186
self-expansion model of love,
    196–197
Self-Expansion Questionnaire, 197
self-healing, 336
self-help, 333
Self-Help That Works (Norcross), 333
The Selfish Gene (Dawkins), 119, 224
selfishness, 223
self-regulation, 122
self-regulatory mechanisms, 176
self-reinforcement, 173
self-reports, 322
self-schemas, 175
Seligman, Martin, 141, 294, 364
Selye, Hans, 265
semantic memory, 96
semantics, 115
sensation, 60
sensing process, 59–72
    early child development, 235
    hearing, 65–66
    overview, 60–62
    perception and, 68–70
    perceptual organizing rules, 70–72
    sight, 62–65
    smell, 67
    taste, 67
    touch, 66–67
sensing process, kinesthetic
    sense, 68
sensitivity, 70
sensorimotor schemata, 236
sensorimotor stage, 237–238
sensory expanded consciousness, 81
sensory memory, 94
separation anxiety, 241
serial position effect, 96
seriation, 242
serotonin, 46, 55

serotonin norepinephrine reuptake
    inhibitors (SNRIs), 55
The Seven Principles of Making a
    Marriage Work (Gottman and
    Silver), 197
sex cells, 230
sexism, 226
s-factors, 109
shaping, 159
shell shock, 273
Sherif, Muzafer, 210
Shneidman, Edwin, 130
short-term memory (STM), 94
siblings, 193–194
side effects, antipsychotic
    medications, 55–56
Siegel, Daniel, 145
sight, 62–65
signal-detection theory, 69–70
signed languages, 116
The Silence of the Lambs (film), 382
Simon, Herbert, 103, 104
Simons, Daniel, 93
Singer, Jerome, 136
situational psychology, 176–178
skill of consciousness, 74–75
Skinner, B. F., 159
Skinner box, 159
sleep, 76–79
sleep apnea, 78
sleepwalking disorder, 78
smart phones, 107
smell, 67
Smoke Detector Principle, 133
SNRIs (serotonin norepinephrine
    reuptake inhibitors), 55
SNSs (social networking sites), 251
social aspect, biopsychosocial
    model, 25
social cognition, 198–202, 243–244
social constructionism, 23
social coping resources, 277–278
social facilitation, 212
social identity, 184–185
social interactionist approach, 115
social learning theory, 173, 219–220
social loafing, 213

About the Author

Adam Cash, PsyD, is a practicing psychologist and Clinical Director of Specialized Psychology Solutions, a psychological services program in Palm Springs, California. He specializes in child psychology, autism, developmental disorders, learning, cognition, and neurodevelopment. He's taught courses in developmental psychology, methods and statistics, substance abuse treatment, and abnormal psychology. Although Dr. Cash's clinical work focuses primarily on children, he once worked extensively with adults and was a full-time forensic psychologist, specializing in prison psychology, violence risk assessment, and sex offender assessment, and he served as an expert witness in trials related to competency-to-stand-trial and not-guilty-by-reason-of-insanity cases. Dr. Cash is the author of *Wiley Concise Guides to Mental Health: Posttraumatic Stress Disorder* (2006). He has expertise in psychological assessment and has conducted several thousand evaluations. He provides medico-legal evaluations for disability and conducts assessment. He is most proud of his marriage to his beautiful wife, Liyona, and the home and family they've built together.

Dedication

To my wife, Liyona, and my beautiful children. Thank you for your love and purity. You are the light; may I stay in it always.

Author's Acknowledgments

I am very grateful to Tim Gallan and Lindsay Lefevere for approaching me to revise this book. I would also like go back and thank the team from the first and second editions as well: Tonya Maddox Cupp, Greg Tubach, and Jenny Brown. Without them, this third edition would not have been possible. Thanks, too, to the children, families, patients, and employees that I work with. I'm grateful for the opportunity to be a part of your lives.

Publisher's Acknowledgments

Executive Editor: Lindsay Lefevere

Project Editor: Tim Gallan

Technical Editors (previous edition):
Professor Robert Howard Ingleby Dale,
Dr. Sue O'Rourke

Proofreader: Debbye Butler

Production Editor: Mohammed Zafar Ali

Cover Image: © Radachynskyi/Getty Images